The
Jersey Sting

The Jersey Sting

Chris Christie and the

Most Brazen Case of

Jersey-Style Corruption—Ever

Ted Sherman

and

Josh Margolin

ST. MARTIN'S GRIFFIN
NEW YORK

www.stmartins.com

Text design by Meryl Sussman Levavi

The Library of Congress has cataloged the hardcover edition as follows:

Sherman, Ted, 1953–
    The Jersey sting : a true story of crooked pols, money-laundering rabbis, black market kidneys, and the informant who brought it all down / Ted Sherman and Josh Margolin.—1st ed.
        p. cm.
    Includes bibliographical references and index.
    ISBN 978-0-312-65417-7
    1. Money laundering investigation—New Jersey—Case studies.   2. Corruption investigation—New Jersey—Case studies.   3. Bribery—New Jersey—Case studies.
    4. Organ trafficking—Jew Jersey—Case studies.   I. Margolin, Josh. II. Title.
    HV6770.A2N574 2011
    364'.109749—dc22

                                                                    2010040313

ISBN 978-1-250-00193-1 (trade paperback)

First St. Martin's Griffin Edition: April 2012

For Rosanne and Karen;

Aliza and Matthew;

Brooke, Julianna, and Rebecca

Contents

Your rulers are rogues, and cronies of thieves,
every one avid for presents and greedy for gifts.

—ISAIAH 1:23

Prologue

Robert Janiszewski, Dewar's-and-water in hand, stood at the bar under a night sky aboard the Lightship Barge & Grill, a converted vessel moored along the Jersey City waterfront. His face said he did not want company. The veteran politician and once-formidable boss of the powerful Hudson County Democratic machine—known by all as "Bobby J"—looked tired and gaunt. It was an August evening in 2001 at the marina at Liberty State Park. The backdrop was the brightly lit lower Manhattan skyline. Bobby J had lost so much weight that some friends thought him seriously ill.

Then, he mysteriously disappeared, only to show up months later as a cooperating witness in a federal sting. His targets were friends, political associates, elected officials, and contractors. Janiszewski had been caught taking a cash payoff from a county vendor in an Atlantic City hotel room during a New Jersey League of Municipalities convention. It is an annual event. Three days of glad-handing, networking, government seminars, and contractor displays for companies selling everything from accounting software to blacktop to municipal services. Outside the convention center, the gathering often hosts golf outings, political dinners, drunken parties, sex, and, at times, corrupt deals that go down behind closed doors.

Deals sometimes captured by hidden FBI surveillance cameras.

Just moments after the cash was slipped to him, Janiszewski was arrested. The payoff had been orchestrated by the FBI. No way out. And then he faced a decision. He could go away to prison for a very long time, or he could make his own deal. When you get caught, the only currency you have is information. That's the way one federal informant described the sensation. Janiszewski reluctantly agreed to wear a wire and spent the next year secretly recording conversations in his car, office, and elsewhere while setting up others not cautious enough to smell the trap.

The covert criminal probe prematurely became public after federal investigators used the tapes in a failed effort to turn a prominent North Jersey developer who had secretly been implicated by Janiszewski. They hoped he would do the right thing and cooperate as well. "That's not what I do," the developer replied.

It was then that Janiszewski promptly left on a "vacation" from which he never returned, ending more than a dozen years as one of the most powerful political bosses in the state. He pleaded guilty and testified against others, including his best friend, and recounted in court how he would get plastic envelopes stuffed full of cash that he would stash away in a file cabinet in his home.

* * *

Politics and business come together in New Jersey like nowhere else, a universe that looks, sounds, and smells familiar but is at the same time strange and foreign. It is a place where there are few good guys and the ones there often earn little, if any, respect. It is a place where there are real bad guys, actual crooks, colorful villains, and even dangerous characters seduced by money and power. But they are so interesting, engaging, and quick with a tale that they are downright impossible to stay away from.

There are political bosses who, when they're not ordering the assassinations of careers and reputations, are philanthropists and businessmen, running schools and banks and insurance companies and law firms. There are the rabbis who lead cloistered communities and use seminaries as power bases to extract their tribute from the politicians. There are the priests who negotiate communion rights based on political stances. There are the lawyers who (as Al Pacino declares in *The Devil's Advocate,* have the ultimate backstage pass because "the law, my boy, puts us in everything...") know everything about everyone, and get paid for it to boot. There are the bagmen, the go-betweens, the intermediaries who ensure that the skids are greased, the meetings are set, and the beer is cold.

Long before the story you are about to read, corruption seemed to be synonymous with New Jersey—and especially with Hudson County. It is a place once so renowned for stuffing the ballot boxes with the votes of dead people that former governor Brendan Byrne still gets laughs on the dinner circuit when he says he wants to be buried in Hudson "so I can stay active in politics."

At the same time, Byrne, a former judge, notes that corruption is a game fraught with peril for those willing to cross the line. Eventually, he cautions, the chances of getting caught are high. "One of the cardinal rules of New Jersey politics is there's no such thing as a private conversation. Somewhere along the line, you are going to be taped by someone wearing a wire," he explains. "This is why so many political meetings start with a big bear hug—a New Jersey pat-down among friends."

The title of most corrupt state has been claimed by Louisiana, Illinois, even Rhode Island. But seriously, even the feds and the prosecutors agree that New Jersey has few peers. Around the State House, as the Legislature convenes, jokes regularly suggest that yellow crime-scene tape ought to wrap the whole building. Around the state, people generally accept the reality that graft is just part of life—sort of unavoidable, like a traffic jam on the New Jersey Turnpike.

In the last decade alone, one governor resigned in a gay-sex scandal, the state's only medical school was taken over by the feds because of fraud and corruption, and officials from Atlantic City to Bergen County have been put behind bars or are awaiting trial. Jersey's history is one of legendary graft and fraud. Mayors are constantly getting indicted. One former state senator faked his own death in a Bahamas scuba-diving accident to avoid prison, a fate that finally overtook him after a two-year cat-and-mouse game in which he taunted authorities as he hid out in the open with his photographer girlfriend, enjoying a life on the run that took them from the luxury ski slopes of the Alps to sunny Mediterranean beach resorts, on a string of phony passports. He was finally captured in the tiny island republic of the Maldives off the west coast of India, where he was running a chain of highly successful dive shops.

"These guys are for sale and they let you know it," declared one former political operative. He recounted tales of Sharpe James, the former mayor of Newark, who would throw his support to those who rented the offices of the Sharpe James Civic Association for three months (and who spent twenty months at Petersburg Correctional Complex in Virginia as federal inmate 28791-050, before being released last year to a halfway house).

Another former key Essex County legislator sought $5,000 from one gubernatorial campaign for rent of his legislative storefront office just for Election Day. "How much am I going to get?" he demanded. They didn't need his district office. But they could afford to pay him to go away. They offered him $3,000. He took it.

James, who was one of the state's most influential politicians during his five terms as mayor and two as a state senator, would later be convicted of illegally steering city land to his mistress, Tamika Riley. She, in turn, made hundreds of thousands of dollars by quickly flipping the lots instead of redeveloping them, as required under the terms of the land sales.

A colleague of James, State Sen. Wayne Bryant, was once among the most powerful men in the New Jersey State House. He wielded tremendous influence on how the money flowed in Trenton and from Trenton as head of the Senate Budget and Appropriations Committee. He, too, went to jail, after he was convicted of funneling millions in public funding to the state's medical university in exchange for a sham job to boost his pension.

Mims Hackett, the mayor of Orange and a state assemblyman, admitted he accepted a $5,000 bribe and bilked taxpayers by filing phony travel receipts after he was ensnared with ten other elected officials in yet another FBI sting involving public contracts for insurance brokerage and roofing services. Dressed in a charcoal gray suit, Hackett brought his wife, their six children, and other family and friends when he was finally sentenced. "My wife and I always have tried to be good Christians," Hackett told the judge. "We worked tirelessly for the people of Orange. A large part of what happened I now know was unlawful. I had no intentions of doing anything wrong on my part."

Then there was Paterson mayor Marty Barnes, who went to jail on the strength of secret tape recordings, along with photographs of the mayor frolicking with prostitutes at a Brazil resort and evidence of kickbacks, free clothes, trips, furniture, even a new pool with a waterfall. All of it came courtesy of a flashy sewer contractor, a onetime music promoter who first began soliciting municipal contracts throughout the state by wrapping $100 bills around his business cards and hiring scantily clad women to attract attention to his booth at—where else?—the League of Municipalities convention in Atlantic City.

The contractor, Jerry Free, a slick Tennessee salesman, used a powerful mix of campaign contributions and a lineup of influential friends to become a major player. With his quick talk and free spending, Jerry and his company, United Gunite, paid off generously and profited richly from no-bid deals. He was sentenced to six months of house arrest and three years' probation after he helped federal prosecutors go after the elected officials he had once courted.

* * *

For a long time—in Ted Sherman's case, three decades; in Josh Margolin's case, more than a dozen years—the two of us have uncovered and written about much of that corruption for *The Star-Ledger*, the largest daily newspaper in the state. We have traveled the underbelly of New Jersey politics, law, and business. And we have taken up residence in a place where truth really is stranger than fiction.

The book you are about to read is a product of that work: of relationships built, of trust earned, and of history pieced together like a massive, ten-thousand-piece jigsaw puzzle with no picture to guide us. It is all true. It was fashioned from dozens upon dozens of interviews—both on and off the record; from thousands of pages of documents, transcripts of federal wiretaps, court records, and sworn depositions; and the invaluable assistance of some people who, for the sake of their careers, livelihoods, or lives, have refused to be named or take any credit whatsoever.

It goes without saying that a reporter is only as good as his sources. We are truly lucky and gratified that so many who have so much to tell confided in us so eagerly. What you are about to read has been researched and checked and verified by every possible means. Many of the conversations we report come out of depositions, legal briefs, surveillance recordings, or starkly frank transcripts of meetings and calls. Some of them were contained in criminal complaints filed by the U.S. Attorney for New Jersey. Much of it has remained secret by court order—until now.

Where conversations have been re-created, it is owed to the specific and detailed recollections of those in the best positions to report them and confirmed by others. Where thoughts and opinions are reported, these are the actual thoughts and opinions as expressed by the very people we attribute them to, as best recalled by those who were actually present or in some cases were part of a conference call. Just because we name someone does not mean that that person has spoken to us. In order to protect the confidentiality of our sources, we cannot say who gave us information—or who did not.

Where we are able to specify our sources, we do.

Most of all, know that this account doesn't come only from law enforcement or the so-called white hats. After all these years, we are proud to say that plenty of shady characters trust us, too, and we are grateful for that. This story would be incomplete without their help.

As this is being written, the story is continuing to unfold. Some of those charged have pleaded guilty. Others have gone to trial. Many are awaiting their day in court. The legal battles may well go on for years. The investigation—as the feds love to say—is continuing.

Along the way, we learned there were case-threatening mistakes, internal turf battles, targets caught taking money but never charged, and sudden changes in direction that surprised even the prosecutors. No one could have predicted that this investigation would turn out the way it did, when it did.

What led to this point is replete with drama. It's a narrative spanning from New Jersey and Brooklyn to Israel and Hong Kong. It's a story revolving around one man's so-called schnookie deals, a Yiddish term coming from the word "schnook": someone easily imposed upon, victimized, or cheated. It's a tale of greed, corruption, betrayal, ambition, politics, religion, money, and morality, set in the rich tapestry of New Jersey, with its incredible views and awful smells and fascinating people. It may well have determined who became governor of New Jersey.

This is an inside account of one of the largest-ever federal sting operations in U.S. history and the case that led to a massive roundup of elected officials, politically connected operators, Orthodox rabbis, and members of their communities, culminating in one of the strangest and most dramatic days ever in New Jersey . . .

1

⋖┼┼┼►

Everyone in New Jersey Was Arrested Today . . .

It began in the early-morning hours of Thursday, July 23, 2009.

On a warm day that would turn overcast with scattered rain, climbing to near 80 degrees in the summer humidity, more than 300 FBI and other federal agents were in position across the metropolitan area well before the crack of dawn. Deployed from Brooklyn and Jersey City to the wealthy beachfront enclave of Deal along the Jersey Shore, it was an invasion force about to execute a coordinated assault of military-style precision, a takedown that would shatter New Jersey's political landscape and reach all the way into the governor's office, while tearing apart an insular Orthodox religious community that had long shunned outsiders.

For nearly three years, the FBI and the U.S. Attorney's office had been trolling for corruption in one of the nation's most corrupt states, and this was D-day. It was all about to come down.

Some news organizations had already been tipped off that "something big" was going to happen. In the second-floor newsroom of *The Star-Ledger*—New Jersey's largest newspaper—editors were deploying their own army of staff, mostly operating on educated guesswork and cryptic conversations with sources on just where to send them. They knew there were going to be some high-profile arrests and that it was going to be big, but they had no idea just how crazy it was about to get. Something about political corruption and a Brooklyn rabbi, sources had suggested, in a state already well known for its scandals.

New Jersey, after all, was where its governor had resigned after announcing one day that he was gay, and had put his male lover in a sensitive security post for which the guy was wildly unqualified. It was the state where the mayor of its largest city was currently in federal prison for steering lucrative land deals to a woman with whom he had been having a torrid extramarital affair. Where the powerful head of the state senate's finance committee was in prison as well, for steering millions in public funding to the medical university that had given him what prosecutors called a no-show job. A state where a leading Republican candidate for U.S. Senate would go to jail after disdaining a federal inquiry into his election financing, declaring to an informant—who unfortunately for him was wearing a wire at the time—that the heavyset U.S. Attorney pursuing him was just "a fat fuck who knew more about cookbooks than law books . . ." Where more than 200 people had been arrested in recent years on corruption charges large and small, from county executives and freeholders to mayors and legislators and, of course, a couple of backroom political bosses.

Even those who were about to get arrested that morning did not seem to have a clue they would be the next stars of that classic New Jersey ritual: the televised "perp walk."

Peter Cammarano III, a rising star in New Jersey politics, was only in his twenty-third day as mayor of Hoboken, following a tough, hard-fought runoff election in the once-blue-collar Hudson County city that long ago had served as a soundstage for the famed film classic *On the Waterfront* but now a growing preserve of young urban professionals ferrying across the river to work in Manhattan. An attorney and former councilman who specialized in election law and worked for one of New Jersey's most politically connected law firms, Cammarano was seen as the future of the Democratic Party. He had spent the night before celebrating his thirty-second birthday, looking as if he had not a care in the world.

He "tweeted" cheerfully on July 22: *I plan on bartending tonight @ the Hoboken's St. Ann's festival, look forward to seeing the residents and visitors of Hoboken tonight . . .*

He shook hands and mixed drinks. Then later in the evening, he pulled out his iPhone and posted his last "tweet" before the knock came at the door the next morning: *I would like to thank everyone today for the birthday wishes, hope everyone had a great time at the opening night for St. Ann's feast—10:08 PM Jul 22nd from Echofon . . .*

Democratic state assemblyman L. Harvey Smith, 60, was not even in New Jersey that day. Smith, also on the public payroll as a Hudson County undersheriff—a political patronage appointment that only goes to those with the right connections—was a onetime Jersey City mayor and councilman who had just tried, and failed, at another mayoral bid. On this morning, he was vacationing in Virginia.

Mariano Vega, the Jersey City council president, might have had a tougher time sleeping the night before. The 60-year-old veteran Democrat had been visited by FBI agents at his home in the Van Vorst Park historic district of the city the previous day. The feds wanted to know about a meeting he might have had with a developer just 13 days earlier. Vega looked carefully at the picture of the guy. Someone who had been recorded telling Vega he had an envelope stuffed with $10,000 full of cash, and recorded passing that to a middleman; kind of thing most people would probably remember.

"I don't recognize him," Vega told the feds. He was lying and they knew it.

In Brooklyn, along Ocean Parkway just off Kings Highway, some were already on their way to Shachrit, the morning prayer service at Congregation Shaare Zion, one of the largest Orthodox synagogues in New York and center of the close-knit Syrian Jewish community.

Traffic was still light in Jersey City. Miles to the south in Deal, along tree-lined streets of the quiet suburban town, there was not a hint that anything was amiss. The cable guy could be seen on one block. No FBI vans. No agents in blue windbreakers. No guns or handcuffs.

The FBI likes to target its high-profile arrests early in the day, when people are just getting up and not yet really thinking about much more than breakfast. There's less of a chance that anyone is going to do something stupid, like reach for a gun or run, or be warned that there's about to be a knock on the door. In this case, only a handful of the accused, like Vega, had been questioned the night before by the FBI. Most did not realize they had long been targets of a federal investigation. Few had lawyers yet. Soon they would all need one.

The arrests had been planned for at least a month, zeroed in on a date long etched onto the calendar. The FBI had brought in additional agents to augment the myriad arresting, search, and interrogation teams fanned out across New York and New Jersey. IRS agents were there as well. Acting U.S. Attorney Ralph Marra likened the gathering storm to the 1944 Normandy invasion; there would be a lot of troops in the field, and once he gave the go-ahead, he could only hope that nothing would go wrong. "The ships are out there; they're on their way. You're not calling them back," he explained.

That morning, the 56-year-old Marra rushed through his cornflakes and blueberries and headed north up the Garden State Parkway to the office in downtown Newark. There wasn't much for him to do that had not already been done.

A mile away, Weysan Dun, 54, the special agent in charge of the FBI's Newark Division, was already at his post, where he had been camped out since about 4:30 A.M. He surveyed the command center on the twelfth floor of the high-security FBI building, the tactical headquarters for the operation that was about to be launched. The large, long, windowless room was packed with people, some sitting at black and silver computer terminals, others talking by phone with agents in the field.

Dark SUVs and plain sedans were being parked in still-dark neighborhoods as the homes of suspects were quietly surrounded in the predawn. Nobody was expecting anyone to run, but you never knew. If the most dangerous thing in law enforcement is a nighttime highway stop, a close second is bursting in for a surprise arrest or to serve a warrant. Like always, everything was supposed to be played completely by the book. But no one knows what will happen in the field.

Dun, in a starched white shirt and tightly knotted maroon tie, had left his dark suit jacket back in his expansive office down the hall. The command center was filled with a buzz of 20 different conversations going on all at once. A large American flag hung from the wall in back of him. To his left, a big white status board held a grid with the names of 44 targets carefully written in dry erase markers. In the back, by the microwave and a sports trophy case, someone had set up breakfast trays of bagels, muffins, juices, and hot coffee. And donuts.

More than a month earlier, Dun had declared an "Office Special," in an all-hands-on-deck e-mail bulletin to everyone in the division, alerting agents and support personnel to block out this day and keep their calendars clear. Those not directly on the case had no idea what was coming down. Some would not be told of their assignments until just before the arrests would be made. Unscheduled vacations? Canceled. Now they were gathered in what almost looked like the firing room for a moon shot, with dozens of people seated at carefully aligned rows of tables—each with a different responsibility for a piece of the operation. Legal. Intelligence. Media.

Under the recessed fluorescent lights overhead, there was a nervous energy after months of preparation. *Organized chaos,* Dun thought to himself.

The sun was now up. His seat was at a long table stretching across the front of the room and he had been reviewing the final preparations of what was to come.

"Quiet!" someone finally called out. The conversations immediately stopped. It all now was in Dun's hands to call the final order. Go or no-go? . . . The former Army intelligence officer with a DJ's voice took a last look at his wristwatch, second hand ticking out the last moments. It was exactly 6:00 A.M.

The command supervisor looked expectedly at Dun. "Requesting permission to execute," he said. That was the protocol.

Dun nodded without hesitation. "Execute," he replied in his calm Midwest voice.

The order immediately went out by radio to the waiting teams of agents spread throughout New York and New Jersey. *"All units. This is the command post. You have the authority to execute your warrants."*

It remained silent in the room, except for the soft rush of the ventilation blowers in the background. Dun could only imagine the sudden scramble of agents, the echo of footsteps on the run acting immediately upon his command, like the offensive line of a football team poised tightly on the line of scrimmage and then exploding forward on the snap. The operator handling field communications raised her microphone again and she repeated the order three times: *"Execute . . . Execute . . . Execute . . ."*

In Deal and in Jersey City, in Hoboken and Brooklyn, the federal agents—both FBI and IRS, joined in some cases by local cops—immediately went into action, knocking on 44 doors in synchronized unison.

On East 8th Street between Avenues U and V in Brooklyn, Paulina Ajkobyan had gotten up early to take out the garbage. It was still quiet, at the time in the morning when the loudest sounds outside might be the occasional barking of a dog, the grinding of a garbage truck, or the slamming of a car door. When a conversation on the street can carry far down the block.

She paused at the top of her small porch in the neighborhood of modest brick homes. Unable to go back to sleep, she rested for a few moments before going back inside. As she sat, she saw a light brown car pull up the tree-lined street. A man and a woman got out. She could see both were wearing dark blue vests with the letters FBI emblazoned in yellow on the front.

"I think, 'Oh, this [is a] problem,'" she later told a reporter in broken English.

Two more agents quickly arrived and all four headed up the street, entering a two-story duplex with a broken scooter in the yard, chipped red paint on the stoop, and peeling white paint on the wrought iron over the windows. They knocked and then headed up a crooked linoleum-covered staircase. A short while, maybe 15 minutes later, they came back down the street, this time leading someone Paulina did not recognize, a "big fat man" she called him, already in handcuffs. They put him in one of the government cars and drove him away.

A group of Jersey mayors were among the first to be brought in. There was Cammarano. Looking dazed and bleary-eyed, the married father with a two-year-old girl was the young face of an old city and, despite the cuffs, was dressed the part in blue button-down and khakis as he was taken from a car into this hulking FBI headquarters alongside the heavily industrial Passaic River, just off McCarter Highway in Newark. Soon joining him was Secaucus mayor Dennis Elwell. Then a growing stream of other public officials, building inspectors, and political operatives. Afterward would come the rabbis, Hasidic real estate developers, and Israeli expatriates from Brooklyn.

News of the arrests quickly began to leak widely. On WNBC-TV, the local New York NBC television station, a bulletin flashed: *Breaking News: Dozens of corruption-related arrests are taking place across New Jersey this morning. Several Mayors are in custody . . .*

The news radio stations picked it up. At *The Star-Ledger*, the story quickly went up on the paper's Web site, as photographers began transmitting the first photos back from the FBI building. No one was saying how many more there would be or when it would stop. The initial numbers were about twenty. Then thirty. And the arrests kept coming.

Reports, later proved wrong, suggested a massive political bid-rigging scheme. An FBI spokesman cryptically said only that the investigation involved a "high-volume international money-laundering conspiracy." No one was explaining how that all fit together. None of it made sense. What could a group of rabbis from Brooklyn have to do with hard-core pols of Hudson County, New Jersey?

It got stranger still. Sources told reporters that one of the suspects was also allegedly involved in an illegal human organ–selling ring—a suggestion that some brushed aside as sounding too ludicrous to possibly be true. "Someone's got to be smoking crack," one reporter declared.

Twenty search-warrant teams stormed homes and offices in New Jersey and New York, recovering large sums of cash and other evidence. Twenty-eight bank accounts were seized on the confidential orders of a federal judge. The state's governor—unpopular and sitting atop a Democratic Party increasingly infected by corruption—was not spared, even as he was stuck slogging through a vicious reelection campaign. The office and home of a high-ranking member of his own cabinet were searched.

New Jersey governor Jon Corzine had a front-row seat from the high-priced confines of his luxury penthouse condo on the southeast corner of Maxwell Place in Hoboken. The first-term Democratic governor, onetime U.S. Senator, and former CEO of Goldman Sachs could only stare at the flat-screen television as he paced while one Democrat after another in real time was walked into FBI headquarters, each step echoing into Corzine's campaign. Just two floors down from the governor in the very same condo building, Michael Schaffer, a commissioner on the North Hudson Utilities Authority, was being arrested.

Corzine seemed already defeated as he conferred on the phone and remained frozen before the television. Handcuffed Democrats—people he had shaken hands with, supported in campaigns, and given money to help win elections—were being marched into custody, heads bowed down as if looking for a hole deep enough in which to hide.

"Is there anyone there we *don't* know?" the governor slowly demanded.

One of those on the conference call wondered aloud, "Maybe the rabbis?" It wasn't meant to be a joke.

The numbers of those arrested, meanwhile, kept changing, as reporters and TV news crews scrambled to keep up with a story that still did not quite make any sense. It quickly began to flash around the world. At one point, cars were backed up four deep with suspects outside the brown brick FBI building. Photographers watched one agent slowly escort an elderly rabbi, hands clutching a siddur, or prayer book, inside.

One by one they walked into the front door, accompanied by agents, and led to a door on the right and then down a pale yellow corridor. A temporary processing center had been set up on the first floor in a charcoal-gray-carpeted room often used for FBI press briefings and classrooms. The JABS, or Joint Automated Booking System unit—normally in a detention area off the garage—had been moved there and an agent took the hands of each, rolling fingertips over a scanner that would digitally transmit the prints to the Bureau's central computer. The camera flashed for mug shots. Full face. Side view. No one smiled. Then each was moved to a waiting area off to the side for an interview with pretrial services. It was there where they could call for a lawyer, if they had one.

They no longer had titles. They were not mayors or councilmen or rabbis or building inspectors. They were now prisoners.

Mindful that most would not have eaten that morning and some were elderly, Dun had ordered that snacks be set up for them as they waited. Hershey bars. Water. Bagels from a kosher bakery. Hours later, they all began coming out again, still handcuffed, on their way to the federal courthouse. So many that U.S. Marshals were forced to transport them in a big blue military bus borrowed from McGuire Air Force Base in South Jersey.

It would be called one of the most memorable perp walks in New Jersey history. Men and women. Young and old. Some well-known, others a mystery. Some were in open-neck polo shirts, others in jeans or sweat suits. One ranking Jersey City official was showing off her cleavage. Others were in shorts. The Orthodox men shuffled uncomfortably in black pants and white shirts, wearing black coats and steel handcuffs, their ritual shirt fringes blowing in the warm summer wind.

By lunchtime, there was a rogues' gallery like no other. And, of course, a Who's Who of the state's best and most expensive criminal lawyers—in their $2,000 suits—began their parade in and out of the courthouse where their new clients were making first appearances before a federal magistrate. Three mayors. Five rabbis, including Saul Kassin, the frail 87-year-old spiritual leader of Sharee Zion in Brooklyn, looking anxious and fearful. Vega, the first Hispanic to sit as president of the Jersey City council. A deputy mayor. Failed mayoral and council candidates. Real estate developers. Two New Jersey state legislators. One insurance executive who had already been convicted for his role in an insider-trading scam that reached from the governor's office in Trenton to the elite world of the leading law firm Skadden Arps. Political operatives and Hasidic Jews from the bucolic community of Monsey, in Rockland County, New York.

A longtime political consultant, who had already quietly agreed to roll over on his pals, was there as well, though he would mysteriously die days later—after word began circulating that his allegiances had shifted.

The Web site Gawker.com quickly summed it all up: *"Everyone in New Jersey was arrested today!"*

The charges ranged from corruption and bribery to money laundering and conspiracy, in a complex sting operation that spanned from Hoboken to Israel. In a state that prides itself on its history of scandal and colorful mobsters, no one had ever seen—or imagined—anything like this. The tall pile of criminal complaints described in graphic detail the bribes that had gone down in diners, living rooms, and parking lots, taken by the assemblymen, by the mayors, by housing inspectors and authority commissioners. Many of the players had been locked in a series of tightly contested Hudson County elections, apparently more than willing to take money being offered without any questions.

Rabbinical scholars acting more like crime bosses than religious leaders were being accused of laundering millions through synagogues, charities, and yeshivas. Some had money-counting machines in their offices. It was like *GoodFellas*—at shul. Indeed, the brazenness of the intertwined schemes played out in stark terms and in languages that included English, Yiddish, Hebrew, Aramaic, and yeshivish slang—captured by hundreds of hours of hidden surveillance tapes recorded by the FBI and noted in the criminal complaints.

Cammarano, for example, sat down at a Hoboken diner that past May and talked about a $5,000 payment with a mysterious informant whom authorities would not immediately identify. The informant had a cover story portraying himself as a big-spending developer willing to pay cash to grease the way for building approvals.

The informant told others he had cash to burn. "There's people like Democrat, Republican, but I'm in the Green Party; I don't like any conflicts, you understand?" He was playing Joe Pesci. Tough-guy mob movie language from someone who was the only one in the room that knew they were all starring in a production secretly recorded for an FBI greatest hits reel.

One candidate for city council, desperate for campaign funds in a tight runoff election, nervously laughed. "Green is like gold, right?"

"That's right, I don't have gold in my house, but green I have. So, you know, if it's okay with you, you know, maybe I'll do five thousand and another five after the election," the informant promised.

It was clear the scheme had a wide reach. Some would later step forward and acknowledge that they had been targeted as well. They were identified only as "Official 1" or "Official 2" in the criminal complaints but were not immediately charged.

One story making the rounds told of an apparent target who allegedly figured it out. A Hudson County mayor who supposedly was set up with the informant in a restaurant and told to name his price. The mayor, according to the story, took a napkin and scribbled something down, before he got up to leave without a word. The informant looked at the paper, crumbled it up, and followed him out. Federal agents rapidly moved in to recover the evidence. The napkin said: *Go fuck yourself.*

Did it happen? No one knew for sure, but it was repeated over and over, by word of mouth, among political insiders and lawyers, eventually taking on the ring of truth as much as anything else in the strange case, while other elected officials came forward and admitted they, too, were lured with offers that they turned down. That story was not among the most outrageous of reports.

As it turned out, the illegal human organ–selling operation—the rumor that sounded unbelievably preposterous—was indeed a part of the sting. The FBI had nailed a Brooklyn real estate broker for running a black market organ donor scheme, proposing the sale of a human kidney through his Israeli connections. And he had done it before. Many times, he claimed.

The transcripts taken from the criminal complaints against the rabbis sounded like a script from an episode of *The Sopranos*. At one point, one rabbi was told by the FBI's informant that the proceeds of a $50,000 check came from "that guy who was holding, uh, my, uh, money for me on that Florida insurance, uh, scam that I did."

"Okay," says the rabbi. "Give me a couple days."

Another rabbi was caught explaining that they would use code words to schedule meetings to arrange cash transfers. Dollars were *gemoras*. As in "how many *gemoras* would it take?" The *gemora* is actually a part of the Talmud, the section that contains the rabbinical commentaries and debates from two thousand years ago. It is said to have been handed down to Moses at Mount Sinai. The irony was boundless.

Money was exchanged in paper bags, in boxes of breakfast cereal, and in plastic garbage sacks.

* * *

The afternoon press conference in the U.S. Attorney's office on the seventh floor of the Peter W. Rodino Federal Building in Newark, directly across from the federal courthouse where all the defendants would eventually arrive, was packed with media from all over the country. Just a quick PATH train ride from New York, the event brought out crews from all the major broadcast and cable news networks. Newspaper and radio reporters from around the region. Even international press. TV cameras jammed in the front. Reporters squeezed tightly along the sides. In the back, prosecutors and others from the office, there to hear their boss.

The press releases being handed out listed the nearly four dozen people who had been arrested. But it wasn't the press advisory that had brought all the media there. It was the photo of the rabbis in cuffs, one in a long dark coat and black hat, being led onto the blue Air Force bus behind a string of suspects.

The rabbis were being charged with operating a sophisticated money-laundering network by funneling millions of dollars through charitable institutions and schools with which they were associated—an international tax dodge involving transactions routed through Switzerland, Hong Kong, Australia, and Israel.

With the politicians, it was simple payoffs. The classic Jersey-style political crime. Some of the bribes to elected officials were paid through political contributions, the complaint said, often through "straw" donors who wrote checks in their names or businesses to create the façade of complying with campaign finance regulations. Other bribes were simply cash stuffed into envelopes.

The rabbis had really nothing to do with the politicians, and vice versa. Neither side knew each other. Prosecutors said the case was actually a two-track investigation connected only by the same informant, a man who moved easily among the worlds of the Orthodox Jews, development deals, and Jersey politics.

The rabbis included Eliahu Ben Haim, of Long Branch, the leader of a synagogue in Deal, whose sphere of influence extended from the Jersey Shore to the Middle East. He had long-standing connections to the right-wing, ultra-Orthodox Shas Party in Israel. The connections were not just political. He had raised large sums of money for charities run by Shas founder Rabbi Ovadia Yosef, once a chief rabbi of Israel, and his son Rabbi David Yosef.

Rabbi Saul Kassin, a soft-spoken man and author of several books on Jewish law, was charged with money laundering as well. So was Rabbi Edmond Nahum, of Deal, both of them well-known in Syrian Sephardic community of about 75,000 strong that stretches from the neighborhoods of southern Brooklyn to the beachfront homes of Deal, where many spend the summers.

* * *

Ralph Marra had long served behind the scenes as a prosecutor, and then a top administrator in the office under Chris Christie, the U.S. Attorney who had stepped down eight months earlier to run for governor. Where Christie was larger than life, Marra was a low-key guy with a taste for cooking, hard rock, and surfing. He had spent most of his career in the U.S. Attorney's office and had prosecuted every sort of case, from crooked street sweepers to wannabe jihadists.

A lifelong Democrat, Marra had long ties to Hudson County, a place steeped in corruption dating back a century or more. Frank Hague, one of the state's first political bosses and the storied mayor who ruled Jersey City at the same time Tammany Hall controlled politics in New York City, somehow parlayed a city salary that never exceeded $8,500 a year into an estate estimated at more than $10 million at the time of his death. Marra freely speaks of a grandmother telling stories of shakedowns at a family-owned bar in Hoboken.

"I vividly remember her showing me—I must've been nine years old—one of her best friends had another saloon. She'd take me in the back and show me where they used to stuff the ballot boxes," he said.

Marra liked to tell how he used to bring his kids into the voting booth when they were young, instructing them to vote the Democratic line, "skipping the crooks." They would ask, "How will we know?" And he would say, "By the time you're old enough to vote, you'll know."

Marra had faced the press before, but nothing like this, usually leaving the spotlight to others. This time, the lights were on him as he walked to the podium, accompanied by Dun and members of his prosecution team. Marra knew how to give a sound bite.

"For these defendants, corruption was a way of life," Marra began. "They existed in an ethics-free zone." Marra said the politicians willingly put themselves up for sale and "clergymen cloaked their extensive criminal activity behind a façade of rectitude."

Privately, he admitted that despite the serious nature of the allegations, they had to laugh over the sheer chutzpah of it all. "It's sort of hilarious at the same time," he allowed.

Now in his carefully tailored suit jacket, Dun had joined Marra and looked somber in front of the press. Cheerful and often self-deprecating in private, the FBI special agent was all business. He was not smiling. He knew there were going to be questions about the rabbis, as well as charges that the case—first green-lighted by Christie, a Republican—seemed to have targeted mostly Democrats.

"The fact that we arrested a number of rabbis this morning does not make this a religiously motivated case. Nor does the fact that we arrested political figures make this a politically motivated case," Dun said. "This case is not about politics. It is certainly not about religion. It is about crime and corruption."

There was immediate political fallout. As Marra and Dun answered questions, Joseph Doria, the popular commissioner of the state Department of Community Affairs, was in the process of stepping down. Not two years earlier, Corzine had begged Doria to join his cabinet. But Corzine and his advisers felt Doria could not be saved after a team of FBI agents searched his office and another descended on his home. "I have not done anything wrong here. I answered their questions. That's all," Doria said during a brief moment with a reporter. But even that was too much for Corzine to take. Doria, who was never charged, was gone by the end of the day.

Two assemblymen were both asked by leadership officials to resign their legislative committee posts. Residents in Hoboken, Secaucus, and Ridgefield all demanded their mayors step down. Protestors started taking to the streets.

Locked in a battle for his career in a campaign against Christie, the governor, pale, angry, and grim faced, said he was sickened to learn of the arrests. Standing next to the state's attorney general, Anne Milgram, Corzine looked ready to kill. "Any corruption is unacceptable anytime, anywhere, by anybody," he declared, calling the scope of the corruption simply outrageous. "There's no other word that fits than 'outrageous.'"

* * *

Even as the effects of the arrest rolled over New Jersey like successive tidal waves, what was not clear was how it all came down. The press releases only said that investigators had the assistance of a "cooperating witness." The U.S. Attorney's office refused to disclose who that was. The criminal complaints only identified him as "the CW," who had been charged with bank fraud in 2006.

In fact, it was all tied together by that one man, one individual who became the focus of what would become a 29-month sting operation, with twists, turns, and characters that might have been taken directly from the pages of an Elmore Leonard novel. Wearing a hidden wire and being followed closely by FBI special agents, the CW would tell associates and longtime business partners that he was working a new scam. "Schnookie deals," he called them, aimed at outwitting the IRS and his creditors in the wake of his arrest for trying to pass $50 million in worthless checks.

"I have a handbag business. I make knockoff, you know, bags, you know—like Zegna, Canali. They make fancy pocketbooks. . . . See I make 'em for like twenty dollars. I sell 'em for a hundred dollars," he said as he lured people into his government-sponsored trap: a cover story to explain his desperate efforts to launder cash from what would turn out to be nonexistent businesses using FBI money. What would not come out until months later was that among those he went after were his brother's father-in-law; an investor in an unrelated Ponzi scheme; religious rivals of this father; and political officials whose roles in office were as foreign to him as the hierarchy of the Catholic Church.

The scripts changed for the politicians. The CW took on an assumed name and became a fast-talking, seemingly reckless Orthodox Jewish real estate developer with a loose wallet, loose lips, and a plan to put up big high-rises on what seemed to be impossibly tiny tracts of land. If anyone bothered to look closely, they would have realized quickly the informant was full of it. But no one checked. To the politicians, the CW was just another businessman willing to pay off anyone to get the jobs fast-tracked.

It did not take long to connect the dots. There was only one person who fit the description. One person who had been charged with bank fraud in 2006, who was well-known in the Sephardic Jewish community in Deal.

Solomon Dwek.

The son of a well-respected Monmouth County rabbi, Dwek was a big, chubby young man—some called him cherubic—with a receding hairline his yarmulke could not cover and thin, wire-rimmed glasses that barely seemed to fit his face. Married with five kids, he had served as the vice president and chief executive of the Deal Yeshiva and was a major contributor to political candidates. He had given thousands of dollars to the election campaign of Pres. George W. Bush. He had shaken hands with Dick Cheney.

As head of a real estate company called Dwek Properties LLC, he claimed more than 200 properties in Central New Jersey and investments as far south as Florida, including two luxury condominiums in Miami Beach at the private community of Aqua at Allison Island. Through a string of partnerships, he owned medical buildings, houses, and condos and was involved in several major development projects. He had money in a floating casino down in Florida. He was by all indications a very wealthy man who gave generously to charity, including his father's religious school. There was an arts center that he had funded, named after him and his wife, Pearl.

But the multimillion-dollar real estate empire had all come tumbling down one day in April of 2006, when Dwek went to the drive-thru window at the PNC Bank in Eatontown and for some inexplicable reason deposited a phony $25 million check drawn from an empty, closed account and then transferred all the funds out before the Pittsburgh-based bank discovered the massive fraud. The next day, he tried to do it again, with a second bogus $25 million check. PNC would eventually file suit. A month later, on May 11, Dwek was arrested at his home by FBI agents and detectives from the county prosecutor's office, charged with bank fraud, a crime that carried a maximum penalty of 30 years in prison and a $1 million fine.

It made all the papers. To many who thought they knew him, it made no sense. Why would a guy with so much just throw it all away like that? How did he think he was going to get away with kiting one $25 million check, let alone two?

Not long after, he filed a massive bankruptcy petition, involving dozens of creditors, lawsuits and countersuits, and continuing allegations of fraud. While all that was happening, he made a fateful agreement in hopes of cutting the amount of time he would spend in federal prison. He would secretly cooperate with prosecutors, launching a nearly three-year investigation that only now was coming to light.

On the day of the massive arrests, Dwek vanished. At his low, sprawling ranch on a quiet side street in Deal, the door was answered that morning by a domestic worker, who had little to say. Inside was a woman carrying an empty suitcase.

Dwek, it seemed, was gone.

2

⊷†┼†⊶

The Rabbi's Son

Solomon Dwek was musing aloud about an old scam he had once run—
one he had figured out after discovering that most banks were more interested in giving money than in learning where any of it went. He would
take out huge loans for property that did not exist, just by making up the
block and lot numbers. The bank often did not do a title search. They
didn't check anything. If a loan officer questioned it, Dwek would just say
they had mixed up the numbers.

"The property wasn't exactly there," he was telling Moshe "Michael"
Altman, a real estate developer doing deals in Hudson County, who did
not yet know he was being worked by Dwek in a new scheme. "Those were
the 'good ole days.' Three years ago."

Altman laughed. "I should have met you four years ago," he said.

Four years earlier, Dwek had been a big man in real estate, buying dozens of properties at a time, sometimes on little more than a whim. He
loved the wheeling and dealing. "It was thrilling. Satisfying," he would
later recall. It beat gambling in Atlantic City. He never put money down at
the tables. The action was far better in real estate. Condos in Israel, luxury
homes down in Florida, commercial buildings in New Jersey, and a dinner
cruise boat converted into a floating casino that was still docked some-
place—he wasn't quite sure where—were part of a portfolio that on paper
was easily worth $400 million.

He had just sort of fallen into the real estate business. Dwek grew up in
an extremely Orthodox home in Deal, a quiet, affluent Jersey Shore resort
town more than an hour's drive south from Manhattan in fast-growing
Monmouth County.

Over the years, Deal had become a de facto summer colony for the
growing Syrian Sephardic community in Brooklyn. The insular group

shunned publicity like the plague. The Syrian Jews were different from the Ashkenazi emigrants from Europe who originally spread from the Lower East Side of New York and whom most American Jews can trace lineage to. For one thing, the Syrians did not typically speak Yiddish. They spoke Arabic. The Community's traditions and religious customs—rooted in Aleppo, some 220 miles north of Damascus—also were different. Their foods were Middle Eastern. They even cursed in Arabic. Unlike the ultrareligious Hasidim with their black hats and long coats and refusal to mingle with the world at large, these Sephardic Jews came from a culture of merchants, peddlers, and deal makers, bringing with them the commercial traditions of old Aleppo. They interacted far more widely with the secular community, assimilating, in their dress and business dealings with outsiders. Among themselves, though, much of their business was done on handshakes and understandings, without bothering to put anything in writing.

They lived together, worked together, and kept one another's secrets together. Charity and fund-raising was part of the Community's busy social scene. Weddings were as intimate as one can make with 1,000 guests or more. Tithing to the synagogue was a common practice.

Some of the Community's alumni were household names. Actor Dan Hedaya, pop singer and dancer Paula Abdul of *American Idol* fame, and American fashion designer Isaac Mizrahi. Eddie Antar, once widely known as "Crazy" Eddie, was also a Syrian Jew. Antar's New York–based home electronics business advertising "insane prices" had crashed decades earlier, but the fame he won from his over-the-top TV commercials and steep discounts to consumers lived on. He remained a New York icon. Eddie, though, was not a point of pride for the Community. After he was caught up in a spectacular fraud involving the skimming of millions off the books and falsifying profits to pump up his company's stock, Antar fled to Israel in an effort to avoid prosecution. He was eventually jailed; the company went bankrupt and was sold off for its parts.

Far more well-known than the personalities were the businesses and investments spawned by the Community. Jordache, known for their jeans. Rainbow Shops. Century 21, the popular department-store chain in New York. The Children's Place. The Duane Reade drugstore chain. Midtown Equities, one of the leaseholders of the World Trade Center site.

Like its commercial alter egos, the Community's wealth was not hidden. In Brooklyn, modest houses prized for their location in walking distance of the synagogues on Ocean Parkway routinely sold for millions of dollars before being torn down—to be replaced by imposing mansions costing millions more. It was all about location. Those in the Syrian community were willing to pay a million or more for a modest duplex near Shaare Zion and then pour double or triple that amount to rip it down and rebuild, rather than spend far less money on a penthouse on the Upper East Side.

Driving through that part of the neighborhood is like slipping into an exclusive gated complex without the gates. On one corner of Avenue S and East Fifth Street is a stately brick mansion with colonnade pillars and a slate roof. Even larger homes dot the streets nearby, with low brick walls, imposing portico entrances, and red Spanish tile. Some are sandwiched into spaces between the many far more humble duplexes along the street that can only be awaiting the right price to be sold and torn down as well. On just about every block are parked the silver and black SUVs of a security service with yellow light bars on top. Strangers wandering in the neighborhood will very quickly be questioned about what they are doing there. Essentially, the residents have their own private police force.

In New Jersey, the old Victorians of Deal had been taken down over the years, replaced by stark, unaffordable modern beachfront houses or, in some cases, Mediterranean-style villas that seem to echo off the architectural brick and red Spanish tile of the fanciest homes in Brooklyn. Dwek got into a discussion on the phone one day with a newcomer—a Hasid from Brooklyn who remarked at the size of the homes in Deal as he drove, marveling about there being so much money floating around despite the recession.

"Recession, schme-cession," Dwek replied, almost with disdain. "Not for the Syrians."

Like most Orthodox communities, the Sephardic enclaves are encircled by an *eruv*, a wire or line meant to symbolically define the boundaries of a home. Jewish law prohibits work on Shabbat, or the Sabbath. For the observant, that means not being able to carry anything—such as keys, books, or babies—except within the home or an enclosed "private" area. An *eruv* basically extends the confines of a home to whole neighborhoods, including streets and sidewalks, allowing women to push baby carriages to synagogue on Saturday mornings. For the Syrian Jews, though, the *eruv* could be viewed as impenetrable as a stone wall. No one crossed it. Theirs was a closed society, bound together by a 1935 edict set down by Saul Kassin's father against intermarriage with those outside the Community—even Jewish converts—on pain of permanent exile.

The rule contradicts Jewish law. The biblical figure of Ruth, after all, is celebrated as a Jewish convert and the great-grandmother of King David. But the edict was viewed as critical to perpetuating the Syrians—known colloquially as the "SY" community—and in fact has been undeniably successful in keeping it intact. They try to keep it hermetically sealed from outside influences and they have done a very good job. Families have suffered because of it—even Kassin's own daughter Anna, who has not seen him since she was banished by her father decades ago after she married a non-Jew. Yet the intermarriage rate, which some believe is one-in-two in non-Orthodox communities, is nil. There is virtually no assimilation.

Few talk to outsiders about the Community for fear of being shunned. Those who do often will not use their names. "It's a very, very tight community," explained Sammy Antar, who grew up in Brooklyn and was once very much part of it and now wants nothing to do with the Syrians. The cousin of Crazy Eddie and the former chief financial officer of the now-defunct electronics chain, Antar was sitting at an upstairs table at Angelo's Pizza on Broadway in Manhattan, beneath the blue and yellow marquee of the Ed Sullivan Theater, where David Letterman's show is taped. Reflecting on the origins of his community, Antar said many were forced to leave Syria after the formation of the state of Israel in 1948, but they had been forever shaped by living for generations among a hostile Arab population. "It was a community that had to be cohesive for survival."

The traditions of the souk and the Middle East were never abandoned in the New World. Antar, who admitted his own guilt in the fraud committed by his cousin decades earlier, now advises auditing firms, companies, and law enforcement agencies on how to detect white-collar crime. He said it is a given that taxes for many in the community are viewed simply as money to be stolen.

Many businesses deal in cash. "It is an off-the-books culture," Antar explained. Some are involved in international trade, where he said it is easy to create fake invoices to overstate or understate transactions for jeans, electronics, or kids' clothing. Crazy Eddie's was not the only business born in the community known to cook its books, then or now. "There is a large subculture in the community that says 'fuck the government,'" he said.

Dwek himself did not come from a rich family. His father, Rabbi Isaac Dwek, a prominent and highly respected religious leader, came to this country from Syria at the age of 14 and headed one of the first and largest Syrian congregations in Deal—the Synagogue of Deal on Norwood Avenue.

If the Syrians were an insular enclave in Brooklyn, Deal was even more separate, and equally wealthy. For decades, the Brooklyn community had migrated every summer to the Jersey Shore town of Bradley Beach, about fifty miles south of New York. In time, many with money began buying property in nearby Deal, putting up modern houses and even more modern synagogues.

Erica Brown, scholar-in-residence for The Jewish Federation of Greater Washington and an adjunct professor at American University and George Washington University, grew up in Deal and remembered the rapid Syrian influx in what is still a lovely, spacious small town.

"There were stories of people being offered large bags of cash for their homes," she recalled. At first, most sent their children to the public schools, and Brown still laughs at how one of the new kids was asked to name the seven continents. There was North America. South America. Europe . . . And Brooklyn. Which in fact was the center of the universe.

For Brown, there was a sense of separation. The newcomers began taking over local businesses and stores. She had Syrian friends, yet there were parties that she knew she would never be invited to. As she points out herself, "I was a J-Dub," the term the SYs use privately, and derisively, to refer to Ashkenazim—shorthand for the *J* and the *w* in the English word "Jew." Yet she did not feel left out or excluded. It just wasn't her world. "I didn't see a dark side to it. It was something sweet," described Brown. "I was intrigued by the way the community functioned. They relied on each other. It was a very intense and vibrant community."

At the same time, though, she began to zero in on the hypocrisies she saw as she herself grew more Orthodox in her own beliefs and traditions. "I would have a strict way of looking at it, but they had accommodations that helped them navigate the secular and religious world."

For example, she said Syrian families would go to an Italian restaurant, which was not kosher, and bring their own cheese to put on pizza, as if that made it all right. They would go on Saturday during the summer to the Deal Casino, the big beach club, and buy lunch with "Shabbat Tickets," which was simply paper script or coupons that were used so they did not violate the rules of not exchanging money on the Sabbath. But the food they were buying in a way as to not violate the laws of Shabbat was not even kosher. It seemed odd.

* * *

To many within the Community, Solomon Dwek was known simply as The Rabbi's Son. It conferred upon him an aura of trust, said Ken Cayre, a wealthy former music and software executive and another high-profile member of the Syrian Jewish community, and also the uncle of Dwek's wife. Cayre, a multimillionaire many times over, would invest a great deal of money with Dwek over time to put into real estate.

"I've known him for many, many years. He's never done anything that I would consider unlawful," Cayre said in sworn testimony as part of a later bankruptcy proceeding. "He's the son of a rabbi and I just had a trust in him."

Would he have any reason to question the morals or the ethics of someone he knew to be the son of a rabbi?

"No." Cayre shook his head. "No."

Isaac "Ike" Franco, another investor, was even more direct.

"I'm a person that does due diligence and is really on top of his game when it comes to doing business," said Franco, the president and CEO of Franco Apparel Group, a children's clothing manufacturer with a reported $80 million a year in sales. "I trusted him. I believed in him. I wanted to believe in him."

In a culture that values knowledge and piety, where the center of community life is the synagogue and the school, there is something different about being the son of a rabbi. Always has been. "You have to understand, I . . ." Franco paused for a moment. "His father performed my wedding. His father is someone that I care about. And for me, it was probably one of the reasons why I trusted him and I didn't do further due diligence on a lot of things."

The third of eight children—five sons and three daughters—Dwek, like most others in the Community, did not attend public schools. He went to religious institutions from the time he was a young boy. Elementary school was the Lakewood Boys Cheder, a large institution with students from kindergarten through eighth grade, located in nearby Ocean County.

In elementary and high school, there were some secular classes in the afternoon. Maybe two hours a day. As he got older, it was as much as 12 hours a day of Judaic studies. There were no sports, no recreation, no time off. "I never played baseball," he has said of his early life. "No running around. No music. I regret it tremendously."

(Curiously, months after Dwek started talking with the U.S. Attorney's office federal charges were filed claiming the Lakewood school had submitted false statements to obtain nearly $1 million in excessive government payments under the National School Lunch Program. The feds said more than 1,100 preschoolers were receiving meals at ineligible and unapproved sites. Prosecutors say the timing was a coincidence. Dwek, they say, had no role in the matter. The school admitted no liability and agreed to pay a $1.2 million settlement.)

Dwek's Bar Mitzvah at the age of 13 was in Jerusalem. He was the firstborn son, and when he got older he was sent to an Orthodox Jewish boarding school in Riverdale, the upscale neighborhood nestled in the northwest corner of the Bronx. An Ashkenazi school, Yeshiva of the Telshe Alumni was well-known and respected, with roots that could be traced back decades earlier to an institution destroyed by the Nazis in the Lithuanian town of Telshe. "I would sleep there and come home not too often," Dwek recalled during a deposition. "I think my father and my parents decided this was the best school for me. I wasn't that happy, to tell you the truth, in the beginning, but I got used to it after a while."

It was an all-boys school and he studied mostly Torah every day. In conversations with people he knew, Dwek brushed it off. "I was thirteen. It was the top school and my father wanted me to go there. So I went there."

Years later, Dwek in fact sent tens of thousands of dollars to the school after he began raking in big money in real estate.

After graduating, he attended rabbinical college for two years. It was not a seminary to prepare rabbis and it was not a school that gave out degrees. He never applied to college. Nor was he much interested in becoming a rabbi. For that matter, he was not particularly interested in school, period, claiming the only reason he went to rabbinical college was that ultra-Orthodox women wanted to marry scholars. Dwek was no scholar. It seemed he was just a guy on the make.

He was not a particularly good student at that—claiming the only way he graduated was to bribe a teacher with $50 after he failed math. "That's how I got my high school diploma," he claimed under oath.

One year when he came home to New Jersey from school on a religious holiday, he met Jack Adjmi, a longtime family friend with homes in Deal and New York. Adjmi, now dead, was in the rag trade. He was the owner of a major New York–based apparel company whose brands included Skechers, Fila, Champion, and Beluga—suppliers to some of the biggest retailers in the world. But he also dabbled a little in real estate and he had a proposal for The Rabbi's Son. There was a house for sale down the block from the Dwek home. Adjmi asked the teenager if he had seen it.

"Sure." Dwek shrugged. So what? He had not paid much attention to it.

"How would you like to go into a partnership with me?" suggested Adjmi.

Dwek did not have two cents to put together. But he listened to the old man.

"I'll buy it. You renovate it. Then we'll rent it out for the summer, or we can sell it."

Dwek quickly took him up on the offer. Over time, Dwek grew very close to Jack, who became a mentor and father figure as Solomon began playing the real estate game. While he never took financial courses in school, he was street-smart and picked up things quickly as he got involved with Adjmi.

"Jack didn't have too much experience or knowledge in the real estate business, but we worked together," recalled Dwek, who learned through experience. "I bought my first properties with Jack before I was nineteen and a half and before rabbinical college, but we just learned on the job." Sometimes, he said, Jack held the buildings in his own name. Sometimes, he said, Adjmi held them in a family trust. Sometimes the buildings were held in the name of a company.

"It was different. There were a lot of different properties," Dwek said. There were never any contracts between them. No partnership papers. Just a handshake and an understanding.

"You trust me. I trust you and you don't need anything in writing with me," Adjmi repeatedly told him, The Rabbi's Son would later recollect. "I'll never hurt you."

If Dwek had ever made the same promise, it would not be one he kept. It would only be later, much later, before anyone would learn that Dwek had been ripping off his uncle and the Adjmis for millions upon millions of dollars over the years. That, more than anything, led to a fateful showdown years later in the fourth-floor conference room of a Hackensack law firm that would bring down Dwek's house of cards within a matter of days.

* * *

"Solomon was a snot-nosed kid who hung on the apron strings and worked with Jack," Kerry Green, a building contractor who for a time did a great deal of business with Solomon Dwek, told the *Asbury Park Press*. "He was Jack's legman. He went out and found a few deals."

Jack put up all the money on all the early deals. There was financing, but it was Jack's money, Jack's financing, and Jack's cash. Dwek, still very much a kid, then driving a 15-year-old Buick LeSabre, had nothing to invest but his time.

"My husband used to—he was very good about helping boys out, other boys, and he met Solomon and I think that he bought a few pieces of property with him when he was . . . when Solomon was very young," recalled Adjmi's widow, Rachel Adjmi, in sworn testimony. Other than that, she said, Solomon had no shares of her husband's business. "Absolutely not. Never," she insisted. "My husband would never allow anyone to be involved in our businesses—anyone, anyone, anyone. Even people that are like family. Our business is only mine and my children's and his and that's the way it was."

In the beginning, Dwek said he and Adjmi would get loans from New York–based Republic National Bank, which had deep roots in the Syrian and Lebanese Jewish communities and was especially favored in New York City's Orthodox neighborhoods.

Republic had been founded by Edmond J. Safra, the secretive Beirut-born banker and philanthropist whose empire catered to a wealthy international clientele. Extremely religious, Safra was a major supporter of Jewish causes, and his name remains one of the most recognizable in Sephardic communities, where synagogues, buildings, and community centers have been named after him or his father—including one in Deal.

Republic, when first trying to find a foothold in New York, made a name for itself as well, in its aggressive efforts to gain new depositors—becoming one of the first banks there to use giveaways, such as TV sets, blenders, and toasters, to those who deposited funds for extended periods of time.

When Safra finally sold the bank in 1999 to HSBC Holdings of London for $10.3 billion, it was the largest foreign takeover deal for an American banking company. But just before the sale to HSBC, Safra, who had been suffering from Parkinson's disease, was killed in a strange predawn fire that swept through his luxury Monte Carlo penthouse. The news stunned many and led to unfounded speculation that he had been the target of the Russian mob. A private nurse later admitted he had set the blaze in hopes of emerging as a hero.

When the institution was ultimately acquired by HSBC, the world's biggest private bank, one executive with knowledge of the transaction said HSBC had no idea what it was buying. There were stories about HSBC brass touring Republic's New York headquarters and throughout the building seeing mezuzahs, the encased Scripture that observant Jews place on all doorposts. Not knowing anything of the culture they were marrying into, the new people thought they were looking at small video cameras.

"Boy, you guys have really good security here," one executive said.

Dwek would attend closings at Republic's branch in Brooklyn's Williamsburg, and Jack would borrow 70 percent or 80 percent of the purchase price, putting up the balance in cash.

"I don't remember which one was the first one, but I remember I bought a few houses during a short period of time," said Dwek. The deal he had with Adjmi remained verbal. According to Dwek, any time he bought a property, he was to acquire it on behalf of the Adjmi family. When they sold the property, after they got back their principal they were supposed to give him 20 percent of the profit.

"That never happened. But that was a deal I had with them," he said. "I found the properties. I negotiated the properties. I leased the properties, fixed the properties, built the properties a lot of times, and sold the properties at times, too. They weren't involved—I don't think they ever sold their own properties."

Dwek also began working with Barry Kantrowitz. The two first met in 1993, when Dwek purchased his first single-family home on his own in Ocean Township, near Deal. The transaction was handled through Kantrowitz's office. Later, as Solomon began buying more and more properties, he continued to use Barry for a time but then started using a competing broker, cutting Kantrowitz out of hundreds of thousands of dollars in commissions. He finally called Dwek up one evening and they arranged to meet. "You're putting me out of business," Kantrowitz complained.

"That was my intention," Dwek said without apology. "I'm sick of paying you and everyone else in Monmouth County billions of dollars in commissions and not making money. Why should I continue to do this? I have my own people that could do the same job as you."

"Well, you're not a real estate salesperson or a broker," Kantrowitz reminded him.

Dwek had never really thought about getting a real estate license himself. It meant first becoming a salesperson for three or four years and then becoming a broker. He had considered it once in passing but let it drop.

Looking for a solution to his problem, Kantrowitz eventually put an offer on the table. What if they went into business together? "I have thirty years of experience and we'll go fifty-fifty in Barry Associates, LLC, and we'll branch out. You only have one office. I have one office. We'll open up a whole bunch of offices."

Dwek thought about it briefly and then shook hands on the agreement. It made sense for both of them. There was nothing on paper, but he would tell the bankruptcy trustee later that there was an understanding. "I owned verbally. I had a deal with him, fifty-fifty."

The two eventually became close friends and confidants. At least for a time.

* * *

At 23, Dwek met Pearl Sutton, a petite dark-haired woman four years his junior. Where he was heavyset and overweight, taking Lipitor every night for his high cholesterol, Pearl liked to work out at the gym. Pearl's parents were members of his father's congregation. He was looking to get married and she was available, so he had a friend call her parents on his behalf. That's the way it was done in the religious community. A meeting was arranged and they shared a Coke in a hotel lobby in Long Branch. The courtship was short, maybe seven or eight dates, before they decided to marry.

Following Sephardic custom, they named their children for close relatives. Their oldest was Isaac, named for Dwek's father. Solomon's first daughter was named for his mother, Raizel. Then came Milo and Jack, named for Pearl's parents. A fifth child would come along later. They called him Moshe—Hebrew for Moses.

As Solomon began expanding his first real estate dealings, Dwek's father put him on the payroll of the Deal Yeshiva, the Jewish day school the rabbi had founded with his wife, Solomon's mother. The rabbi was the *rosh yeshiva* (head of the school), overseeing Talmudic studies but not concerning himself with the day-to-day operations. That was his wife's responsibility. "You talk to Raizel with the small problems. You come to me with the big problems," the rabbi would tell staff members.

Solomon was made vice president of the school, initially at a salary of about $40,000. The compensation would quickly grow to more than $200,000 a year. Solomon's wife was also made an employee. As a secretary, she was making $100,000, according to federal tax filings. Hers seemed to be a no-show job, said teachers at the yeshiva. They could not recall ever seeing her there. Dwek's office was not even in the school but rather in a small two-room tan brick building about the size of a trailer located on Brighton Avenue, adjacent to the synagogue.

The school's business office had no lobby or reception area. Nothing on the walls. Dwek's Formica-topped desk was in the front, and there was a door to the back where Amy Annecharico, his assistant and bookkeeper, could be found.

Some remembered Solomon as shy, soft-spoken, and reserved, although he was not a hard person to like. "He doesn't speak much," Rabbi Dwek told school administrators. "Don't take it personally."

One teacher said Solomon had a subdued sense of humor. "Sometimes he wouldn't look at you in the eye," he said.

Others noted Solomon would more often than not be following the stock market on the computer in the tiny school office, an undecorated warren strewn with stacks of documents. There were no pictures. Not even of his kids.

Bankruptcy court filings charge that Solomon began using the school as his private piggy bank and, eventually, to launder money. While he contributed millions to the school, checks drawn on the school's payroll account were later traced to Dwek's own companies, to construction and title firms and to a landscaper. There were payroll checks written out to S. Dwek, Dwek Properties, Amboy National Bank, PNC Bank, Pax Construction, Carroll Construction, Imperial Title & Marble Co., Inc., Eatontown TV, and Partusch Lawn Service. Other payments were found to be related to capital improvements on Dwek's own properties. Dwek also transferred funds to the Deal Yeshiva using his American Express cards. The documents suggest he was effectively laundering tens of thousands of dollars out of his business dealings by contributing money to the yeshiva and then taking out salaries for him and his wife, while covering his living and other expenses by having the school pick them up.

Much later, during the first of the criminal trials that Dwek would testify at, he was very matter-of-fact about the money-laundering and tax evasion scheme he ran out of the school. His job, he said, was to raise money and there were a number of deep-pocket donors in the Sephardic community willing to write big checks to the yeshiva. He was the one who would solicit them. But the money would come with a catch, he explained. They would give him a check but wanted most of it back in cash. The yeshiva could take a 10 percent cut of the transaction. He could take a commission for himself. The donor got the rest back clean, while writing it all off on that year's income tax return. From Dwek's perspective, it wasn't a bad deal.

"I was trying to retain these donors," he said unapologetically. It kept the donors happy, put money in his pocket, and still brought in money for the yeshiva. A win-win-win situation for everyone but the IRS. He got quite good at it. Eventually, though, he couldn't handle the amount of money being converted. It was too much to deal with out of the school budget. He had to find others to help him launder the money being shoveled in. People who could handle $50,000 at a pop.

* * *

The Dweks' lifestyle ranged from Costco to Lexus. They would shop at Shloimy's Kosher World in Lakewood. Dwek wore $13 white short-sleeve cotton shirts he bought at T.J.Maxx, a big-box discount store.

Yet they thought nothing of vacationing at the exclusive Phoenician resort in Scottsdale, Arizona. He owned a $1.9 million home north of Miami in Aventura, Florida, sandwiched between a golf course and a marina.

They lived in a $1.6 million, 4,600-square-foot six-bedroom home in Deal, with custom marble and wood floors, separate maid's quarters, and six bathrooms. At one point, Dwek, by then in bankruptcy and facing millions in judgments, had three Lexus luxury cars and a Jaguar S-Type parked in his driveway.

"Do you and your family need four cars?" a lawyer asked.

"No," Dwek allowed. "Three cars would do."

* * *

The land deals continued to grow, at first modestly and then, it seemed, with almost reckless abandon. Ocean Township councilman Christopher P. Siciliano, who also works as a real estate agent, watched as it all went into overdrive. He would often see Dwek at the bagel shop in the small strip mall near his own real estate office, and Dwek would be constantly on his cell phone. On the road, Dwek, now in a leased Cadillac, would have one hand on the steering wheel and the other on the phone in his ear.

"He exploded on the scene," Siciliano said, remembering the initial purchases of a few commercial properties. But then it seemed to go from a sound business plan to an obsession, a crazed Monopoly player going through the board game and buying everything—offices, retail space, residential buildings, even a funeral home—without a thought to how it was going to be financed before passing Go.

As he toured the area one morning, showing off some of the properties that started going into Dwek's portfolio, Siciliano gestured out the window at the many small, undistinguished suburban tract homes on the side streets off Monmouth Road while he navigated. "This is ground zero. This is Solomon Dwek territory."

Many were modest houses aimed at first-time home buyers, properties that Dwek bought at prices far more than they were worth and then never sold. Because he was overpaying, he could not flip them. But he could leverage them, and that's what he began doing, taking out additional loans atop properties that were being artificially inflated in price. He would rent them out, said Siciliano, or let them sit idle while continuing to buy everything that came on the market. The commercial properties might get a quick slap of paint, but little more. Along busy Highway 35, Dwek had a Denny's restaurant, a blue-roofed Starbucks, and a Subway sandwich shop. There was a paint factory in a small industrial park that to this day sits empty.

Siciliano couldn't figure it out. Nobody could. "There was so much money going in, I thought there was money laundering going on," he said candidly.

One place still sticks out in his mind. It was a little blue carriage house on the back lot of another property that could not have been more than 900 square feet, if that. Dwek was ready to buy it, sight unseen, for $530,000. It was a ridiculously high price for what the property was. "Why would somebody do that?" Siciliano wondered aloud. "It was worth at least one hundred thousand dollars less."

Basically, Dwek created his own market. People would sell to Solomon because he would pay more, buying up everything for prices far above the going rate. He was paying unbelievable returns to investors and had no shortage of takers.

Suddenly Dwek had become like his father: sought after for advice, successful, the center of attention. Sure, Solomon's sphere was not God and good works but condos and colonials. But that didn't matter, because the chubby kid with the glasses was now a man of respect.

He became the director of a bank at the age of 29: a start-up called Monmouth Community Bank. He was a major shareholder of the holding company, with 5.4 percent of the shares of its stock. The prospectus painted a picture of a successful entrepreneur:

> Solomon Dwek is known for his commercial real estate ventures having facilitated the leasing and sale of many high profile commercial properties in the State of New Jersey. Mr. Dwek became a member of the board of directors of Monmouth Community Bank on December 17, 1998, and has served as a member of the board of directors of the holding company since its inception.

Another board member was Philip Konvitz, an aging longtime Monmouth County political power broker who resigned from the board after being named in a 13-count indictment that accused him of bribing former Asbury Park councilman James Condos in return for Condos' support on development issues. Charges were later dismissed after medical experts agreed that the 92-year-old defendant was suffering from Alzheimer's disease, dementia, and atrophy of the brain, and was deemed unfit to stand trial.

Dwek gave hundreds of thousands of dollars to charity. Not just to the Deal Yeshiva, which was also paying his bills. And not just to Jewish charities or those within the community, like the private ambulance service connected with the Orthodox. He donated more than $30,000 to refurbish the Lumia Theater in Long Branch, home of the New Jersey Repertory Company, which named its 60-seat black box stage the Pearl and Solomon Dwek Little Theater. Gabe Barabas, one of Lumia's founders, told *The Star-Ledger* that he approached Dwek to make the donation and met with him briefly two or three times to seal the deal. Barabas said Dwek seemed interested when he heard the theater would be used to produce plays for children.

"He struck me as a quiet person," Barabas said. "Just a simple, unassuming man."

Dwek never returned to see a play. He only dropped by once, to see the theater after the renovations were complete. "He said, 'Very good,' or something to that effect and left as quickly as he came," Barabas said. "He always seemed to be in a rush. It was almost like a little tornado went through."

He also paid for the construction of a granite monument to honor Frank Caltabilota, a West Long Branch college student killed in the January 2000 dormitory fire at Seton Hall University that led to the deaths of two others and left three students with terrible burns. There was also a $5,000 contribution cited on Dwek's 2005 federal income tax returns to a Brooklyn rabbi by the name of Mordchai Fish, who would be among those arrested by the FBI four years later for laundering charitable contributions in the federal sting operation.

* * *

Records show Solomon became a prolific contributor to political campaigns as well, from mayors to the president of the United States. Larry Bathgate was a heavy hitter within Republican circles who made a fortune many times over through astute land investments in rural farmland properties in Central and Southern New Jersey. A former New Jersey Republican finance chairman, he was a key fund-raiser—not only for the GOP but also for schools, charitable institutions, and other causes—with a Rolodex filled with other wealthy friends and business contacts who could be counted on for their generosity to one another's causes.

With strong ties to the large Hasidic community in nearby Lakewood, New Jersey, Bathgate met Dwek in the midst of a property dispute involving a land contract that Dwek sat on and then tried to hold up in court. Bathgate didn't try fighting it through litigation. That would have dragged on so long that he would have effectively lost just by waiting for it to play out. There was a better way. He took it directly to a rabbinic court, a Beth Din, literally a house of judgment. Dwek never showed up for the proceedings and lost by default. Before the ruling could be advertised, Dwek personally apologized to Bathgate.

As they spoke, Dwek, who knew of Bathgate's friendship with Pres. George W. Bush, told him he would be very interested in attending the next political fund-raiser he held. Turned out, there was one coming up in Lakewood. Vice Pres. Dick Cheney was scheduled to come to New Jersey to harvest cash for the Bush-Cheney campaign coffers. The event was scheduled for March 2004. Those able to put together at least $10,000 for the president's reelection—from personal contributions up to the campaign finance limit, and whatever could be bundled through friends and business partners—would be invited to participate in a roundtable with Cheney and have their picture taken with the vice president. It sounded like a good idea to Dwek, who was immediately agreeable. "Okay, put me down," he said. He wrote out a check for $2,000 and his wife matched it. He also gave an additional $25,000 to the New Jersey Republican State Committee.

The fund-raiser was held at the Chateau Grand, an aging banquet hall on Route 9 in Lakewood that had once been home to a German restaurant and still bore vague aspirations to being a Bavarian village. It was not a fancy place anymore. The parking lot blacktop ran right to the edge of the building and the interior had seen better days. Inside, ice sculptures of GOP elephants and American flags graced the serving tables. Off to one side were tables of strictly kosher food for Orthodox donors from Lakewood. On the other, guests nibbled on decidedly non-kosher hors d'oeuvres such as shrimp kebabs and bacon-wrapped scallops.

Cheney, flown in to Lakehurst Naval Air Station aboard Air Force Two, loved Lakewood. Driving in, his caravan passed pickup trucks with gun racks. Pulling up to the barn-like banquet facility, the vice president told Bathgate it reminded him of Wyoming. Even better, the fund-raiser, attended by 700 people, brought in more than $600,000—a haul that would be celebrated at the highest echelons of the Bush campaign. The state's Republican elite were also all there, including former governor Christine Todd Whitman.

Dwek got his picture, standing with a big smile alongside the vice president, blue tie slightly askew with his collar loosened, flanked by the American flag on the left and the buff-colored flag of New Jersey to the right.

According to Dwek, he raised a great deal of money for the president's campaign. "I don't recall if it was ten—ten thousand dollars, twenty thousand dollars, or twenty-five thousand dollars. Probably somewhere between ten thousand dollars and fifty thousand dollars, if I had to estimate," Dwek said. "I gave him a check, I believe, from my personal account." Despite the financial support, he did not appear to be particularly partisan. Dwek gave evenly to Democrats and Republicans. There were checks to Bush and to Democratic senator Robert Torricelli of New Jersey. To Republican senator Orrin Hatch and to New Jersey Democrat senator and senate president Richard Codey. Over a 10-year-period, Dwek and his wife gave nearly $200,000 in campaign contributions. He claimed to have met President Bill Clinton.

* * *

Dwek's apparent success in real estate attracted others in the community, who began investing with him. Among them were Ken Cayre; Manny Haber, president of the apparel firm Fleet Street; Ike Franco; and Rabbi Eliahu Ben Haim, the son of another respected rabbi and a family friend whose daughter was married to Dwek's brother.

Cayre had made a fortune in the record and video business. He and his brothers had created SalSoul Records, named for its blend of salsa and soul, and moved early into video with a company called GoodTimes, which marketed cheap children's videos through Walmart. Cayre described the deals being offered by Solomon as a "profit participation" arrangement. In one of them Dwek, Cayre said, had come to him saying he was able to buy a number of properties from Meridian Health, a Neptune, New Jersey-based health care system. The plan he outlined was to buy the land on their behalf and eventually sell the parcels to them—flipping them at a profit.

"We had made up a profit participation agreement where I would get a percentage of the profits in return for putting up some monies, certain monies," explained Cayre. "He supposedly put me on the phone with some official from Meridian. That was about the only due diligence I did. I was relying mainly on trust and on my past knowledge of Solomon to be an honorable person, and I didn't do as much due diligence as I wish I did."

Cayre never saw any documentation. He never asked for any. He did not request any appraisals from Dwek, did not contact any closing attorneys concerning the transactions, and did not attend a single closing. If Cayre had, all sorts of warning flags would have been raised. According to court filings, he wired $12 million to Dwek on June 30, 2005, from his account at HSBC Bank and an additional $2 million from a separate account at Mellon Bank, based on a promise from Dwek that he would receive a quick $1 million profit in 10 days. Twelve days later, he received $15 million back—all his investment, plus the $1 million he was expecting. Easy money.

In August, Cayre wired Solomon another $3.6 million in connection with a property on Montgomery Street in Neptune, New Jersey, based on the pledge that he would see a $200,000 profit in three days. He got back $2.5 million two days later and another $1.3 million within five days, netting the $200,000 that was promised. He was hooked.

But afterward, he said subsequent dealings did not go nearly as smoothly and he slowly began to get suspicious that things might not be as they seemed to be.

Franco was also a participant in the Meridian deal that Solomon was promoting.

"He took me to the hospital, showed me, actually, a plaque that he had donated to the hospital—gave them over one million dollars in donations, and that he had a very strong connection with the president/CEO of Meridian," recalled Franco.

"How are you getting these deals?" Franco had asked.

"I have a special relationship," Dwek explained. "I'm outsourcing these locations for them. I have a track record, a history with Meridian."

Franco never spoke with anybody at Meridian. He asked Solomon about it but never pressed him on it. "I'm a busy person running a business," Franco said. "As long as Solomon was really running the deals, I didn't have any need to be meeting with these people."

Joseph Dwek, the brother of Rabbi Dwek, was married to Jack Adjmi's daughter and also took notice early on of his nephew's success. Joey, who had first introduced Solomon to Jack, was a top executive with Adjmi's company. He knew children's clothing, not real estate, but he could see the kid was doing great. Joey wanted in on the action. "You're my nephew. I don't know anything about real estate. Maybe you can put me into some good real estate deals," he recounted years later for a room full of lawyers trying to untangle those deals.

Someone asked, "What made you interested in doing real estate with Solomon?"

Joey did not flinch. "Make money," he answered. "Because the whole community does real estate, so I thought it's interesting to get into. Real estate was hot then. I had some money to invest. I said, what's the best thing to do but invest with a person that knows what he's doing in real estate, and he seemed like he knew what he was doing in real estate, and I trusted him fully."

Solomon very quickly offered Joey a building interest, but had no hard sell. He sketched it out without elaboration, showing his uncle only the bottom line.

"I have a building that became available. It's this address and it's this amount of money," Dwek told Joey. "This is your return. Do you want to buy it or not?"

The terms were the same that Solomon had with Jack Adjmi. Solomon would receive 20 percent of the profits from the sale of the properties purchased by his uncle. Joey Dwek did not even look at the property or examine any of the paperwork. He took his nephew on faith, and said so with some embarrassment much later on. "You're not gonna believe this, but I really trusted him fully," he said ruefully. "I bought all of them. He sends me the contracts. I send him money. I wire the money out. I never saw any of the buildings."

That was the beginning.

To Joey Dwek, there was little reason to dig deeper. "You trust a guy who's your nephew. It's not like a stranger. 'Come. Show me the building you're buying. I want to see it. Where's the money going? Where's this?' It's my nephew," he explained. "They say *mishpocheh*."

Mishpocheh. Hebrew for extended family.

And among the Syrian Jews of Brooklyn and Deal, all of the Community was *mishpocheh*.

3

⊸+✦+⊹▸

The Schnookie Deal

Monday, April 24, 2006, was on the cool side of the fifties after a miserable weekend of heavy rains that had inundated New Jersey and threatened to continue spilling into the new week. In Eatontown, a few miles to
the west of his home, Solomon Dwek was in deep shit. As he drove down
busy Wyckoff Road behind the wheel of his dark blue Lexus, he could
only think about the options he had left, and none of them looked very
good.

One of his business partners was threatening to cut his balls off, and
Dwek was pretty sure he was serious. His uncle Joey was coming to the
realization that Solomon had screwed him out of $60 million. HSBC, the
bank that had lent him $20 million to buy several properties in the Jersey
Shore town of Neptune—and had actually let the loans go through without ever checking what he had done with the money—finally discovered
the scam and was ready to call the FBI. But first they all wanted their money
back. All of it.

It had not really taken too long to get to this point, Dwek would later
reflect. As his real estate empire began to grow, he began to notice that
no one was really watching what he was doing. No one even seemed to
care. It was an up market, and the banks were lending money with few
questions. One bank didn't record any of their mortgages like they were
supposed to.

"They never attended any closings. They never saw a title or an appraisal .
or a survey of a property and it didn't seem like they were interested in
looking," he recalled. "I don't know what the bank was relying on. What
I do know is if the bank did thirty seconds to do due diligence . . . they
wouldn't have done the loans."

He was buying properties like crazy. As long as the market continued to soar, it really didn't matter what he paid for anything. Wait long enough and he was bound to make money on it at some point. Unless things tanked in a hurry. Even when they did, he still believed he had an ongoing business. "You could call me an addict," he explained later.

His uncle and most of the other investors did not have a clue about what Dwek was investing in, and even Jack was too busy with his own business. They gave Dwek money and he signed notes for unbelievably good returns. To most of them he was sure he was really little more than a steady source of pocket change.

* * *

Dwek was not certain of the date, but there were so many deals going on and funds being commingled from one project to another that he saw an opportunity. It was simple, really. He began to just make things up. "I don't remember any specific details of what I told them, but the Adjmis and Joseph Dwek might have invested money in properties that they thought I was buying and I wasn't really buying them," explained Solomon. "They put up deposits on certain properties that either I wasn't buying or didn't exist."

It was not all that difficult. The key to it all, he claimed, was Jack's longtime chief financial officer, Eli Seruya. According to Dwek, Seruya controlled all of the money being put into his real estate transactions by Adjmi and Joey Dwek and concocted a scheme to get a little bit more out of the deal.

No money left the Adjmi companies' account without Seruya's approval. So if Solomon told Jack or Joe Dwek he needed a wire for a million dollars to buy a property, he would call Seruya, who would make it happen. "Without him giving the blessing, no money left the Adjmi accounts or the Joey Dwek accounts," Solomon said when questioned under oath during his bankruptcy proceeding. "If I told them I was planning to buy a property, they would call Eli to see if it was a good deal. If Eli said 'no,' then the deal was dead."

The way Dwek told it, Seruya also saw an opportunity. According to testimony by Dwek, Seruya told him sometime between 2001 and 2003, "Look, I'm not working for free." So Dwek said they reached an agreement. Dwek began building significant kickbacks into the deals by greatly inflating the prices of the properties he was buying. If he bought a property for a million, he would create paperwork to show it cost more, much more. Seruya, he said, would wire the money for the inflated amount and they would divvy up the proceeds.

"He would not bless the deal without the kickback," he said. "I gave him on one deal seven hundred and fifty thousand dollars back," Dwek testified.

They didn't keep records per se. In that particular case, Dwek claimed, Seruya wrote on a yellow Post-it: *January, February, March, April, May, June—75.* It was the only paperwork to show Dwek needed to pay out $75,000 a month.

Dwek claimed that at one point he also put down thousands of dollars in deposits, all in Seruya's name, on several condominiums in Meron, a small community 25 miles away from Tiberias in northern Israel.

Seruya has denied it all in court depositions.

The 2004 and 2005 sale of two properties on Belmont Avenue in Long Branch was typical of their deals, Dwek claimed. He said he bought the two on Adjmi's behalf for $400,000. But the paperwork showed six properties being acquired for $1.8 million. Dwek said he and Seruya split the difference. It was that easy.

That wasn't the only scam, Dwek said. If no one was looking, who cared if the properties were even there? He began putting together paper real estate deals for properties that simply did not exist. One was on Corlies Avenue in Neptune. It was a flower shop and he had absolutely no idea who actually owned it. "It was a fictitious deal. I never bought it. I never sold it. I never owned it," said Dwek. The only thing that mattered was that the bank thought he was buying it and was willing to give him mortgage money.

Other times, he would get lots of people to invest in properties he already owned. It was like Max Bialystock in *The Producers* telling Leo Bloom he sold twenty five thousand percent of their Broadway show to investors. "Max," Leo sadly informs him. "You can only sell one hundred percent of anything . . ."

* * *

Dwek, meanwhile, was fast getting in over his head. His monthly expenses—between paying off fictitious profits to those who were investing with him and maintaining his buildings—were rapidly overtaking the money he was making in rents. No matter what he did, he was coming to the cold, hard fact that he would never be able to pay back any of the money he was taking in. "I believe it started sinking in sometime in 2004," he confessed after it all came apart.

He started taking out bigger and bigger loans—not just from investors but also short-term lines of credit from banks—to cover the returns he was promising and the mortgages he already owed. Some of the loans were for the purchase of buildings or land he already owned. Others were for phantom properties that no one would ever find on a tax map. Incredibly, no one from the banks seemed interested in confirming anything he told them. He said as much while being grilled by an attorney for HSBC Bank over a multimillion-dollar loan on yet another fraudulent deal that only came to light long after it was approved.

"At the time that you borrowed the money from HSBC, did you tell them it was a Ponzi scheme?" asked the attorney.

"No, of course not," Dwek replied coolly.

"Did you tell them that you didn't intend to repay the loan?"

"No, they wouldn't have lent me the money if I did, I think."

The attorney was persistent. Well, did Dwek tell the bank the loans would not be used for any legitimate purpose?

Dwek did not raise his voice or show any sign of emotion. If he was at all smug, his face remained blank. "I didn't tell them it was a Ponzi scheme, but they didn't bother to ask or make inquiry where the money was going, what the use of the funds were, and if I was taking the money and paying it back to a Ponzi investor. There was no due diligence," he said. "If they looked at my financial statements for ten seconds they would have realized I was committing a fraud on the bank and they wouldn't have lent me the money. They would have realized I was operating the Ponzi scheme."

* * *

Amboy Bank, a private community bank based in Old Bridge, New Jersey, was one of the institutions lending millions of dollars to Dwek. In fact, George Scharpf, the bank's president and chief executive officer, was surreptitiously investing his own money into Dwek's ventures, the bankruptcy trustee later alleged.

Amboy was a relatively small banking institution with strong political ties to the powerful Middlesex County Democratic organization, the machine that gave birth to the career of former governor Jim McGreevey. In January 2003, the bank and Scharpf were fined for helping bank executives expense their political contributions to candidates. According to the Federal Election Commission, 11 senior bank officers wrote off $55,322 in campaign contributions on their expense accounts between February 1996 and January 2002. Scharpf, who donated nearly $28,000, made the majority of the contributions.

It was also the bank that McGreevey, fresh from his 2001 victory in the race for governor, turned to in trying to help a senior aide obtain a mortgage for a condominium. The assistance would prove to be front-page material in the wake of McGreevey's stunning 2004 announcement that he was gay and would resign. The aide who needed the mortgage was Golan Cipel, McGreevey's controversial homeland-security adviser who forced the governor's resignation by threatening to sue McGreevey for sexual harassment. (At the time, Cipel was trying to buy something closer to the governor's mansion in Princeton.) Amboy gave Cipel two mortgages totaling $171,000, thanks largely to the governor's intervention, with McGreevey vouching for Cipel and then showing up with him in person to move things along.

Dwek's relationship with Amboy began back in 1999, when he started borrowing funds to finance the purchases of individual parcels of property. By 2004, he was forwarding multiple real estate contracts of sale and loan requests to Amboy on a weekly basis. In one three-month period, for example, Dwek requested at least 35 different loans from Amboy, including 8 contracts totaling nearly $1.4 million. According to documents filed in the bankruptcy court, the loans were routinely granted with minimal underwriting or due diligence. He was also purchasing delinquent third-party loans from the bank, including loans collateralized by real estate being foreclosed by Amboy. "We were partners in the good and the bad," remarked Dwek.

The loans, however, were edging toward Amboy's legal limit of what could be lent to a single borrower and Amboy attempted to put on the brakes, waiving prepayment penalties and other fees to encourage Dwek and his partnerships to reduce their total outstanding debt, according to a lawsuit by the federal bankruptcy trustee. Yet a few months later Dwek approached Amboy and Scharpf for a $10 million line of credit, ostensibly to acquire more property. According to the federal bankruptcy trustee, despite the limits, the bank issued the loan commitment that September, secured by an investment account owned by Dwek, which had already been pledged as collateral for a totally separate loan made to a relative, said the trustee.

Dwek didn't stop there. In late September, he met Scharpf at Amboy's offices and told him he needed a loan of $20 million to make a down payment on a $91 million deal to purchase a building at 30 Broad Street in New York, a landmark Art Deco office tower in the financial district whose tenants included the New York Stock Exchange.

"It's too expensive to purchase outright," Scharpf told Dwek.

But Solomon said he had a plan to generate some easy cash. He wasn't going to actually buy the property. He just needed to secure a purchase contract and then he would flip the building for a quick payday.

According to the bankruptcy trustee, Scharpf bought into the plan. He not only agreed to give Dwek the money but also wanted in on the deal. He agreed to give Solomon $7 million in a personal loan. Scharpf never spoke to the seller of the building or Dwek's attorney, according to the bankruptcy trustee. He never requested a real estate appraisal or copies of any leases. He never even preconditioned the loan on evidence that the funds would be used in connection with 30 Broad Street. If he had, he would have learned that the proposed purchase contract only required an initial down payment of $1 million, not $20 million.

But then again, Dwek wasn't planning on using the money on the Broad Street building. He needed the money to pay off investors to keep his operation going. A Ponzi scheme can only work as long as fresh money is coming in so the older investors can reap what they believe are investment profits. Dwek wasn't really buying and selling real estate anymore. He was borrowing armfuls of cash to cover the investment returns he was paying out.

"The money came in from investors and banks and most of the money went back out to investors and banks to fuel what I was doing," Dwek said. "It was like you steal from Joe to pay Ike . . ." Dwek was short every day. "Unless I went to the well every day to get money, I couldn't have met my obligations."

Even after Scharpf wired him the money, Dwek continued to push for another $13 million from the bank. *I am only looking for a short term loan for an opportunity that came my way,* he wrote Scharpf.

A week later, Dwek sat down with Scharpf and Kenneth Greco, an Amboy loan officer, to discuss the loan. They agreed to $10 million, secured by three properties that Dwek claimed represented $3 million in equity. According to the bankruptcy trustee, Amboy still failed to perform any due diligence. No title searches. No paperwork. Dwek only provided Scharpf with an unsigned copy of a purported purchase agreement that did not reflect the actual business terms agreed to by Dwek and the seller. Scharpf was also hesitant to submit the loan for approval to the bank's loan committee. "Out of an abundance of caution," Scharpf said, he would hold the collateral mortgages in escrow and talk to the loan committee at a later date, according to one of the trustee's lawsuits.

"Do you want the mortgages recorded?" asked Greco.

"You didn't hear me," Scharpf snapped. "No committee. No recording." He told Dwek that if it was discovered he was personally lending money to him and participating as a partner in investments that were partially funded by loans from Amboy, he would have serious legal issues, according to the bankruptcy trustee's lawsuit. The bank president said the consideration for the three mortgages would be shown as $1 on the books, "so that no one knows what went out the door."

Scharpf was contacted by the authors but declined to comment about the matter, and to this day he has not been charged with any wrongdoing.

None of the money that went out the door was used on the 30 Broad Street property. It, too, went out to pay off other investors.

And then, Dwek really began to stumble.

* * *

While his initial investments had quickly paid off, as early as April 2005 Ike Franco was increasingly suspicious about what was going on. Franco bore a passing resemblance to Brad Garrett, the actor best known for playing Raymond's brother in the TV series *Everyone Loves Raymond*. The hard-driving apparel industry businessman who once worked for his own brother had become wealthy in his own right, overseeing a New York–based company that that gotten into the licensing game early, marketing sports brand clothing through agreements with Major League Baseball, the NBA, the NCAA, and the National Hockey League.

Franco, or Ikey to most people, knew Dwek and his father well. Franco's sister, Evelyn, had worked for the Deal Yeshiva. He had given Solomon $1.5 million to purchase a property in Neptune, which he was told was going to be quickly resold for $3.6 million. He was supposed to get back $300,000. "When I was refinancing these deals through my bank, there was a due date of when these loans would be paid back, so that's how we worked on the—when it was due, based on what Solomon put in the contract," explained the executive in a deposition.

The money never came in, and Franco was caught short at the bank to repay the money he had borrowed and then loaned out to Dwek. He shot an e-mail to Solomon:

> Shlomo *[Hebrew for Solomon]*, I know you mean well but we are not dealing with the closing of a property, it is my business we are talking about here. Bottom line is I need a certified/bank check to be delivered . . . by 9 am the latest on Monday Morning, so it can be immediately deposited into my account. This is not a joke. Not only have I been fined, but I am losing credibility with the bank as well . . . Not for nothing, but you should have picked up the phone to call me. The fact that you did not call after numerous requests knowing I was hanging is unforgivable.

Solomon quickly responded, blaming the bank. He claimed to have repeatedly rewired the money and offered to get Franco a bank check:

I think I made you a lot of money until now and how many millions more to come. I don't control this. I was in meetings all day with them looking at 13 buildings. I couldn't talk. Thanks—

Franco was incredulous. What kind of bullshit was that? He tapped out a quick response:

I have NEVER heard of a wire being sent 3 times and never reaching its destination. Not only have you defrauded and deceived me, I now look like an idiot . . .

Yet Franco kept giving money to Dwek. Ikey explained to those questioning why he just didn't fold his cards and walk away that there was always more than one deal going on with Dwek. "Solomon was a little bit convoluted in his style of funding," Franco said. Sometimes they would have two deals on the table and Dwek would fund the second deal prior to the first and then credit it back to the first.

Still, while Franco had doubts, he later told lawyers investigating the transactions that he chalked it up to Dwek being either disorganized or very complicated. "I didn't want to believe he was dishonest. I really didn't want to believe that," Franco recounted. The thought occurred to him. But he still didn't believe it.

Franco was facing growing pressure from other partners and lenders as to why things were not closing on deadline. "What's going on?" they asked him. "You know, I don't know this fellow. You know him. Is he dishonest?" Franco reassured them that Solomon had always paid every deal they had done and never gone back on his word. "He's just been running late, or he's maybe doing too many deals that he is in over his head," Franco told them, he later said in a sworn deposition. "But he'll make good on it."

Solomon kept giving Franco dates when things would be paid. Then a few weeks later it finally would be, or sometimes it was paid much later.

Dwek saw it differently. Franco, he said, "always told them that I was running a legitimate business and two minutes before that he was telling me I'm a crook and a liar, a cheat and a thief, and he was going to kill me."

Franco began ramping up the threats when Solomon did not deliver as promised. According to public filings, by December of 2005, the e-mails were an angry tirade in the shout of all capital letters:

I STILL DO NOT HAVE ANYTHING IN MY ACCOUNT! THEY ARE CALLING ME EVERY 5 MINUTES AND NEED THIS RIGHT NOW!!!!! IF I DON'T SEE IT IN THE NEXT TWO MINUTES I'LL STRANGLE YOU.

Two weeks later, he laced into Dwek again:

I AM GOING TO KILL YOU IF YOU DO NOT CALL ME RIGHT THIS MINUTE! I MEAN IT!

In another, he told Dwek:

LET ME TELL YOU ONE THING: YOU BETTER HAVE THEIR 20M WIRED IN THE MORNING EARLY G-D HELP YOU OTHERWISE!

(Observant Jews don't like writing out the name of God.)

* * *

Joey Dwek thought he was doing well by his nephew. Solomon, though, was continuing to milk his uncle dry. The agreement, as Joey understood it, was that in return for putting together acquisition packages, he would retain Solomon as property manager and would make charitable contributions to the Deal Yeshiva, where, not coincidentally, Solomon was drawing a sizable salary. At one point, Joey asked Solomon why he was sharing so many good deals.

"I got three hundred deals. I'm making a lot of money. Don't worry about me. I'm okay," Solomon reassured Joey. "I want to take care of my uncle."

What he didn't know was that his nephew was not only siphoning kickbacks out of the sales, he was also doing fake mortgages. And even when his uncle asked for documentation and was repeatedly put off, no red flags went up.

"I always asked. I asked him constantly," said Joey Dwek. "He said, 'It's buried in paperwork. We did maybe three hundred deals. You can't push me. You can't hound me. I've got so many things to do. I'll get it for you.'"

Any alarm bells go off? Like this shouldn't be that tough?

"Who would think in a million years that it's all a bluff?" replied Joey. "You wouldn't think in a million years."

He did not appear to get suspicious until early March of 2006, when Joey said he got a call from Ken Cayre, who left an angry voice-mail message letting him know that his nephew was involved in some criminal fraud. Joey could not immediately reach Cayre, so he e-mailed Solomon to ask what was going on. Dwek brushed it off:

He is kidding around. I just called him. Relax he still loves me. Thanks.

What happened with him? *[Joey asked.]*

Dwek e-mailed back:

we bought a building together. i want to sell for a big profit. he doesn't/ I made up with him. Ignore him. thanks

Joey persisted.

Where's the fraud?

Dwek replied that Cayre thought he had signed the contract against his will. But the fifty-fifty deal was going to turn over $1.8 million. There was no problem, said Joey's nephew:

he's happy now. thanks

Solomon's uncle sounded less than convinced:

It didn't sound that he was kidding.

Joey Dwek said he later found out Cayre had been taken care of through a stock transfer. Solomon's reassurances to his uncle were all lies. Asked about the exchange and the $1.8 million Solomon alluded to, Cayre replied, "I have no idea what he's talking about."

Other lenders were not so easily put off. Signature Bank actually discovered in late 2005 what it believed to be a fraud. With the amount of short-terms loans going through, bank officials had told Dwek they just could not continue going on without having appraisals done or title work.

"That's fine, no problem," he said.

So they ran a title on a property he claimed to be buying. They discovered Dwek already owned it. Then they hired a private investigator to look into some of the other deals. Dwek tried to bluff his way through it.

"Jersey's backed up in recording properties," he said. That part was true. The hot real estate market had led to long delays in many New Jersey counties. While deeds, mortgages, and other land deals were supposed to be recorded daily, some counties were months behind. In some offices, hundreds of unopened envelopes might be piled up as home owners refinanced their mortgages because of low interest rates. It was an invitation for fraud across the state, since there was no way to see whether a property had been purchased until weeks, maybe months, after the transaction. Dwek also insisted that the surveys were mixed up or that he had misinterpreted. The block and lot numbers were inadvertently switched. That worked for a while. And then the bank went and looked for itself.

"The guy who went out to see what the deal with the properties were came back with a photo of the property being a trailer that was on the market for seventy-five thousand dollars," Dwek later told attorneys digging into the matter. "I gave them a song and a dance."

"You gave the bank a song and dance and they believed you?"

"No," he admitted. "They wanted to hang me."

"What was the song and dance that you gave to the president of Signature Bank that resulted in their not suing you?" one of the attorneys asked.

"I told him I'll pay him back in a couple of days or a week or two weeks. I don't recall the exact time frame. And, you know, he was very upset that the bank was defrauded and I think he was worried about the bank and his client. I just told him I'll pay him back."

"So you did not lie to him?"

"Oh no—no, I didn't lie to him on that call. I was caught pretty much," Dwek said. "What else could I do? There was a picture of the vacant lot with the trailer parked there, and a 'for sale' sign. I didn't deny it."

The bank demanded its money back, declaring that it would no longer do business with him. "I told him whatever I told him, but I got him back the money eventually," he said.

Yet it was Dwek's growing portfolio of similar schnookie bank loans that ultimately caught up with him.

* * *

Dwek began executing a series of loan and credit agreements with HSBC Bank—some through Franco, others through his uncle. One of the purported deals was to buy the Deal Golf and Country Club, a huge expanse of land just a block from Solomon's home. He proposed to turn it into a new subdivision of luxury homes.

The Deal Golf Club dated to the early 1890s, when railroad financier George Washington Young purchased 135 acres in West Deal to build an estate and established the first golf course at the Jersey Shore. It eventually was organized as the Deal Golf Club in 1898, and a clubhouse was built on the site, which remains the oldest in continuous use in New Jersey. Among its members were Robert Todd Lincoln, the son of Pres. Abraham Lincoln; Colo. George Harvey, editor of *Harper's Weekly;* and William C. "Will" Durant, who founded General Motors.

Tight with narrow fairways, the historic course, now surrounded by multimillion-dollar homes, would be worth a fortune to developers if they could ever get their hands on it. Only problem was, the club was not exactly for sale. Members had received a letter from club president William C. Barham notifying them of a "*bona fide,* credible offer" to purchase the club, but it gave no specifics, saying only the pitch was of significant value and came from a "financially sound group of investors." The investors were ostensibly being put together by Dwek. As would be seen later, this phantom deal would prove very useful to Dwek.

Other HSBC loans were earmarked for investment properties that Dwek said he was buying and reselling at a quick profit. But it was another variation on his old game. Dwek already owned the buildings he told the bank he was buying. HSBC did not immediately perform title searches and did not know these were fraudulent loans, according to the bankruptcy trustee. Dwek already knew he was probably not going to be able to pay the loans back. Before the ink was dry, Solomon was promising returns to investors in the hundreds of millions of dollars. By now, though, he had a sinking feeling in his stomach that no matter what he did, he wouldn't be able to pay back HSBC or Franco or anybody else.

"I didn't have a cash flow. I didn't have positive cash flow from any income-producing properties just to cover my overhead," he said. "Forget about investors. My bleed every month was at least two million dollars to three million dollars. My income was under a half a million dollars before I had to pay any Ponzi investments back. Paying my mortgages and stuff."

His wild ride was about to come to a crashing end.

* * *

By early 2006, HSBC finally got down to obtaining title documents on Dwek's mortgages. Attorney Anthony Yeh, who had represented HSBC on four loans, had failed to get property appraisals on the buildings Dwek was supposedly financing. At the same time, the bank never recorded the debts. His heart pounding, Yeh immediately called up Dwek. "I just ran title and we realized that you own the properties and you have all the mortgages on them," Yeh said in a panic. Something was screwed up and didn't match. The bank did not hold the mortgages on the properties Dwek had said he purchased.

"I'll pay them back if I'm able to," said Dwek, downplaying the issue. No worries. It would be fine.

But it wasn't fine. How could it be fine? Yeh was hanging with one hand over a bottomless pit. He was screwed. He could lose his job or even his law license. He began calling Dwek 10, 20 times a day when Solomon failed to cover the loan. "Where's the money? Where's the money?" Yeh kept asking. "The bank violated its own policies."

(In August 2008, Yeh was questioned under oath about the mortgages and why he didn't do what he was supposed to for his client, HSBC. Initially, Yeh said he had no reason. Then he declined to answer because of attorney-client confidentiality.)

At the same time, Franco was getting angrier and ramping up the pressure on Dwek.

"He used to call my house midnight or two in the morning yelling and screaming like a madman threatening to kill me, kill my wife, kill my kids, cut off my balls, things like that literally," Dwek testified.

Franco was under the gun with Signature as well, over the failure to deliver title policies on the properties Dwek had bought. Plus Franco had cash shortfalls—including a $5.2 million wire transfer that Dwek had promised to make into Ike's account. The money never arrived, and on April 11 Franco shot him a new e-mail:

IF THE 5.2M IS NOT IN MY ACCOUNT IN THE NEXT 5 MINUTES I WILL COME THERE AND BREAK YOUR NECK!!!!!!!!!!!!!!!!!

By now, Dwek was thinking it just might not be an idle threat.

* * *

HSBC was also putting its own pressure on Franco's neck. It was looking for repayment of a separate $20 million line of credit, and on Friday, April 21, bank executives were in communication separately with both Dwek and Franco. Solomon had promised to wire the funding to HSBC but again gave them an incorrect reference number. He always gave incorrect reference numbers when he needed to buy more time. "Ike, he's losing total credibility," Nat Marotta, one of the bank officers, told Franco.

Franco, still in Florida that week for the Passover holiday, told Marotta,

"Listen. I'll be back in New York. I'll come to the bank and I'll make sure Solomon comes to explain himself Monday."

Franco immediately called Dwek. "The wire's being sent," Dwek insisted. "It's in the wire room. It's going to be sent out."

There was nothing more Franco could do at that point. There was no communication between the two over the weekend. Both were Orthodox and neither would have picked up a telephone or his BlackBerry on Shabbat. They were effectively in radio silence. On Monday morning, April 24, Franco, now back in New York and still angry, reached out again for Dwek. "What's happening? What happened on Friday?" Franco demanded. HSBC wanted answers today. "What happened to the wire?"

"I'm checking," insisted Dwek. "I'm going to let you know."

"They want us to come in this afternoon. You need to be available," Franco said. "Four o'clock."

Dwek said he would be there.

But Franco was not that easily put off. He was angry. "How could you say a wire went out and it didn't go out? How can you not be sure?"

"I'll explain it to you when I see you," said Dwek. He was very abrupt.

Franco told Dwek to meet him at his office that morning so they could discuss it before going over to the bank. Dwek begged off.

"I gotta be in Jersey this morning. Some closing," Dwek said.

As he hung up, Franco was convinced more than ever there was something definitely wrong. For Dwek, there was. He was now out of time and out of money. He was desperate. His markers were getting called. The banks wanted their money back. Franco wanted his money. And there was more coming due to Dwek's investors. If he did not think of something quick, the game was going to be over quicker than a gunshot to the head.

Then it came to him. Dwek had kited checks before, and the bank always let it go after he covered them. Only thing was, this would require a very, very large check.

*　*　*

The wet weekend had given way to a rainy morning. The appointment with Franco at the bank in Manhattan was not until the afternoon, so Dwek had a few hours to kill, enough time to make a side trip.

Dwek had been banking at the PNC Bank branch in Eatontown for years. He was the landlord of two of the bank's New Jersey branches and was well-known at the Eatontown office. He moved a great deal of money in and out of his accounts every week. He usually went to the drive-thru window. That way he didn't have to get out of his car.

Michelle Penix, the teller supervisor at the branch, was filling in at the bank's drive-thru window that afternoon, talking to Dorothy Lassik, the branch manager, when Dwek pulled up to the window at about 2:00 P.M. Penix didn't see him at first, until the pneumatic tube *whooshed* and a delivery box dropped in. She pulled out a check and a deposit slip inside. It was a handwritten check to SEM Realty, one of Dwek's companies, drawn on a separate Dwek business account in the name of Corbett Holdings II, LLC. The amount was $25,212,076.35. Double the price of many corporate jets.

Because of the amount, Penix handed the check to Lassik. It was a PNC check, No. 1059. "You know, Solomon's outside making the deposit," Penix finally said.

Dwek, black yarmulke on his head, sat behind the wheel of the blue Lexus idling at the far drive-up window. They all knew Solomon. He would come in two, three times a week. "If you know of any buildings for sale, you know, bank buildings for sale, something, let me know," Dwek once told Lassik.

Penix punched in the account number into her terminal. *Closed status,* the computer reported. There was no balance to cover the deposit. Under the bank's policy, she could not accept the check.

"This account is closed," she said aloud. She put everything back in the box to send it back to him and then turned on the microphone at the window. "Solomon, this account is closed," Penix said.

He nodded his head. "Corporate is reopening the account for me," he replied through the open window of his car. "It's okay."

She turned off the speaker and went back to the terminal, looking at Lassik, who was standing there and heard everything he said. Lassik had been through issues with Dwek before. Solomon frequently overdrafted his accounts. As many as 80 times before this, millions of dollars at a clip. There was never that much concern about it, the bank later concluded, because he always came in and deposited money to cover the overdraft. Still, she had warned him about it. A year earlier, though, PNC—concerned about the amount of wire activity involved in Dwek's account—had actually opened an investigation into his transactions. There were suspicions of check kiting, an old bank fraud that played the float by writing checks from accounts with insufficient funds and then covering the shortage with another rubber check from another bank before the first check bounced. It was the lowest of low-tech crimes, barely a generation removed from three-card monte in Times Square.

The internal probe went nowhere, with investigators concluding that the rapid-fire movement of money was simply part of the nature of real estate. On a document, someone had scrawled: *large wire activity due to the purchase and sale of properties.* Lassik recalled a bank security official telling her, "Solomon Dwek is well-known. He is who he is. There is no reason to shut him down." It was their gold seal, as far as she was concerned. The bank also made substantial fees on the overdrafts and wires. There were a few times, though, that it would hold up payment if the money was substantial. Maria Quintana, the branch's business banker, had spoken to him about the fees, suggesting that he move the money to an account that would earn credits to offset those charges.

"It's not an issue," Dwek said of the fees. He didn't care about them.

Penix waited with the check, as if to ask, *What do we do?*

Lassik seemed to be talking to herself. "You know, corporate is reopening the account," Lassik repeated. That was all she said, Penix recalled later.

After a long pause, Penix took the check and electronically deposited it, sending back a receipt. Simple as that. Lassik did not stop her. No hold. No discussion. Much later, attorneys and prosecutors would be struck by the fact that there was no conversation at all. Just an everyday deposit—for $25 million.

Dwek pulled out onto Wyckoff Road and headed up the Garden State Parkway to New York.

* * *

The 4:00 P.M. meeting at HSBC in New York was tense. Ike Franco was there. So was George Wendler, the bank's chief credit and risk officer, with a number of other bank executives. Wendler had recently had throat surgery and could not talk. He had an electronic voice box that he typed into and it would speak for him, so the meeting took some time. He said the bank wanted immediate repayment on a $20 million loan taken in October.

Where's the money? typed Wendler.

"I have it," said Dwek.

Why didn't you send it to us?

"I am. I will. Some mix-up. I will take care of it."

Wendler was not easily mollified. This was a lot of money they were talking about. "You know, I do business with you, with your uncle and you," he told Dwek. "You're jeopardizing your reputation with the bank and you're jeopardizing your good standing with us."

Despite it all, the financing for the Deal Golf Club purchase was still in play. Nobody knew the membership had voted the month before against selling the club. Wendler only said everything would be on hold until

Dwek took care of the outstanding loan. "We're not doing anything with you until you clear up this balance," Wendler said.

"I do have the money," Dwek told him again. "You want me to provide it?" He asked to use the speakerphone in the office and called PNC's toll-free customer account line, entering his account number and pass code. The automated system confirmed a balance of more than $25 million. No matter that most of it was unavailable. No one asked where the money had come from.

"You'll have the money in the morning," promised Dwek. "I'm just waiting for certain things to clear."

"If I don't have the money by the morning I'm going to go through our attorneys," threatened Wendler.

Solomon walked out. Franco had not said much during the meeting. Once they left the bank, he turned on Dwek on the street. "What's going on here? If you have the money—I don't understand. If you have the money sitting in your account, why are you not sending this money to them? Why are you playing this game?"

"I'm gonna take care of it," promised Dwek again.

Franco still thought the Deal Golf Club purchase was real and did not want to lose it. And he needed HSBC to finance it. He just couldn't figure out Solomon's angle this time. "You have the money sitting in PNC. So why wouldn't you pay back HSBC?"

Dwek was cool. As Franco would reflect later, Dwek didn't even look nervous. "Just make sure you get the money back to them like you said," Franco said.

"I will," Dwek replied.

"Otherwise," continued Franco darkly, "there's going to be big trouble for me—[and] you." It was a 10-minute conversation. Franco went back to his office. Solomon went to his car.

If he had any hesitation in his mind over what he was about to do, Dwek has never admitted it out loud. He didn't even think it was that big a deal. Just before 9:00 A.M. the next day, he called up the PNC wire department from his office at the Deal Yeshiva. PNC, he knew, offered its customers next-day availability on internal bank check deposits. He had done this hundreds of times before. The call was routed to a center in Pittsburgh or Philadelphia, and there was a set script everyone followed: *PNC Wire. Your call is being recorded. My name is* [first name]. *How may I help you?*

All Dwek had to do was provide his account number, his name and pass code, the recipient, and the amount. He had $25 million on account, at least until the bank discovered the check was no good. So he borrowed it. He figured it was like a short-term IOU that would get repaid before anyone was the wiser. He began wiring the money out.

One of the wires paid off the $20 million loan he owed with Franco at HSBC. A second $2.2 million wire went to pay off Ken Cayre. Two other wires totaling $590,000 were sent out to Valley National Bank and Citibank.

In Dwek's mind, it was just a temporary stopgap. He fully expected that HSBC would reextend the $20 million he had just repaid for the golf course deal. It was just a technicality. The money would then go right back to PNC to cover the overdraft. No harm, no foul. It was no more than an off-the-books loan that would be covered once he got through with HSBC. "It wasn't like I was running away with the money. It wasn't a big event," he told people later. "I was trying to get money from other sources."

Franco knew nothing of the wires. Dwek never called him or told him to check with HSBC, and he did not follow up. Ikey was getting ready to fly out to Milwaukee that night for a big meeting with Kohl's Department Stores.

* * *

About an hour and a half later, Dwek was back in New York for a second round with HSBC Bank. This time his uncle, Joseph Dwek, was there, along with his brother-in-law, Mark Adjmi. Joey also brought along Eli Seruya as his financial adviser.

Before he was summoned, Dwek's uncle had not even been sure what the meeting was about. Joey had been in Israel for Passover the week before, getting a mysterious e-mail on his BlackBerry that Friday from Mary Pan, a senior vice president at HSBC:

> George will like to meet with you on Monday if you are available. He comes in early but please advise what is convenient for you. Looking forward to seeing you.

Joey had his own $25 million loan outstanding with HSBC for another one of Solomon's property deals. The money was not yet due, but Joey was already thinking the worst after months of funny business with Solomon's other deals. He e-mailed Solomon from Israel, including a copy of the message from Pan:

> You better have answers for me of when we are paying down the 25m. I do not want to ruin my reputation with the bank. I cannot and will not lie to the bank.

That Monday he tried calling Solomon, but his nephew—who was never without his cell phone—would not return Joey's calls. The meeting with Wendler was pushed back to Tuesday. Joey e-mailed Solomon, telling him to be there:

> We are on for 10:30 tomorrow per Mary george wendler wants to see me. she told me you sent her leases unsigned. they are worthless. I ask you to please attend, my name and reputation is on the line . . .

Pan, who did not speak at the meeting, had only told Joey there were issues with the documents the bank had and would not go into detail. Wendler, still speaking through his electronic voice box, expressed concern over the loan. He echoed Pan, saying HSBC had found discrepancies between the properties Solomon had purchased and the title work. HSBC wanted properties to secure an outstanding $25 million credit line.

Solomon had to come up with the collateral. Dwek nodded. "I will do that," he agreed.

There was a yellow legal pad in Wendler's office. Solomon ripped a page off the top and began writing notes. The bank executive had a long list of things he wanted to see.

Deed, copy of deeds, Solomon scrawled. *Plus title, plus evidence of sale plus deeds plus proof of funds.*

One deal at a time.

Get mortgages on four parcels.

Get list of No. mortgages with 45 properties, income producing.

Close Park Avenue by June 20, 2006. He crossed that out and then wrote: *June 30, 2006.*

Solomon wasn't that talkative. "Let me speak to my uncle and let me see what I can do and then I'll get back to you," he said.

Joey sat there shell-shocked as he suddenly began to comprehend what his brother's son had been up to for so long. The bank had let the loans go through without checking that the properties were there. And Joey had given a personal guarantee. There was no collateral and now he was on the hook for the money. *This is a no-win situation,* he thought.

After the meeting, Joey confronted his nephew at the corner of 40th Street and Fifth Avenue. "What's going on here?" Joey asked. Did Solomon actually not buy properties?

Solomon did not answer.

Joey stormed off to his office and called his lawyers. Adjmi made a call to Solomon's father, Rabbi Dwek, to tell him everything.

* * *

At PNC, it was a crisis. The Pittsburgh-based bank was trying desperately to figure out what was going on. Dana Bryant in loss prevention called Michelle Penix at the Eatontown branch. "You took a twenty-five-million-dollar deposit. What happened?" Bryant asked.

Penix retold the story, adding, "Dot was standing right there." Dorothy Lassik.

"She was?"

"Yes."

Loss prevention wanted the branch manager. Immediately. But Lassik had just left for a meeting, so Penix filled her in. As she spoke, Penix pulled up the account and could see the wires that had gone out. Twenty-five million dollars. Gone. Bryant instructed her to call Dwek right then and find out what was going on.

Dwek's cell phone number was on the account. Dial. Ring. Voice mail. He didn't immediately answer. But then he called her right back. "Solomon, this is Michelle," she said. They knew each other. There's a problem, she told him. "That account was not reopened. The money's not there."

"Oh, don't worry about it. I have more money," Dwek said. Again, totally cool. "I'll take care of it."

Penix called back Bryant and related the conversation. "Okay," said Bryant. "Keep me posted."

Later, Penix got another call, this time from PNC's North Asbury office. Dwek had just gone there to deposit a second $25 million check. Penix did not hesitate. "Reverse that deposit!" she instructed. "Because we are having a problem right now with that." Then she called loss prevention to alert Bryant. No sooner had Penix hung up than she got another call from Dwek. He had been looking at the account online from his office and knew what had happened the moment she shut him down.

"I see you reversed that deposit. You're not letting it go through?"

"Solomon, I just told you, you could not do that. That account is closed. And the money is not there."

He thanked her and ended the call without any further discussion.

PNC was now trying unsuccessfully to reverse the wires from the first check to HSBC. They called Franco's office, and his assistant got through to him in Milwaukee. "Ikey, something's weird," she said. "PNC's requesting for us to return the wire that Solomon sent. Can you call up Solomon and ask him what's going on here?"

Franco had never heard of a bank making a wire to another bank and then asking for the money back. He called Solomon and finally got through to him later that day. "What's going on?" Franco demanded.

This time, Solomon was no longer calm. "I need you to help me," Dwek said. "I need you to help me get twenty million dollars. I gotta get this money put into PNC."

Franco didn't understand. "What are you talking about? You have the money at PNC. What do you mean, you need to put money into PNC?"

Pointed questions. Vague answers.

"I have to replace the funds. The funds that I had there were not cleared from the other bank. I need to get twenty million dollars." He asked Franco if he could talk to one of his business partners who had participated in earlier real estate deals. Even now, Solomon was trying to keep the con going.

"You want me to help you? You want me to go out on the line and speak to somebody and help you? I need you to be straightforward with me," Franco told him. He wanted information on all the properties that he held with Dwek. Titles. Locations. Everything. Finally Franco was doing his due diligence—millions of dollars too late.

Now Dwek was in a $25 million hole with no way out of it. There was only so long he would be able to hold off PNC before it all closed in around him. He needed a lot of money in a hurry.

* * *

That Wednesday night, Dwek met again with Joey and Mark Adjmi down the Jersey Shore at Solomon's office to see if he could cut a new deal with his uncle. Again, Solomon asked him for $20 million. "I cut a check. It didn't cover," he said. He wasn't very specific. "I need twenty million dollars to cover the shortfall; otherwise I'm in big trouble," he pleaded. He said only that he had deposited a check and thought the funds were going to come in to cover it.

His uncle shook his head. He was in no mood to negotiate. "You gypped me. You conned me," he told Solomon. "There's no way we're going to give you twenty million dollars."

"I'll give you properties for it," offered Solomon.

"Nothing doing. I'm already in the hole sixty million dollars," Joey shot back. Dozens of properties that were supposed to be bought in Joey's name had been put in Solomon's portfolio. Joey had been cheated and he was beyond pissed. "Forget about it. I'm not giving you no twenty million dollars."

Solomon never followed up with the additional collateral and Joey's homes in Brooklyn and Deal were now on the line because of his personal guarantee. Joey e-mailed Solomon late Thursday:

> I thought you gave them more collateral . . . they weren't supposed to attach mortgages to both my homes. I am very upset, what is going on???? Do you want to leave me Bar Minan *[God forbid]* on the street with my kids while you take the money for your own personal use? What Chuzppahh!!!!!

(A federal bankruptcy judge years later did not believe Joey's claims that he had no idea what his nephew was up to. Solomon had taken out a $1.5 million mortgage on his uncle's summer home in Deal, but after their confrontation Joey insisted his signature was forged on the loan documents and refused to pay back the money. That led to a lawsuit. Joey came up short. The judge found Joey had been aware of the mortgage but did nothing about it as long as he was making money.)

Franco was back from Milwaukee that Friday and agreed to meet again with Dwek. Franco again asked what Dwek planned to do with the $20 million.

"Just help me get this taken care of," Dwek urged. It was the first time, Franco reflected later, that he had ever seen Dwek nervous. "If I don't get this taken care of, I'm going to go to jail. I need your help. I need your help."

"I'll help you," Franco said finally. "Just get me the information you've been promising me for the last month and a half."

"We're fifty-fifty in the golf course," Dwek reminded him.

Franco still was convinced the golf course deal existed and that Dwek had just gotten himself into a situation. The golf course itself was there and Ike thought the property value was tremendous. It looked to him like a very lucrative deal and he still believed Solomon.

"Get me the information," Franco said. "I'm not going to stick my neck out until you do."

Sunday, promised Dwek. "I'll get it for you by Sunday."

Sunday came and went. On Monday, Dwek called again, begging for help. Franco told Dwek there wouldn't be any money until his outstanding investments were secured.

Dwek's last slim hope was now his uncle. After a flurry of calls with Adjmi and Seruya, Solomon thought they had reached an agreement. He would sign over a long list of properties he had faxed to Seruya. Out of that, Joey Dwek would extend $20 million to pay back PNC.

That Tuesday, he drove with his father, the rabbi, to the office of Joey Dwek's lawyers in Hackensack, a run-down town of law offices and government buildings seven miles from the George Washington Bridge. Adjmi had called Solomon and told him to be there by 10:00 A.M. They kept him waiting until maybe 1:00 or 2:00 P.M. before bringing him into a big conference room. There were seven or eight lawyers and paralegals. They had stacks of documents, deeds for properties Dwek held that they wanted signed over to his uncle for nominal consideration, of between $1 and $10 each.

The rabbi cautioned his son, "Have you ever closed on property without an attorney?"

"No."

"Then don't sign anything. Call an attorney,"

But Dwek was out of time. He recalled his uncle's attorneys kept saying they had to "beat PNC to the punch." Solomon agreed to sign, convinced that after he signed the deeds his uncle would wire the money to cover the overdraft. "There wasn't too much talking other than sign here, sign there. Like that. I was very busy signing," he recounted later.

The properties, 129 of them, all went into a new entity Joey Dwek had created. It was called Yeshuah. Hebrew for "salvation." Joey had come up with the name.

After he signed everything, Solomon asked Adjmi when he would receive the $20 million. "Call me tonight," Adjmi said.

Dwek left with his father and they drove to the law offices of Lowenstein Sandler in Roseland to talk with Michael Himmel, one of the state's top criminal defense attorneys. That night, Dwek called his uncle and made one last try to extricate himself from the abyss.

"I need to give the money to PNC, to wire the money in," Dwek told Joey.

"Go fuck yourself," his uncle snapped.

Adjmi, Dwek said later, also dismissed him and told him he wasn't getting a cent. "I ain't giving you the money," said the son of Solomon's old mentor, Jack. It was a very short phone call. Dwek and Adjmi never spoke again.

Yeshuah would provide no salvation this time.

By now, PNC had filed a Suspicious Activity Report, or SAR, with the Financial Crimes Enforcement Network of the U.S. Treasury. Incredibly, the bank was still offering Dwek a last way out. "You own a lot of properties. If you give us collateral, like thirty-five or forty million dollars in properties that are unencumbered, we'll take a mortgage on them and give you time to pay back the debt," a bank official advised.

Dwek agreed, asking them to fax over the paperwork. But he had no properties to sign over any longer. He had already given everything to his uncle.

The Rabbi's Son went home and waited for a knock on the door. He knew the FBI would be coming.

4

─◄┼ ┼ ┼►─

You Have No Idea What You're Messing With . . .

PNC finally took Solomon Dwek to court on May 3. The bank had put a
settlement on the table, but Dwek, to no one's great surprise, never showed
up to finalize it. Embarrassed by the $25 million loss and figuring that all
the money was gone, PNC execs pulled the trigger on a lawsuit. Their
only play now was to recoup whatever they could by seizing Dwek's properties.

Before filing the papers, they did a quick records search and identified
at least 60 properties that could be targeted—or so they thought. No one
at the bank had any idea yet that Solomon already had signed over most of
that real estate to Uncle Joey just days earlier. None of the properties had
been recorded yet with the county clerk.

* * *

The Monmouth County Hall of Records is located in an office along a
tired downtown strip in Freehold, New Jersey. Bruce Springsteen's Freehold. There, in the chambers of the chancery division of state superior
court, a PNC Bank lawyer from Morristown named Dennis Kearney met
with Judge Alexander Lehrer seeking an order freezing Dwek's assets. If
the empire was collapsing, PNC wanted its piece first.

Lehrer, a longtime lawyer and pillar of the Jersey Shore legal community, was a tough-talking former prosecutor—essentially a district attorney
for the county—with a bone crusher of a handshake and a made-for-the-
front-page personality. It was not uncommon for lawyers to call him
Crazy Al Lehrer and not worry that he might hear it. He wasn't Crazy
Al just to the lawyers. Other judges knew it, too.

In one case, the state appeals court reversed Lehrer and ordered a lawsuit between two former law partners be sent back to superior court. The

appeals court also took the unusual step of ordering that the case be assigned to a different judge, after Lehrer just flat out mocked the matter from the bench. Lehrer never tried to hide his feelings about the case and said that mocking was in fact his goal when he said things like "let's spend sixty thousand dollars in legal fees for me to determine whether or not one lawyer owes another lawyer twenty-four thousand dollars."

In another reversal, the appeals court ordered Lehrer to reduce a $3 million jury verdict for a Jersey Shore man who sued a Chicago clinic after his treatment for sexual dysfunction was botched. The treatment left the man with a three-day erection that could be ended only with surgery, which resulted in impotence. The appellate panel said the size of the award "shocked the court's conscience."

Lehrer announced that the appeals judges "know how I feel about this case. I've already told them. I didn't think three million dollars was enough." Then he trimmed the sum. By just one cent. To exactly $2,999,999.99. The higher court was not amused. Lehrer was publicly chastised for a "demonstrated unwillingness to comply with our instructions."

Yet Lehrer was also known for a can-do, why-the-hell-not kind of attitude. So there were the moments when he won public acclaim, like the time in 1999 when he forced feuding developers to resolve their litigation and finally begin putting back together the monstrosity that had become the dilapidation and repeatedly abandoned redevelopment of the oceanfront city of Asbury Park. "There are very few times in life when we can really make a difference," Lehrer announced. "All we need is for someone to say, 'Enough—let's stop the litigation.'"

Kearney, PNC's lawyer, was an established figure among the "A-list" of North Jersey attorneys. He was a former prosecutor with a lucrative partnership at a big law firm who could tell a story. Over the years, Kearney had given up his taste for locking up dope dealers and murderers and became expert in the far more financially rewarding specialty of representing banks in New Jersey courts. What he was seeking here, however, was the most unremarkable of judicial orders: a temporary hold on Dwek's assets so PNC could get its $25 million. If he couldn't cough up the dough, PNC would ask Lehrer to begin liquidating Dwek's assets.

PNC—already struggling to explain the Keystone Kops farce that allowed one check to be drawn on a closed account and saw a second one nearly go through—just wanted its money back. Even PNC couldn't believe the unbridled level of stupidity demonstrated by the Dwek incident. But the bank couldn't just run off and hide, because of the sheer scope of the loss.

The legal play in Freehold was supposed to be mundane. Banks always want their money back. Courts typically play along. With the list they had compiled, Kearney and PNC figured Dwek had enough of a financial and real estate portfolio to cover the bill.

"This was a garden-variety check kite," according to one of the bank's people involved in the case. The problem was PNC was just seeing the tip of a very large iceberg. Nothing about Dwek was as it appeared. Not his loans, his properties, his charity, or his investments. The $25 million at stake was just a small part of the vast scheme Dwek had played that had yet to come to light. In fact, a very small part.

Lehrer read and then reread Kearney's filing before the hearing. *This is bizarre,* he thought to himself. The complaint, Docket No. C133-06, was 21 pages of short sentences, numbered paragraphs, and lawyerly language almost impossible to believe. Kearney mentioned the drive-thru, the two checks, and, of course, Dwek's ludicrous explanation that "corporate" was reopening the account. Bizarre wasn't the half of it.

Typically, the judge did not even look at the parties on the front page of a complaint. It was immaterial to the facts being presented. But he quickly began to get a picture of what was going on. The Syrians of Deal were no strangers to Lehrer. As the county's former top lawman, Lehrer had built a politically necessary relationship with the Community, and it turned out to be invaluable decades earlier when tensions with the local cops threatened to boil over. At that time, the police decided to shut down a Sunday night reception because of noise, but the unintended result was that an old man in the crowd died of a heart attack amid all the commotion. It was the kind of problem that could cripple or end the career of a politician. Lehrer knew everything was riding on that case and he recalled overseeing it himself—from investigating the cops to watching the grand jury refuse to indict to observing the ensuing anger of a wealthy, influential voting bloc.

* * *

Through his years as a lawyer and later a judge, Lehrer—like the rest of the bench in Monmouth County—saw case after case connected to the Community. As night follows day, the cash just kept coursing through the matters like blood rushing through unrestricted arteries. Judges don't like to talk in those types of generalizations out loud—it's unbecoming and could lead people to question their impartiality. But no one who spent any time in Monmouth County legal circles could avoid noticing the cash that was washing up along the Shore in Deal. Million-dollar homes in the names of old ladies with five-figure salaries on their tax returns. Divorces that pitted wives wrapped in minks against husbands driving Maseratis, both sides claiming poverty and cat-food dinners as their chartered planes were being fueled up for shopping trips to Europe.

Lehrer presided in an ornate throwback to a regal era in American law. Light blue with white trim, an etched ceiling, and leather chairs, his courtroom lent an air of importance to the cases that were decided in it. But that day, Lehrer and Kearney were stuck in a backroom, thanks to ongoing building reconstruction. With Kearney in front of him, the judge finally took his seat in an empty, awful courtroom. The jerkwater courtroom, some called it. It was a brief hearing that attracted no notice. There were no reporters, no other interested parties. Dwek also had failed to appear. It was quiet. And calm.

The Dwek empire was worth easily somewhere between $300 million and $500 million on paper. Lehrer did not know anything of the Ponzi scheme. Almost no one yet knew that Dwek's empire was a combination of quality real estate and a house of cards. Everyone had been making money and, in fact, getting rich as long as new investors pumped in fresh cash. But the judge knew that freezing and liquidating Solomon's assets likely would put dozens upon dozens of people—most of them still unknown—at risk of losing some or all of their money. Widows who had entrusted their life savings to Dwek, would-be real estate barons who had been looking to cash in on the housing bubble, even some local businessman who had bought land with Dwek and go-go bars with other guys.

Kearney and Lehrer knew each other well. So it was more than just judicial dramatics when the judge finally put the papers down and stood nose-to-nose with the attorney.

"You have no idea what you're messing with," Lehrer said flatly. The ominous warning was neither explained nor understood. It was an understatement, in any event. With a stroke of his pen, Lehrer froze Dwek's assets.

The next morning a news report appeared in the local paper, the *Asbury Park Press,* carrying details of the lawsuit. "Dwek bilked PNC out of $25 million in a single day," the paper quoted Kearney as saying. Dwek could not be reached for comment. Himmel, his attorney, said only he had not seen the judge's order and that he had been in communication with the bank.

Yet according to some of the lawyers in the case, Dwek still didn't even think the end had arrived. Just one more deal, he figured. Another round of good luck. And back in business. "You know what your problem is?" he asked one of the bank attorneys months later. "If you only had waited twenty-four hours, I would have paid you off. I woulda had you covered . . ."

Himmel, though, already knew what was coming. And despite his bravado, so did Dwek.

                                                                    * * *

Special Agent William Waldie was considered one of the best undercover agents the FBI ever had in New Jersey. One of the federal prosecutors called him the Magnificent Waldie. He just never seemed to stop. Colleagues say he was usually up at four in the morning, at the gym by five, and frequently worked seven days a week.

Originally from New Jersey, Waldie graduated from college with his CPA before landing a job with the FBI more than 20 years earlier. Serving time in the Washington field office, he finally came back home to the Newark Division, where he was assigned to the white-collar crime squad.

One of his first headline cases had been a major international money-laundering operation being run out of the Cayman Islands. But what he had been focusing on almost exclusively for much of the past few years had turned into a systematic takedown of corrupt political officials in Monmouth County in Central Jersey, a sting that became known as "Operation Bid Rig." The wide-ranging investigation initially had been carried out by an undercover informant who took on the guise of an owner of a demolition company looking for big contracts in exchange for fat envelopes of cash. Waldie accompanied the informant, most of the time in disguise. "Sometimes I had a beard, sometimes a goatee, and sometimes I was clean-shaven," he said. "No one ever spotted me. There's a way you do it that you avoid detection."

It led to a sweeping set of cases against mayors, councilmen, and other officials that overtook the fast-growing county at the northern reach of the Shore. Dwek had not been a target in that long-running probe but somehow was always oddly close to the people who were getting arrested. There was a property deal for a proposed senior citizen condominium project that had gotten Waldie particularly interested in Ocean Township. Two lots totaling just over eight acres grew in value from $330,000 to $4.25 million in four years, after zoning changes and planning approvals were granted under a crooked mayor who went to jail. One of those transactions involved Dwek and Barry Kantrowitz, his longtime broker, who was questioned but also was not accused of any wrongdoing.

"I was the guy who took the risk," Dwek told reporters after the FBI scrutiny became public. "If anything, I was a fool and sold too cheap."

Much later, Dwek acknowledged in bankruptcy depositions that Kantrowitz had called him up and told him the FBI was snooping around. "He said the FBI came to see him and they were asking him questions about dozens of individuals and my name came up," recalled Dwek. "He said they were asking about a lot of people and about a lot of properties."

No charges were filed that time, but there had been more sinister talk tied to other federal investigations of moving a lot of money around, involving mysterious Israeli connections. The FBI also had been told that Dwek had paid off a mayor and possibly others, but there wasn't enough there to take to court.

As Waldie sat in the FBI's Red Bank office, the walls of his small cubicle decorated with family photographs and football memorabilia from the Miami Dolphins and Alabama's Crimson Tide, he looked over the PNC Bank report. He sensed an opportunity. Then he went in to see Edward Kahrer, the assistant special agent in charge who had supervised the Bid Rig investigation from the start.

"Remember Solomon Dwek?" Waldie asked.

* * *

Just over a week after PNC went to court, the FBI, the IRS, and members of the Monmouth County Prosecutor's office arrived unannounced at Dwek's home on Crosby Avenue in West Deal. They knocked on the door and said they had a federal warrant for his arrest in the PNC Bank fraud. Bill Waldie was among them.

It was 6:00 A.M. on a damp, chilly day, but Dwek had already been up and dressed. Pearl, still pregnant with their fifth child, had also been awake for a while, although the kids were still sleeping. Before he was handcuffed and put in the backseat of a car for the drive north to Newark, Dwek called Himmel. Dwek said very little. Brought to the FBI building through the basement entrance off McCarter Highway, The Rabbi's Son was led to a small, windowless room. They took his fingerprints, his photograph, and, of course, his belt.

Over at the U.S. Attorney's office, the case had already been usurped by Assistant U.S. Attorney James Nobile, head of special prosecutions (the official name for the public corruption unit). A legend in the office, Nobile was quiet and meticulous—mysterious even to those with whom he worked. He wrote memos in a maniacally neat handwriting that looked like it was printed on a machine. Jimmy Writing, they called it. The memos were done in felt-tip color pens, with each color seeming to be some kind of code to him and him alone. He wouldn't explain what the colors meant.

Nobile forgot nothing and saw pathways in cases that others would often overlook. By far one of the most capable prosecutors in the office, he commanded a respect that led few to challenge him—including his own bosses. He wanted Dwek for special prosecutions but refused to say exactly why. What nobody knew was that Waldie and Kahrer had already spoken with Jimmy and told him what was coming. They were convinced it was an opening for a bigger play.

Typically a bank fraud would have immediately been sent to the commercial crimes division of the U.S. Attorney's office. This seemed like an open-and-shut case of check kiting, and some in the front office questioned why Jimmy would want any part of it. Nobile insisted. Dwek "is a name I'm interested in" was all Jimmy would say.

Eventually he was given the okay to take the matter and he quickly assigned it to Brian Howe, a young prosecutor on his unit. B-Howe, as everyone referred to him, was immensely popular in the office. He wasn't sure how he got his nickname. It was just something that developed at the U.S. Attorney's office. When Howe was growing up, friends used to call him Howey.

The intense man with a wicked sense of humor made his way around the office in a motorized wheelchair. Howe had been paralyzed in a dirt bike accident as a 14-year-old kid. An athlete who once excelled in football, basketball, and baseball, he went riding one day in the hills of the Ramapo Mountains near the New York State border in far northern New Jersey. Sliding off a muddy trail while trailing his brother, his wheel hit a boulder. Howe pitched abruptly over the handlebars and into a tree, breaking his neck. Rushed to the hospital, he stopped breathing at least once. There were bouts of pneumonia. Finally, doctors said he would probably live, but he would never walk again.

It wasn't until after months of rehabilitation and life-threatening surgeries that he was finally able to return to school in a wheelchair. But Howe was a smart kid. He graduated first in his class, going on to Princeton University and then earning a law degree at the University of Virginia. He landed a prime clerkship with U.S. District Judge Dickinson Debevoise and went to work for a Newark law firm, before getting hired by the U.S. Attorney's office in 2000—long his ultimate goal.

Howe viewed his disability as a non-issue, which had embarrassed more than one judge before his face became known around the federal courthouse. The first time Howe represented the office in a case, he was an intern. A judge called for appearance and each of the attorneys stood to give their name and whom they were representing. With Howe's wheelchair hidden under the table, the judge mildly chided him for failing to stand and show his respect to the court. "Counsel, it's a little hard to hear you up here," the judge said.

Paula Dow, then an assistant U.S. Attorney (who would later become the Essex County Prosecutor and then the state's attorney general), whispered to Charles McKenna, another assistant U.S. Attorney who was in the courtroom, wondering if they should pass a note to the judge.

"Let the judge embarrass himself," McKenna directed in a low voice.

When it was Howe's turn to address the court, he wheeled over to the lectern in the middle of the room. The judge suddenly realized what had happened and immediately apologized.

Howe shrugs his disability off. "Do I wish I was still running around? Absolutely," he said. "But I am by no means the only one who has battled adversity. Everybody does. My thought process has always been to keep plugging away. The most angst and hurt was for my parents."

Howe's office was in a corner of the special prosecutions section on the seventh floor of the federal building in Newark, just down the hall from Nobile. The walls were beige, a full-size American flag hung limply on a pole, and there were two framed letters of congratulations from FBI Director Robert Mueller, pictures of Howe's three young kids, and drawings they had done. The view outside the window looked down at Broad Street, and his office had paper everywhere. He had a fairly normal-looking cherrywood desk, made by federal prisoners on special order. It was extra high to allow room for his wheelchair to fit underneath, and it had no drawers so he could maneuver.

Putting the criminal complaint together days before Dwek's arrest, Howe dropped by the office of Michele Brown, the chief counsel for the U.S. Attorney's office. "Do you have any 'go-bys' for bank fraud?" he asked her, referring to the boilerplate documents with the appropriate language to file charges. "What's up?" she asked as she went looking for them.

He told her about the case. The drive-thru window. The $25 million check on a closed account. The deposit that nobody questioned after Dwek assured tellers that he had spoken to "corporate." Brown couldn't believe it. Not so much that someone had tried to get away with it, but that the bank even allowed it. Legitimate home owners had a tough time getting a mortgage, and this clown walked into a bank and was handed $25 million on no more than his say-so.

* * *

Appearing after his arrest before U.S. Magistrate Judge Mark Falk in the old federal courthouse in Newark, Dwek—his feet shackled and hands cuffed behind his back—repeatedly tugged at his black pants to keep them from falling down. The initial appearance was intended to set bail. It was a short, 20-minute session during a lunchtime recess in a court that was typically a flurry of motions, bail hearings, and a seemingly endless stream of initial appearances by sullen defendants. Falk's fourth-floor courtroom was rather plain, in contrast with much of the rest of the building that also served as the city's main post office. The original walls had been covered over with flat wood paneling. Overhead was a low, suspended ceiling with recessed fluorescent lights. Pale yellow carpeting stretched across the room. A single American flag stood to the left of the bench and a row of windows to the right framed the gray skies outside and a less-than-scenic part of the city.

Appointed a magistrate judge in 2002, Falk, who once represented Bruce Springsteen in a civil complaint filed by former roadies of the rock star, was calm on the bench. Down-to-earth with a pleasant and polite demeanor, the judge had seen a fair amount of corruption defendants—many of them just recently from Dwek's own backyard—parade through his court on their way to trial. This was just another case. Himmel told Falk that his client was trying to resolve matters with the bank. "They are working to make PNC whole," Himmel said.

As Dwek stood with his lawyer, his father, Rabbi Dwek, and other family members sat behind him on the dark wood benches of the long courtroom. Howe called Dwek a "significant flight risk," arguing before Falk for $10 million in bail. It was not an idle fear. With Dwek facing 30 years or more, the U.S. Attorney's office had real concerns that he would skip town and reappear in Israel, as Crazy Eddie Antar did 15 years before.

"Judge, he has deep roots in the community," countered Himmel. There were seven siblings and four young children, and a fifth child due in the next several weeks. "If ever there was a situation of someone who is not a flight risk, it is Mr. Dwek." Himmel added that Dwek had extensive landholdings and no prior arrests.

Falk was not persuaded. He set bail at $10 million, secured by $3 million of equity in the Deal homes of Dwek's mother-in-law, Milo Sutton, and his sister-in-law. Both Dwek and his wife were ordered to surrender their passports. Travel was restricted to New Jersey and New York. Afterward, Himmel tried to put the best face on it that he could as he left the courtroom and spoke with reporters outside. "The government has made some allegations involving criminal behavior. We view this as a civil dispute," Himmel remarked. "I'm disappointed that it got this far."

Michael Drewniak, the public information officer for the U.S. Attorney's office, put out a news release later that Thursday afternoon:

Prominent Monmouth County Real Estate Developer
Charged with $50 Million Bank Fraud Scheme

NEWARK—A Monmouth County real estate developer was charged today with scheming to defraud PNC Bank out of $50 million, U.S. Attorney Christopher J. Christie and Monmouth County Prosecutor Luis A. Valentin announced.

Solomon Dwek, 33, was arrested this morning at his Ocean Township, Monmouth County, home on a criminal Complaint by Special Agents of the FBI and investigators from the Monmouth County Prosecutor's Office. Dwek appeared before U.S. Magistrate Judge Mark Falk, who ordered Dwek to post a $10 million bond secured by equity totaling $3 million in the Deal homes of his mother-in-law and a sister-in-law. Magistrate Falk also ordered Dwek and his wife to surrender their passports.

Dwek, a Monmouth and Ocean County real estate developer and vice president of the Deal Yeshiva School in West Long Branch, is charged in the Complaint with defrauding PNC Bank in connection with his deposit of two $25 million checks drawn on a Dwek account that had been closed and had a zero balance . . .

* * *

The next day, with the news of the arrest spreading throughout the state, all hell broke loose in Lehrer's courtroom in Freehold, which was now center stage in the ongoing drama in the case of *PNC Bank v. Solomon Dwek*. The hearing already scheduled on the bank's application to freeze Dwek's assets was set to begin, and the full extent of Solomon's far-flung problems were now becoming very clear. Panic was in the air.

With the PNC lawsuit and Dwek's subsequent arrest, Dwek's operation had gone from 90 mph to 0 in seconds. Everyone who had ever done business with him realized they were now on the hook or had skid marks down their back. Even business interests unrelated to Dwek were at risk, the partners realized, because the court might decide to freeze and liquidate all their assets under the theory that the partners' assets were Dwek's and they belonged to the banks that had showered mortgages on the developer.

The Community itself was in an uproar, yet many were still supportive and citing his charity.

Without realizing it, Kearney had filed a case that was unprecedented in New Jersey legal history. The size and scope would later be equated to one of those massive "toxic tort" cases like the Erin Brockovich matter in California, where kids were dying from cancer and large conglomerates were forced to pay billions. Here Lehrer was being asked to oversee a record-setting fire sale in state court—a court that was nowhere near prepared to handle it—without any of the federal bankruptcy statutes and assistance to help. He had no idea what would happen, who would come out of the woodwork, or how it would all end. One thing was certain: a circus was about to begin.

Before the day got started, Lehrer already knew there were going to be a lot of lawyers seeking to intervene in the case. He vacated his own courtroom for the one occupied by the county's chief judge. It was the largest courtroom in Freehold and still it was not large enough. People were piled into the jury box and the courtroom door was obstructed by bodies. Only Dwek himself was not there. Looking around at the more than 100 lawyers, bankers, real estate developers, investors, former partners, self-described victims, and reporters jammed into the court and into the hallway outside, Lehrer smiled thinly as he welcomed "the state bar association" to the proceedings.

Kearney had arrived late to the 11:30 A.M. hearing, but Lehrer immediately spotted him as he squeezed through the doors. Lehrer gestured to him.

"Up here, Mr. Kearney. You've got the twenty-five-million-dollar seat right up front," the judge said, instructing Kearney to make his way through the crowd. "You're the guy who started this thing."

The attorney felt like he had just stuck his hand in a beehive, later telling a reporter, "A week ago, it was just me in a courtroom, by myself, with the judge. Seven days later you have half of the Monmouth County Bar Association in the courtroom . . . I don't think anyone anticipated that."

Relishing the moment and the attention and the adrenaline of it all, Lehrer had some proclamations to make from the bench. "There is absolutely no reason to panic," Lehrer said. The only problem was the panic had already set in and was flooding through the courtroom, as bankers jockeyed for a leg up over individual investors and lawyers were worried their personal bank accounts could be frozen and liquidated simply because they were tied up as some minor partner in a minor deal somewhere.

One of the lawyers later got a mysterious call from Jimmy Nobile, the day after a story on the hearing appeared in the paper. "Is this real?" Nobile asked.

"Yes."

Nobile said nothing more. He just hung up.

Lehrer tried to calm the room. "The chaos, speculation, and uncertainty will end here, now," he said. "It is my duty to establish a procedure whereby everybody feels comfortable that they will be heard, that they will be heard quickly, that their interest will be determined quickly, and that we will work full-time, twenty-four hours a day, seven days a week . . . to sort this out so that nobody here gets hurt. If that can be done."

Before calling the court into session, Lehrer had contacted Donald Lomurro, a prominent local attorney, to serve as a "special fiscal agent." Lomurro did not have a white-shoe law firm pedigree. A graduate of Rutgers University, he had gone to the University of South Dakota to get his MBA and then got his law degree there as well. "I am the only graduate of the University of South Dakota Law School that you will ever meet," he joked to a reporter for the *Asbury Park Press* after being brought into the case.

Lomurro's job for the court was to analyze Dwek's portfolio and sell it off as quickly as possible and for as much money as he could. Then, with the court's supervision and approval, Lomurro was to divide the proceeds among Dwek's partners and creditors. Frankly, it doesn't even sound simple. In practice, it was pretty much out of control.

* * *

For almost a week, Lomurro had watched the Dwek saga play out in the news. There was the cashed check, the uncashed check, and Kearney's motion to the court. The lid had been blown off something big. After a long legal career in a county that has a knack for making more than its share of national headlines, Lomurro wanted in on Dwek and was not surprised when Lehrer rang through to his office that spring morning.

His rate was $400 per hour, with others in his firm, from associates to paralegals, receiving as little as $100. "At that time, we had thirty-seven lawyers and I added three immediately when I took the appointment," Lomurro said. "I rented extra space. We called it the 'Dwek Wing.' We set up a war room. Every property was on the wall. Sort of like a detective in a serial murder–type case and they have all the deceased on the wall so the detective is reminded what he's doing. We had every property on the wall and then we had every LLC. You had to understand at all times a scorecard of all the properties."

LLCs, or limited liability companies, are used all the time by developers and other businesspeople to set up new enterprises. They're simplistic corporate structures that can be put together by paralegals working 15 minutes on a computer. And they require little in the way of bookkeeping because the people who own the LLCs—called members—are allowed to record their taxes and expenses through their own individual tax returns. Typically, a builder will open a new LLC with each project so, if one fails, the rest of the landowner's properties remain untouched. It's no different than the way feature films are set up as their own corporate entities, limiting the financial risks to the studios or backers. A real estate operator like Dwek has dozens upon dozens of LLCs, each with different partners, different projects, and vastly different revenue-and-cost structures.

Lomurro, whose early years of work were mostly as a public defender, was exhilarated by the challenge of it all. In the beginning, he would get thousands of e-mails a week on the case. Some of Dwek's investors didn't share Lomurro's enthusiasm, and they weren't thrilled with him personally. People in the Syrian community were nervous about everything being liquidated and of losing their shirts, Dwek said in a sworn deposition in May 2007. "I told them I was going to do everything within my power and my attorney's power to get . . . the best dollar out of each property to get them their funds back."

Evelyn Safdieh—Ikey Franco's sister—harshly criticized the selection of an attorney who she felt had no experience and no track record for selling real estate. She complained, according to Dwek, that she looked at Lomurro's résumé and the only experience she could see was as a slip-and-fall attorney. "He's an ambulance chaser at best. And the last real estate deal he closed was in 1984," she objected, according to Dwek.

Lehrer introduced Lomurro and had all the attorneys, bankers, and investors put their business cards in one box so Lomurro could start the process of cataloging the properties, assets, and possible liabilities. Without any associates with him and armed only with a yellow legal pad, Lomurro had to phone his office to have an assistant rush over with stacks of his own business cards after he quickly ran out.

"That day you understood how many people were at risk," Lomurro said. "There were a lot of lawyers in the room. And then there were unfortunates in the room, people who would tell me their life savings were tied up. A lot of sad stories. The people who get hurt most are the people who get in at the end. They've been sitting, watching others make money. The conversation around them is so-and-so is making twenty percent, thirty percent. So they come in at the end and those were people who were going to get badly hurt. People would tell me, 'I gave Solomon fifty thousand dollars or one hundred thousand dollars and this was our savings. This is what I was going to use to buy a house. This was our last money.'"

As Lomurro listened to the stories, he felt an odd mix of sympathy and astonishment. "We all, since we were five years old, know that if something is too good to be true, it usually is," he said. "So when people would tell me 'I was to get fifty percent or twenty percent or forty percent in six months,' you say to yourself you didn't have to go to law school to figure this was not a good situation."

Attorney Robert Weir, representing Dwek that day, said his client had wanted to work out the claims against him, but his arrest by FBI agents interfered. "Instead of walking in with funds to settle it, we are a little behind it," Weir told reporters after the court hearing. "We're not running away. We're going to address it."

PNC by now learned of the transfer of properties to Joey Dwek and furiously moved to set those transfers aside as fraudulent. In its papers, the bank charged that the transfers were made even as Solomon was negotiating a settlement with PNC. It cited other irregularities. "The notices of Real Estate Settlement were prepared on April 30, 2006, a Sunday— apparently in a scramble to convey the properties before PNC reached the courthouse," the bank charged. "The conveyances are clearly fraudulent and made with the intent to defraud PNC and other creditors."

Joseph Dwek maintained that the properties were all purchased with his money and were rightfully his. "I provided Solomon with millions of dollars to purchase real estate on my behalf," he said in court papers.

The claims against Dwek quickly added up. Within days, Lomurro received more than $310 million in creditors' claims. Atop the list were Uncle Joey and Amboy National Bank. Both filed claims for tens of millions of dollars. Ike Franco said he was owed $30.2 million. Landscapers, businesses, and contractors were also on the list, among them Kerry Green, the owner of Four Star Builders of Neptune, who submitted a $2.1 million claim. In an interview that day with the *Asbury Park Press*, Green said he had built strip malls, office buildings, and single-family homes for Dwek. "He always pays. It's the reason why I dropped everybody and went with him," Green said. "He has [always] been a very honorable client with me until this month, when the rock dropped."

Despite the tangled litigation in the courtroom, Lomurro found that unlike the Bernie Madoff scandal that erupted much later, there was actually very little anger directed at Dwek. In fact, Lomurro was stunned to learn that Dwek's charisma continued to charm his victims even as they saw their financial futures crumbling because of him.

"There were people who continually believed in him until the very end and you would be shocked that they would continue to believe," Lomurro said. "As evidence would unfold, they still would say to me, 'Solomon told me this; Solomon told me that,' and they accepted it as gospel. Most of the people believed that Solomon would make it right, that it would be okay.

They were very concerned because they had a lot at risk, but the majority of the people really believed in Solomon."

Lomurro also found Dwek charismatic. "It's funny, because charisma comes in many forms," allowed Lomurro. "We can all see the six-foot-three dashing politician with the wavy hair who has charisma. And yet you can see Solomon Dwek, who's clearly not a physical presence in any sense, and he has charisma. He clearly has it. It was an overall package."

There were a lot of ways Lomurro saw Dwek's charm and magnetism show themselves. But none was more obvious and pronounced than the one thing that was understood but not seen: his family.

"He was the son of a rabbi. Instantly, he had credibility in the Community, and it's a tight community," Lomurro explained. "A fair amount of people would say, 'It's not within the realm of possibilities he would be untruthful.' It would upset me for people who would come in five months, six months into this project and say 'Solomon says, Solomon says.' And I'd say, 'Look, how can you keep saying that to me?'"

But they would.

5

⊰┼╂┼⊱

"Do I Really Want to Get in Bed with This Guy?"

Mike Himmel was looking to make a deal.

He did not need anyone to tell him that the federal sentencing guidelines in Dwek's case were off the charts. The truth of the matter was, Himmel knew that the government had his client dead to rights. Dwek was easily facing 30 years or more in prison and a $1 million fine. It had been a $50 million bank fraud, and there was absolutely nowhere to go with it.

The U.S. Attorney's office, on the other side, had no incentive to enter into a deal of any kind. To the front office, it was already an open-and-shut fraud case. Dwek was going to jail. When word first came down about the massive fraud at PNC Bank, Howe made his way down the hallway to the office of U.S. Attorney Christopher Christie to let the boss know. Howe told the story again of the bank drive-thru window. The $25 million bogus check. The closed account.

"And they negotiated it," Howe had told him. Then Dwek tried it again at a different PNC Bank branch the very next day, he said, even as he was wiring out the funds."

Christie almost laughed at the thought of it. "A twenty-five-million-dollar check?" he asked, incredulous. "This is a guy I gotta meet."

A big, affable man, Christie had a boyish charm. He had been named U.S. Attorney for New Jersey by Pres. George W. Bush in 2001, amid considerable controversy. As a securities lawyer with no experience in law enforcement, Christie, then 39, had never prosecuted a criminal case and was derided by critics who said his only qualifications for the job were that he had served as legal counsel for the Bush state campaign and had raised a lot of money for the Republicans. The president bestowed upon Christie a nickname that stuck. Bush called him Big Boy. He never liked the handle.

Christie's only previous government service had been as a Morris

County freeholder—an elective office with a name that harkened back to the days when New Jersey was still a British colony. A freeholder then meant a person worthy of land grants, when only men who held their land "free and clear" were eligible to be chosen for membership on the county governing body. It was essentially the job of a county supervisor. Christie served just one term in office, finishing dead last in the Republican primary when he sought a second term. Christie ran for state assembly and lost, and fared no better in a bid for the state senate.

Though he had no criminal law experience, he was always intrigued by corruption. As a high school senior class president in Livingston, a rich suburb to the west of Newark, he went to Washington with other members of a national youth program for a week in 1980 to study the federal government. He was assigned to spend time with Harrison "Pete" Williams, the highly respected Democratic senator from his home state and a champion of organized labor and migrant workers. Williams had fought for a range of social welfare laws and urban transit programs during his more than two decades in the Senate. Christie never got the chance to spend time with Williams, though. On the first morning of the program, Christie awoke to headlines detailing Williams' indictment for his role in the Abscam bribery scandal. It was one of the first big FBI sting operations aimed at public corruption. Undercover agents posing as Arab sheiks were recorded buying off members of Congress and other officials.

"It was my first introduction to New Jersey corruption," Christie recalled wryly some thirty years later, talking about it with a reporter. Christie called the incident hugely embarrassing: "Here was a guy held in such high esteem by so many people and he turned out to be a crook," he told the *Los Angeles Times*. "I spent the rest of the week defending New Jersey against jokes and insults made by other students, and the experience stayed with me my entire life. You think someone is a pillar of the community, but then suddenly the truth comes out and they're hauled away."

A graduate of the University of Delaware and Seton Hall Law School, Christie—who doesn't do things halfway—waged an aggressive campaign for the top federal law enforcement job in the state. The U.S. Attorney is a political appointee of the president, and Christie received widespread backing from prominent New Jersey Republican leaders. Opponents to the nomination, though, argued that Christie was, at best, ill prepared to be U.S. Attorney in an office with a reputation for its independence and known for high-profile cases ranging from espionage and political corruption to white-collar crime and health-care fraud. The executive committee of the Federal Bar Association of New Jersey passed a unanimous resolution urging the president to nominate a candidate with law enforcement experience.

Christie was to succeed Robert Cleary, a veteran prosecutor serving in an acting role after his predecessor, Faith Hochberg, was appointed to the federal bench. Cleary had headed the investigation into the elusive Unabomber, caught after one of the largest manhunts in the history of the FBI. He was a prosecutor's prosecutor; Christie was a pol.

After his nomination, Christie called up Cleary, who would not allow him to come to the office before he was confirmed. The two met instead at a Starbucks on Broad Street in Newark. Christie did a slow burn, and not only because he did not drink coffee.

Despite the opposition, Christie had the support of New Jersey's two Democratic senators, Jon Corzine (who would later become governor and then lose his reelection bid to Christie), and Robert Torricelli. Christie ultimately won Senate confirmation and was sworn in as the state's top federal law enforcement official in January 2002 by U.S. District Judge Joel Pisano, a friend of Christie's, who administered the oath of office during a private ceremony in the judge's chambers in Newark. It was a rough start even before the day was over. When Christie was sworn in Cleary had not even vacated the corner office. He was seen moving files out of the office later that day in a wheeled trolley cart. "He had it in his mind that Chris wasn't going to show up," suggested a former member of the office who had watched it all.

There was a lot of distrust in the office right from the beginning. Nobile immediately sized up Christie as a political hack and ignored him in the middle of a sensitive corruption case involving Jim Treffinger, the Essex County Executive vying for the Republican nomination for U.S. Senate. Christie did not hide his anger. He pulled Nobile outside and pointed to the glass door, where Christie's name was now lettered in gold.

"You see whose name is on the door?" he demanded. "As long as you see my name there, you tell me what's going on!"

Christie went home to Mendham his first day as U.S. Attorney and told his wife, Mary Pat, "I'm the only one in this office who thinks I can do this job."

He began by surrounding himself with a team of well-regarded career prosecutors as his top lieutenants. Ralph Marra was made first assistant. Charlie McKenna became executive assistant. Soon after arriving in January 2002, Christie met with each of the nearly 150 assistant prosecutors in Newark, Trenton, and Camden, restructured the office, and pressed some units for faster results. There were those who left, ruffled by his hard-charging style and short résumé.

In response to critics who said the U.S. Attorney's office too often ignored South Jersey, he appointed a senior-level deputy in Camden. U.S. Marshal James Plousis would later recall accompanying Christie on a visit to the offices of a newspaper editor in Salem County. "He thought this was the first time in history that the U.S. Attorney had been in Salem County," Plousis said.

The new U.S. Attorney began making public corruption a top priority of his office. Christie often explained corruption was key because people need to have faith in their government and its institutions. But it also made for huge headlines and Christie simply loved huge headlines. Within days of Christie becoming the new U.S. Attorney, the FBI arrested Paterson mayor Marty Barnes, who was charged with handing out millions of dollars in public contracts in return for vacation trips, a new swimming pool and waterfall for his home, expensive suits, and other luxury items. Leader of the state's third-largest city, Barnes was accused in a grand jury indictment of illegally skimming from his campaign funds, filing false tax returns, and also charging the city for travel expenses that had already been secretly picked up by contractors. It wasn't Christie's case, developed long before he arrived, but it was the first public corruption indictment to come before Christie, and he spoke out strongly.

"The conduct here is the most reprehensible type of public conduct that you can find anywhere in this country," he declared. "It is personal gratification and financial gratification at the expense of the public, using your public office to do that. And it's disgraceful."

In the years that followed, Christie kept the pressure up. A steady stream of defendants showed up in federal court, with more than 100 other New Jersey public officials arrested and charged with corruption. New Jersey was "an incredibly target-rich environment," Marra liked to say of political corruption.

Indeed, Christie relished his growing reputation, burnished by the arrests and convictions of more than a hundred mayors, councilmen, county officials, and legislators over the years. There had been Newark's mayor. Middlesex County power broker and Democratic state senator John Lynch, who would plead guilty to tax evasion and fraud charges. Treffinger, who was sentenced to 13 months in prison after pleading guilty to blocking a federal investigation and placing campaign workers on the county payroll. It was Treffinger who famously made the "fat fuck" comment in reference to Christie. By the time Dwek made his ill-fated trip through the PNC drive-thru, Christie was in the middle of an ongoing investigation of the state's medical school over a no-work job to boost the pension of a powerful state senator who had funneled millions in grant money to the university. The former Sussex County Democratic chairman had just pleaded guilty in U.S. District Court for using his health benefits management company to siphon money out of a union fund that ultimately went bankrupt.

In Christie's seventh-floor office was a bottle of Mr. Clean household cleanser, emblazoned with a photo of the U.S. Attorney's face on the label. The office itself was a shrine to Christie the fanatic, decorated with all sorts of memorabilia from his beloved New York Mets and a signed Fender guitar from his idol, New Jersey rocker Bruce Springsteen. A Springsteen freak, Christie was known to shut the door before a news conference and turn up the volume on classics from the E Street Band, getting himself juiced before meeting the press to talk about a major arrest. More often than not, it was the song "Thunder Road," and Christie, who once flew to London, England, just to catch a live Springsteen performance, had a tendency to sing aloud.

*　*　*

Himmel, a graduate of St. Louis University School of Law, long ago had been an assistant district attorney in the Bronx and later served as an assistant U.S. Attorney in New Jersey. During his years as a federal prosecutor, Himmel had run a number of high-profile cases that included the convictions of a New Jersey state senator, a former speaker of the New Jersey Assembly, and a series of union officials. White-collar crime was his specialty as one of the state's top defense attorneys.

He was an attorney who very rarely brought people in to cooperate. But following Dwek's arrest, Himmel made a call to Nobile. Himmel knew the way it worked. Give them somebody else and they might drop some of the charges before they went to a grand jury. Even better, it would mean an application with the judge for a downward departure—not a Get Out of Jail Free card but something that could possibly take off significant jail time.

Himmel had spoken about this in depth with his client. "You're an adult. You do what you have to do. You're the one that has to make the decision," Himmel told Dwek. "But there's no turning back."

The problem for Himmel was that Solomon, all on his own, was a big fish, so the feds had little reason to do anything other than punch his ticket to the federal pokey. The defense attorney put some chips out on the table. He had something to offer, Himmel said. Dwek knew people. There was a lot he could talk about that would be of interest to the government.

* * *

Nobody ever played liar's poker with Jimmy Nobile and really expected to win. Suspicious as hell and extremely well-organized, Nobile was a sphinx. He showed nothing. And mostly said nothing. Prosecutors from other divisions were not allowed to socialize with his people on his floor. In fact, when strangers asked him what he did for a living, Nobile would say only that he worked for the government. He refused to use EZ Pass, the electronic toll-paying system, because it left a record showing where one had been. He would not use direct deposit for his paycheck. And prosecutors in the office still recall the day when the fire alarms went off in the Rodino building during Nobile's investigation of Newark mayor Sharpe James. Nobile left the building with everyone else. Then he saw the fire trucks arrive with NEWARK printed on the side and suddenly had to be restrained from running back in to secure his files. He was convinced Sharpe had sent the department to get into his evidence. Only those who knew nothing about Newark would have thought him paranoid.

Nobile had a candy dish in his office that he kept filled for visitors but locked the office door every time he left. He did not have to refill the dish very often.

What Himmel did not realize was that Jimmy was intrigued but not yet convinced. Kahrer and Waldie saw Dwek as a gift and were pushing hard to see if they could get him to turn. Himmel knew none of that, only that Nobile wasn't offering him anything. He was frustrated and felt like he was getting nowhere after weeks of effort, so he finally resorted to calling Christie directly.

The U.S. Attorney is a talker and he was always pretty easy to get on the phone, especially for lawyers with real business to discuss. However, he ducked Himmel's incessant calls. Christie let it be known he just didn't want to talk to the guy. He wasn't sure what Himmel was selling, and he sure as hell didn't trust Dwek. He could not imagine what Himmel could possibly put on the plate, and did not want to hear his pitch.

"It was presumptuous," Christie explained much later. "He had a pitch and insisted on making it to the front office."

Himmel would not let it go. "You want to hear what I have to say. This is right up your alley," he said to Christie, the corruption-buster on the prowl.

"Like what?" asked the U.S. Attorney, after he finally got on the phone.

"I want to do this in person."

In Christie's mind, they already had Dwek solidly on the bank fraud, and it was no small case. The guy was facing too much time and there was little likelihood he was offering anything other than another con. A $50 million bank fraud would mean Dwek was not going to see the light of day from outside prison for decades.

Despite his tenure with the U.S. Attorney's office long ago, some prosecutors there just did not like Himmel. Some called him whiney and self-important, as if his pedigree as a former federal prosecutor—which he threw around like a résumé—gave him special standing. There were some bad feelings left over from the long investigation of Charles Kushner, a big player in New Jersey real estate and politics. Kushner got wrapped up in a tax fraud case that turned into attempted witness tampering when he set up a brother-in-law with a prostitute and sent a videotape of the encounter to his sister, who was set to testify against him. Himmel represented an accounting firm tied to Kushner and there was a belief among the feds that there had been financial records deliberately held back during the investigation.

"Give him the meeting," urged Marra, who supervised some of the office's top investigations and would later step in as acting U.S. Attorney when Christie left to run for governor. Marra had an easygoing personality and a quick smile. Like his boss, Marra was a baseball fan, although he sided with the New York Yankees, and his taste in rock trended more toward punk. There was a huge poster of Chrissie Hynde of the Pretenders on the wall of his office that traveled with him whenever he moved, and he would neither confirm nor deny he had named his daughter for her. But despite his casual manner, Marra was aggressive and willing to hear Himmel out. "We're total opportunists," Marra was fond of saying.

Michele Brown, the chief counsel, agreed with Marra that they should let Himmel come in and make his pitch. "Just talk to him," she said.

Christie remained dubious. "Do I really want to get in bed with this guy?" he asked of Dwek. "He just tried to pass fifty million dollars in bad checks."

But with the rest of his senior staff ready to listen to Himmel's pitch, Christie finally gave in. The meeting was in the afternoon, in the U.S. Attorney's private conference room, just off Christie's office suite in the deteriorating Peter W. Rodino Federal Building in Newark. The structure was named for the late congressman who had presided over the impeachment hearings for Pres. Richard Nixon. The 1960s-era building on Broad Street wore a permanent scaffolding apron around the entrances to protect pedestrians from the occasional falling piece of concrete. Huge concrete planters filled with weeds blocked off the side street in front of the building from traffic, a remnant of the security measures put in place after the Oklahoma City bombing. The conference room was decorated in stark contrast to the rest of the floor's unremarkable municipal-building style. Like the rest of the suite, it was carpeted in a thick blue pile, with accented blue walls. It held a long wooden table, lined by chairs and, while Christie was in charge, surrounded by a career's worth of photos of the U.S. Attorney with family, friends, and the famous. This was where Christie would meet his top aides for regular briefing sessions. It's where he would hold smaller news conferences, the ones involving cases that attracted attention but not the type of media turnout that would bring with it dozens of reporters and a score of TV cameras.

It was the room where once, in December 2004, Christie and his team went so far as to interrogate New Jersey's senior U.S. Senator at the time, Jon Corzine, who had just announced he was running for governor. Unaware of the irony still to come, Corzine, without any public notice, had drawn the attention of the FBI and federal prosecutors after he was found to have been making unexplained payments of $10,000 a month to the wife of former senate president and Democratic political boss John Lynch, who went to federal prison early in Corzine's term as governor. The payments were suspicious but proved to be little more than an inconvenience for Corzine that was never made public.

Christie sat at the head, as he always did, with his jacket off. Himmel sat close to the U.S. Attorney on the side of the table opposite the window. On the other side was the senior staff. Marra was there; so was Brown, together along the window side. At the other end were Nobile and Howe. None of them said much. They never did. They let Himmel do all the talking. It was his "ask," as such meetings were called. They had all been through the routine before. The guy on the other side would try to spin them; promises would be made. It was like pitching a bad act to a talent scout who had heard too many off-key singers, all thinking they were Pavarotti.

"What's with the fucking Mount Rushmore treatment?" one veteran attorney once complained, unnerved by the silence. "Am I getting anywhere?"

Himmel had to come to the table with some specifics. And he told them Dwek had a lot to tell them about corrupt politicians. Payoffs for building permits. Cash given to expedite approvals. But the pitch mostly related to money laundering in the Syrian Jewish community. "This guy can make cases for you," Himmel said. He had access. He knew people.

Himmel would not offer much more. But it would be big-time, he promised. Major money laundering, involving religious charities. Political payoffs. Other stuff. He also insisted on protection for Dwek.

That just raised everybody's eyebrows. What kind of protection did he need from a deeply religious community? Marra just laughed. "Come on, Mike. You're overselling. You're a defense lawyer."

Himmel didn't back down. "My guy's life will be in danger," he said.

"What are you telling me?" demanded Marra. "There's some team of ninjas after your client?"

"I'm telling you—you don't know these guys," warned Himmel. "I'm serious."

They remained noncommittal.

"Okay." Christie finally stood up after about an hour. "Thank you very much. We'll let you know."

After the defense attorney left and was escorted to the bank of elevators, the prosecutors kept the meeting going to talk it over. The argument went around the table. Do they offer any kind of cooperation agreement? Dwek was going to jail. The only question was how long he would spend there. The guy was in a multizillion-dollar jam, said one. Of course he's looking for a deal. And what kind of a cooperator could he be? The best cooperator is not the guy who has been in all the newspapers for a $50 million bank fraud. Dwek's cover was already blown. He had been charged. His name was already out there. Who was going to talk to him? Who wouldn't immediately assume he was wearing a wire? That aside, what was the danger to him if anybody found out? Some remained dubious.

"How do we wire him up and put him out there?" one asked. "He's already been arrested."

Christie agreed. "How are we going to go undercover with Dwek?" he asked, suggesting they had to be dealing with the stupidest people in the world if Dwek wasn't "made" as an informant before he even opened his mouth.

"Give him a chance. Give him a chance," countered Marra. "What's it going to cost you?"

Christie remained reluctant. By now he had been fully briefed on Dwek's history and knew there could be opportunities. But Christie still didn't believe Himmel and did not trust Dwek. Christie wasn't skeptical there was money laundering going on. He was skeptical that Dwek could deliver.

"So what do we want to do? Can this guy give us anything that's worth our while?" the U.S. Attorney asked. "He's working off a ton of time."

Using a cooperating witness in a criminal case is always fraught with peril. Everyone at the table knew an informant had every incentive to push beyond the limits in an effort to make a case for prosecutors that could later backfire. At trial, defense attorneys with a case they cannot win always try to attack the informer as a bad guy selling a story to get out of jail. They howl entrapment. That it was a setup. "Don't convict someone," they plead to the jury, "on the basis of someone who would say just about anything to win their own freedom."

Prosecutors respond that they have to depend on bad guys to catch bad guys. In summations, they urge jurors not to focus on the acts of the informant but on the evidence collected against the defendants. And while entrapment is rarely a defense that works, there are lines that must not be crossed.

Of greater concern was that a cooperator might commit more crimes while undercover for the FBI. It had happened before.

Nobody in Christie's conference room could forget Michael Guibilo. He had been arrested 27 times and convicted of 11 felonies since the 1960s. Still, he was repeatedly released from prison to work as an informant for federal and local law enforcement, testifying against mobsters and drug traffickers and helping uncover criminal plots against two federal judges. His work for the government did nothing to reform him. He returned to robbing banks.

Christie was also all too aware of the controversy over the 2003 criminal case involving Hemant Lakhani, a British exporter, who was arrested in an airport hotel suite near Newark for trying to sell missiles to terrorists to use against U.S. airliners, in a highly orchestrated sting that spanned two continents. It was later disclosed that the informant who set up Lakhani, Mohammed Habib Rehman, was a small-time swindler with a trail of more than $200,000 in court judgments and unpaid debts. John P. Martin, a reporter for *The Star-Ledger,* pored through court records and found that Rehman, who sometimes called himself Haji, continued to work for the FBI—despite warnings to the Bureau that he could not be trusted from a former federal agent who had worked extensively with him.

Putting an informant on the street also risked the possibility of never seeing him again. There was the constant fear that people facing significant jail time for whatever they had done might simply flee in the middle of a sting operation. Informants are also in constant danger of being "outted" or getting killed, and even though the feds really don't care about whether the informants live or die, they are very nervous about the bad publicity that goes along with the killing of a cooperator.

None of these issues was new to any of them. They had had these discussions in the same room not long ago. Unknown to anyone outside the office, federal prosecutors had been secretly working for months on another major case with the help of a cooperating witness involving allegations of a terror cell at Fort Dix, the sprawling U.S. Army base in South Jersey. Earlier in the year, a 23-year-old clerk at a Circuit City consumer electronics store in Mount Laurel called authorities after he was asked to convert a videotape to a DVD and saw what he thought were disturbing images. On the tape, he saw men firing rifles and shouting "Allahu Akbar," Arabic for "God is great." Six men were now under investigation in the case, and the key to it all right now was an Egyptian national by the name of Mahmoud Omar convicted in one bank fraud and suspected in several others.

As the debate over Dwek extended beyond the conference room to others in the front office, the argument continued. Charlie McKenna, a top aide to Christie with a hard-core Queens attitude and an incredible vocabulary of profanities, used many of those same words with the boss, telling Christie that Dwek would just disappear, or call them long-distance from Israel to say good-bye. "Fuck him! He's playing us," McKenna said of Himmel. "He's just jerking your chain."

Thomas Eicher, the deputy chief of the special prosecutions division who had spent three years in Washington on the House Bank investigation that ensnared members of Congress and their staffs in a check-kiting scandal, favored a deal. "There's no downside to it," he told others. If Dwek scored, great. If not, he's still headed to federal prison for bank fraud.

The office had gained much success in some of its high-impact cases involving informants. Lakhani, in fact, had eventually been sentenced to nearly half a century in prison by a judge who said he deserved the harshest possible punishment. Then there was Robert Janiszewski, the four-term county leader in Hudson County who disappeared shortly after that night along the Hudson River waterfront. The onetime Democratic Party power broker, caught on camera taking bribes from another informant, became a cooperating witness himself, spending nearly a year secretly working with the FBI to bring down a number of public officials and developers.

They had also nabbed three sitting mayors, four current councilmen, and a police commissioner on corruption charges—all in a single day—in a long-running probe through Monmouth County, Dwek's own backyard. The busts came after the FBI launched an informant who posed as the owner of a construction and demolition business, paying out cash bribes in exchange for the promise of public contracts.

That case, more than anything else, was the argument for making the deal. Dwek had been on the edge of the investigation they called Bid Rig. He was known to be throwing money around. Something about him just did not add up at the time. "Give it a try," Marra said. "What do we have to lose?" Nobile was also strongly pushing to go ahead.

Michele Brown sided with Marra and Nobile but wasn't as vocal about it. "Let's see what the guy can do," she said.

Howe, a veteran of the Lakhani terror case, stayed silent. It usually took him a while to get worked up.

It was Christie's decision to make, and he wasn't sure. It just didn't sound kosher, he told them. It seemed like a morass, a sinkhole. He had seen the paperwork filed in the bank fraud. Who would possibly want to talk to him?

The FBI, though, was convinced that Dwek could take them to places they had never been. Kahrer, the aggressive FBI supervisor with a long history with Marra, McKenna, and Nobile, continued to lobby for the U.S. Attorney to take it on.

The suggestion of public corruption at play intrigued the big man. After he had announced the arrests of the 11 public officials in Monmouth County the previous February on bribery and money-laundering charges, he received 85 letters in two weeks reporting suspicions of corruption. People were fed up with the state's continuing reputation as the most corrupt place in the country. And, of course, there was the promise of headlines.

Christie decided to sleep on it.

The next day, he told Marra to go ahead.

"Make it a short leash," Christie said. "Let's give him six months."

6

⊶+ + +⊷

Point of No Return

Dwek sat quietly in a conference room at the U.S. Attorney's office as William Wachtel, the New York lawyer representing Ike Franco, interrogated him about why he had stolen $30 million of Franco's money.

"Do you consider yourself to be an observant Jew?" Dwek was asked.

Dwek, wearing the black yarmulke he never removed, could only shrug. "Listen, 'observant' everyone could clarify any way you want," he answered carefully.

"There's six hundred and thirteen rules," pressed Wachtel, referring to the 613 statements and principles of law and ethics in the Torah known as mitzvoth, the law of Moses. "I'm not asking if you're batting .613. Do you consider yourself to be an observant Jew?"

Dwek nodded. "I try to do—to follow, to the best of my ability, the commandments."

"The Ten Commandments?" persisted Wachtel.

"You said six hundred and thirteen. More than ten commandments," Dwek replied. "But I try to follow the commandments of the Torah."

Wachtel had a specific line he was following. "How about the first ten of the six hundred and thirteen? The famous Ten Commandments?"

"I try, to the best of my ability," Dwek repeated. "I don't think I ever killed anyone or kidnapped anyone or stuff like that."

But "Thou shall not kill" was not the commandment Wachtel had in mind, and Dwek, by now, knew where he was going. He had little choice but to answer the questions in the court-ordered civil deposition. "Are you familiar with the section of the Bible known as Leviticus?"

"Yeah. I mean I can't quote verses or anything like that, but I think—I studied it years ago in elementary school," Dwek acknowledged.

. "Well, do you remember the section that says you, quote, 'you shall not steal, you shall not lie to one another'?"

"Yes," he answered simply.

"Have you done your best to honor that section of the Bible?"

"No," said Dwek.

"Why not?"

He was starkly honest. "Greed is probably a simple, short version of answering that question," Dwek said. "Greed, pressure, threats, and stuff like that . . ."

* * *

The exchange, years after Dwek's Ponzi scheme unraveled and his cooperation with the government finally came to light, was an echo of an earlier series of conversations Dwek began with prosecutors in the very same office, in late 2006. After Christie had agreed to a deal with Dwek, a meeting with several of the assistant U.S. Attorneys in the case was set up at the federal building in Newark. Accompanied by Himmel, Dwek went through the metal detectors and took the elevator up to the seventh floor, where he was given a visitor's pass and brought into a conference room. There was not yet a deal on the table, and before anyone signed off on one Dwek had to answer their questions.

While Christie had given the go-ahead to negotiate a cooperation agreement, the U.S. Attorney first wanted to hear exactly what Dwek could provide to the government. Prosecutors wanted to know everything he knew—not only about the crime for which he was charged but anything else they could build a case around. The money laundering his attorney had discussed earlier. The political payoffs.

This was the point of no return for The Rabbi's Son. To be an informer— *moser* in Hebrew—is to be despised and shunned in an Orthodox community. One could not be held in greater contempt than for talebearing against a fellow Jew. It was a tradition that grew out of Talmudic times, when to inform on an already-persecuted community frequently living under corrupt and anti-Semitic rule was to threaten everyone in it. To stand accused of informing to a secular authority could, and did, often result in death to transgressors.

It's an odd edict in a free society, considering the competing premium Jewish law also places on adhering to the authority of the secular government, known as *dina d'malchuta dina* (the law of the land is law): something that was critical to the Jews' existence through centuries of persecutions, holocausts, and inquisitions.

Indeed, the bulk of those even in the modern Orthodox movement have no conflict with the principle, said Ronald Kiener, director of Jewish studies at Trinity College in Connecticut. "The right thing to do is if someone is doing something illegal is that you don't ask the ethicist," he remarked. "You be a law-abiding citizen. That's one of the keys to being [a] mensch."

But he said the ultra-Orthodox have always set themselves apart and the principle of *dina d'malchuta dina* is often set aside. There is a mind-set that they are not bound by "the ways of the gentiles, who have done nothing over the centuries than make our lives miserable." Still, Kiener said there is no real mechanism for carrying out any sanctions against those who rat out others in their community. It is not, he noted, like the Mafia concept of omertà. It's mostly the potential for social ostracism.

For Dwek, to become a *moser* would mean permanent exile for himself, perhaps even his children and wife, from a close-knit community that was the focal point of everyday life. Even if he was to escape prison, it would be inconceivable that he would be accepted into an Orthodox congregation ever again once his cooperation became public knowledge. He would be a pariah.

The fears Himmel had expressed to federal prosecutors about his client's life being in danger might not be that far-fetched. He was about to help federal authorities put others behind bars, in exchange for what he hoped would be a lesser punishment for himself. The Syrians could be a tough crowd. There would be no forgiveness.

Faced with 30 years in prison, Dwek was about to enter into a Faustian bargain. If he wanted to see his children again before the other side of childhood, he would have to trade friends, associates, and other people he had known for years. He had to betray everyone he knew and not look back.

If it gave him pause then, he never showed it. Indeed, he seemed almost eager to toss just about anyone aside—naming names and then carefully spelling them out to make sure there was no mistake. He had no qualms about leaving any of them on the side of the road. People he had done business with, former investors, even those related to him. Like the adrenaline junkie he seemed to be at the height of the Ponzi scheme, he was almost eager to talk.

The initial sit-down was with Brian Howe, Eicher, and several others from Special Prosecutions. Himmel, who was also there, had instructed his client earlier how it would work. They would be asking him questions. Lots of questions. He could not hold anything back. He could not lie. He could not mislead the FBI. And if he did everything they asked of him, then the U.S. Attorney would file what was known as a 5K letter, a recommendation that the judge lighten a convict's sentence because he helped nail other crooks. There were no promises. No guarantees. Even if Dwek cooperated to the full extent, the judge could do whatever he wanted to in the end. But as slim a hope as that was, it was something.

The first day was a short meeting. They called it a proffer. They wanted to know what Dwek was going to offer them. It was mostly a get-acquainted session, with both sides feeling each other out. Dwek later admitted being far more nervous than he was when he passed the $25 million check at PNC Bank.

A longer, follow-up meeting was held away from the Rodino building several days later. Howe, Eicher, and the others did not want Dwek to be seen coming into the federal building. There was always a chance someone might recognize him, and everything would immediately fall apart if anyone suspected he was cooperating. The IRS criminal division was located a few miles away, just off Route 22 in a three-story brick office building in suburban Springfield. They reconvened there. This time some of the FBI case agents were brought in, including Waldie and Kahrer.

The meeting was not taped, but notes were taken. The hours went by. They began grilling Dwek specifically about the PNC Bank fraud for which he had been arrested in May. He showed no hesitation in answering their questions. He readily admitted the check-kiting scheme, which had been fully documented already in PNC's lawsuit.

"What did you do?"

"I wired funds on a closed account just like I got charged with," Dwek said.

"What can you tell us about Joseph Kohen?" Dwek was asked.

Dwek went into great detail about Kohen, a Monmouth County mortgage broker who wrote the $25 million check that bounced. Dwek had asked for Kohen's help in April and had him get on the phone with PNC Bank to claim he was Solomon's attorney. Kohen told the bank he would be sending a wire to cover the $25 million. There was no wire. There was no money.

"They wanted to just get a little more detail with me as to why I had an urgency to wire out the twenty million dollars and the two-point-two million dollars to Ken Cayre and on and on," Dwek recalled.

What did he tell them?

"I told them there were certain threats made to me and I felt compelled to send the money out when I sent it out even though I knew there weren't funds to cover it," he answered. "They had a list of names that they asked me about certain individuals, and if I knew the individual I answered the question. If I didn't, I told them I didn't know."

Prosecutors felt he was not giving them the whole story. He was holding back on a lot of what led up to the check cashing, trying to explain away the real estate scam. One of those at the meeting expressed frustration: "He's playing games. He's trying to con us."

By then, the FBI had begun piecing together the Ponzi scheme that a federal bankruptcy trustee would later detail in a series of lawsuits. As they confronted Dwek with the evidence, he started talking. He talked about the money he had stolen from Uncle Joey and Ike Franco and everyone else.

Then they asked Dwek about all the money laundering he claimed to have had done through the Deal Yeshiva. How it was done, with whom, and how much he had skimmed off the top in transactions dating years earlier.

He told them about others he had used to launder money, including Eli Ben Haim, his brother's father-in-law. Dwek had more than $1 million in cash stashed away—money from the "vig," or take, from all the illicit dealings, money that he said he had given for safekeeping to Barry Kantrowitz, his real estate broker. He talked about all the money he had been paying out to politicians for years. There was a $10,000 payoff to a Long Branch councilman in exchange for zoning approval to build 11 town houses. There was $50,000 to the mayor of one Monmouth County town where Dwek had been doing a lot of business.

Waldie already knew about some of the payoffs. The initial Operation Bid Rig investigation in 2002 had led quickly to Terrance Weldon, then the mayor of Ocean Township, next door to Deal. Dwek had been having difficulty back then obtaining the necessary approvals for a senior citizen development he was backing, Ocean Independent Living. Dwek had not known Weldon, so he had arranged an introduction through Kantrowitz and later admitted in sworn statements he paid the mayor $50,000 in exchange for the necessary approvals.

Dwek ultimately obtained a green light from the township and developed and then sold the property for huge profit.

The FBI had leaned on Weldon early and the mayor quickly turned, agreeing to cooperate with authorities in hopes of cutting down his own prison time. At the time of the Weldon probe, the bribe from Dwek was never publicly disclosed, although the FBI had gone to Kantrowitz and began asking uncomfortable questions. Despite what Waldie learned about the payment, there had not been enough to take it to the prosecutors. Weldon even tried to set up Dwek on tape, but failed.

The Big Rig investigation connected with Weldon was actually still playing out while Dwek was being interviewed by prosecutors that summer. In June 2006, a month after Dwek was indicted for the PNC Bank fraud, a federal jury quickly convicted former Middletown Township committeeman Ray O'Grady of taking thousands of dollars in bribes.

O'Grady had been arrested the previous year, along with nearly a dozen other current and former Monmouth County officials—including the mayors of Keyport, Hazlet, and West Long Branch—all charged with extorting cash bribes and free work from a contractor who was cooperating with the FBI. It was a case that in many ways previewed what was to come with Dwek. Waldie's team of case agents had gone undercover. Two of them, who went by the names of Joel and Vinnie, were a pair of tough-looking guys who ran shotgun for "Duke" Steffer, a mysterious man who had set up a demolition company in Monmouth County.

Duke was a plant. He had gotten into some big trouble with the law down in Florida and the FBI put him to work as a cooperating witness in a sting operation targeting towns along the Jersey Shore. He got to be well-known, driving around in a big, fully loaded black Cadillac Escalade, always accompanied by Joel and Vinnie, who many took to be Duke's bodyguards. No one knew much about him, except that he was quick to hand out fat envelopes of cash to any takers, in an effort to steer no-bid contracts to his company, based out of an office suite that coincidentally was being rented to him by Kerry Green, one of Dwek's contractors.

O'Grady got pulled into the sting when he agreed to meet Joel and Vinnie at a Chili's restaurant on Route 9 in Freehold in October 2004. Sitting at a table over drinks, as Waldie and a partner, Donald Russ, sat just two tables away, the undercover agents told O'Grady they had been working in construction—mostly in Florida and Alabama—before hooking up with Steffer. "Our boss knows that you're influential and he knows that in January you're gonna become the mayor," Joel told O'Grady. "You have a lot of influence. And he knows you're gonna look out for our best interest."

"I could possibly help you out," acknowledged O'Grady.

"Next week, stop by the office," said one of the undercover agents. "We'll give you a little early Christmas gift or whatever . . . Do whatever you want with it . . . You know, show the boss's appreciation."

"Sure . . . okay," O'Grady said.

He then offered a little bravado that would haunt him to his trial and still resonates as one of the more remarkable exchanges in New Jersey's sordid history of corruption, after one of the undercover agents expressed concern to O'Grady over the possibility of getting caught.

"I can smell a cop a mile away," bragged O'Grady.

Joel tried hard not to laugh out loud. Even Waldie was trying to keep a straight face. "We need you," Joel said, playing immediately into it. "We need you like those dogs that go through luggage."

"Well, I don't talk in the open. I don't talk to anybody. You don't do stupid things," declared O'Grady as he was captured on surveillance tape. "Don't take fucking notes. And I don't talk about things on the phone."

The following week, the township official went to the Steffer Demolition office on Route 33 in Neptune and told them he was planning a trip to Aruba. Joel gave him an envelope with $1,000 in cash. "Look out for our best interests," the agent told O'Grady. "When you're the mayor, you know, we're looking for contracts."

O'Grady shook hands. "Let's see how we can work out this partnership."

Joel told O'Grady he wished Duke was there to shake his hand personally.

"They'll be plenty of opportunities, I'm sure," said O'Grady, who became known among the agents as O'Shady. He ultimately took $6,000. A federal jury deliberated just three hours after watching and listening to FBI recordings before voting to convict O'Grady.

Despite his cooperation, Ocean Township mayor Weldon later had the book thrown at him by Senior U.S. District Judge William Walls. In a dramatic courtroom proceeding, Walls rejected calls for leniency by prosecutors. He declared that he was fed up with the seemingly endless parade of New Jersey politicians "hell-bent on corruption" and sentenced Weldon to nearly five years in prison.

Assistant U.S. Attorney Mark McCarren, who had pressed for a light sentence, argued that Weldon's cooperation led to charges being brought against Weldon's accountant, a developer, an engineer, and a local planning-board member. But the judge would have nothing of it. He likened it to Al Capone ratting out his driver.

"As far as I'm concerned, the commission of such crimes deserves severe punishment," Walls declared. "It does us no good to pat him on the wrist."

It might have given Dwek serious pause had he known about it at the time.

* * *

The meetings with Dwek, the FBI, and the assistant U.S. Attorneys went on for several weeks as Dwek unloaded. They talked to him about wearing a surveillance wire and getting others to implicate themselves and were especially interested in political corruption. The money laundering was okay, but Christie wanted politicians on the take.

In July, meanwhile, the FBI and IRS paid a visit to the business offices of the Deal Yeshiva on Brighton Avenue and began combing through Solomon's desk. They also searched an office in Oakhurst where Dwek's real estate records had been kept.

* * *

As Dwek's talks with prosecutors progressed, the civil litigation in Monmouth County over his properties continued, and the case docket grew and grew. The state court system had to set up a special section of its Web site to handle documents generated by the Dwek case.

The fight over assets went well beyond Uncle Joey's properties. In fact, there were business ventures that went far afield of land development in Monmouth County. There was a 116-foot dinner boat 1,100 miles to the south on the Florida Gulf Coast called the *Excalibur.* Dwek said he and Eli Seruya put together a $2.5 million deal to acquire the vessel and, with two other partners, turned it into a floating casino. The idea was that gamblers would motor into international waters and have a turn at roulette, blackjack tables, and slot machines. The business went bust.

Dwek blamed his partners for the failure of the venture. "I kept on pumping money in and money was going out the back door. I wasn't there or Seruya wasn't there to operate it and at some point—I hired a guy to go down and try to operate it for a few months and it wasn't successful," Dwek recalled.

His partners put the business entity into bankruptcy and then the note holder sued him and got a $1.1 million judgment after Dwek defaulted on the loan. The boat was taken over by an operator who turned it into a floating strip club. Dwek still had an interest in the new business, but that failed, too.

The Dwek empire overtook Lomurro's firm as the lawyers became instant experts in real estate. Never before had Lomurro or his associates owned properties, managed them, dealt with tenants' complaints, fixed leaky faucets, or marketed apartment complexes. All of that was now part of Lomurro's everyday life. To get it all done, Lomurro came to depend on Dwek, who played the role of some out-of-body consultant helping his own coroner disassemble his corpse. For months, Lomurro would have to call Dwek to ask things simple and complicated, to get him into the office to go over details or sales issues. And for all those months, Dwek was a remarkably willing accessory to his liquidators.

"He liked the action," Lomurro said. "He was necessary. And properties were moving. If I talked price, he talked price. He wanted to be involved. He would be here. He would stay. We'd put him in a room. I would be surprised if there weren't occasions he wasn't here for ten hours."

During the litigation, he told a reporter from the *Asbury Park Press* that he saw Dwek five times a week. "He's probably in the building right now, negotiating with someone" on a property, Lomurro said, laughing. And as a matter of fact, Dwek, dressed in a dark blue suit and white shirt, could be seen that day through the glass wall of a conference room down the hall in Lomurro's Freehold law office, talking with several lawyers and at least one claimant.

Lomurro at the time said Dwek had a "good eye for property," with most of the properties selling for more than he paid for them.

It went on like that for the next eight months. Lomurro sold and ran a real estate company, Lehrer oversaw the property auctions, and the banks fought each other for better position in the hopes they might see 50 or 60 cents on the dollar of what they were owed. At one point, Lehrer even reached out to Rabbi Saul Kassin, the elderly patriarch of the Syrian Jewish community in Brooklyn, to see if he would be willing to play intermediary among Dwek's creditors. Kassin wasn't interested.

At hearing after hearing, Dwek himself would traipse around the courthouse, putting on a show like he was hosting a kid's Bar Mitzvah or throwing a cocktail party. "Mr. Big Mouth is walking around the courthouse talking to anybody and everybody," one lawyer, still stunned by the display, muttered.

But Dwek remained a man of secrets. Only later did it come out that, while the litigation was proceeding, people were growing desperate and decided to confront him. "A bunch of guys came to his house and said, 'You better make this right, you better make all these payments back to the people you're ripping off,'" according to one insider.

*　*　*

The secret meetings with the U.S. Attorney's office continued into the fall. They were very cautious. At one point, the case against the Lakewood Boys Cheder involving the excessive payments under the National School Lunch Program, which was being developed by another assistant U.S. Attorney who knew nothing of the talks with Dwek, came across Christie's desk for approval. He sent it to Nobile first to make sure it would not conflict with the case now being developed.

Do you have a problem with this? Chris scrawled on a Post-it note.

It came back with a one-word reply in Jimmy Writing: *No.*

By early 2007, Christie gave his final blessing to the deal and Dwek entered into a cooperation agreement with the government on January 25. The eight-page agreement called for Dwek to plead to two criminal counts charging him with defrauding PNC Bank and engaging in monetary transactions in property derived from unlawful activity. The government agreed not to prosecute him on any of the other charges related to the Ponzi scheme, the money laundering, or bribing public officials.

There was no promise of how much time he would spend in prison. On just the first count, he faced a statutory maximum of 30 years. The nature and full extent of Dwek's cooperation would be made known only to the judge. The agreement was signed by Brian Howe and Tom Eicher. Dwek put his name to it with a quick scrawl. Himmel and Christopher Porrino, his co-counsel, signed below a week later. It was filed with the court under seal.

* * *

The sell-off of Solomon's assets, meanwhile, was getting nasty. A two-page declaration of assets filed with the court showed only $1,700 in cash and two luxury cars. "From day one, there's always been a question as to whether Mr. Dwek was being forthcoming," attorney Richard K. Coplon, who represented one of Dwek's investors, told reporters. "It's an ongoing problem to try to track down this man's assets."

The Community was in little mood to compromise with Solomon. His efforts to use $37,800 of his seized assets to pay for tuition to send his kids to a yeshiva were opposed by creditors. Ike Franco's lawyer, in a letter to the court, said flatly that the expense of tuition "should not be borne by Solomon's victims and creditors." Lehrer would not allow the payments. Dwek's brother, living rent free in one of the seized Dwek properties, was also told to pay up or leave.

At the same time, with each new hearing or hiccup, PNC was embarrassed yet again as the ludicrous story of the $25 million check got rehashed as background for news reports and court sessions. In February, two weeks after Solomon signed his secret cooperation agreement with the U.S. Attorney's office, Dwek's creditors finally moved to put him into federal bankruptcy court in Trenton. It was probably the worst move for

PNC if the bank was hoping to get some money back. But it was good public relations, Lomurro said. "The second the case went to Trenton, the publicity was gone."

U.S. Bankruptcy Court Judge Kathryn C. Ferguson wasted little time taking the case from the state Supreme Court. In a courtroom filed with more than 50 lawyers, creditors, and other interested parties, Ferguson said allegations of fraud and malfeasance by Dwek, "permeate just about every aspect of this case."

The property sales of Dwek's empire were frozen. Everybody took a step back to see what would happen next.

As Lomurro was closing up shop, he briefed Charles A. Stanziale Jr., the new federal bankruptcy trustee appointed to manage and sell off Dwek's holdings for creditors in U.S. Bankruptcy Court.

"You cannot believe anything Solomon's telling you," Lomurro told Stanziale. "And you should always assume he's wired . . ."

7

⊷✦✦⊷

Mike from Monsey

The morning of Tuesday, March 6, 2007, was cold and windy, with the temperatures well below normal for that time of year. Dwek made his way north to Union City, a densely packed blue-collar immigrant community in Hudson County straddling the busy Route 495 approach to the Lincoln Tunnel into Manhattan.

After being coached for months by the FBI and the assistant U.S. Attorneys, Dwek had to prove his worth as a cooperating witness. He was now an undercover informant. One of his first contacts would be through someone he had known for years—Shimon Haber, 34, a soft-spoken man whose trim, prematurely gray hair belied his age. The two had done business together in the past. Haber was a member of the Syrian community like Dwek, who knew Haber's family well. Solomon had business ties to Shimon's uncle, Manny Haber, another investor in the Ponzi scheme along with Ike Franco and Uncle Joey. Manny had big money. He was the CEO of Fleet Street, Ltd., a New York–based apparel company on Manhattan's Seventh Avenue in the heart of the fashion district known for raincoats and outerwear. Now one of the many unsecured creditors in the bankruptcy case, he had lodged a $1.6 million claim against Solomon.

Solomon and Shimon had gotten involved more than a year earlier in a proposed condo development deal Haber was trying to put together on a section of Palisade Avenue in Union City, just across the river from New York. At one time mostly Italian, Union City, a place once known as the embroidery capital of the world, had been transformed by successive waves of emigrants over the years—families from Europe and Cuba and then from Ecuador, El Salvador, and the Dominican Republic. Its ethnic restaurants and storefront signs were now in Spanish, proclaiming its

Latino character. There was a Hasidic Jewish community there as well, which kept largely to itself, with its own schools, buses, and ambulances. Unlike the Hasidim of Brooklyn or Jerusalem, those in Union City preferred to stay well below the radar, although they had a good relationship with Mayor Brian Stack.

It was a tough place to build anything. Union City is the most densely populated community in the country, and construction meant buying up old houses or tenements, knocking them down, and then getting zoning approval for something new. The process was fraught with uncertainty in a place ruled from its quaint, Victorian-style City Hall, where politics, favoritism, and connections almost always trumped everything else. This, one had to remember, was where former mayor and state senator Bill Musto had been reelected in 1982, a day after being sentenced to seven years in prison for racketeering. It was also the incubator to the career of U.S. Sen. Robert Menendez, who, while fighting for the city's virtue, reinforced its reputation with his stories of death threats and his history of having to wear a bulletproof vest after helping the feds.

One building owner had been fighting for years to get approval on another condo project, only to discover during his long-running court battle with the city that one needed some juice to make things happen. Former officials readily admitted in sworn testimony that zoning decisions were made long before anyone voted on them. In fact, several former members of the board of adjustment, which voted on variances—needed before any major building project could move forward—testified that decisions by the board were all preordained. They believed those decisions came from Mayor Stack, an old-school Democratic pol who passes out turkeys at Thanksgiving and toys at Christmas, running Union City like an old-time Chicago ward heeler. Stack denied the allegations.

A block down from that proposed condo project, the State of New Jersey had ended up paying $1.8 million for another parcel of land earmarked for a new elementary school after developers with connections hurriedly built a new apartment building on the site. The state claimed the three-story structure, which was never occupied, was erected simply to inflate the price of the land but ended up settling the matter out of court. The apartment building was eventually torn down and the state ran out of money before it could build the school. The parcel remains vacant to this day.

That there was even a demand and market for new housing in Union City seemed odd to a casual observer. There were few signs of wealth. Yet there was an ongoing building boom in the city. Local activist Larry Price, who lives on Palisade Avenue, walked with a visitor through his neighborhood, perched high on the bluffs overlooking the Hudson River. When the trolleys ran here, they needed a switchback track to climb the hill in stages.

"For almost fifty years, there was no development here," Price said. But then the quick ride by bus into New York, the cheap real estate, and the million-dollar view began to get noticed by outsiders. Condos started getting squeezed into odd-shaped lots. Small pieces of real estate were being bought up and assembled for larger projects.

Price these days fights most of them, gaining a reputation as a thorn in the side of developers. "I get bribe offers all the time." He laughs. "I've turned down serious money."

Once, a project proponent suggested a token payment to just go away. As a payoff, it was almost an insult. "Why aren't you offering me more?" Price demanded.

"We know you're not going to take it," the guy conceded.

"Yeah, but it's a matter of respect," Price told him, laughing out loud as he recounted the conversation. Even the good guys worry about their street cred in Hudson County.

After a short stroll, Price arrived at the corner of Palisade and 10th Street, where Haber and Dwek had been planning to develop their project. Haber purchased one house and then a second one. He had proposed a condo development of 150 units, Price remembered, as he pointed out the site with its modest homes of brick and plain siding. "Can you fit one hundred fifty units there?" he asked, and then answered his own question: "If you build it high enough you can."

For that, they would have needed major zoning concessions from the town.

Dwek had been an equity partner in the project. Between 2005 and 2006, he had sent $745,054 to Haber, according to bankruptcy court filings. The two also wrote out a number of campaign contributions to Stack for his state assembly race in October 2005. Haber gave the mayor $2,600, the maximum allowed. Dwek himself wrote out at least $5,200 in checks to Stack's campaign committee: one for $2,600 from his company, Dwek Properties LLC, and a second individual contribution for another $2,600 in his own name.

But the project never got off the ground. It did not even go before the city for approvals. A woman whose home was between the other properties refused to sell, and Haber was left with two unconnected parcels that were useless to him without the piece in the middle.

* * *

When the FBI finally unleashed Dwek, the agents gave him a cover story, one that sounded plausible, although he had been lying like this for years. The only difference was that this time he had a rapt audience, listening and watching his every move on the surveillance video.

Haber was the first target. Dwek called Shimon, telling him he was looking for development opportunities in Hudson and a way to grease the skids to make it happen. He also needed someone to take a check from one of his businesses and turn it into cash. Haber knew all about the PNC Bank fraud. Everybody in the Community did, and he was well aware that his uncle was one of Dwek's unsecured creditors. The bankruptcy case had been filed just a month before. Despite Dwek's troubles, though, few in the Community had completely turned their back on him. He had a wife and now five kids to feed. And he was still The Rabbi's Son.

Whatever Solomon's problems, the Community always supported its own. Dwek's mother-in-law had put up her house so Solomon could make bail back in May. As his business sank deeper into bankruptcy, he still talked with investors from the Community, assuring them that he could make them whole. They still wanted to believe him. Even if they didn't like or trust him, they wanted their money.

Haber agreed to hook Dwek up with another big player in Hudson County real estate, Moshe Altman, who claimed to have some level of political juice. Altman also had ties to several religious funds that could help him move money without the bankruptcy trustee catching on. For his trouble, Haber was about to be thrown under the bus—with Dwek backing up a few times to make sure he had run over him.

While both Altman and Dwek were involved in real estate, both about the same age, and were members of Orthodox communities, they did not know each other. The two were from totally different worlds. Dwek was Syrian Sephardic. Altman, in his late thirties, was a so-called black hat Haredi: a member of the sizable Hasidic community of Monsey, New York, whose business was putting together development deals in Hudson County. He knew and was known by some of the key political players, including Stack.

Despite his previous involvement with Haber in Union City, Dwek did not know much about Hudson County. Most of his real estate business had been down along the Jersey Shore, miles to the south, in the vicinity of Deal. The difference between Hudson County and the Shore is the difference between Manhattan Island and Manhattan, Kansas—the same country, but worlds apart.

"I had some other property in Ocean County like in Toms River and Brick Town and other places, but the majority dollar wise, most of them—most of the properties were in Monmouth County," he explained in a deposition.

Asked about the business he had done in Hudson, he shrugged. "What towns are they there?" he asked. "Can you name me a town? I'll tell you."

Jersey City?

"I don't think so."

Hackensack?

"I one time tried buying a gas station in Hackensack."

One of the lawyers pointed out that Hackensack was actually Bergen County. Dwek readily acknowledged he had no sense of geography for the region, whose key selling point was its commanding views of Manhattan and easy access into the city. "I need towns. I don't know counties," he said flatly.

Wired by the FBI for both audio and video, Dwek was a walking multimedia platform as he trudged up the stairs to Altman's second-floor office in Union City. Everything Dwek said and saw was digitally recorded. He also had his cell phone. Even before all this, he always had it up to his ear or would be forever texting someone. During his sit-down with the agents weeks earlier, he would be texting while talking, answering questions from the trustee about the sales of properties or sending a message to Pearl at home. Now the cell was a direct connection to the agents. What no one would know until much later was that Dwek was constantly texting his handlers on the cell phone as well, as he worked the sting.

While Waldie and his team of FBI special agents, which now included Don Russ and Sean McCarthy, were outside on the street, ready to get him out if things went bad, Dwek was left on his own to spin his story. He admitted being nervous. "I always had fear that it would be exposed. There was obviously risk," he later told someone. "I was nervous every time."

Solomon was essentially selling to two separate audiences. He had to be convincing to get Haber and Altman to swallow his line. And he had to show the government that he could deliver what Himmel had promised.

Upstairs, Dwek explained what he was trying to do. He needed to get money out of his bankrupt real estate empire without anyone catching on. "Question is," asked Solomon, as the three of them sat in Altman's office, "if I bring in money, how many of these guys can convert it? No?"

Haber gestured to Altman, sitting at his desk in the same uniform black pants, white shirt, and black yarmulke they were all wearing. "Talk to him," Haber said. "He has the washing machines."

They all knew what a washing machine was, and it had nothing to do with clean clothes. Money is traceable and crooks can't afford to have their cash traced. Criminal proceeds—whether from drug dealing, cash taken out of businesses to avoid the tax man, illicit deals, or organized crime—are typically funneled through a variety of legitimate accounts, businesses, and sometimes charities to make the money untraceable. Dwek, as vice president of the Deal Yeshiva, had been more than happy to take checks from donors in the name of philanthropy and convert the money back into cash for them. Who cared? Call it money laundering, but the yeshiva got to keep 10 percent and he took his cut as the facilitator.

Altman, it appeared, would be able to do the same, although the kind of money Dwek was talking about was no small amount. The newly minted federal informant told Haber and Altman he wanted to pull tens of thousands of dollars out of his real estate holdings before it was all swallowed up by lawyers and creditors.

You need more than a washing machine, Haber said. "You need a Laundromat."

If it was a lot to Altman, he didn't say. His office, on the tight block where parking is always at a premium, was on the second floor of a two-story storefront directly above the JP Laundromat at street level.

You want a Laundromat? Altman asked. "They got one down there," he said, gesturing out the security bars of the office windows that looked out onto Central Avenue. Dwek, though, kept to his carefully written script. He had to talk out loud about the mechanics of going between check and cash and whether one of Altman's contacts could do the job. That was what Dwek had rehearsed. Both Haber and Altman had to know the proceeds were illegal and that Dwek was laundering the money to evade detection. If the feds were going to bring charges, just laundering the money wasn't enough. The launderers had to be aware that they were helping someone hide cash brought in illegally.

Moshe Altman had someone in mind.

"He converts from green to check . . . whatever?" asked Dwek.

"Solomon needs a converter," Haber translated aloud. Not just someone to exchange one check for another, but someone who would take a check and give him cash—"green," as Dwek liked to say.

Altman nodded. His guy was a converter, just like a bunch of similar guys he knew in Israel, he said. He'd get it set up.

Two weeks later, Dwek's name was back in the news. Joseph Kohen, 37, the mortgage broker Dwek implicated during the proffer meeting, pleaded guilty in the bank fraud against PNC Bank. Under questioning by Brian Howe, Kohen admitted he made the $25 million check that had been made payable to SEM, a Dwek company, and that he had later called PNC Bank on Dwek's behalf—falsely claiming to be his attorney and promising to wire sufficient funds to cover the $25 million check that had just bounced.

The proceeding was not kept quiet. The U.S. Attorney's office put out another news release. If that was a warning sign to Haber and Altman, it went unheeded. It seems stupid even now, but New Jersey is a crowded, busy place and it's hard enough getting your own business done, much less worrying about someone else's.

The next week, they all got back together at Altman's Union City office. Dwek was again wired for sound and video. "You still need a washing machine?" Altman asked.

"Yeah," said Dwek. "But not all in one shot. I'm talking twenty to fifty now."

"Which way it is going?" Altman asked. Checks? Cash? How was it to be converted?

"I have checks."

Twenty thousand to fifty thousand dollars in checks that he wanted converted to cash. That was a lot of green in one shot. Altman seemed suddenly nervous. He lowered his voice to a whisper. "Do me a favor," he said in a low tone. "Just write."

Dwek took a scrap of paper and scribbled for Altman:

1. Check to who?
2. How much do charge? 10% is fine.
3. How long to wash?

Altman took the paper and responded to the first question: *Gmach Shefa Chaim.*

A *gmach,* sometimes transliterated as *gemach,* was essentially an Orthodox charity. The word came from an acronym of the Hebrew letters *gimmel, mem,* and *chet,* which stood for *gemillas chasodim,* or "acts of kindness." There are literally hundreds of kinds of gmachs in Orthodox communities. They could take the form of a free loan fund to help those in need. Sometimes it could be an organization, a community chest of sorts that is there to lend things out for free, such as brides' dresses, baby carriages, or party tables.

In this case, Gmach Shefa Chaim was an account at Valley National Bank that held over $500,000. This was the washing machine, a tax-exempt charitable account that no one would ever take a second look at. When federal agents would later search Altman's office, they would seize eight bundles of blank checks from the gmach accounts, as well as four hard drives and a laptop computer that, they said, contained the charity's books and records.

Altman did not answer the second question. As to the third, he wrote: *1 wk to 2 wks.*

Dwek understood. Then he spoke aloud again. He knew he had to get this part down for the surveillance tape. Waldie and Kahrer and the prosecutors had repeatedly drilled Dwek about establishing that what he was asking was illegal and that the targets of the investigation had to acknowledge that.

"Because of the bankruptcy court, no one can know nothing," he warned. "I've got to declare all assets."

That included, he said, anything of value. Even cars, watches, furs, firearms, jewelry, and suits. Altman and Haber said they understood.

Meeting again in May, Dwek pressed Altman on how much he could handle through the charitable fund. "What's the numbers? Just tell me the numbers," Altman said.

Dwek had rehearsed this with the FBI, too. He claimed there was a silent partner who owed him money from other deals. There would be checks ranging from $25,000 to $100,000 that he wanted to convert to cash.

"I can handle it," Altman assured Dwek. "It could take a week. Ten days. It depends. It's not all taken out right away. So it can take two weeks."

Not long after, Dwek came back to Altman with an $18,000 check.

"I don't need a copy," Dwek said. "I don't keep records."

Altman agreed that was for the best. As Dwek handed over the check, he spun the tale he had rehearsed earlier with the FBI, which had put up the money through a front company, BH Property Management. It turned out Dwek was well suited to his new job. "Basically, this guy owes me money from bank deals. Schnookie bank deals no one knows about and no one could know about," Dwek said. "This guy's a partner of mine." He told Altman to expect another $50,000 next week that he would need converted to cash.

"Okay, very good," said Altman, who said his contact would take a 15 percent cut from the transaction rather than the normal 10 percent, because the amount of money from the transaction was low. Altman told Dwek that his own contact in the deal—the converter—had wanted to know where the check came from, but said he had kept Dwek's name out of it.

"I keep my word," said Altman.

"Good," said Dwek, talking again now like a mob character on *The Sopranos*. It had to be kept hush-hush. "Number one, I have the bankruptcy thing. Number two, I have at least one hundred thousand dollars a month coming from money I 'schnookied' from banks for bad loans. This guy can't know nothing."

"No problem," Altman assured him. Dwek gave him another $75,000 check on the account of BH Property Management, which the FBI had set up as a shell company more than five years earlier out of Brick Township, New Jersey, as part of the Operation Big Rig. Three days later, the check, No. 1023, was posted to an account maintained by Valley National Bank in the name of Gmach Shefa Chaim.

* * *

As he shuttled back and forth from Union City, Dwek continued to work with the lawyers untangling his web of real estate deals in bankruptcy court.

The federally appointed trustee in the case was veteran attorney Charles Stanziale, who had handled a number of complex, high-profile cases before—including Tower Air, which he operated in Chapter 11 for seven months, using a fleet of leased 747 jets on worldwide charters. He was co-counsel representing Trump Entertainment Resorts in a Chapter 11 reorganization restructuring of $1.8 billion of debt. And he had been bankruptcy counsel to John Z. DeLorean, the once jet-setting auto executive whose DeLorean DMC-12, with its distinctive stainless-steel body and gull-wing doors, was immortalized as a time machine in the movie *Back to the Future*.

Stanziale seemed made for the job of shepherding the Dwek bankruptcy—and even more so after the fact. A Newark native with a prep-school background, Stanziale knew New Jersey politics better than anyone. His wife was the daughter of Congressman Peter Rodino, of Watergate fame. A member of the Catholic lay organization the Order of Malta, Stanziale sprinkled his conversations liberally with Yiddish.

Stanziale knew Dwek only by reputation and had no idea what had led to the bankruptcy. In Stanziale's mind, Dwek was simply a wheeler-dealer. When Stanziale finally met him, Solomon came in by himself. To look at him, Stanziale recalled, was to think he just came in off the streets of Brooklyn. He wore his usual white shirt, black pants, black orthopedic shoes, and yarmulke. He didn't look like a businessman. And he sure as hell didn't talk like a businessman. Stanziale offered him coffee, but Dwek politely declined. Then the new trustee put it directly to Dwek, in words Stanziale did not mince, like a hard-boiled cop talking to an unreformed street punk to make sure they understood each other.

"Don't mess with me and I won't mess with you—and don't think I can't do it," warned Stanziale. "You're going to have to cooperate with me. If I want information, I expect to get it. Quickly and honestly. If you don't, I can go to the court and hold you in contempt."

Stanziale had inherited a mess. One of the reasons a trustee had been appointed was because the creditors had raised allegations of fraud. At the same time, he believed there was no law for what the state court had been doing in appointing a fiscal agent with unlimited power. Funds were being commingled, with no differentiation between creditors from one deal to another. There were no investor documents. Much of what had been negotiated had been based on a handshake, with nothing on paper. And for a time, Stanziale wasn't sure Dwek was being truthful with him, despite his tough talk.

In the very first meeting of creditors in Trenton, it was clear to Stanziale that Dwek's empire had been built on a house of cards. "You could see he was getting money and using it to pay off others," Stanziale recalled. "Many properties were of marginal value or unoccupied. So there was no cash flow to pay the mortgages."

He confronted Dwek. "This is obviously a Ponzi scheme," Stanziale said. Dwek didn't deny it. "Yes," he said.

* * *

The bankruptcy case seemed to be consuming most of Dwek's time. In late June on a Friday morning at eleven o'clock, he sat down for a court-ordered deposition in the case in Newark in the law offices of Duane Morris LLP, the attorneys for the creditors committee. He was there with his bankruptcy attorney, Timothy Neumann. No one knew Dwek was now cooperating with the government, and the FBI agents who constantly shadowed him were nowhere in sight. He talked about going down to Florida with his family for Passover in early April. He flew down on JetBlue. He also told them he never went to Brooklyn. "I don't like that town," he declared.

Asked if he had worked since the bankruptcy petition was filed, he replied, "No. I don't do any outside work."

"You don't do any outside work, so do you do anything?"

"Yeah, I'm busy full-time," said Dwek. "I've been very busy, to say the least."

It was an inside joke and, of course, only Dwek knew why it was funny.

A few days later, on June 26, Dwek returned to Altman's office. One of Altman's business partners, Itzak Friedlander, was there waiting for him. Altman had stepped out, said Friedlander, handing over a white plastic bag containing the cash in return for the $75,000 check. Dwek was still counting it when Altman returned, about twenty-five minutes later. There was $54,800 in the bag. "It's short," Dwek complained. Even with the fee arrangement the two had struck, he was owed another $8,950. Nobody seemed that concerned.

"I'll get the rest to you again in another day or two," Altman promised.

Dwek nodded and gave him a check for another $50,000, again drawn on the account of the FBI front company and made out to the gmach. "More money from one of my schnookie deals," explained Dwek. "Your guy should convert this more quickly."

Altman laughed. "You're right. I should teach him the business," he said. Moshe Altman knew the business. Very well, it appeared. One day, as Altman counted large bills in his Union City office, Dwek looked on. "Why don't you use a cash-counting machine? It would be easier," Solomon mused aloud from the other side of the desk.

Altman shook his head and continued to count the money. "See, if you have one, it means . . . ," he trailed off. "Well, you don't want somebody who goes to the office, sees one, and says, 'Hey!'"

* * *

Back in Newark, videos from the surveillance operation were being reviewed each day by Howe and others in the U.S. Attorney's office. There were detailed notes of each meeting and the corresponding tape. Howe kept the master collection of Dwek recordings. Eventually it occupied almost an entire wall of his office. Dwek had been hooked up with a tiny video camera on his shirt, just below his chest—possibly disguised as a button—that captured his own view of the table as he discussed payoffs, cash exchanges, and development deals. The surveillance system, which was called the HAWK, had been developed by an outside vendor.

It was a far cry from the days when the FBI would look for ways to conceal what were then state-of-the-art Nagra tape recorders on informants, observed William Megary, now retired from the Bureau, who once ran the Newark office. The miniaturized Nagra recorder, while small, was still big enough to find if you were looking for it and did not pick up sound very well in restaurants—where people were most likely to talk, especially in Jersey's landscape of diners. Surveillance tapes would carry the rattle of dishes, waiters taking orders, and the din of talk echoing in the room. The sound was so bad, defense lawyers on trial would spend hours on cross-examination debating what had been said.

For years, the FBI tried to steer informants in sting operations to the relative quiet of a car—where audio- and videotape recorders could be far more easily concealed—or hotel rooms, where the infamous Abscam payoff that netted Sen. Pete Williams went down nearly 30 years earlier.

The new technology carried by Dwek seemed light-years ahead. The video was not set up in a room. He was carrying the camera himself. And the sound quality was very good. No more straining to interpret the words of those being recorded. Their gestures, inflections, smiles, and expressions were all captured.

Still, the images captured by Dwek were odd. The camera often would catch forkfuls of food coming in at mouth level, as well as unnecessarily intimate views of the urinals of a men's room, where the discussions continued. The images were in black and white, sometimes tilted strangely depending on how Dwek sat or moved, but the sound was crisp and clear, and Solomon quickly got the hang of what prosecutors were seeking—sometimes too quickly. He didn't always follow the script. He was fearless and would sit down with anybody, but there was a general feeling that he thought he was far smarter than the agents and was sometimes hard to control. He would compliment himself after seeing the tapes. "How'd you like that? That was really good, wasn't it?" he asked prosecutors after one meeting with a target.

In fact, Dwek made some in the U.S. Attorney's office uncomfortable as the case grew. Prosecutors became very nervous about the fantastical tall tales he would spin. They "told him to down it down a bit." But he wouldn't.

"The guy is not readily controllable," one fed complained.

Still, as time went on, everyone conceded Dwek had an undeniable talent as an undercover operative. He became very astute at picking up any hint of something prosecutors could use later, as the case would eventually move from money laundering to corruption. Summaries of each setup were generated in nearly real time, and the videos would be distributed as DVDs to a select few within the U.S. Attorney's office. Despite their concern over how often he strayed from the script, the feds marveled at Dwek's ability as an informant and how cool a customer he was. "Put this guy on the witness stand," said one. "He'll take down any lawyer. He'll run fuckin' circles around him."

* * *

Not everything was perfect, though. Soon after Dwek began working with the FBI, the informant's former driver reported to the Bureau that among

Solomon's activities outside the law, he visited frequently, though irregularly, with prostitutes in Manhattan and New Jersey. Tales of illicit sex and high-end call girls don't surprise the hard-bitten FBI and federal prosecutors, and as one prosecutor said, "there are always call girls swirling around in white-collar cases." But the issue with Dwek could pose a problem because, as the agents were told, Solomon's exploits occurred both before he started working for the feds and while he was already undercover. If true, it meant that Dwek was breaking the law while being protected by it.

The driver, Herman Nagar, a former Israeli soldier who drove and handled all sorts of errands for Dwek's father, started working for Solomon in 2004. Nagar told his story to the feds as well as the creditors going after Dwek in bankruptcy. A full dossier on Dwek's activities was compiled for the creditors' lawyers by a former FBI agent.

As Nagar told it, Dwek carried stacks of $100 bills in his glove compartment and would take four or five of them every time he went into one of these liaisons. Typically, the visits in the summer would be on weeknights at Pandora's Box, a well-known S&M club on West 26th Street in Manhattan. In the winter, the visits were to West Broadway in Long Branch, usually on Saturday nights when the Sabbath ends earlier.

Nagar was not brought into Dwek's confidence about the visits and Dwek never explained what they were. To the driver, Dwek said only they were "business meetings." But Nagar said he grew suspicious, especially about the Manhattan stops, because they were always to the same place, and "you don't go into a business meeting or a closing at eleven o'clock at night," the driver told the feds, "with four hundred or five hundred dollars in cash and no papers in your hands!"

Nagar claimed that one night he called the contact number Dwek left for him in the car and the phone was answered by a woman explaining he had reached Pandora's Box.

The FBI asked Dwek about Nagar's claims and Dwek denied them, repeating that his visits were strictly for business purposes. Under oath, he denied them again. The FBI investigated Nagar's claims and determined that there was no substance to the accusation.

* * *

Every morning in Newark, Christie was briefed on ongoing cases by one of the divisions of the office, set up under a six-month schedule. They were meant to keep Christie current on what was going on. And on those days the special prosecutions unit gathered to talk about developments in their ongoing cases, the meetings tended to be long. Christie always liked to hear from Special Prosecutions. These were the investigations that generated the headlines, and the meeting dominated Christie's schedule on those days. They would begin with the hot-button case of the moment, such as an ongoing trial or a recent arrest. There was no formality to it. If the meeting was set for a Monday during football season, it would begin with talk about what the Jets had done the day before. During the summer, it would be about the Mets and Yankees. Not long after Dwek was launched, Christie sat down at his conference table one day to meet with Nobile and Howe.

"What do we got today?" Christie asked Nobile.

Nobile gave very complete reports. The ever-secretive chief of the special prosecutions unit looked over at his list of cases to give updates on progress. And at the beginning, Dwek was not at the top of the agenda. There were other cases being worked. Finally Jimmy came to Dwek. "We've got Mike from Monsey," Nobile said.

Christie looked over, puzzled. He knew Nobile listened to New York sports radio WFAN-AM, where callers typically introduced themselves by first name only and from where they were calling. Like Rob from Teaneck. Joe from Bayonne. Ron from Manhattan. But Christie didn't get the joke.

"Who's Mike from Monsey?"

Nobile almost mouthed the name without saying it aloud, as if it were a state secret, even in here. "Dwek," he said.

Oh. Of course!

Dwek was from Deal. The Monsey connection was Altman. And Nobile was unlikely to use anybody's real name to code an operation. Christie shrugged. Jimmy being Jimmy again. From that point on, though, Dwek became known in the front office as Mike from Monsey. Nobody called him Solomon Dwek. He was always Mike from Monsey.

On the street and outside the U.S. Attorney's office, Dwek had no idea he was Mike from Monsey. At one point later, one of the money launderers came up with his own name for Dwek. Nervous over doing business with someone who had been charged in a $50 million bank fraud, he gave Dwek a street name to use around some of the money couriers who did not know him. He began calling him David Esenbach. It was a pseudonym Dwek would soon adopt as his own as part of the sting.

As Dwek grew proficient, he prepared to set up one of his own employees closer to home. Charles Amon, also known as Shaul, lived in Lakewood Township, another large Orthodox community far to the south of Union

City. Amon and Rachamin (Rocky) Nahem worked for one of Dwek's companies, managing the 70 homes Solomon owned in Lakewood and collecting their rents. Dwek knew that Amon frequently paid off one of Lakewood's building inspectors and told him he wanted to pay off the guy to illegally convert a house into a commercial office. Again, the video would capture all of it.

It was chickenshit stuff, but it had potential. Christie liked building inspectors. After a career in politics, Christie knew inspectors were rarely free agents. They kicked up money to their bosses, and it was another line of investigation that could lead to something bigger. Amon, who would plead guilty less than five months after his arrest, talked freely to Dwek of slipping money to Jeffrey Williamson, a Lakewood inspector.

"I used to take care of him and sometimes he'd go crazy," Amon explained to Dwek. "I tried every inspection he failed me. I gave him fifty bucks. One hundred bucks. But I knew if I had something that would have failed, I gave him the one hundred."

Williamson never explicitly asked for cash. He said, "Why don't we do lunch?" It did not mean he was looking to eat. He was looking to get paid.

Amon would play along. He would give Williamson money, saying it was for the "holiday," but whatever holiday it was intended for was usually months away. "He didn't want to ask you point-blank that he was shaking you down?" asked Dwek.

"Right."

Christmas always came early for Williamson. Amon estimated that Williamson performed approximately fifteen to twenty inspections a day and accepted payoffs for "half of them."

He could also get greedy. Amon had slipped Williamson $100 once and he still kept raising issues, stalling for more cash. But the property manager wasn't about to up the ante. "I paid him a hundred for this; I'm not doing it again," Amon said of the incident to Dwek. "I'm gonna become a sickness."

Amon had already given Williamson the bribe to look the other way. To keep paying him for the same inspection would only raise the price the next time around. So Amon sent his own message. He didn't say anything. He just pulled out a single $20 bill and bluntly held it out to the inspector.

Williamson flashed with anger at the insult. "Should I tell the office you're bribing me?" he demanded.

Amon stared him down. "Should I tell them that you took bribes before?" he responded evenly.

Williamson stood for a moment and then walked away without taking the additional cash. "You passed," was all he said of the inspection.

"Will he take a payment directly from me?" wondered Dwek.

Amon could have laughed in his face. It had been less than a year since Dwek had been arrested on the PNC Bank fraud, and there wasn't anybody in Lakewood who didn't know that.

"He's gonna be extra, extra precautious with you," Amon said with utter conviction.

* * *

For a while, the U.S. Attorney was satisfied with progress on the case. The money-laundering deals with Altman were going down week after week, without a hitch, for months. Money was going back and forth, but it began to become clear that it was not going much further than Altman. Christie was starting to get impatient with the whole thing. At one of the morning briefings, he wondered where it was all leading.

"How much more money are we going to launder?" the U.S. Attorney asked. He wasn't really that excited about it. He had agreed to go forward on the expectation that this would eventually turn into a political corruption case, but all he could see was tens of thousands of FBI dollars going into a black hole. Altman had been promising Dwek that he could get to Stack, but nothing had come of it. The elusive Union City mayor was like Moby-Dick. They were hunting something they could not find.

"I think Altman is full of shit," Christie eventually told his team. Others in Special Prosecutions were coming to the same conclusion. Although they had the gut feeling that he knew more than he wanted Dwek to see, Altman did not want to be cut out of any deal, they believed. He was a middleman and wanted everything to go through him.

Finally in July, as they were still considering whether to pull the plug, Altman came through. Not with Mayor Stack. There was a Jersey City building inspector Altman claimed was willing to be bribed. This was some progress, Christie told the team. As in the case of Williamson, a corrupt inspector frequently led to others higher up the food chain.

John Guarini, a Republican candidate for Congress in 2006, was the cousin of a former Hudson County congressman and had enough connections to get on the public payroll as a property improvement field representative for the Jersey City Department of Housing, Economic Development and Commerce. He was a character straight out of a Damon Runyon tale. A bald guy, quick with an expletive, who would give you the shirt off his back. Guarini could be very, very funny and always seemed to be looking for an angle.

Guarini also had a surname with its own curious place in the annals of political double crosses. While in Congress, his cousin Frank Guarini was working to get some program off the ground in North Jersey despite the perennial claims of poverty from the powers-that-be on Capitol Hill. So Frank Guarini not only developed the project, but he also found the funding. Then he took the whole package to Chicago congressman Dan Rostenkowski, the legendary chairman of the Ways and Means Committee. Rostenkowski was impressed and liked the funding plan—so much so that he appropriated it for himself and an entirely different program that he wanted established. Guarini got nothing, except a D.C. term of art: to be "Guarinied" is to have another member of Congress take your funding source for his own pet project and leave you with nothing more than the stupid smile on your face as you realize your pocket has just been picked.

Altman put his Guarini on course for another colossal double cross. "In terms of getting zoning and getting approvals [on properties], John's the man," Altman assured Dwek. Altman said he had made payoffs to Guarini in the past for various issues.

On a rainy Wednesday morning, Dwek met Guarini at a building Altman owned in Jersey City. For the first time, Dwek adopted an alias he would use for rest of the sting operation. He took the name the Altman crowd had given him, becoming David Esenbach, a developer from New York who had done a lot of work in North Carolina, New York, and Florida. His cover this time was that he was looking to expand his portfolio into New Jersey, and Jersey City in particular. He did not change his appearance in any way. He was still the balding, casually dressed Orthodox guy with a black yarmulke and wire-rimmed glasses so small they perched on his face like old-fashioned pince-nez spectacles from the nineteenth century.

Dwek told Guarini, then 59, that he had his eye on several development properties in Jersey City. "I'm looking for a comfort level on zoning and other matters," Dwek explained. He did not want to be bogged down for years on municipal approvals and wanted to make sure the way was clear before he put millions of dollars into a project.

Guarini suggested that he was not going to be an issue. "You're not gonna have any problem with anything with me," he said earnestly. "Whatever we have to do, I can get done."

Jersey City at the time had been coming off one of the largest building booms in its history. Top developers, including Donald Trump and suburban home builders such as Toll Brothers and K. Hovnanian Homes, were putting in thousands of new residential units. The tallest building in New Jersey, the Goldman Sachs Tower, designed by renowned architect César Pelli, had been planted along the waterfront just a few years earlier. With so much new construction, they were calling the downtown area around City Hall a gold coast, permanently transforming a city once left for dead.

The project Mr. Esenbach had in mind was a high-end 23-story luxury condominium project at 740-760 Garfield Avenue in Jersey City, where units would be going for $500,000 each.

It was a ludicrous proposal. The site was in an industrial area of the city, next to a toxic, chromium-contaminated property long slated to be cleaned up. Anyone familiar with that part of Jersey City would know that nobody was going to be building much of anything there, and certainly not luxury condos. Anyone who drove by would see tired old two-family homes, an auto body shop, and a car wash. And anyone who checked the tax rolls would see that the site was zoned R-1, which does not allow for a building with more than two apartments.

Ernest Thompson, a retired trucker who rents an apartment there, later laughed when told of the project after the sting came to light. "Nobody's going to spend no half a million here," Thompson told the *Jersey Journal*. "It's not that kind of area."

City officials later said that to build the project Dwek was talking about, the planning board or city council would have to change the zoning or the area would have to be designated as blighted. Whether Guarini knew, or for that matter even cared, was never an issue. He told the man he knew as Esenbach that getting approvals for Garfield Avenue would not be a heavy lift. Guarini told Dwek that he could help obtain approvals for additional units at the Garfield property. "Worst-case scenario," Guarini said. "We have to put in for a variance, go before the board of adjustment. We present the set of plans. The whole bit. But I get the blessing from everybody up above for that to go through."

The two headed to the boiler room as they talked. Down there, Dwek pulled out two stiff white FedEx envelopes, each containing $10,000 in cash. The open envelope flashed briefly to show the money inside, like a magician telling his audience that he actually did have something up his sleeves.

"You know, we got there, ahh, twenty," he said.

"Okay," said Guarini, taking the envelopes.

It's a deposit, Dwek said. "But I'll make you a rich man. You take care of me, I'll take care of you."

"Absolutely." Guarini beamed. "You got my undivided attention."

"I got a handshake? I got a handshake?" Dwek asked. Was it a deal?

"Yes. Yes," said Guarini. "Absolutely." He gave Dwek his cell phone number. "I'm around all the time."

The inspector then briefly looked around the boiler room, as if mindful of his own role that he was playing. "Everything looks good here," he said.

That, too, was captured on Dwek's surveillance recording.

That same day, Dwek also met with Jeff Williamson in Lakewood at the R & S Kosher Delicatessen in Lakewood, where corned beef, chopped liver, and kishka (a traditional type of stuffed kosher sausage filled with matzo meal, onion, spices, and suet) dominated the menu. Despite Amon's assertion that the inspector was going to be extra precautious over any dealings with Dwek, Williamson did not seem to be the least bit concerned over taking money from Solomon. At their first meeting months earlier, Dwek was clear in his intentions. He wanted to turn a residential property into commercial office space. The rents would be higher.

Unlike Guarini, Williamson actually had some real concept of the way things looked. Williamson told him to find a property that would not stick out like a sore thumb. A place nobody knows about. Like the deli, the property needed to look kosher. "If it's a corner lot, you might be able to get away with it," Williamson said.

Dwek showed him a list of properties and Williamson suggested some that would escape close scrutiny. "Just don't make changes that would be too dramatic," he suggested.

Dwek and Williamson then went together to the unoccupied women's bathroom in the restaurant. Dwek pulled out $500. "This is for the holiday coming, you know, whatever," he said awkwardly. "That's just to start. It's five hundred dollars, but you can count on me for whatever it is; don't worry."

"It's not necessary," Jeff protested halfheartedly.

"No, keep it."

Williamson pocketed the money. "I do what I gotta do," he said self-consciously.

"Your reputation supersedes you." Dwek smiled, misusing the word, possibly deliberately. "You don't gotta say anything. Don't worry about it."

At a follow-up meeting, Williamson explained how he worked: "I'm gonna overlook painting. I'm overlooking cosmetics." But the building inspector on the take still had his standards, he told Dwek. "Life safety," he said, "I can't overlook. It's real simple. As long as they have smoke detectors, carbon monoxide alarms, and a fire extinguisher, I'll pass them."

"You'll close your eyes to everything else?" asked Dwek.

"Well, I'm giving—I'm giving time . . . not making a big deal," Williamson explained. This time, he told Dwek he was not looking for payment. "I'm involved in too much crap right now, between running for the Assembly and work on a building committee for a synagogue."

The day Dwek settled with Guarini, he came to an understanding with Williamson. Meeting again in Lakewood, Dwek told Williamson he simply would pay him a flat $1,000 a month in cash to make sure there were no problems with any of his properties. "You do the right thing by me, I do right by you," explained Dwek.

8

⚊╉╉╊⚊

Religious Retreat

Arye Weiss was expecting Dwek when The Rabbi's Son came to his door in the Borough Park section of Brooklyn. He had a green box of Kellogg's Apple Jacks cereal waiting to be picked up. Inside the cardboard box was more green: roughly ninety-seven thousand dollars in tightly wrapped cash bundles.

"I didn't count it," said Weiss, as if it were just a box of kids' breakfast cereal with a plastic toy inside. He just had taken out $3,000 owed for the commission.

Dwek started targeting rabbis and religious charities very soon after his early meetings with Altman and Haber, playing out the money-laundering scam he knew well as head of the Deal Yeshiva. Altman was just a Laundromat. The religious charities had a broad reach that was almost impossible for the IRS to detect. The way it worked, contributors wrote checks to the charities or, as in this case, Jewish congregations as well. The money would then come back to the contributor in cash, minus a 10 percent commission. Sometimes the charity would directly pay the bills of the contributor, so that no money actually changed hands. I give you $500 and you pay my landscaper $400. Keep the change. Or the funds would go offshore to a company tied to the contributor.

The contributor got a big tax write-off and most of his money back. The yeshivas got the money they needed to operate. The IRS got nothing. To many, it was quite simply a victimless crime. Who cares, they figured, if Uncle Sam gets his money or not?

The widely practiced tax dodge was an area Himmel originally outlined for prosecutors when he first came in to negotiate with Christie months earlier. One bank executive who deals with Israeli accounts privately said such transactions were common in many Orthodox communities. He cited thousands of checks going into one synagogue with only 100 members and checks going out the next day in turn, less 10 percent: "It is a dirty little secret in the banking industry."

It was not a new phenomenon. A decade earlier, two Orthodox rabbis and ten others were charged with laundering $1.7 million in drug profits through a yeshiva and synagogue for Colombian dealers. Also, it was not a scam limited to the religious charities of Orthodox Jews. Ellen Zimiles, a leading expert in anti-money-laundering programs, saw similar transactions going in and out of churches in Bogotá, Colombia, when she was an assistant U.S. Attorney in Manhattan. "Any place where there is a tax deduction is open to this type of scheme," said Zimiles, who now tracks such activity as a fraud risk consultant.

Israel is an epicenter, according to New Jersey attorney Ari Weisbrot, who has spent years tracking down funds stolen from one of his clients and laundered through a string of charities. "The best way to hide your money is offshore, and for the Orthodox, offshore is Israel."

It didn't hurt that Israel was light-years behind in modernizing its money-laundering laws and had become something of a Wild West by the late 1990s, observed Yael Grossman, a Tel Aviv attorney and head of the Israeli Bar's committee on money laundering.

Dwek admitted under oath that he had been laundering money for years as vice president of the Deal Yeshiva. Even before he started working there, he would go around as a kid with his father, the rabbi, to ask for support from the wealthy members of the Syrian community for the school, where most sent their children. After Solomon left rabbinical college, his main job at the yeshiva was to call up supporters for money. Tuition was not enough to keep the school open, and many gave generously through their private foundations.

But Dwek soon found there were several donors looking for a little accommodation. They were willing to gives big checks to the yeshiva, but they also wanted to use the school to cash out additional funds. Sort of like writing a $75 check to the supermarket for $10 in groceries and getting the rest back in fresh new bills. Only this was illegal. It was all off the books, except for the original donation itself, which they planned to declare on their income tax returns. "I was trying to retain the donors," Dwek explained in court much later on as to why he agreed to do it. He would take the check, keep 10 percent for the school, as well as a nice cut for himself, and return the rest to the donors. "There was greed involved." He shrugged. "The Deal Yeshiva got a cut and I was making money."

Even better, the cut he was taking was off the books as well. He had pulled more than $1 million in cash out of the Deal Yeshiva, stashing it with Barry Kantrowitz long before Dwek had been arrested in the PNC Bank fraud, and later confided to the trustee in his federal bankruptcy case that he told Kantrowitz to keep it for him in case authorities ever came looking for him.

But there reached a point where even the Deal Yeshiva could not handle the amount of money that "donors" wanted to exchange. The school did not have that large a budget that so many large checks could flow through without raising suspicions that money laundering was going on. While the IRS was not really looking, the kind of money Dwek was being asked to handle would have quickly required a bank to file a currency transaction report to authorities for transactions over $10,000. His donors were looking to structure $50,000 to $100,000 in exchanges. Even the most dense bank examiner would take a look at that and immediately know something was up.

While the amount of the donations going in would not have aroused suspicions, the money going out, earmarked as operating expenses for the yeshiva, would have raised all kinds of red flags. So Dwek said he began spreading out the money to others in the Community who launder larger sums and took a cut as a middleman for the referral. Some of them, he said, were rabbis he had known all his life. Eli Ben Haim, the principal rabbi of Congregation Ohel Yaacob, also in Deal. Or Edmond Nahum, who, with Dwek's own father, was a rabbi and served as the cantor at Deal Synagogue, a modern, soaring house of worship that served the Sephardic community, located on the corner of Brighton and Norwood avenues.

* * *

Nahum, in his fifties, with a long gray beard, dark hair, and glasses, ran several charitable tax-exempt organizations in conjunction with the synagogue, including Ahabat Haim Vehesed and the Deal Kupot. In June 2007, Dwek arranged a meeting with Nahum that was secretly recorded for the FBI. "I have a check for you from a guy who owes me money from a while ago—ten thousand," said Dwek. It was clear he wanted cash back, under the usual arrangement, this time to keep the transaction hidden from the bankruptcy trustee.

Dwek suggested making the check out to the Deal Kupot, a synagogue-based charity fund that he had been using for years for legitimate charity giving. Typically, he would forward money to the account and Nahum, who was in charge of the fund, would issue individual charity checks to other organizations at Dwek's instructions.

"I would tell him to write a check to, like Rabbi Hillel, and he would write the check to the sum that I told him to write to. Just like the Jewish communal fund work—same way," Dwek explained in a deposition.

Rabbi Nahum had check-signing authority for the Deal Kupot but had recently created a new fund—Ahabat Haim Vehesed—and suggested Dwek write out the check to that one. Saul Kassin at Shaare Zion might also be able to help, Nahum said of the older rabbi who headed the large Syrian congregation on Ocean Parkway in Brooklyn. Money frequently flowed between Kassin's and Nahum's accounts.

"That's a good way to get rid of money," said Dwek. It made the paper trail much more difficult to follow.

"Exactly," agreed Nahum. Still, the cantor had limits. There was another guy, he recalled, who had wanted to run $200,000 through Nahum, but he drew the line. That kind of money would draw the attention of the government. It was too much for him to handle.

The following week, Dwek went to Nahum's office at the Deal Synagogue and gave him two bank checks for $10,000 each. One was made out to the Deal Kupot and the other to Kassin's organization. The money, Dwek claimed, came from an associate who wanted to launder it through the religious charities.

"The guy gave it to me because he wants a write-off," said Dwek for the surveillance tape. "Like everybody else."

Nahum again told Dwek that Kassin received many checks every day. "Hundreds of thousands a week, no?" asked Dwek.

"At least. More," said Nahum. "He's got a staff to help him with the accounting."

The check to Kassin was mailed to his home in Brooklyn. Dwek was looking not for cash this time but for a check to another company from Kassin's charity that served simply to disguise the source of the funds. The fee to convert it would be between 5 percent and 10 percent. They included a stamped envelope addressed to Dwek. The company he wanted the return check made out to was an FBI front.

* * *

The following week was busy for Dwek. Tuesday, June 26, he was up in Union City to meet with Altman. That same day, Dwek had arranged to meet Ben Haim. Eli had come to the pulpit later in life. The son of a highly respected rabbi and scholar, he served as principal rabbi at Ohel Yaacob in Deal. But he had been in business with Dwek, long before Solomon had gotten himself in trouble, funneling millions of dollars into real estate deals. From 2004 through March of 2006, just before Dwek's arrest, Ben Haim had given Dwek $3.1 million and gotten back $3.6 million in profits, bankruptcy filings show.

Ben Haim had deep ties to Israel. He was very close to Rabbi David Yosef, a son of Rabbi Ovadia Yosef, the founder of the right-wing, ultra-Orthodox Shas Party in Israel. Ben Haim was also active in the Yosef family's Yechave Daat organization, reported *Haaretz*, Israel's oldest daily newspaper. David Yosef was the head of the Yechave Daat Yeshiva in Jerusalem.

Dwek himself had connections to David Yosef as well. He had a signed, contractual agreement with the younger Yosef to donate hundreds of thousands of dollars to Yechave Daat. In one of his tax filings, Dwek agreed to contribute $100,000 "to bet midrash Yeschave Daat" for each volume of the Halacha Berura that David Yosef translated into English. In return, Yosef ageed to publish two thousand copies of the book and set aside special pages of dedications in each volume.

Halacha Berura is the renowned work of the late Rabbi Avraham Isaac HaCohen Kook, also a onetime chief rabbi of Israel, which explains Jewish law and tracks each rule and stricture to its original Talmudic source.

Dwek met Ben Haim at his home in Elberon, another beachfront community adjacent to Deal, and gave him a $50,000 check drawn on the FBI front company. He made it out to Congregation Ohel Eliahu, a charitable organization Ben Haim headed. "The check came from the guy who was holding money for me on that Florida insurance scam that I did," Dwek explained to the rabbi.

"And you need forty-five thousand dollars?"

Yes, said Dwek.

Ben Haim said there wouldn't be a problem. It would take a couple of days. The money would go through a contact in Israel he had met more than four years ago. Dwek didn't know whom Eli was talking about. "IM," said Ben Haim. "He washes money for people. He washes money for people here." In fact, there was a delivery of cash he had to pick up that week in Brooklyn and Dwek offered to pick it up for him, but Ben Haim seemed hesitant. He was expecting a large delivery.

"Half a mill?" asked Dwek.

"Yeah."

* * *

Dwek had a deposition in Newark on the bankruptcy case at eleven o'clock the very next morning. He then returned to Deal to meet Nahum, escaping to the coolness of his air-conditioned office at the Deal Synagogue on a record-setting day when it hit 93 degrees. Dwek had more money he wanted to convert. "Kassin is big," Nahum reassured him. He would have no problems converting the money.

"So if I have, like, you know, fifty thousand dollars a month for the next three months, he can handle it, no problem?"

Kassin would be able to do it, Nahum said. "If I give it to you, he'll do it right away?" Dwek asked.

"Yeah. Sure."

"That's what he does?"

"Yeah. That's what he does," said Nahum simply.

The two met again the next day, this time outside the synagogue. Dwek gave Nahum a $25,000 check already made out to Kassin's charity. "I've got a couple of hundred thousand dollars that no one knows about from the bankruptcy," Dwek explained once again, his words caught on the surveillance tape being monitored by the agents nearby. He proposed a long trail to throw anyone off the scent of the money. He would give the check to Nahum, who would give it to Kassin in Brooklyn. Kassin would make out a check to Eli Ben Haim and Eli would give him the money.

"No problem," said Nahum. "As long as they don't ask questions."

Not to worry, said Solomon. "I've got a silent partner." Solomon's partner would get a tax write-off and Kassin and Ben Haim would both earn a 10 percent fee. Solomon would keep the money out of the hands of the bankruptcy trustee.

"This way I can live. I have no problems."

He had another check to deliver to Ben Haim—one for $50,000. And once again, Dwek went through the script for the surveillance video. "I've got a lot more money available out of silent partnerships," he explained. "This way they get a write-off. It's good for them. I get the money back. So this way there's no trace, through you, and it works out for everybody. The court doesn't know. The trustee doesn't know. No one knows nothin'."

As Rabbi Ben Haim ran the bills he had in exchange through a cash-counting machine, he talked of another guy who had been dealing in far bigger figures. He was due $495,000. "He has money in Hong Kong from the kickbacks from the factories," Ben Haim explained. The money was being wired through Israel to "IM."

It was an international business. IM had more than a hundred customers and they all wanted to hide their money. The checks went from Ben Haim to Israel and then the cash came back through Brooklyn. "You see the merry-go-round?" asked the rabbi. "This guy's been doing it for twenty, thirty years."

He would later marvel at IM's connections: "Did you know that he had me in the last four years send out wires every time to a different place in the world to a different name? It's unbelievable. I never saw anything like it."

"In Israel?" asked Dwek.

"No, all over the world . . . All over the world," said Ben Haim. "From Australia to New Zealand to Uganda. I mean every country imaginable. Turkey, you can't believe it. All different names. It's never the same name. Switzerland, everywhere, France—everywhere. Spain . . . China . . . Japan . . ."

* * *

The transactions with the two rabbis continued over the summer on a weekly basis, with tens of thousands of dollars from the FBI's account going through the religious charities of Ben Haim and Nahum, Dwek reiterating each time that the cash was dirty and being kept out of the bankruptcy court. At one point in August, Dwek slid into Ben Haim's car with a $75,000 check, made payable to Congregation Ohel Eliahu. "This is seventy-five from that bank schnookie deal. And I have one more seventy-five from him—we got a half million from a bank," Dwek said.

Ben Haim asked aloud what he should tell the feds if they finally came asking about where the check came from and then answered his own question. He would just say someone mailed him an anonymous donation. The pickup point for the cash, meanwhile, kept changing. It could be in Queens. It could be a hotel in Manhattan. "It could be anywhere," said Ben Haim. "Lately, it's been Borough Park." IM wanted Ben Haim to open an account in Geneva for a special customer who was planning to deposit as much as $30 million per year. Ben Haim would receive $1.5 million in commissions.

On Monday, August 6, Dwek was back with another big check. "This is a check for, uh, fifty thousand from that, uh, bank, uh, schnookie deal," he told Ben Haim, who had $67,500 in cash waiting for Dwek to complete the money-laundering transaction from the $75,000 check he had handed over the previous week. The rabbi told Dwek he could pick up the cash for this go-round in Brooklyn on Tuesday or Wednesday. The contact this time was Arye Weiss, who operated a cash house from his home.

"He sits there all day, and he's going to have it tonight. So tomorrow, you can get it," said Ben Haim. "In the five years I'm with IM, maybe I saw over a hundred different people."

Dwek didn't make the trip immediately. Tuesday, he was tied up with his money-laundering connections in Union City, making another deal through Friedlander, the Altman associate. Dwek had another $50,000 of

FBI money coming, which he delivered the next morning. He repeated his warning that the proceeds came out of his PNC Bank fraud and told Friedlander to keep the source of the funds secret from whomever he was using to handle the transaction. "Just don't tell him my name or anything, because this is money that I 'schnookied' from the bank, and I have the bankruptcy . . ."

Friedlander raised his hand. "I'm not saying anything," he said. Pulling out his phone, he called his contact to set up the exchange. "I'm gonna push it," Friedlander promised Dwek over the call. "I'll call you."

Later in the morning, he got into Brooklyn to do the pickup for Ben Haim, walking out with the money in the Apple Jacks box. "I'll count it and it should be okay," said Dwek. "Maybe we'll have some more to pick up next week. We'll see."

It was a non-stop series of exchanges. That same day, Dwek stopped by Nahum's synagogue office with another $50,000 to forward to Kassin and two $5,000 checks made out to the Kupot and to another Nahum charity, Ahabat Haim Vehesed. Nahum, though, was starting to get concerned. He had gotten a call recently from a woman at the bank where the checks were being drawn. He did not like the attention. Dwek tried to reassure him. "This is from my partner that doesn't know nothing where the money's even going, 'cause, you know, I can't—the bankruptcy—that nobody can know anything," he said. "I don't go to the bank. I don't show up anywhere on any paper. My name's nowhere. They don't know who I am."

Dwek, dangling the fees coming out of the transactions, reminded Nahum that Kassin would get 10 percent, or $5,000, of the $50,000 being laundered. Still, Nahum seemed reluctant.

"No problem for sure?" he asked.

"I don't say anything to nobody. You don't say anything to anybody, and that's it."

A few days later, Dwek was back again in Deal for another exchange with Nahum. "Wait a few days to let the check clear," Nahum recommended.

No problem, agreed Dwek. He would be back next week with another bunch of checks. It was a large amount of money again. Put most of it through Kassin, said Nahum.

"Kassin is the best," Nahum said, telling Dwek to think about going through a number of rabbis instead of just one transaction that could attract attention. "I think it's better. You know why? The more it's spread, is better."

"Yeah, no question," agreed Dwek. "This way no one can see anything."

Nahum also told him to try Rabbi Mordchai Fish in Brooklyn. "Fish can do a million dollars—under the ground."

Dwek, who knew Fish, expressed doubts. "He's unreliable," he said.

"Fish is good," insisted Nahum. "Promise him something."

* * *

Ed Kahrer's office in Red Bank held a collection of FBI pins, a photo of J. Edgar Hoover, and the Bureau's imposing seal—with the motto, Fidelity, Bravery, Integrity—mounted on the wall. A graduate of Hudson Catholic High School in Jersey City, Kahrer had been hooked as a kid by the long-running TV series *The FBI*, which starred Efrem Zimbalist Jr. Kahrer wanted to be like Inspector Erskine and joined the Bureau right out of college in 1982.

Among the framed newspaper clips in the office from some of the big cases Kahrer had been involved with over the years was a photograph of Kahrer back in 2001, as kidnap victim Anna Cardelfe, a six-year-old from Spring Lake snatched from her home 24 hours earlier, was reunited unharmed with her family. "Greatest moment of my career," Kahrer would say of the photograph. "To give a child back to her parents . . ."

He and Waldie would talk every day of the Dwek sting operation. Kahrer had grown up in Jersey City and when he was in high school had seen Mayor Tom Whelan arrested in a multimillion-dollar kickback scheme involving city contracts. Now nothing surprised Kahrer. Not the rabbis. Certainly not politicians willing to take cash.

Dwek's efforts to pay off someone in Hudson County began anew as he got Altman and Haber to attempt a setup in Union City. It was an effort to resurrect the stalled Palisade Avenue project. The approach was going to be through a campaign fund-raiser for Union City First, the Democratic political committee controlled by Brian Stack.

Haber had already contributed to the committee. He sent a $1,200 check to the committee for tickets in February. So had Altman. "You've got to pay for more tickets," Haber told Dwek.

Despite the bankruptcy, which monitored everything he was spending, Dwek said it would not be a problem. "I can get you a check probably," he said. "I have a management company that doesn't show up anywhere."

"You need four thousand dollars," said Haber. "Give it to Moshe and he'll send it through some charity."

Dwek shook his head. "I don't need a gmach," he said of the fund he was already using to launder checks for cash. "I can do a check straight. I don't show anywhere. It's an offshore management thing."

* * *

A week later, Altman sent a text message to Dwek's cell phone, telling him he would be meeting with a go-between for Stack, and told him to bring another "10." Altman wanted another $10,000 in checks to give to the campaign. Dwek did as he was instructed, bringing a $4,000 check written on the account of BH Property Management, the FBI front company, and another $6,000 that he had written as a check to Gmach Shefa Chaim.

The fund-raiser was that evening in Union City. Altman reintroduced Haber to a Stack representative: "Shimon Haber. You met him before."

"I've heard things about you. Good stuff."

Dwek shook hands. "We want to invest a lot of money in the city," he said, leaving no question about his intention. "We want to make sure everyone does the right thing by us."

"I understand," said Stack's middleman. "We want development. We want people that come up with good projects."

Dwek immediately brought up the money. "I gave him ten thousand dollars," he said of Altman. "Four thousand dollars is for the committee and six thousand dollars to him, which he'll get to you this week." Dwek would structure the money through straw donors to get around campaign finance limits. He said he did not have any limits as to what he would put on the table.

Haber and Altman were taken aback by the directness of Dwek's approach. "Ay, ay, ay. Too much talking. You can't talk to them like this," Altman complained later.

Haber agreed. "You gotta start slow with these guys," he said. The developer did not let it drop. He met with Dwek later, telling him Altman was very upset with how open he had been. "He thinks you're a fool for wanting to put your face into the picture at this stage," Haber said.

Haber couldn't understand it himself. Dwek had federal criminal charges pending against him and here he was trying to openly bribe a public official to get a project approved. "I don't understand why you want to put yourself in jeopardy?" Haber snapped. "So hide. It doesn't make a difference!"

* * *

Saul Kassin was a revered figure in the community. The chief rabbi of Shaare Zion, a synagogue located on Ocean Parkway in Brooklyn, Kassin could trace his ancestry back to fifteenth-century Spain. In 1994, he had succeeded his father, Jacob S. Kassin, to become head of the nation's largest Syrian Sephardic Jewish congregation.

In late October, Dwek arranged to meet Kassin at his home in Brooklyn, a modest two-story brick house with a small patch of manicured grass in the front and air conditioners in several windows. Dwek had a $25,000 bank check with him. The story was the same: "This is from some partnerships that I have with people where I'm not—I don't show up too much."

Kassin retrieved a large accounting ledger from another room and began to write out a check to Dwek.

"So there's ten percent for you and then ninety percent back to—I need a check back to Eli Ben Haim, Congregation Ohel Eliahu, please."

"Is that tax deductible?" Kassin asked of the organization, his words caught on surveillance video.

"Of course."

"Why don't you just go to Ben Haim?"

The question was not just business. Ben Haim was *mishpocheh*. Family. Kassin was Ben Haim's uncle. The rabbi's father, Jacob Kassin, had been Ben Haim's grandfather, one of the founders of the shul in Deal that Ben Haim now led.

Solomon danced around the question. "I did a lot of business with him already. I don't want too many checks to him, you know. It doesn't look good, so. He has a lot of business. Eli is too big. He's doing too much business, this guy."

Kassin asked him again about the partnerships.

"I don't show up on the paperwork because I don't need to show up. I need to keep everything quiet now," said Dwek. "So it's make a donation and then a check to Eli. This way there's no trace or anything. I have to live you know. This way, I give ten percent and then on ninety percent I'm able to survive."

Kassin seemed to barely be listening. He completed writing out a check for $22,500 and gave it to Solomon.

Dwek returned to Brooklyn again in December and then in February, but Kassin seemed to be getting increasingly nervous about the exchanges. In December, the U.S. Attorney in Los Angeles had announced the arrest of Grand Rabbi Naftali Tzi Weisz and his executive assistant, or *gabbai*, Moshe Zigelman, both members of the Spinka sect, a small Hasidic denomination within Orthodox Judaism named for the Romanian town where the group first originated. The two Brooklyn men were charged with orchestrating a massive money transfer system stretching from Los Angeles to Tel Aviv, in a scheme that very much mirrored Kassin's own operation.

Kassin was well aware of the arrests. The story was in *The New York Times* and on the Web and carried by all the Jewish papers. The 37-count indictment alleged that Weisz and Zigelman had solicited millions of dollars of contributions to several Spinka charitable organizations, with promises of secretly refunding up to 95 percent of the contributions to donors. The donors, of course, claimed the full amounts of their contributions on their federal income tax returns. Six others in California and in Israel were also charged.

In some cases, the contributors received cash through businesses that operated in and around the Los Angeles jewelry district. Others were paid through wire transfers from Spinka-controlled entities into accounts secretly held in Israeli banks. The international accounts manager at United Mizrahi Bank and a Tel Aviv attorney were both charged with setting up accounts that would allow the Spinka contributors to obtain loans from the Los Angeles branch of the Israeli bank, secured by the funds in Israel. Five Spinka charitable organizations—Yeshiva Imrei Yosef, Yeshivath Spinka, Central Rabbinical Seminary, Machne Sva Rotzohn, and Mesivta Imrei Yosef Spinka, all based in Brooklyn—were also named.

It was only later learned that the whole scheme unraveled after a longtime Spinka contributor, Robert Kasirer, a wealthy Beverly Hills lawyer, agreed to cooperate with authorities in return for a lighter sentence after he was jammed up in a multimillion-dollar health-care fraud investigation in 2004. According to prosecutors, the transactions involved a series of transfers between a paper corporation and banks in Los Angeles and Israel. In one example, they said Kasirer, who had been a big contributor to Yeshivath Spinka, created an offshore corporation on Nevis, the small Caribbean island east of Puerto Rico, and then opened an account in a Tel Aviv bank in the name of Capital Realty Associates. Most of the money he gave to the school was subsequently kicked back to his offshore account in Israel, after the Spinka charity received its cut. Kasirer then took out a loan in the name of one of his businesses from the Israeli bank and paid it down with the funds already on deposit in the Capital Realty Associates account.

After Kasirer began wearing a wire for the government, the money laundering took on different forms, including a New Zealand trust administered by a company in Switzerland.

A few days after the Spinka indictment, Dwek went to Brooklyn with a $25,000 check to exchange. Kassin again asked why Dwek did not go through Ben Haim. "I do too much business with him," insisted Dwek. He also had a new cover story. He was counterfeiting designer handbags, he claimed. His family had to eat.

"I have a company here in New York. I don't have my name—I have partners, and we make handbags, pocketbooks, this and that," he said.

"We take handbags, and we put on different labels like Prada, Gucci, and stuff. They're false labels."

Kassin still seemed to pay little attention to what Dwek was saying, as he wrote out a check in exchange for the one on the FBI account that Dwek gave him. He did not ask again about the handbags and did not seem to care. The routine was the same a few months later in February. When Dwek walked into Kassin's dining room, there were several men, some of them speaking in Hebrew, writing checks to and from Kassin's charitable organization. As in the past, Dwek was carrying the hidden video camera, recording everything that was seen and said. The counterfeit-handbag story was still part of Dwek's cover and he repeated it once more for Kassin, who might have already forgotten that Dwek had said it earlier. But Solomon wasn't repeating it for the rabbi. He was repeating it for the surveillance tape. The targets always needed to acknowledge they were laundering "dirty" money.

"We make the stuff and then we switch the labels and we have Gucci and Prada . . . and we're making money," said Dwek. "I just have to get it around the bankruptcy . . ."

This time Kassin questioned Dwek further. Where did the check come from?

"I have a company. I don't show up on paper," he said, describing himself as a silent partner. "Any time that we make money, they give me a bank check and then I—you give me a check back. Then Eli Ben Haim gives me the cash. I'm able to survive until the bankruptcy, uh, is finished."

Kassin held the check. What if someone comes knocking at the door someday and asks about the check? "What if someone comes and asks me, 'What's this? This money that you're taking?'"

"It doesn't come back to me. My name is nowhere."

Kassin again asked only why Dwek did not go through Ben Haim.

"I did a lot of business with him already," Dwek said. "I don't want too many checks to him, you know. It doesn't look good, so. He has a lot of business. Eli is too big."

Kassin wrote out the new check, apparently still thinking of the Spinka rabbi, now facing lengthy time in federal prison.

"I am very careful now," said the old man, his words caught on tape.

9

◄+◆+►

Kidneys and Fish

Nobile was talking about Mike from Monsey in his regular case update with Christie and his senior staff, reviewing the ongoing money-laundering operations with Kassin and Ben Haim. Christie was bored, leaning back in his chair. He was tired of the whole thing and he told them so.

"How's he helping us? Where is this going?"

All Christie could see, he told Nobile, Howe, and Marra, was an end-game where they would go in and raid a bunch of synagogues. It was not where he wanted to be and it was certainly not the home run that Dwek and Himmel had advertised. Millions of dollars in FBI seed money were being laundered, but the charges were not going to get much better. Wrap it up. Go on to something else.

But Nobile had an ace up his sleeve. This time, the special prosecutions chief had something new to talk about. The team, he said, had stumbled upon a black market kidney transplant operation and Dwek could take them in.

Reawakened, Christie sat up. "What?"

There was someone in the Orthodox community in Brooklyn broker-ing human kidney transplants for about $150,000 a pop. As the story went, the broker would find donors in Israel and for the right price hook them up with people who needed transplants for operations here in the United States.

"You're kidding me," Christie said.

They were not. The broker's name, Nobile and Howe said, was Levy-Itzhak Rosenbaum. He was Hasidic—not Syrian—and though Dwek did not know him personally, he had heard about Rosenbaum through others. In fact, Dwek was aware of a number of people who had indeed bought their way onto the transplant list, including his own grandfather, who he said had paid for a kidney through Rosenbaum. There were others as well, including a major banking executive.

Christie turned to Michele Brown on his left. Having never seen anything like it crawl across his desk before, Christie said almost jokingly, "That's definitely against the law, right?"

Brown, his chief counsel, nodded. She had done the research. "Yes." It was illegal to broker a transplant.

The law actually dated to 1984, when a Virginia physician, after losing his license over a Medicare/Medicaid fraud conviction, announced plans to establish the world's first organ-brokering service. Dr. H. Barry Jacobs, who established a company called the International Kidney Exchange, proposed charging from $2,000 to $5,000 for his services. Donors would get up to $10,000 for a kidney, with the cost paid by the recipient. Oh, and they would also be out one kidney and have to deal with the risks and complications that went along with the process.

The outrage was immediate. Several states moved to immediately outlaw the sale of human organs. On Capitol Hill, a Tennessee congressman named Al Gore introduced legislation banning such sales, and Utah senator Orrin Hatch sponsored similar legislation in the Senate. The National Organ Transplant Act became law in 1984, spelling out the prohibition, though leaving the issue somewhat vague: "It shall be unlawful for any person to knowingly acquire, receive or otherwise transfer any human organ for valuable consideration for use in transplantation." No one had ever been prosecuted under the statute. If the Dwek prosecutors made a case, Rosenbaum was going to be a first.

Christie did not authorize it right away. It took several months to get the U.S. Attorney's office to sign off on the approach before launching Dwek.

Federal tax records showed Rosenbaum had ties to a Brooklyn-based charity organization called Kav LaChayim [literally translated, "path to life"] United Lifeline. The returns filed by the non-profit organization showed Rosenbaum listed as president and a brief description of its focus as meeting the medical needs of children. But Rosenbaum claimed to have had more than a decade of experience meeting the medical needs of other clients—those looking to pay for healthy kidneys.

While it is illegal to profit from the sale of organs, there is in fact a thriving marketplace for those seeking to connect with potential donors. There are more than 84,000 people on waiting lists for kidneys and the available supply comes nowhere near meeting the demand. Pleas for help can readily be found on social-networking sites such as craigslist and Facebook. The non-profit Web site MatchingDonors.com is like many others, serving as a clearinghouse to match up possible donors and recipients through postings such as these: *Please help me save my son, Please help me live longer,* and *I need a kidney to rejoin my wife and young son.*

Rosenbaum apparently had his own network of connections and was known as the man to go to in New York. Short and a little overweight, with a full gray beard and matching moustache, he was described by one Israeli who met him as very Orthodox but "jolly and very off-color." Like Dwek, Rosenbaum wore a black yarmulke at all times.

Dwek called Rosenbaum in mid-February of 2008 on a Friday, just before the start of the Sabbath and a couple of days after he had showed up at Kassin's home with the $25,000 check from the bogus counterfeit-handbag business he claimed to now be running. Dwek's secretary, he told Rosenbaum, had a desperately ill uncle, Teddy Moses. Uncle Teddy needed a kidney transplant to live. Rosenbaum, who had a very heavy European accent that was almost unintelligible on the FBI wiretaps, invited Dwek to come to his home in Brooklyn.

The "secretary" was actually an undercover FBI special agent. She took on the name of "Sarah," the biblical mother of the Jewish people, and used the Hebrew pronunciation to say it. Sarah worked out of the New Jersey office, which was unusual. The FBI did not like to use local agents in undercover operations. You don't want to be posing as someone and then run into a target while shopping for groceries or standing on the checkout line at Costco. But she could pass as Jewish, which was part of the cover.

Dwek and the undercover agent drove to Brooklyn, where Rosenbaum lived in a large three-story brick home on 21st Avenue in the Flatbush neighborhood that he had subdivided into two condos. There were graceful wrought-iron balconies and a grand bay façade on the second level, set on a street of far more modest houses.

"I'm in real estate," said Rosenbaum by way of introduction. He had told neighbors he worked in construction.

Dwek introduced Sarah as "my secretary for, like, twelve years."

They immediately got down to business. Uncle Teddy, said Dwek, was "having some kidney issues. He's on dialysis."

Wired for video and audio as always, Dwek immediately made it clear why they were there: "He needs to, you know, organize to buy one and we need to find how we can do this. I told him I'd take care of the financial arrangements."

"So who is the needy one?"

"My uncle," Sarah told Rosenbaum. In addition to a name, the FBI gave him a critical condition—the kind of detail necessary to make the scam look real. "Teddy" had polycystic disease. Rosenbaum was not a doctor, but kidneys were his business, so he knew what that meant. Polycystic kidney disease is a genetic disorder, leading to the growth of cysts that eventually fill with water-like fluid. The kidneys, which are about the size of a fist, filter wastes and fluid from the blood to form urine. When cysts form, they can enlarge the kidneys, resulting in reduced kidney function and sometimes kidney failure. When that happens, patients may require dialysis or a transplant.

Dialysis, however, is just not all that well tolerated. It makes people very tired and it is very time-consuming, which is why most patients on dialysis prefer the idea of a transplant. Older people, though, are often not considered candidates for transplants, and several of those Dwek knew about in the Syrian community who arranged transplants through Rosenbaum never would have made it to a transplant list. Even if they did, there was no guarantee of a kidney.

The undercover agent told Rosenbaum her uncle, who lived in New Jersey, had been on dialysis for several years and was on the transplant list at a hospital in Philadelphia. How, she asked, could Rosenbaum help?

The way it worked, he explained, was that he would send a blood sample to find a matching prospective donor. One of the first things transplant surgeons look for is a cross-match for donor antigens. A positive cross-match shows the donor and patient do not match. A negative cross-match means there is no reaction between donor and patient, allowing a transplant to proceed. "If you want to arrange it faster, then I bring the donor over here," Rosenbaum explained. "The hospital is the authority who decide it's a match or not. Not me, not you, not him, not nobody."

The hospital would screen any potential donor carefully for various ailments and diseases before authorizing a transplant. Even if blood type is identical, the genetic makeup and the size of the kidney are factors that could weigh against going ahead with an operation.

"I'm doing this a long time," he said carefully, as his words were recorded by Dwek. "Let me explain to you one thing. It's illegal to buy or sell organs. So you cannot buy it. What you do is, you're giving a compensation for the time—whatever—he's not working."

The key, he said, was to concoct some kind of relationship between donor and recipient. Make up a story that would hold up under questioning. "The hospital is asking what's the relationship between the donor and the recipient," he said. "So we put in a relationship—friends, or neighbor, or business relations—any relation."

"Cousins? Third cousins?" Dwek asked.

No. Rosenbaum shook his head. "You wouldn't go to cousins. The recipient is not going to be investigated, but the donor is investigated. So if you start with family, it's real easy to find out if he's not. It's not the family, because the names and the ages and who is who—it doesn't work good." He brushed aside the problems, though. "Putting it together is the easy part," he said. "The one thing you should know, that it's not something you can talk about freely."

Dwek then asked what it would cost.

"The price with what we are asking here is one hundred and fifty thousand dollars," said Rosenbaum.

Dwek brought up the name of a patient they both knew. One in the Syrian community who had gone through Rosenbaum. He had only been charged $140,000, noted Dwek.

Rosenbaum just laughed. "I knew that was coming," he said. Bargaining, however, was not on his agenda. There was no need for that. It was a seller's market. If you didn't like the price, where else were you going to go? He said half of the total cost would have to be paid up front, with the rest due when they got the donor to the hospital. "I'm not a surgeon, and once I get a donor here it's beyond my control," Rosenbaum told them. "But I take care of the guy after the surgery also."

"What do you mean?" asked Dwek.

"I place him somewhere," said Rosenbaum. "You have to baby-sit him like a baby because he may have a language problem, maybe not."

The donors typically came from Israel. Some of them recent immigrants. Many of them desperately poor, they needed the money.

"There are people over there hurting," Rosenbaum explained. At the same time, there were payoffs and expenses to be spread about. "Schmear" was the term he used. Like a bagel and a thick schmear of cream cheese. The donor had to be paid, and the doctors in Israel who would examine the donor, and then the expenses in preparing the visa work, and paying the donor's expenses in the United States.

"One of the reasons it's so expensive is because you have to schmear all the time," Rosenbaum said. He told Dwek and the agent he would accept cash as payment.

The following week, Dwek and his secretary returned to Rosenbaum's house. Sarah, the agent, said she had more questions, although she was following another script put together by the U.S. Attorney's office for the surveillance video. They wanted it to be very clear that Rosenbaum knew he was doing something illegal. At Rosenbaum's home, Dwek's secretary said her uncle was worried about others finding out about his purchase of a kidney.

"Let me explain this to you. It's illegal to buy. It's illegal to sell," Rosenbaum said once again. That's exactly what prosecutor Mark McCarren, who was running this part of the case for the U.S. Attorney's office, wanted to hear when the DVD was played back in Newark. Rosenbaum was oblivious to the trap. Instead, he dug a deeper hole for himself, trying to reassure his new clients. It was the donor, he said, who would be the one facing the questions. "They're going to investigate him, not you, not your uncle. He's going to speak to a social worker and a psychologist to find out why is he doing it. And it is our job to prepare him," Rosenbaum explained.

Dwek prompted him to continue: "What kind of story would the donor give them?"

Rosenbaum said he would be creative. "I put together the story by seeing your uncle, seeing him. Could be neighbors, could be friends from shul, could be friends from the community, could be friends of, of, of his children. Business friends," he said. "They all come from Israel."

He gave them the name of one recipient who had received a kidney transplant four years earlier, and offered to give them other references. Other recipients willing to talk about the process. One of them had an appointment at the hospital in just two weeks for testing. Rosenbaum told Dwek and Sarah he was an Israeli currently living in Wisconsin.

The two finally got up to leave. Sarah told Rosenbaum she would obtain blood samples from her uncle.

The next day, the FBI agent used a phone number Rosenbaum had given her and contacted one of his earlier kidney transplant customers, in her role as Dwek's secretary. The former patient, a resident of New Jersey, acknowledged that he paid Rosenbaum cash for the kidney and the operation had been done at an out-of-state hospital about a year earlier.

Why do you think the donor was willing to give up a kidney? the agent asked.

"I guess he needed the money."

* * *

The following week, Dwek was back to his money-laundering routine with the rabbis, but the initial contacts with Guarini from the previous July were finally beginning to bear some fresh fruit for prosecutors. And not a minute too soon. Despite the kidney investigation, Christie was by now set to close up shop on Dwek and have the special prosecutions gang get back into the business of nailing crooked pols.

On March 10, 2008, Guarini met Dwek again, this time on Montgomery Street in Jersey City. It was a cold day and the building inspector climbed into the car of the man he knew only as David Esenbach. Good news, he told Guarini. He was about to enter into a multimillion-dollar real estate contract to develop the luxury condo complex on Garfield Avenue, the supposed luxury condominium. No matter that it was on the edge of that chromium-contaminated wasteland. No matter it was hell and gone from the part of Jersey City where big money was putting up Class A buildings. If Guarini had checked on that, he didn't say so now. Dwek told him he had also just closed on a big project in West New York, another crowded Hudson County city—but complained he had lost a significant amount of money because he "didn't know anyone" there.

"I don't want to be stupid in Jersey City," Dwek told Guarini, as the scene was recorded. "Money is not a problem."

Reminding the inspector of the payment he had made to Guarini months earlier, Dwek told him he didn't mind doing that again to keep Garfield Avenue on track.

"Approvals won't be a problem," the older man said. "Just sign the contract. I can have a meeting with somebody concerning what you, what you want done and get an answer from him right then and there."

Esenbach warned his new friend "to be careful" when he called him on the phone and to refer to the payments—what he called the grease—as "invitations."

"We're not gonna do nothin' illegal," declared Guarini, who by now wasn't inspecting much of anything, either. He had failed to get his plumbing sign-off from the state Division of Community Affairs. So the powers-that-be had made him a taxi inspector instead. But he agreed that after getting the "grease," he would get Dwek an answer regarding his concerns about the Garfield property.

That Sunday, Guarini met with Dwek at the Broadway Diner in Bayonne. Guarini was working Dwek as much as Dwek was working him, touting his influence. The typical approval process for development in Jersey City, he said, could take six to eight months. He could cut that to maybe 90 days. "With me, it's a guaranteed yes," he boasted. "All you gotta do is take care of me. I'll bring you to all the principals that'll be in charge—they'll guide us through everything."

"Do I pay them directly?"

"No," instructed Guarini. "I'll take care of it. I told you I take care of everything."

To the feds, the city inspector seemed to have recognized the gravy train and did not need anyone else to get on board. He kept telling the informant that everything should go through him. Guarini also told Dwek he had someone who could help get him the approvals he wanted. A Jersey City official who might play along. The guy he had in mind was Maher A. Khalil, the city's assistant director of health and a member of the zoning board, who, Guarini said, would "do the right thing" and "get things done."

"Is he on the same page?" asked Dwek.

"He's on the same page," Guarini assured Dwek. Khalil would take cash.

* * *

Later that week, there were two more cash exchanges again with Rabbi Nahum at his office in Deal. There would be a larger check the following week, Dwek told Nahum. "I'm getting money from a silent partner in New York," Dwek said.

He set up the meeting with Khalil and Guarini the following Wednesday, again at the diner in Bayonne. Before Khalil arrived, Dwek took out one of his familiar FedEx envelopes and flashed it once again to show the money inside. "This here is ten thousand dollars," he said. Payment for Garfield and another project that Dwek wanted to speak to Guarini about.

While they waited, Guarini gave Dwek a quick rundown on Maher Khalil. He not only was on the zoning board, but he also knew the right people to help with any development interests in Jersey City.

Good, said Dwek. "I've got another envelope in the car with ten for him."

Guarini suddenly stopped Dwek, raising his right hand to slow him down. Not so direct. Guarini wanted to be the gatekeeper. "I'll take care of everything," he said once again. "Khalil is on board."

Dwek told Guarini not to worry. "I'll give it to you after the meeting," he said.

Khalil was balding, with dark eyes and a slouch to his stance. He had once sat on Jersey City's Ethical Standards Board, until it was disbanded over political infighting that saw many members boycotting its meetings—including Khalil himself. A Coptic Christian who later became Mayor Jerramiah T. Healy's liaison to the city's large Egyptian community, Khalil was earning a meager $50,000 a year at City Hall in a job he never seemed to be at and thought he deserved more money, more authority, more respect. And he needed the scratch now more than ever because Khalil and his wife were about to have their first child.

Guarini saw Khalil entering the diner and made the introductions.

David Esenbach, he told Khalil, was developing property around Jersey City. "He's a very big developer," Guarini said, outlining the details of the same 750-unit luxury condo project Dwek claimed to be building at the Garfield Avenue site. Again, no one thought anything about the lunacy of what he now claimed would be a 43-story luxury tower on a chromium hot spot overlooking the New Jersey Turnpike. Nobody even looked to see who owned the property.

Dave talked about development deals he had done in New York and down south. None of it very specific, all of it well into the tens of millions, and nobody ever asked any questions. He talked non-stop, not really eating anything and not really saying anything, either. "Before I make a two-hundred-million-dollar investment, I want to make sure all the boys are on board." You're on the zoning board, he said to Khalil. Can you help me "to slide through with no problems?" Khalil allowed that he might but suggested that Esenbach not "show up at zoning board meetings," as "people might ask questions." (What Khalil neglected to say was that if Dwek had shown up at meetings, he'd have learned quickly that Khalil's pull with the board was gone, as his tenure as a zoning official was expiring that same month.)

Staying invisible was fine with Esenbach. Later, as they left the diner and took in the parking lot, Dwek told Khalil that he had an envelope for him that he would give to Guarini "so there won't be any problems." Dwek then pulled another FedFex envelope from the trunk of his car with $10,000 in cash and gave it to Guarini.

Two weeks later, Dwek got together again with Guarini at a bar in Jersey City. Dwek had another envelope for him. Another $10,000 in cash. The building inspector, meanwhile, had been looking out for the developer and had some inside information to share. "There's a property on Ocean Avenue," he mentioned to Dwek. "It's already been approved for forty-two units."

Dwek played his role. "With you, I can get like eighty or one hundred units?" he said to Guarini.

It was not going to be hard, Guarini believed. "I think we can get eighty units without a problem."

The FBI was not interested in actual investment properties. That meant real money and actual applications before the council and other city agencies. Nobody was actually developing anything and a decision had been made early on that they would never get to the point where they would actually buy any property. They couldn't allow anyone innocent to be hurt in a fraudulent transaction. But Dwek took the information and gave Guarini his envelope, like an animal trainer tossing a silvery fish to an eager dolphin who had just jumped from the water through a hoop. "This here is another ten big ones; that's for today's meeting and on account of Garfield," Dwek said. He had taken to calling the payoffs "the FedEx thing."

Guarini took his reward. "You're gonna need me for everything," he stressed one more time.

* * *

Thursday, May 8, 2008, was a cool and wet day in New Jersey. The FBI had been busy elsewhere in the state that morning. A series of early-morning raids across Jersey targeted a number of high-ranking members of organized crime, including Andrew Merola, reputed to be a member of the Gambino family, and Martin Taccetta, the alleged former underboss of the Lucchese crime family's New Jersey faction.

In Jersey City, the undercover operations with Dwek went on and the informant caught up again with Guarini and Khalil at a restaurant. David Esenbach rarely ordered much from the menu. Sometimes a salad. Maybe a fruit platter that he would pick at. Often he just pulled some chocolate out of a pocket. The man liked chocolate. In fact, at one lunch meeting much later on in the sting, Dwek went all the way with his appreciation for the sweeter things in life. While the others ordered lunch at the Light Horse Tavern in Jersey City, he got chocolate bread pudding *and* a separate dessert plate of devil's food cake. He was especially fond of the chocolate *tartufo* at Casa Dante, one of the Italian restaurants favored by the pols.

With Guarini and Khalil, Dwek was still pressing them about who could help speed up approvals for Garfield Avenue. He wanted people who would do the right thing by him. "I can't go into town naked," David Esenbach insisted. "I need to know who needs to be taken care of. Just tell me how much. I'll get those envelopes to them." Whatever it cost, he said, would be no problem.

Khalil did not like the talk at the table. Like Haber, Khalil thought the developer was getting a little too direct. You should be careful, Khalil warned. It could land you in big trouble. But Khalil agreed to introduce Esenbach to "the right people." He had someone in mind. A fixer with ties to those in power. His name, he said, was Joe Cardwell.

As they talked, Guarini got up and headed for the men's room. While he was gone, Dwek casually asked Khalil if he had gotten the $10,000 he left for him with Guarini.

"No," Khalil said.

Dwek thought about that for a moment and then excused himself. Guarini was still in the men's room when Dwek walked in. "Did you give the envelope to Khalil?" he asked him privately.

"Yes. Of course," said Guarini.

One middleman was double-crossing another in a pattern that would repeat itself over and over. It was a huge problem for prosecutors if they ever were to make a corruption case against Khalil or anyone beyond Guarini. No one had seen or acknowledged bribe money going to the official. But there was an easy way to fix it. A couple of weeks later, Khalil drove all the way to Toms River, about an hour down the Garden State Parkway from Jersey City, and met Dwek in the parking lot of a diner. The man Khalil knew as Esenbach gave him a FedEx envelope.

"This is the money John was supposed to have given you back in March," he told Khalil. There was $10,000 in cash inside. Dwek made sure to remind anyone listening to the surveillance tape that it was dirty money, being given in exchange for Khalil's influence on the zoning board in connection with the Garfield Avenue project.

"Thank you so much," Khalil said, caught on the wiretap.

"Spend it wisely," the developer instructed.

"I'll try. Thank you so much."

* * *

While Dwek worked the corruption sting, the money-laundering operation still continued to expand through a widening group of contacts being made in the Orthodox communities, including both Sephardic and Hasidic rabbis in Brooklyn and Deal. Dwek—back to being The Rabbi's Son under his real name—shuttled constantly between New York and New Jersey. He was still moving a lot of money with Ben Haim, and the rabbi was moving it all through IM, thousands of miles away.

At one meeting, Ben Haim was running $300,000 through a cash-counting machine in his office—money that Dwek had brought back in a bag from Brooklyn the previous day. It was a surreal scene on tape. In the background were scholarly books on Talmudic studies. And there was Ben Haim, running cash through a machine as if he had been doing that for years. Ben Haim mentioned that he owed IM about two hundred thousand dollars.

"Does he pester you about it?"

"No. He trusts me."

As with Kassin, Dwek also changed his cover story on the source of the money he was laundering. He brought up the counterfeit handbag operation that he had spun for Kassin in Brooklyn. Sitting in Ben Haim's black Lexus outside the rabbi's home in Elberon, Dwek had a $50,000 bank check he wanted to convert to cash.

"Business is very good," he said, describing how he took fake labels to sew into knockoff designer bags. "Prada, Gucci, boom, boom, boom. I put up four hundred thousand principal. These are only my profits."

It couldn't be traced to him, Dwek reiterated. It was all from out of the country. "We have the factory. We make the stuff in Brooklyn, but we off-shore it," he said. "There's no trace, no nothing. So all the profits are hidden."

After hearing the story, Ben Haim demanded a higher percentage off the top to complete the transaction. Dwek protested, "I'm a repeat customer! Your best customer, no?"

Ben Haim was quiet for a moment. "No," he responded in a hushed tone.

"Why? 'Cause you've got guys who do a million dollars a month?"

"No, that was once upon a time . . ."

Ben Haim got out of his car and retrieved a bag from the trunk. Inside was a box with logos from *Power Rangers,* the live-action TV series for kids featuring colorful costumed heroes who battle bad guys. The box held tens of thousands of dollars in bundles of cash, and the rabbi pulled out $45,000. Business was good, he told Dwek. IM "called me up fourteen times. He says, 'I got another three hundred [thousand]. You want it?'" Ben Haim said, closing the trunk. "I declined the offer, but I have orders for Sunday. I don't have enough."

Despite the pile of cash still left in the Power Rangers box, it wasn't enough to cover the customers he had waiting on Sunday. He asked Dwek what his needs were. "You want to do a hundred [thousand] next week?"

"Let me see how much, what our profits are next week," he said.

* * *

While pushing the limits of what Ben Haim and Kassin could handle, Dwek found himself beginning to do a lot of business with Mordchai Fish, a rabbi in the Hasidic community whom Nahum repeatedly urged him to use. Fish operated several charitable tax-exempt organizations, including one called BGC and another called Levovos, and Dwek had sent money to him long before his arrest in the bank fraud. Solomon had even declared a $5,000 contribution to Fish on his 2005 federal income tax. There was no declaration as to whether any of that was kicked back, like so much of the money Solomon was laundering now.

Fish was the rabbi of a small shul—a *shtiebel* (literally "little house") in Yiddish—Congregation Sheves Achim in Brooklyn. He wore wire-rimmed glasses, had a white beard that looked spun from cotton, and carried a heavy Eastern European accent. At times he sounded like an eccentric loving uncle and anyone listening to him on the phone would think he was always talking of religion, taking pleasure in the Jewish festivals that dot the calendar and the social occasions like weddings and engagements. He raised money for a variety of charity projects in Russia, including the building of a ritual bath, or *mikvah*. None of it sounded very sinister, and much of it caught on the surveillance tapes was hard to understand at all. Most of it, though, was in code.

Fish was a nervous, furtive guy reputed to have cash couriers operating all over Borough Park, the ultra-Orthodox enclave, in Brooklyn. Of all the people Dwek had been dealing with, Fish was by far the most paranoid over getting caught—and certainly the most organized. Prosecutors watching the surveillance video could not believe his intensity over evading possible detection. It was crazy. At one point, he went to a *mikvah* to discuss business in a changing room. He was constantly swapping phone numbers and repeatedly gave Dwek new SIM cards for his cell phone to thwart the possibility of a government wiretap. A SIM card is a portable memory chip that activates the phone and holds personal identity information and the cell number. Switching it out is like having a new phone. But it did not matter. Fish could have thrown away Dwek's cell phone. Everything was being recorded by the FBI's hidden surveillance camera.

Driving with Fish through Borough Park one day to pick up $50,000 in laundered cash, Solomon started calling out loud the cross streets they were passing. They were being followed by the FBI and he was like a locator beacon, broadcasting their location as the agents listened from blocks away to stay out of sight.

Fish suddenly hushed him.

"I'm nervous now . . . Don't even say the street in this car."

"There's nothing. I had it swept," Dwek assured him as they drove, well aware that the car was wired and the FBI was listening to every word. "Don't worry about it."

Fish was unconvinced. "Swept, shmept," he muttered.

He never mentioned the word "money." They were dealing with one network, Fish explained one day, and they both needed to be very careful what they said. "It's a whole chain," he told Dwek. And when speaking with members of anyone from the network on the telephone, "Everything is code."

When Fish spoke of cash, the word he used was *gemoras*. At first, it meant nothing to the FBI, but The Rabbi's Son knew well that it was a reference to part of the Talmud—the collection of Jewish law and tradition that explains the Five Books of Moses—containing rabbinical commentaries. In the TV series *The Sopranos*, New Jersey mobsters used pasta references as a substitute for cash, so $1,000 was one "box of ziti." To Fish and his money-moving friends, the box of ziti was instead one *gemora*.

A recorded call to Fish in New York was typical of the conversations. "I'm bringing, uh—fifty-five *gemoras*, and then I'll see you," Dwek said awkwardly, like a kid stammering over Pig Latin. He was bringing $55,000 in cash.

A few weeks later, he said his purported partner in the counterfeit handbag business had more money to siphon out of his bankruptcy case. "I think he wants to do a lot of *gemoras* this week. So maybe a hundred *gemoras*, maybe more." Fish also used a Hasidic version of Spanglish to make it so the uninitiated would have no idea what the hell he was talking about. In one sentence alone, Fish would refer to cash as a *gemora*, use Hebrew numbers to say how many he was changing, and then agree to meet by saying the day of the week in either Yiddish or Hebrew. For anyone raised in the Orthodox world, the amalgamated lingo was second nature. For FBI agents and prosecutors used to midwestern Presbyterianism or even New Jersey Catholicism, it might as well have been Icelandic rap music.

Fish even had a code for a money-laundering meet. "We'll learn together," he would say. Meaning, they would be studying Torah.

When Fish would call and get Dwek's voice mail, he wouldn't leave messages. Well, he would, but not the way one typically would. For 30 or 40 seconds—sometimes longer—Fish would sing into the phone Hasidic songs about Torah and peace, devotional, repetitive "humming tunes" with few words, called *niggunim* in Hebrew typically used to aid in meditation during prayer or Torah study.

* * *

The routine with Fish was the same as with Ben Haim and Kassin. Ten days after his meeting with Khalil in Toms River, Dwek got together with Fish and the rabbi's brother, Lavel Schwartz, in a home on Hooper Street in Brooklyn.

Williamsburg was a difficult area for the FBI to operate in. The Hasidim, like the Syrians, were another insular community where strangers quickly stood out, even if they donned the white shirts, black pants, and yarmulkes that were ubiquitous in this part of the city. It was here that one of the FBI undercover agents shadowing Dwek was confronted on the street one day. Whatever the agent did that made him stand out was never made clear. His cover wasn't blown, but it was clear he didn't fit in the community, said one of those connected with the investigation. "He had to hightail it out of there."

Fish and Schwartz knew Solomon and were well aware of what had happened in New Jersey. Dwek did not make any secret of it. He had brought with him yet another $50,000 check, supposedly from the bank fraud.

"I had twenty-five million from PNC," he said, recounting exactly what had been printed in the newspapers more than a year earlier. Well, not exactly. "I gave twenty million dollars to HSBC. I took five million. I sent it offshore."

He claimed he had a guy holding the money for him, doing whatever he asked with the funds, and cashing it out slowly. "I don't wanna do too much at one time."

Fish took the check and Dwek asked who would deliver the cash in exchange. "Yolie," said Fish. "Yolie Gertner. "I not only do business with him. I have four or five guys."

"I'm not going to tell him I have two million dollars," said Dwek.

"Don't say anything."

Gertner came by a few minutes later and then disappeared again with Dwek's $50,000 check. As they waited Fish's cell phone went off, and as he turned away Dwek continued the conversation with Schwartz for the surveillance video, talking about the difficulties he was having with the ongoing bankruptcy proceedings in New Jersey, again to establish what they was doing was wrong.

"Any money I make, it goes to the bankruptcy, to the court. I can't make money," he complained. "Before the whole thing happened, that, that five million dollars I took from the bank schnookie—now it's . . . I have nothing else."

Ten minutes later, Gertner was back with a package containing thousands of dollars wrapped in bundles. Dwek and Schwartz began to count the cash.

"If anyone ever asks you, you didn't see me. You understand? No bankruptcy, no bank schnookie, no nothing. Don't say nothin' to nobody," Dwek warned Gertner.

Fish pulled Dwek aside and told him not to talk to Gertner. "He doesn't even know your name!" Fish hissed. After the fees had been taken out, Dwek had $42,000 in cash given to him. He stuck it in his pockets.

* * *

The next time they met, again at a house on Hooper Street in the Hasidic section of Williamsburg, Brooklyn, Dwek had an $80,000 check payable to another charity. He went back to the counterfeit handbag story: "profits from that label thing. You know I invested four hundred thousand in that company where we switch the labels from the Prada, the Gucci, and stuff like that."

Fish could care less. "Yeah, yeah, yeah," he replied.

But Dwek persisted. It was important for the surveillance wire that Fish knew where the money was coming from and that it was *profits* from an illegal operation. "I invested in this label, you know, company. We make pocketbooks, handbags, and stuff. The business is very good now because the market's down—economy's down—and everyone wants to buy. Instead of spending a thousand dollars for a Prada bag, we sell it for two hundred dollars. Gucci bag. Three hundred dollars. It's twelve hundred dollars in the store."

Fish said nothing. His brother, Schwartz, and Gertner, the courier, were inside the house. Gertner took the new check and again disappeared somewhere. They would give him $68,000 in exchange for the $80,000 check. For the first time, Fish asked directly about the origin of the funds.

"That's the profits from the label and some of the interest—the profits from the bank," said Dwek, immediately on script. "All of the money came from my partner. The partner gets the money, and he washed it back, you understand?" Dwek told Fish he had invested $400,000 in cash in the counterfeit handbag business and the bankruptcy court was unaware of it. The merchandise was being manufactured by undocumented workers in a sweatshop in lower Manhattan.

The explanation seemed to satisfy Fish. Then he gave Dwek another new SIM chip for his cell phone.

* * *

Six months after meeting with Rosenbaum, Dwek and the undercover FBI agent took another crack at the kidney broker. In the U.S. Attorney's office, no one was calling the broker by his name. He just became known to everyone as "Kidney Guy." On Monday afternoon, August 18, 2008, Dwek called Kidney Guy on his cell.

"It's Schlomo Dwek," he said. "Are you around Wednesday afternoon or Thursday just to sit down for a few minutes?"

He wanted to talk again about setting up a transplant for his secretary's "uncle." They left it up in the air, but Dwek called back on Wednesday a little after two in the afternoon and they agreed to meet the next day at Rosenbaum's home. The broker had a few loose ends to tie up, but one thing was important to him and he insisted on getting an answer before they proceeded. It wasn't a medical question.

"She's Jewish?" he asked about the secretary. Then he asked again.

On Thursday, Dwek and the agent returned to Kidney Guy's home and he brought them downstairs to the basement apartment. Playing the role of secretary, the agent talked about the condition of her supposed uncle, who she said had been receiving dialysis three times per week over the last couple of years.

"What type of blood is he?"

"O positive."

Dwek asked Rosenbaum if he had a doctor in Israel who checks out donors and makes sure they are able suitable candidates.

"I got a guy over there," he assured them. "Any donor has to be very healthy, and has to be tested for any disease." The blood type must also be a match. And her uncle would need to meet the donor before proceeding. It was essential for the cover story that the two were able to play it like they knew each other. The stories of both the donor and recipient had to coincide, and on that point, Rosenbaum declared, "so far I've never had a failure."

Not only would her uncle be tested, but a blood sample of the recipient would be sent to a lab as well.

"So there's a doctor that's putting it together, sending it to the lab, I guess?" asked the undercover agent.

Yes, said the broker. He added that he had an associate based in Borough Park who took blood samples on behalf of an insurance company for whom he worked. Rosenbaum always paid him in cash for handling blood samples of would-be organ recipients.

The price was again put on the table. It would be $160,000, with half paid up front. Rosenbaum's primary expenses were incurred early in the process, he said. He wanted cash, but Dwek had only four checks with him drawn up in the amount of $2,500 each. Rosenbaum agreed to take the checks, but he wanted another $70,000 in cash paid up front as part of the 50 percent deposit.

"Who do I make them out to?" asked Dwek.

Rosenbaum gave Dwek the name of a congregation but then told him to leave the checks blank and said he would call him when he filled in the name of the payee.

A few days later, Dwek reached out to Rosenbaum. "Those checks, you make them out yet?" he asked.

"Yes."

"You want to fax me a copy? Let me know the names so I can tell my bookkeeper."

The checks were made out to another charitable organization, Ach Tov Gemach, and deposited at a Wachovia Bank branch in Brooklyn, according to FBI records. "Ach Tov" is a biblical reference from Psalm 23, the Psalm of David that begins: "The Lord is my shepherd, I shall not be in want . . ." It ends with the phrase *Ach tov vahesed / Yird' funi kol y'mei hayai.* "Surely goodness and mercy shall follow me all the days of my life . . ."

* * *

Soon after the money was deposited, Dwek called Rosenbaum again. "You want to know when the guy's going to come to you?" he asked the broker.

"Yes."

Dwek told him he would check with his secretary.

"Listen, the sooner the better, because I want to start moving, I have to start with the tests," Rosenbaum said, his voice betraying his impatience.

The Bureau, however, was in no rush to bring this one home. It was time to give the fictitious yet beloved Uncle Teddy some serious medical complications. Nothing that would kill him. Just enough to put everything on hold for a while. On Wednesday, a few days after Labor Day, Dwek called up Rosenbaum.

"I spoke to Sarah, my secretary, and she called her uncle there, Teddy Moses. He's having a little bit of problems this week. He has a little bit of fever; he has a virus or something. So I'll call you when I hear back; hopefully, next week or something he'll be better and then I'll have him come up there."

"He has a virus?"

"He thinks he has a virus. He's going to see his doctor later on, I don't know, he has like a low fever, one hundred or one hundred and one. He just wants to wait until he feels a hundred percent before . . . ," Dwek trailed off.

"Yes, he has to be one hundred percent," agreed the kidney broker.

"We have to wait a week or two until he feels one hundred percent."

"A week or two?"

"Yeah, you know, he wants to regain all his strength. Probably a week, you've got to figure."

"Okay."

Dwek reassured him, "I'm on top of it and I'll bother her every day and I'll let you know exactly when he's better and he has the energy and everything to come up."

They were back on the phone again three weeks later, as Dwek continued to string Kidney Guy along.

"Tell me what's going on. I started to arrange some things. What's going on?" Rosenbaum asked again. The informant now had more questions about the procedure and Rosenbaum was glad to patiently talk it all out again.

"You recover . . . but it takes time," he said. "Takes two to three months." In fact, everything takes time, he noted. It takes months to get a person and bring him over here, and then over here it takes months.

Dwek, though, was looking to really slow things down, just as Rosenbaum was growing increasingly eager to get it going. The broker called Dwek in late October and left him a message, trying to find out what the holdup was. After consulting his FBI handlers, Dwek quickly called back and got Rosenbaum's voice mail to let him know that Sarah's uncle was not getting over his medical problems as quickly as everyone had hoped.

"Isaac, good morning. Schlomo returning your call," Dwek said on the message. "I spoke to my secretary this morning and her uncle, Teddy, is back in the hospital. I'm not sure exactly what the problem is. We don't think it's too serious, but he's having some problems. So once hopefully he gets out and gets better I'll call you. In the interim, don't do anything, don't bring anyone over, and don't do anything, don't order anything, until you hear back from me."

While the feds wanted to keep things going, they did not want Rosenbaum bringing over a donor. They didn't want Rosenbaum starting tests and they certainly did not want their sting to lead to any unnecessary medical procedures that could potentially go wrong. That would only complicate things. There was absolutely no way they were going to actually arrange a black market kidney transplant and let the charade run until they were forced to stop it at the last minute—when it could be too late. That would jeopardize the entire sting operation and put some poor unsuspecting donor in the middle of a mess orchestrated by the Justice Department. Dwek could also be immediately exposed.

Anyway, the FBI figured it had the goods on Rosenbaum through the meetings and wiretaps. A half hour after Dwek left the voice message, Rosenbaum called back. What the hell is going on?

"This guy, Teddy, is back in the hospital," Dwek told Rosenbaum. "We don't know what's wrong with him. We don't think it's anything serious, but you know, don't do anything yet. Don't bring anyone in or anything until you hear from me."

"This guy, what's his problem?"

Dwek was vague, just telling Rosenbaum to hold off temporarily until he gave him a call.

"The reason I'm calling you so much is the thing I don't have what to work with. Sometimes I have to go look for it," said Rosenbaum in his heavy accent.

"I understand you have people that might be a match or something."

"Yeah."

It was getting serious now. They really couldn't have Rosenbaum bringing over a potential donor. Only weeks before leaving the U.S. Attorney's office for good, Christie himself gave the final order on the Rosenbaum case: intent to broker a kidney would have to do, because taking things any further just could not be allowed.

The FBI was told to put the brakes on the whole thing. Two days before Thanksgiving, there was a new and grave medical crisis to give them all a time-out. Dwek called Rosenbaum a little after 7:00 P.M. Teddy Moses had suffered a "mini-stroke" that past Friday, he claimed. "He's doing a little better, but he wants to put everything on hold until he has therapy and recuperates. So it's not good news," Dwek told the kidney broker. He made light of the constant delays.

"You know, one thing after the next with this guy," remarked Schlomo. "First he's sick; then he gets a virus; then he's in the hospital; now he has a mini-stroke. I don't know what to tell you. It's crazy. These things are never simple, right? These things are never simple. I thought I'd help the lady out. Impossible."

At the other end of the line, Kidney Guy seemed to accept Dwek's newest line of bullshit but still wanted to know more after all the runaround with this client. "I would like to meet this guy once just to see you know, to talk to him," he told Dwek. "I'm willing to come over. Just tell me where and when."

"Okay, we'll set something up," promised Dwek. "I don't know if the guy's walking, what the story now is. I guess, these people, once something goes wrong with them, everything happens, one thing after the next. It's like my grandfather. Same story. Every week, something else. Everything's on hold now. Crazy."

10

⊶╂ ╂╂╼

The Fixer

For 20 years, Joseph Cardwell was one of the go-to guys in Jersey City. If you had a project that needed approvals or you wanted access to key officials or a patronage job was something you sought, Cardwell was your man. He was known as a "fixer."

Increasingly, the FBI field agents and prosecutors trying hard to focus Dwek on political corruption found they were in need of someone like Cardwell. The feds long believed that Cardwell and his ilk were the bagmen responsible for greasing the political skids with cash. Believed but could never prove. Now, if only the feds could get Dwek inside with Cardwell and others like him, they would be able to serve up to Christie the political corruption counts that were promised as Dwek fought to put off his inevitable prison sentence.

In Hudson County, fixers are key to getting almost anything done. "Reliable middlemen," as Ralph Marra, Christie's top lieutenant and eventual successor as federal prosecutor, would later describe them on live television.

Want a meeting with the mayor? Need a sit-down with the congressman or the candidate or the council president? You need a guy with the right rep and the right set of phone numbers? Someone who can open doors and decode the political landscape?

A fixer was someone who could tell a developer that money in politics does not signal philosophy but is a necessary business tool and it's nonpartisan. As one insider explained to Dwek on an FBI wiretap, he needed to "take care of both guys," spreading his money between competing political candidates to hedge his bets, as David Esenbach navigated a city government as foreign to him as a third-world dictatorship.

There's no real job description for a fixer, and they don't usually call themselves that. They are consultants. Or political strategists. In the movies, George Clooney's Michael Clayton was a fixer in the form of a smooth big-firm lawyer who handled everything from immigration problems to a top client's driving mishap. Even Yankee tickets. For foreign correspondents in need of a native guide, a fixer is a combination translator and road manager hired by news organizations to help work through red tape and recalcitrant (and corrupt) bureaucracies in far-flung countries.

And in politics, they're people like Cardwell and Jack Shaw, compared by some to the Tibetan Sherpas who guide explorers through the Himalayas. They are loyal to no one but their best client of the moment. In other words, their only loyalty is to themselves. They're people who know the details and plot the strategy but are liable to turn on their clients for nothing more than the right price.

Some are dapper; some are disheveled. Sometimes the fixers are lawyers or lobbyists, sometimes both. Some of them build confidence through rapport, others by the sheer force of their arrogance or the power of the unspoken threat (*use me or don't bother trying to get anywhere in this town*).

They are especially easy to come by in New Jersey's cities where the politics is layered thick with agendas difficult to understand—much less manage—and animosities that are old, entrenched, and different block by block. In Hoboken, for example, a fixer needs to understand and navigate the divide between born-and-bred residents and the new urbane class that has transformed the city into Manhattan West. But even among those groups there are subpopulations, and the fixer has to be able to manipulate them all. In Jersey City, it's even more delicate—and, therefore, potentially more lucrative. There's the upscale you-can't-touch-it corporate and yuppie section along the waterfront and then there are the working-class black and Hispanic neighborhoods on the other side of the New Jersey Turnpike Extension whose leaders carry sway at City Hall.

Often unseen, fixers do surface sometimes. Sometimes in grand fashion. In the middle of the heated 2006 U.S. Senate race, Democratic incumbent Robert Menendez was running against Tom Kean Jr., the son of the popular former governor. The election pitted the First Family of New Jersey against the child of Cuban emigrants who had clawed his way to the top of the political food chain. At the time, Menendez—the de facto political boss of Hudson County—was trying to run away from a pedigree that can kill a candidate in the white-bread suburbs of New Jersey horse country. Then the recordings surfaced. Menendez's fixer, best friend, and attorney, Donald Scarinci, was heard pushing a psychiatrist to hire another doctor after the shrink complained he was having trouble getting his county contracts signed.

The story and the characters were as bizarre as any comic-book writer could dream up. Playing lead was the shrink himself, Dr. Oscar Sandoval. He wore cuff links and heavy TV makeup. He moved from expert testimony in courtrooms to political meetings in backrooms and he was always wiring himself up. He passed bribes, worked as a government informant, and, when his 15 minutes of fame arrived, relished every second as his secretary—boobs pushing desperately to escape her overextended blouse—ushered reporters into Sandoval's cluttered inner sanctum two at a time for hours at a clip. Sitting in Sandoval's waiting room for an audience, you couldn't help but get the feeling you had arrived in a cartoonish brothel, sandwiched between a church and Kennedy Boulevard in Union City.

"If you can take this guy back, and do something with him, that would be a favor to the congressman," Scarinci could be heard on tape telling Sandoval in reference to Menendez, a member of the House of Representatives at the time. "If you can deal with Dr. Ruiz and make him happy, Menendez will consider that a favor; if you can't, then that's okay . . . [From] my point of view, it makes sense for you because it gives you protection."

Scarinci was summarily ousted from the Menendez campaign and went into hiding through the end of the race.

The best of the fixers, though, are quite simply invisible to anyone who doesn't need to see them. They set up meetings, drop off the money, work the press (anonymously, of course), and often signal to the powers-that-be who's on what side on any given deal. They are like casino hosts, found anywhere there's politics and money and government and people who need to navigate through them on the way to a payday. The only qualifications are a Rolodex and an appetite for diner food and watered-down beer—two of the staples in the fixer's diet.

In New Jersey, developers always hired fixers. Hospitals put them on retainer. Even medical schools, law firms, and venerable Wall Street investment banks hired fixers. So did young pols looking to make their moves up the political ladder. Now, Dwek was about to buy one for the FBI.

* * *

Khalil, as he had promised several weeks earlier, introduced Dwek to Joe Cardwell, on a warm July morning at a restaurant in Jersey City. Despite

Guarini's efforts to control everything, the investigators needed to move up the chain, not just from diner to diner. Paying everybody through Guarini was a dead end if they hoped to pull anyone higher up into the sting. A building inspector might be a trophy for some rookie assistant DA, but New Jersey's feds hunted big game and had been in that end zone many times already.

The deal with Khalil was the same as with Guarini. The more people Khalil brought to Dwek, the more money would come flowing his way. Before the Cardwell meeting, Khalil was given an envelope, documented by the surveillance video. Inside, $10,000 in cash. The cash incentives turned Khalil into a bounty hunter of sorts. He repeatedly told Dwek he needed the money and landed one fish after another, constantly complaining about how much he was getting paid at City Hall and the always out-of-reach promotion he so desperately wanted.

Khalil knew a payday when he saw one and he treated Dwek like the developer/informant was the Second Coming. He would say "God bless you" when Dwek moaned about how hard he was working, and Khalil would revel in the high times Dwek (actually the FBI) would host for his little band of insiders: trips to Atlantic City, long lunches and expensive dinners at some of New Jersey's best-known places. Neon lights and a bullhorn couldn't have made Khalil's sucking up more obvious. He was simply Grade A perfect for the sting. In so many ways, he did Dwek's job for him, even manufacturing a backstory on his own at one point that he and Dwek had known each other and worked together for nearly a decade. It was the kind of detail-rich fiction that convinced others Dwek was a trustworthy crook—one with whom they could do business. And when other conspirators voiced second thoughts about the goofy Jewish developer with the fast talk, the FedEx envelopes stuffed with C-notes, and a fictitious private jet, it was Khalil who kept their fingers in the pie. When Denis Jaslow, a prison guard turned elections investigator on Dwek's payroll, started worrying, it was Khalil who calmed him down.

Khalil, who knew tons of people through politics, now was motivated because of the cash Dwek dangled. He also had a city job that required little or no actual work. Opportunity, inclination, and access. Three for three and the feds knew it. The hook was baited. Khalil was in the water.

* * *

Entering the diner for the Cardwell sit-down, Khalil gave Dwek a brief lowdown on the fixer who'd be sitting across from him. "He's connected,"

Khalil explained bluntly. Joe, he said, had ties to a number of state and municipal officials. Cardwell's role would be as a consultant who could make sure that state and local government officials were "on board" with Esenbach's development plans. Finally spotting Cardwell coming inside, Khalil introduced him without understatement. "Here's one of the most powerful men in Jersey City," he proclaimed.

An African American with black wire-rimmed glasses, close-cropped hair, and a graying moustache, Cardwell was a big man with a warm smile and a singsong cadence to his chatter. He had always been an incredibly affable guy, and unlike many in a political world where the most volcanic tempers win, Cardwell never got outwardly mad, never blew his stack, and never vowed revenge. Oh, he would get angry and get even. He just kept it quiet until he was ready to make his move. The problem for Cardwell was people didn't trust him or how he made things happen. Including his friends. Especially his friends. They knew firsthand how things worked.

Cardwell's name was legend around New Jersey, even if most people in politics had never met him. He was the key adviser to Jersey City's first black mayor, Glenn Cunningham, and campaign manager to Cunningham's widow, Sandra, who now held the state senate seat left vacant after Glenn's unexpected death. Cardwell was a ward boss. And producer of huge voter turnout in the precincts he controlled. He was Svengali to former Jersey City mayor Gerald McCann, who was convicted in 1992 and did time on federal fraud charges. And Cardwell was publisher of the outrageous, flamboyant, and often manufactured-out-of-whole-cloth *Urban Times News* newspaper.

Cardwell carried himself as a consultant and "lobbyist" for developers and, indeed, that was the portfolio that yielded him the bulk of the money he flashed around town and in Atlantic City. But "lobbying" and "consulting" don't begin to describe how it was that Cardwell came into his cash and did his business.

Take Roseland Properties, the major real estate firm based in leafy Short Hills, the upscale enclave 12 miles and a world away from downtown Newark. The company had apartments for rent in Jersey City and was getting clobbered in the columns of the *Urban Times News*. Then Roseland started advertising in the paper. Bye-bye bad press.

The same went for Cardwell's clients. If Cardwell was on the team and the clients were current with his fees, you could bank on no problems from the *Urban Times News*. Those who did have problems with the paper were those who either wouldn't hire Cardwell or wouldn't play ball. Or, worse, had a falling-out with Cardwell and his late partner, Bobby Jackson.

One was Alex Booth. The onetime chief attorney at City Hall in Jersey City was a well-liked guy and the brother of Jay Booth, who had been an adviser and confidant to Glenn Cunningham dating to when the mayor was New Jersey's U.S. Marshal. Alex Booth became a target of Cardwell in the earliest days of Cunningham's tenure as mayor of Jersey City. A hold-over in the job of "corporation counsel," Booth had deep support on the city council and among Cunningham's adversaries, and he and the mayor began battling almost as soon as the curtain went up on Cunningham's administration. Soon, Booth was fighting a two-front war, one in the open at City Hall, the other with Cardwell and his organization. It wasn't long before the *Urban Times News* "reported"—without the slightest shred of anything approximating facts—that Booth was related to Abraham Lincoln's assassin, John Wilkes Booth. In a city as racially and ethnically diverse as Jersey City, the specter of connection to the death of the Great Emancipator gave the word "nightmare" new meaning.

Entertaining as that was (for everyone except Alex Booth), it was only an appetizer. As Cunningham's power grew, so did his ambition for more of it. He was sitting in the seat of the legendary Jersey City mayor Frank Hague and believed the office entitled him to the status of undisputed ruler of Hudson County. Traditionally, the mayor was the top official in the county, empowered to control patronage and contracts from tiny East Newark to West New York. But the power dynamic had shifted in Hudson when Republican reformer Bret Schundler took the mantle of mayor for nine years at the same time Robert Janiszewski was consolidating his authority as Hudson County Executive. The county executive spot is bigger and has more official power than mayor of one community, and Bobby J, as Janiszewski was known, put that into practice. Alas, Bobby J went off to jail and Schundler left office, and so Cunningham wanted to be the top dog, believed he should be the top dog, and barked at anyone standing in his way.

The person on the receiving end was Bob Menendez, then still a Democratic congressman. Once locked in a power struggle with Bobby J, Menendez unified his control over Hudson County in the vacuum left by Janiszewski's fall. An impatient competitor, a sharp arguer, and a go-for-the-jugular politician, Menendez always fancied himself capable of becoming a national player and saw in the mirror nothing less than a U.S. Senator-in-waiting. None of his aspirations, however, could be possible if he lost control of his home turf. Control it he did, mainly through the unofficial, backroom work of Scarinci and through the official channels of the Hudson County Democratic Organization.

Menendez found himself standing squarely in the path of Glenn Cunningham's ambitions, and it was not long into Cunningham's term that war between the mayor and the congressman broke out. Cunningham challenged Menendez and his allies for control of the Democratic machine and beat Menendez's handpicked candidate, L. Harvey Smith, for the party's nomination to the state senate. Cunningham also went on television to assail Menendez and Scarinci for trying to put him down and keep him down.

Cunningham's war was Cardwell's war. If Cunningham could take over the Hudson County Democratic operation, a massive budget and fund-raising operation would come along with it, and that could mean millions for Cardwell as paid operative and party consultant. Enter the *Urban Times News*. With reporting techniques that make the *Weekly World News* seem like *The Wall Street Journal,* Cardwell's paper set off to light Menendez on fire. Week in and week out, the congressman was pilloried in print, and for the most part, he and his people dismissed it. That is, until the *Urban Times News* "reported" that Menendez's girlfriend at the time—who had been his aide—was pregnant with Bob's love child and that she and Menendez's ex-wife had had a public argument. Even those closest to Cardwell acknowledged there was not a shred of anything accurate to the story, but it quickly became legend in New Jersey politics.

It addition to the scare tactics used to get advertising and the political score settling, Cardwell's paper also came up with a novel method of securing the lucrative legal notices that pay a lot of the freight at smaller newspapers: run the ads without contract and then charge the government agency after the fact. Repeatedly, the *Urban Times News* copied legal notices from *The Star-Ledger*'s sister paper, the *Jersey Journal,* and then charged Jersey City thousands for the ads. A lot of that money was paid.

Even before he opened the newspaper with his crazy buddy Bobby Jackson, Cardwell was known for his political acumen. As he ran Glenn Cunningham's campaign for Jersey City mayor in 2000 and 2001, Cardwell would routinely meet with a key group of insiders to plot strategy, fund-raising, and tactics every other Sunday evening at Manhattan's ritzy Tribeca Grill. Ironically, Jay Booth was part of the cozy cabal.

"It was a lot of firepower," recalled state senator Ray Lesniak, an adviser to Cunningham and a top-ranked Democratic power broker who has lived more than nine lives in state and national politics. "Even back then, I was taking issue with their lack of record keeping, whether in the campaign, [fund-raising] reports. They were sloppy with requirements. But it was like I was speaking a different language."

That type of record keeping was perfect for Dwek.

* * *

As they sat together in the Jersey City diner, Dwek outlined his phantom luxury condo project on Garfield Avenue and how he wanted to grease the skids to move it along. Khalil suddenly reminded Cardwell that everything at the table was under-the-table. It was hardly necessary.

"All my business is confidential," Cardwell declared, his words picked up by the tiny video camera Dwek was wearing and witnessed by the team of FBI field agents sitting nearby at one of the tables, carrying on a conversation as if oblivious to anything else.

Waldie, Russ, and McCarthy and the other special agents who accompanied Dwek everywhere were never seen, anywhere—even the time that two of them had inadvertently been seated in a restaurant first and found themselves unexpectedly placed adjacent to Dwek and their targets when a hostess slapped down a sheaf of plastic-coated menus at the empty table immediately adjoining theirs. It was not the way the agents liked to operate. They wanted to be close but far enough away to be ignored. The agents, a man and a woman, had to pretend they were husband and wife, quietly talking and laughing to each other as if over some private matter, while their informant played his role, pretending he didn't know them.

Cardwell told Khalil and Dwek that he knew what buttons to push. "You don't need to know how I do something. All you need to know is whether it got done."

Dwek smiled. He told Cardwell he was looking to engage someone who could guarantee that he would obtain permits and approvals from Jersey City.

"I don't guarantee," boasted Cardwell. "I just succeed."

There was a lot of truth in the boast. "Joe is a 'hustler,'" one of his confidants said. "In the best possible sense. He hustles. And it's Hudson County."

Cardwell knew the numbers and the people and he made his calls and contacts as fast and aggressively as he could. If Dwek ordered up permits for Garfield Avenue, then that's the agenda, he said. He would just go and do it. After the meeting with Cardwell, Dwek gave him an initial down payment. Dwek took out a FedEx envelope—the type that by now was an immediate signal to anyone who knew David Esenbach that payday was here. Inside was $10,000 in cash. It was all caught on the surveillance video.

* * *

Two weeks later, Jersey City corruption was in the news, but it had nothing to do with the still-secret sting being run by the FBI. A state grand jury indicted a former Jersey City municipal court chief judge on charges of dismissing eight parking tickets for a female companion and a former court administrator. Both the judge, Wanda Molina, and the administrator, Virginia Pagan, stepped down a year earlier as the investigation widened. More evidence of the state's culture of corruption that continued unabated, even as people were being arrested.

That same day, Dwek, as David Esenbach, and Cardwell were meeting alone to talk at length about the Garfield Avenue project. Dave had big dreams and big financing. The condo development was $180 to $200 million in investment, he claimed. There was an unwritten percentage that developers sometimes set aside to make things go smoothly with officials. With the tape running, Esenbach said he was fine with paying between $200,000 and $300,000 in "up-front" payments to officials to assist in obtaining approvals. Cardwell suggested he talk to Carl Czaplicki, a former chief of staff to Mayor Healy, now running the city's housing and building department—the place you go for construction permits. "Carl is one of my guys," Cardwell claimed. "He's been with me for about nine years."

Dwek was fine with that but wanted to make it clear just whom he wanted to meet. He only wanted to be introduced to government officials willing to take money in exchange for expediting his approvals. Cardwell said he understood.

* * *

Over the next week and a half, Dwek was again playing as Solomon Dwek, continuing to exchange checks and cash with his money launderers.

Kassin was back at his summer residence in Deal, where the Syrian population swells every year from 1,000 to over 6,000 during the months of July and August as families escape the city and move whole households from Brooklyn. Dwek reached the rabbi at his home on Monmouth Drive, about a block and a half from the beach.

"Hi, Schlomo Dwek calling."

"Who?"

"Schlomo Dwek . . . Ummm, I have a check I need to get exchanged. I was wondering if I could come by sometime."

"What is it, a bank check? You want to come today or tomorrow?"

Dwek brought over a $25,000 bank check made out to one of Kassin's charitable organizations. Again, wired, Dwek talked of profits from his knockoff handbag operation. The rabbi took the check and exchanged it for a $22,500 check made out to Friends of Yachave Da'at, a charitable organization operated by Ben Haim.

The same week Dwek met with Altman in Union City and Nahum in Deal. The fictional designer handbag knockoff operation was going very well, Dwek told them. None ever asked to see a sample.

* * *

At the end of July, Dwek and Cardwell again met at a diner in Jersey City and exchanged war stories. Bribes, suggested Cardwell, were just a way of doing business in New Jersey. He recalled one official who had been pressing hard to be paid off. "You have to take care of what you got to take care of," Cardwell reminded Dwek.

Dwek outlined his theory out loud, and for the surveillance tape. Before he developed in a particular town, he wanted to "own" officials in that town. He simply built those "soft costs" into the projects.

It wasn't a lesson Cardwell needed to be taught. "I understand what soft costs are," he said, cutting Dwek off. Then Cardwell got back to Czaplicki. "Carl is a player," Cardwell noted, promising to vouch for Esenbach with Czaplicki.

"Would he be happy with five thousand dollars or ten thousand dollars?" asked Dwek.

"I don't know."

"Tell him that I will do the right thing." Dwek also agreed to match whatever he gave to Czaplicki with a payment to Cardwell. His finder's fee.

Before they set up the Czaplicki meet, Dave Esenbach arranged a casino junket to Atlantic City for Khalil, Cardwell, and Alfonso L. Santoro, the 70-year-old Democratic leader in Ocean County who had come into the group as the latest sting target in the political corruption track of the investigation. Dwek was working him to score some new introductions outside Hudson County.

It was a collegial weekend retreat for the middlemen. For the FBI, it was a key opportunity to cement the trust Cardwell, Khalil, and Santoro had for the informant. Everyone brought along their women, including

Dwek—but the woman who accompanied him was not Pearl. There was not a chance the FBI would send his actual wife on a sting operation, even if she knew what was going on. His spouse for the trip was another FBI undercover agent who called herself Leah—taking the biblical name of another of the mothers of the Jewish people.

Dwek played the role of travel coordinator, acting like he had high-roller business hooks into the Borgata Hotel Casino & Spa, the new, 2,000-room complex with marble bathrooms, huge chandeliers, and gourmet fare by Bobby Flay and Wolfgang Puck. Dwek told the fellows he had already booked "massages for the women for Tuesday morning" at Borgata's renowned spa.

The boys all needed some hand-holding. Khalil wanted Dwek to make reservations for him because he had reached his credit card limit. Then Cardwell called with his own problems. There were no rooms at the high-end hotel. No problem, said Dwek. Ask for a room at the Borgata's Water Club tower, a separate opulent boutique-style hotel with floor-to-ceiling water views, an indoor court of bamboo and palm trees, and a two-story spa with heated massage tables. "Couple of bucks more, but who cares?" he told Cardwell. Dwek was always generous on the FBI's tab.

While the others were at the gaming tables, Dwek sat down with Santoro, who agreed to set up a meeting with Assemblyman Daniel M. Van Pelt, a Republican legislator in Ocean County. Dwek dutifully doled out a cash bonus, handing Santoro $1,500. He said he also had connections with attorney George Gilmore, the chairman of the powerful Ocean County Republican Committee who in November 2009 would run an Election Day operation that would put Chris Christie in the governor's mansion.

The informant separately met with Cardwell at the casino to discuss how to approach Carl Czaplicki, who had power and authority over both the building and planning departments in Jersey City, not to mention his considerable influence everywhere else in the Healy administration. Dwek again reiterated to Cardwell that he was looking for takers. People he could "own."

The meeting with Carl was already scheduled at a pricey Jersey City restaurant later in the day. The plan was that Cardwell would excuse himself from the table to go to the men's room when Esenbach was ready to flash the cash with Czaplicki, but he said that he would first run it all by Carl. "I'm not trying to do anything wrong. Get you to do something that's not right, or illegal," remarked Cardwell.

"I don't want to do anything stupid," replied Dwek, his words still being captured by the HAWK. He told Cardwell he just wanted Czaplicki to help him with approvals. Dwek asked again if Czaplicki would be "insulted or anything" by giving him "ten or twenty."

"No. But I'll test the water first." The real price, Cardwell explained, would actually come due later. If Carl wanted "some help" for the mayor in the upcoming election, then "you have to help the mayor," Cardwell said.

Dwek thanked him, promising to bring two envelopes to the meeting according to the surveillance video. One would be for Cardwell.

Checking out of the Borgata, Dwek drove up from Atlantic City and headed north. It was a day that had been dampish and in the seventies. The meeting with Czaplicki was at the Liberty House Restaurant, a dramatic and expensive setting against the sparkling backdrop of downtown Manhattan, perched at the water's edge in Liberty State Park in Jersey City. Among the featured menu entrées was a pan-fried Parmesan-herb chicken, cedar-planked Tasmanian salmon, and double-cut white marble pork chops with maple-whipped sweet potato. Dwek ordered salad.

Carl had a boyish face, slicked-back hair, and a goofy-looking lopsided grin. Never accused of any criminal wrongdoing, he had parlayed his political connections over the years. He had scored an appointment to the Passaic Valley Sewerage Commission, long a patronage pit where commissioners gave out jobs like candy. His brother was put on the payroll and quickly was given big salary increases as an administrative clerk for the public authority. And after Czaplicki was married in 2003, his new wife was also hired and became the highest-paid account clerk there.

Before Czaplicki arrived at the meet, Cardwell reassured Dwek he had spoken to Carl about the kind of arrangements he was seeking, convincing him that the guy was on board. Amid the bustle of the restaurant, Carl finally walked in and was introduced to David Esenbach.

At first, the meeting seemed to go well. Esenbach talked about the mythical Garfield Avenue project. He spoke again of the need to have access and not be sandbagged in the approval process. Time was money and he was willing to do whatever it took to short-circuit any delay. "I need your help," Dwek told Carl. "I don't want to come in naked." He told Czaplicki that he did not want to get shafted and needed a guy to help him and did not want to be treated like every other developer.

Carl assured Dwek that he would have "access" and that his job was to "smooth" everything "forward" and not let the bureaucracy slow things down. "If I can fast-track matters, then I will," he said. "I only want what's good for Jersey City."

As the meeting wound down, Czaplicki finally got up to leave. Following behind him, Dwek murmured quietly with Cardwell. "Is he cool?"

"Yes."

"Will I be embarrassed?"

"No."

As Dwek caught up with Czaplicki in the parking lot, he told him he had something for him in the car. "I don't do that," said Czaplicki stiffly, before it went any further. "You can deal with Joe." The city official told Dwek there would be events and tickets for the upcoming Healy election. "Joe knows the playing field," he said.

The FedEx envelope stayed in the trunk of Dwek's Lexus. Back inside the restaurant, Cardwell asked Dwek how it went with Czaplicki. "Did he take it?"

"No."

Cardwell tried to brush it off. Carl was just being cautious, he said, but trusted him. "He doesn't know you. I'll handle that. I'll warm him up."

Three days later, the two men met again in Jersey City. Cardwell told Dwek it had all been ironed out. Czaplicki, he said, would help with Dwek's approvals. The money would just have to go through Cardwell.

The FBI had no way of knowing whether this was a scam by Cardwell, or Czaplicki being extra cautious. Dwek had no choice but to give the money to the fixer, who took two envelopes—each containing $10,000 in cash.

"Carl is not a private guy, but I am," said Cardwell. So Czaplicki, he explained, had to be more careful and they had to do things his way. "In his position, he can't be a fool." At the time, the fixer said there was a bright side to all of this. They did not need anyone else in Jersey City government to help with Esenbach's approvals, because there was only one person over Czaplicki. And Cardwell knew how to get there.

Cardwell would later explain that he never intended to take a bribe or pass a bribe. He only took the cash because Esenbach owed him money for the consulting work he was doing.

Czaplicki was never charged with any wrongdoing.

* * *

A week later, political corruption was again on the front page of *The Star-Ledger*, totally unrelated to the sting operation. The FBI raided the law office of Bergen County Democratic Chairman Joseph Ferriero, one of New Jersey's premier political power brokers, seizing and carting off boxes full of documents. Agents also searched the Hackensack law office of Dennis Oury, an attorney for the Bergen County Democratic Organization and a partner in Ferriero's consulting firm, Government Grants LLC. The search warrants sought documents regarding the consulting firm, which holds contracts with local governments in North Jersey. Ferriero's attorney, Joseph A. Hayden Jr., told the paper his client cooperated fully with authorities. (More than a year later, Ferriero would be convicted of conspiring to secretly profit from government grants obtained by the consulting firm on behalf of towns where he exercised political pull. That conviction, though, was thrown into limbo with a U.S. Supreme Court ruling on June 24, 2010, and ultimately vacated in July.)

But the remainder of August was mostly downtime for the political side of the sting operation, as many of the FBI's targets were now gone, headed for Colorado or Minnesota with the start of the national political conventions.

It wasn't until a few days after Labor Day that Cardwell caught up with Dwek again at a Jersey City restaurant. Cardwell reiterated that Czaplicki would "take good care of" Esenbach but told him that Carl still had not taken the $10,000 in cash. He claimed that he wanted Cardwell to use the money to buy tickets for a political fund-raiser for the mayor.

"I explained the whole nine yards to Carl," he told Dwek. "He'll do the right thing."

Cardwell told him not to worry. He would give the money back to Esenbach before he would let him get screwed. This was not going well for prosecutors, and they knew it. They wanted Cardwell and believed he would take them all the way but so far they were out of luck. Still, they had to go along for the ride.

Just before Rosh Hashanah, the Jewish New Year, Cardwell met with Dwek once again and said he had given Czaplicki $2,000 in connection with a political fund-raising event.

"You have to do it in drips," Cardwell explained.

Trouble was a drip like that was simply a legal campaign contribution—or close enough to one that there was no way they were ever going to indict someone over it.

* * *

Not long afterward, Nobile and Howe came knocking on Christie's door. "There's a problem," Nobile told him.

Dwek, it seemed, had come up with a new scam behind their backs. Seeking to cash in on the $50,000 in campaign contributions that he had helped raise for President Bush, Dwek—still a secret federal informant—had approached Republican fund-raiser Larry Bathgate to talk about seeking a presidential pardon on the check-kiting scheme that had brought him here, before Bush left office. Bathgate, Dwek knew, was one of the heaviest of heavy hitters in Republican politics in the country—a former national party finance chairman and confidant to both Pres. George W. Bush and his father. Pardons were not the kind of thing Bathgate did, and he told Dwek he couldn't help him. Bathgate referred him to White House Counsel Fred Fielding.

The conversation rocketed back to the feds.

Dwek had already agreed to plead guilty to the PNC Bank fraud and had been working with the FBI and U.S. Attorney's office for more than a year. Now the son of a bitch wanted a pardon? Christie was flabbergasted and pissed off.

"You've got to be kidding," Christie said angrily to his prosecutors when they told him. It was a little late to be making a Hail Mary pass. (At the end of Bush's term, one of the few pardons the president did grant was to Isaac Toussie, a Brooklyn developer and coincidentally also a member of the Syrian community who was facing prison in a real estate swindle involving shoddy homes sold to inexperienced first-time buyers in poor neighborhoods. The uproar over the action—which came after Toussie's father donated $28,500 to the Republican National Committee—led to the extraordinary step of the pardon being withdrawn within a day of being announced.)

The feds had no idea what the hell Dwek was doing with Bathgate. Was Dwek actually seeking a pardon? That would be bad enough. Or was he trying to set up Bathgate without official clearance, even though the fundraiser had not been implicated in the case? Bathgate was a pillar of New Jersey's public life and a figure who could single-handedly make or break a Republican's chances to win the governorship.

No matter what angle Dwek thought he was playing, Christie just flat out hit the roof. Dwek wasn't just threatening the investigation. He had a signed deal with the U.S. Attorney's office, which had held off prosecuting him. If he hadn't, The Rabbi's Son would very likely already be sitting in a federal prison.

Christie told Nobile and Howe to get hold of Dwek's lawyer immediately. He wanted Himmel reminded—in as many four-letter words as possible—that his guy had entered into a cooperation agreement with the government and couldn't just run around New Jersey talking to just anyone about whatever he wanted.

"Get this guy under control," Christie thundered.

Dwek quickly backed off and never filed the paperwork for a pardon.

* * *

Through the end of 2008 and into 2009, Khalil continued trying to put Dwek in touch with anyone who could possibly be interested and also those who might be in a position to help the developer named David Esenbach win approvals in return for bribes. Khalil was not always successful, especially in the early stages.

One particular swing and a miss disappointing to Dwek's FBI handlers was Mario Drodz. The former mayor and councilman in Belleville, a blue-collar Essex town on the Newark border, wanted to get Dwek in with the elected officials there, surveillance tapes show. But Drodz just couldn't get them on the same page after a badly botched meeting at town hall.

Drodz was operating outside what would become Dwek's core area, but the plays were made during the summer of 2008 and the feds were just as willing to follow Khalil's leads to nearby Essex County. Drodz was advertising that he could help Dwek get quick and easy construction approvals from Mayor Raymond Kimble and his aides. Kimble, once seated opposite Dwek, realized something was wrong—especially as Dwek kept saying he wanted to avoid the normal permit process. Kimble was ticked at Drodz for arranging the meeting and they haven't spoken since.

Later, Dwek explained how it all went wrong in Belleville. "I got a feeling that this mayor guy isn't a player like I like him," Dwek lamented to Edward Cheatam, another Hudson County political operative, on January 27, 2009. "I didn't like what I heard from the guy. He wasn't willing to do anything; he wasn't a player . . . he wasn't the type of person I think was worthwhile."

The FBI was also trying hard to get into Ocean County as a result of the connection Democratic Party leader Al Santoro brought to the case. Late in the afternoon on Monday, October 6, Esenbach gave Santoro a call. "Wondering if you could, I don't know, either reach out to that Van Pelt guy or have George [Gilmore] put a call or something. I want to make a meeting with that Van Pelt guy," he said.

George Gilmore was the unquestioned political overlord in the usually quiet county along the Shore. The chairman of the Ocean County GOP, Gilmore was a lawyer and a player and a critical cog in the wheel of the state's Republican Party—one of the most important and powerful leaders. Only two months earlier, Gilmore had been one of the chief New Jersey delegates to the Republican National Convention in Minnesota, where Christie's brother Todd and best friend, Bill Palatucci, were quietly pushing

Chris' political agenda. By the time 2009 would end, Gilmore would be credited with driving up voter turnout so incredibly that his county handed Christie the victory in the governor's race.

Inside the U.S. Attorney's office, however, the talk wasn't about voter turnout or the convention or the best way to secure continued GOP dominance in Shore communities. The discussion was about bribes and whether Gilmore was on the take. Santoro, the executive director of the barely existent Ocean County Democratic Committee, convinced Dwek—and by extension the FBI—that Gilmore was dirty and that Dwek's alter ego Esenbach would need Gilmore's help if he wanted to develop anything in Ocean.

Keenly aware that Christie came from the tight-knit world of big-money GOP power players, Jimmy Nobile was concerned that Gilmore might be too close to Christie for anyone's comfort. Nobile walked the well-worn path from his office to Christie's on the opposite end of the seventh floor of the federal building in Newark. Nobile closed the door. "Listen, let's talk through recusal," Nobile told Christie. You know Gilmore, you've met with Gilmore, Nobile said to his boss. Was this a problem? Could Christie separate the Gilmore he knew from the man they were seriously thinking of arresting?

Nobile wasn't instructing the boss to get out of the case. He just didn't want to jeopardize either the investigation or Christie by allowing the U.S. Attorney to stay involved if he had a conflict of interest.

Christie never denied his long-standing "acquaintanceship" with Gilmore, as he described it, and he said it was plainly true that the two of them used to have lunch once a year or so to keep in touch. Christie called in Ralph Marra and Michele Brown, and together with Nobile they hashed out the issue. Whether or not to take himself out of a case is a decision made by the U.S. Attorney, and Christie decided his relationship with Gilmore would have no bearing on his judgment. Then Christie said, "If he's taking, take him. I'm in."

At that point in the investigation, Gilmore had become the biggest corruption target on the books. However, Ocean was a dangerous diversion for Solomon Dwek and the FBI. The informant had done real estate business in Ocean too, and the *Asbury Park Press,* which covered his fall from grace, circulated there. Now the feds wanted to put David Esenbach there, in a place where everyone knew him as Solomon.

* * *

After a series of false starts and reschedulings, Dwek and Gilmore met. Gilmore had also reached out to Dan Van Pelt, a member of the state assembly who was in the final months as mayor of the Shore community of Ocean Township. "Listen, Al Santoro has a client who owns property in Waretown," Gilmore told Van Pelt. "They really want to meet with you. I'd really appreciate it."

Young and new to the Assembly, Van Pelt was eager and he was in debt. And after years as a politician and town administrator of nearby Lumberton, he knew how the game worked. The call from Gilmore was not an invitation to a social gathering like some Sunday afternoon of daiquiris. Gilmore was giving him instructions. "Bottom line is: the county chairman calls, you go," Van Pelt recalled later. "I refer to him as Darth Vader. He can have that kind of impact on your career."

The meeting was held at Gilmore's law office in Toms River. "It was obvious to me the goal here was the county chairman, not me," Van Pelt said. Gilmore was the real big fish. Esenbach wanted to explore the idea of high-density construction outside of the so-called town center in Van Pelt's community. The area was zoned for low-density residential, but more important, Van Pelt and Gilmore knew Esenbach could have a problem pursuing the bogus concept he was pushing.

"Doesn't Solomon Dwek own that property?" Van Pelt asked the bearded developer in the yarmulke sitting right there.

"Yeah, that's Solomon Dwek's," Gilmore agreed.

Dwek froze. Then the adrenaline kicked in and his mind moved. He knew that both Van Pelt and Gilmore were aware of the collapse of Dwek's empire, the bankruptcy, the arrest. But it was clear they did not connect with the face. Dave Esenbach blinked and then calmly shut the door, keeping the conversation moving. "No, no, no," he said. "The bank has it."

Gilmore would not meet with Dwek again. The feds never determined whether the Ocean Republican was just too honest or too smart. It didn't matter to them. Gilmore was out and Van Pelt was the target of the moment. Van Pelt met with Dwek over and over going into 2009. They toured the area; they met at restaurants; they spent time together in Atlantic City.

At one point, Van Pelt even brought his wife—a local divorce lawyer and part-time municipal judge—to dinner with Dwek and Santoro at Il Giordano in Toms River. Esenbach began talking about projects in Jersey City—none of which were real. "I went in front of the planning board. Built two thousand units by the Goldman Sachs building across the street. I have two properties, a parking lot and a warehouse. And I want to tear the warehouse down. Put up a thousand units in each one," he said. "One meeting, half hour, I'm in and out of there. It's unheard of. Fifty, fifty-two stories each. Oh yeah, it's great. Redevelopment and all."

It was unheard of because none of it was true.

Van Pelt and his wife owned a mansion way beyond their means. They brought in nearly $250,000 a year, but they liked living at a higher standard, driving Mercedes-Benzes and trying their luck with online casinos. They were $900,000 in the hole when the predator David Esenbach/Solomon Dwek moved in.

He's just another jerk-off developer, Van Pelt thought to himself of Dwek. *Who cares if he keeps saying things like "I'll make it worth your while"? If this were an Italian guy or an African American, I wouldn't bother listening. I'd just get up. But this guy, Esenbach, he's a Syrian Jew. This is how their community works. It's all cash and it's all fast. It'll be fine.*

On February 21, 2009, Van Pelt took $10,000 in cash from Dwek. Van Pelt later would tell the jury it was a consulting fee. On May 19, 2010, a jury called him a liar, convicting him on bribery and extortion charges. It took just 11 hours of deliberations.

* * *

In November 2008, Barack Obama was elected president and the clock began running out on Christie's tenure. The U.S. Attorney was a presidential appointee, nominated by the younger Bush seven years earlier. As with all 93 U.S. attorneys across the country, Christie was expected to step aside with the election of a Democratic president. In a two-page letter to Attorney General Michael Mukasey, Christie tendered his resignation on Monday, November 17. A short time later, he was gone.

It was no secret Christie was already considering a run for governor of New Jersey the following year, but he would not announce his candidacy at the time. "It was time for me to say good-bye," was his only comment as he walked into a Newark restaurant, surrounded by a gaggle of reporters.

Democratic governor Jon Corzine called Christie "a strong contributing actor" in the efforts to rid the state of graft. But Corzine was unwilling to cede all the credit to the prosecutor likely to challenge him in the coming year. "The governor has been clear about the need to confront all of the challenges we face in the ethical environment as it exists in this state," said spokesman Sean Darcy.

No one outside the U.S. Attorney's office had a clue of what was yet to come. Even Christie, who left his job when the number of targets in the

Dwek case was really in its infancy, was unaware of how it would expand exponentially. But with Ralph Marra named acting U.S. Attorney succeeding Christie and Solomon Dwek on the make for bad guys looking to buy into his sting, a tsunami of a case was only months away from crashing into a steamy New Jersey summer.

11

◄┼┼┼►

The Man from Chicago

For months, Dwek had been going up the ladder making political connections. Altman had taken him first to Guarini. Then Guarini, the Jersey City building inspector, brought him Khalil, who was the connection to Cardwell. Finally, Dwek and his FBI handlers hit pay dirt, though they couldn't know it at the time. In December 2008, Khalil introduced Dwek to Ed Cheatam, another low-level Hudson County operator with political hooks.

A retired cop with the Port Authority (the agency that operates the New York and New Jersey tunnels, bridges, and airports), Cheatam had served as vice president of the Jersey City Board of Education and was very close to Democratic state assemblyman L. Harvey Smith. The legislator himself was a major political player: a former council president and leader of his own political faction, who had served briefly as acting mayor. Inside the U.S. Attorney's office, prosecutors could not stop laughing about Cheatam's name.

"Could you imagine this guy goes to trial?" asked one after Eddie first came into the picture. In one of his early meetings with David Esenbach, Cheatam agreed to help the developer nail a contract for tile work with the school board. Another FedEx envelope with $10,000 in cash changed hands. Cheatam thought the delivery method clever. If anyone asked, he explained, he would just claim that he had received plans or an interstate courier package.

"I appreciate it," said Cheatam, taking the envelope. He told Esenbach he could introduce him to "the right people" in Jersey City. Those who could be trusted. People with access. Just the kind of people who would be useful to an outside developer looking to turn a profit in Hudson County.

Cheatam was thinking of Jack Shaw.

* * *

Of all the fixers and middlemen connected to the Dwek case, none would prove more critical or colorful than Jack Shaw. By the time he was arrested, Shaw had fallen off the radar screen so completely that some political insiders expressed surprise that he was still alive. As he sat in the lockup, people said he looked like he might keel over any second. When he walked out that afternoon, reporters and photographers new to New Jersey politics thought he was some second-tier crazy uncle who had gotten caught up in a big game. Only the experts and old-timers recognized the old guy. They knew that Shaw, once upon a time, had been one of the greats.

It was a remarkable fall from where he had once been, from the perch he occupied a generation earlier. At that time, he had been the premier political strategist in New Jersey—the Karl Rove, the James Carville, the David Axelrod of his day.

A raconteur who looked like Santa Claus, or an overgrown leprechaun with his strawberry blond hair and beard, Shaw was a mix of old-school political thug and new-age campaign operative. He loved JFK and was a believer in the science of modern PR and voter-turnout techniques. In his youth, he favored tailor-made suits and shirts, $100 ties, and shoes that were always polished.

When Shaw first met Dwek he explained, on an FBI wiretap, that Jersey made him feel at home. "This is the only place in the country that I have found to be like Cook County . . . Chicago. That's why, that's why I think I get along with people out here." It was the type of line Shaw had used over and over since arriving in Jersey.

Everyone knew he was a Chicago guy. Shaw liked to offer fanciful stories about family wealth that sprang from open-pit coal mines in southern Illinois and to boast he had been the personal assistant to Chicago's legendary mayor, Richard J. Daley. To this day, people refer to Shaw's stories of relations with the Daleys as political science fiction conjured up by a fabulist. Daley's son Bill, who was President Clinton's commerce secretary and is now White House Chief of Staff, said Shaw's name meant nothing to him. He was quick to offer that people were always trying to lasso themselves to Mayor Daley. Truth is there was at least some connection between Daley's crew and Shaw and it was on display in St. Louis in 1975 when, at the Young Democrats national convention, Shaw made it clear to those around him he was getting his marching orders directly from the mayor's gang in Chicago.

Shaw occasionally would drop references to three sisters he talked to, a brother he hated, and a tour in Vietnam that he didn't like to discuss (the National Archives has no record that Shaw ever served in Vietnam or anywhere else). That was about all the personal history he would betray. "You could never get anything out of him about himself," said one of Shaw's friends. You certainly could get nothing out of him about why he left Chicago for New Jersey.

"He bullshitted a lot about what he did in Chicago, how good he was, how close to the Daleys he was. You never really knew if it was true," remembered George Zoffinger, a onetime major Democratic power player in New Jersey who had been close with Shaw. "There was always a lot of bluster, a lot of 'we know how to do things in Chicago.'"

As it turns out, Shaw didn't quite know how to do things in Chicago—at least not well enough to stay out of trouble. By the time he arrived in Trenton and Jersey City, Shaw had already caused and escaped his first scandal, in Cook County. Shaw had been the president of the Young Democrats of Illinois when the group stopped filing financial reports and its records disappeared. The Illinois Board of Elections started investigating. So did the Cook County prosecutor. The cover of the C Section of the *Chicago Tribune* announced on March 21, 1977: "Young Democrats hunt ex-leader, fund records." The story said $50,000 was not accounted for and it was believed that Shaw had mishandled the money.

The tall and husky Shaw surfaced in Jersey in the early eighties with his unfiltered cigarettes (if he was low on cash, he'd buy cut-rate filter butts and tear off the filters), an affinity for collecting military miniatures—historical metal figurine soldiers that he would painstakingly paint and detail with tiny, fine-point red sable brushes—and a level of bluster that gave new meaning to "Windy City."

Shaw was a master of diner politics with nicotine-yellowed fingertips he tried to disguise with manicures, and he immediately merged onto the fast lane in New Jersey. He plied his trade first on the failed Democratic gubernatorial bid of Congressman Bob Roe, then on the U.S. Senate campaign of Barbara Boggs Sigmund (sister of TV news personality Cokie Roberts and daughter of the late House of Representatives majority leader Hale Boggs). Soon Shaw found a winner, signing on with U.S. Sen. Frank Lautenberg and serving as director of his state office—the unofficial political eyes and ears for the wealthy senator whose only political experience was his ability to write checks and spell the word "politics." When Gov. Tom Kean ran for reelection against Essex County Executive Peter Shapiro in 1985, Shaw was working Shapiro's team.

"Jack fit into the mold of one of the classic New Jersey political archetypes," Shapiro remembers. "Jack was the big-city operator. Many people in urban New Jersey politics believe elections are won by putting together the right guys in the diner. Jack's one of those guys." The right union leaders and small-town mayors and political operators and, of course, the activist women who bring out scores of friends eager to stuff envelopes, knock on doors, and cold-call voters.

Shapiro today is a finance whiz who admits he maxes out at one glass of wine and always took off before the real hardball conversations began. Jack, he said, was a big eater and a big drinker. "Chummy and a little scary," he recalled. "Jack was able to promise, to imply, to threaten. He was physically large and the key part of it was he could get things done."

Kean, a blue-blooded Republican who much later garnered international acclaim as leader of the 9/11 Commission, had been elected governor by the slimmest margin in modern history. Four years later, he chalked up reelection by the widest spread ever. Unable to seek a third consecutive term because of state limits, Kean in 1988 was preparing for a future that would make him a college president and elder statesman. The New Jersey governorship tends to switch from Republican to Democrat in eight-year cycles, so it was said to be "inevitable" that Kean's job would go to a Democrat—the very same Democrat Kean had narrowly defeated back in 1981. South Jersey congressman Jim Florio.

Onetime boxer, hard-edged kid from Brooklyn, and a product of the powerful Camden County Democratic machine, Florio always wanted the title of governor. By the time he was preparing to run again, Shaw seemed to have gotten on at the ground floor of a winner. He was Florio's guy and was presumed to be the campaign manager-in-waiting—and potentially chief of staff in the governor's office—as he was overseeing one of those laughably named political front groups set up to allow Florio to campaign for office without officially filing candidacy papers.

The organization was called the Committee for a Safe and Clean America. It might as well have been named the Not-So-Secret PAC Dedicated to Jim Florio's Future. Shaw was seen as the most indispensable player in the effort. Shaw was present in the State House during the odd meetings in 1985 deciding that Shapiro would be the party leader to play the role of sacrificial lamb because it was obvious Kean would win reelection going away. That same year, Shaw plotted Florio's bizarre "I'm-not-running-this-time" speech on the floor of the state assembly, which actually attracted more reporters and guests than the average kickoff rally.

It was Shaw who devised the "air of inevitability" strategy that carried Florio through the campaign. Shaw's point was to make everybody in politics and media believe that Florio had the nomination and the governorship locked up and, by the time anyone realized it, the prize would be Florio's. Seemingly simple now, the strategy was revolutionary at the time. It was based on the circular logic: *you need to support Florio because he is going to win.* And, once he had all that support, *there is no way he could lose.*

"Florio had a lot of confidence in him," recalled Ray Lesniak, whom Florio had named state Democratic chairman and who much later was a key fund-raiser for Bill Clinton and Al Gore. Florio's mantra, Lesniak said, was that the team does whatever Jack says the players should do.

Shaw was the quarterback who called some of the most important plays in the political life of Jim Florio. At the top of that list was Shaw's role in making former state assemblyman Robert Janiszewski the county executive in Hudson County, one of the most influential positions in the state. Janiszewski was plotting a bid to return to Trenton in the hope of restarting his career. But an insurgent effort for Janiszewski would have spelled civil war in Hudson and posed a serious threat to some of Florio's top allies. A fight in Hudson was just unacceptable to Florio. A fractured Democratic landscape in the Democratic county would have added untold complications to the gubernatorial campaign and would have forced Florio to take sides and make enemies when he needed friends more than anything else.

Working 18-hour days, Shaw convinced Florio to barnstorm around the state's smaller and more heavily Republican counties. The candidate and some Democratic Party leaders thought it a waste of time, but Shaw insisted that it would allow Florio to make the relationships that down the road would lead to a steamroller of endorsements from county party chieftains. Shaw said over and over that he couldn't care less that Sussex County in the north and Cape May County in the south couldn't chalk up a dozen Democratic votes between them. Both had Democratic chairmen, he argued. And when it came time to announce who had the most organizational support in a Democratic primary, those chairmen would be worth their weight in gold. Shaw was right.

Shaw also convinced Florio—a divorced workaholic with the image of a "stiff"—to announce his engagement to his then-girlfriend, Lucinda. First, Shaw implored Florio that Lucinda was a political asset as an attractive teacher who was far more palatable than the candidate himself in Republican suburbs such as Morris and Somerset counties. Also, the logic went, someone who's engaged is seen as more romantic and less stiff. Plus, Shaw wanted to use an engagement as a fund-raising opportunity, which is exactly what he did with a huge, high-dollar event thrown to honor the happy couple in Princeton. To the political brain trust around Florio, an engagement was also viewed as the perfect elixir to put an end to rumors of the candidate's womanizing.

More than anything, though, what impressed Jersey political operatives most about Shaw's work for Florio was the organization he put together for the 1988 Democratic National Convention in Atlanta. Michael Dukakis was the party's nominee for president and the White House was open after eight years of Ronald Reagan. But that was just totally beside the point for Shaw and Florio. Every four years, the presidential-nominating conventions serve as the unofficial coming-out parties for New Jersey's gubernatorial candidates, whose campaigns begin right after the presidential voting ends. The state's delegations are basically captive audiences of political opinion leaders, and Shaw made it clear to the Florio operation that it was an opportunity that wouldn't be missed. Shaw arranged for vans to shuttle party leaders and their spouses to the convention hall, to go shopping, to play golf, to find a watering hole. Wherever the hell they wanted to go, Shaw and his Florio gang were glad to do the driving. If a member of the Jersey contingent walked out of the delegation's headquarters at the Embassy Suites Hotel, Shaw or one of his people was at the ready: "And where would you like to go today? No problem, hop in." The destination could have been Mars.

Shaw arranged for every reporter covering the delegation to have private face time with Jim and Lucinda, and he made sure that every delegate's wish was his command. "Today, you'd call it 'networking,'" one Democratic operative said. "He didn't call it that. But that was him. Always relationships. To Jack, you didn't make a phone call if you could meet in person at the diner. And I don't know what he thought about e-mail, but he would've hated e-mail."

All over New Jersey, Shaw was there with Florio at the diners, the ugly backrooms, the shot-and-a-beer taverns. Shaw dealt with the precampaign politics of labor groups. He guided the candidate through the minefield of ethnic communities and regional clashes. "Jack made Florio the candidate in 1989," the operative said. But when it came time to start the final leg of the political marathon—the one in the spotlight of national press and thousand-person rallies—Shaw was mysteriously cast aside.

Three thousand miles away from New Jersey, the phone rang in the London flat once owned by newsman Peter Jennings. The dashing ABC correspondent had sold the place after moving to the New York anchor desk of *World News Tonight*, but the Notting Hill home was still known in the neighborhood as Jennings'. By 1988 it was the property of Shaw's pal, George Zoffinger. The loud, brash bank-turnaround expert always quick to shout "fuck!" who got rich by fixing up troubled lending institutions so they could be sold off, was in England on assignment with the old First Fidelity Bank. He and his small cabal of friends and associates were essentially an adjunct of the Florio campaign.

Zoffinger was unsurprised to hear Florio's voice on the other end of the line. He had just finished firing the top First Fidelity executive in Britain because that guy had been making unsecured loans to the Palestine Liberation Organization (unacceptable with First Fidelity's depositor base in the Jewish bastions of New York, New Jersey, and Philadelphia). There were a couple of quick pleasantries and then the governor-in-waiting got to the point—something he was pretty bad at in person and only marginally more skilled at on the phone. Florio didn't want to talk to Zoffinger. Florio told Zoffinger to get Jack Shaw on the line.

"Jack was going to be campaign manager," Zoffinger later said. "But Florio called and told him he was out. That weekend, Jim announced he was bringing in other people to run the campaign back in Jersey."

To this day, Florio tells people he never fired Shaw. That Shaw quit. Technically, that's true. Florio told Shaw that morning that he would have someone else run the day-to-day and Shaw should continue humping as the key guy in the field. Just without the big title. All the work, none of the glory. Shaw wouldn't stand for it, so he walked.

Shaw cut ties with Florio and split with his friends who stayed with the campaign, though he still managed to show up at odd times during Florio's reelection effort four years later. No one knew what Shaw did or why he was invited to whatever meeting he was sitting at, but that's not all that unusual, really. In big-league New Jersey politics, you don't ask a lot of questions. Election laws require campaign officials to know who's donating, how much, who owns the phones you're talking on, whether the donuts on the table were paid for and, if they were, who paid, how much they cost, and whether they were purchased as part of the primary or general election accounts. But those very same campaign people want to report as little, and know as little, as possible. So no questions.

Shaw's falling-out with Florio was bad for the would-be governor and some of his closest political allies believe he might well have been more successful and won reelection had he kept Shaw on the inside. Worse, the split turned out calamitous for Shaw. Soon afterward, Shaw confided to only those closest to him that he had been diagnosed with spinal cancer in the lower back. He was known for disappearing for days at a shot, and this time he knew he had to have surgery and it would take him out of commission for a while. The word was he was returning to Chicago for an operation. The surgery ended up being done in Houston and then Shaw returned to Jersey in a wheelchair, nearly bedridden for months.

Two years later, Shaw hit Zoffinger up for $8,000 for another medical trip home. The money was never discussed again and certainly never paid back. "He got sick and indicated he had to go back to Chicago for treatment," Zoffinger said. "It was implied it was some kind of cancer. I never called him or bothered him for the money and I thought, frankly, it was gone."

Shaw recovered and slowly began turning up at meetings at the state Democratic headquarters and he hooked on with other top pols. He opened a firm in Jersey City and called it Rifka Consulting. It was a reference to his girlfriend's Hebrew name and was selected so no one would know what his company did or what the name meant. Rifka is the Hebrew name for Rebecca, the biblical mother of Jacob. Among Shaw's most important clients was Joe Doria, the state assembly speaker at the time, who had taken pity on Shaw after Florio cast him off. Shaw grew close to labor leader Edward Pulver and even closer to Bob Janiszewski.

* * *

Bobby J rose to prominence as a political reformer believed to be well on his way to New Jersey's governorship after his short stopover as the Hudson County Executive. He was going to be the man to finally clean up Hudson County and restore its status as the kingmaking center of North Jersey. Janiszewski quickly invited Shaw to join his crew full-time. Shaw was named executive director of the Hudson County Democratic Organization, chaired by Bobby J and the two of them, along with Janiszewski's longtime friend Paul Byrne, began spending their days and nights together. They'd strategize and drink and play the angles. And they would do cocaine, according to friends of both men and federal investigators who had Janiszewski in their sights. There were women. Lots of women. Lots of parties. Plenty of cash to pay for it all.

Tales of their exploits were legion. Development money had started pouring into Jersey City and fat cats from all over wanted to get in good with Bobby J and his team. They seemed to be the best. The parks were getting cleaned up; the potholes were getting fixed; it truly looked like Hudson County was back. And, if the boss and his guys played hard, that was okay because they worked hard. Money was everywhere. Much of it was legal, donated to Janiszewski's campaigns or the county organization or any one of a dozen accounts he controlled. Much of it was illegal: cash that came in big numbers and was quickly hidden or spent on women, booze, or blow.

"Shaw, Janiszewski, and Byrne were stealing hundreds of thousands of dollars," said one person close to the organization.

Shaw was a political man-about-town. He was driving around in his big, well-polished cars (he preferred a Chevy Caprice Classic over a Caddy or a Lincoln), wearing his custom-made suits, and showing his face at all the right places. He would represent Hudson's powerful Democratic organization at events around the state. With Joe Doria running the Assembly, Shaw would travel to Trenton when the Legislature was in session to hold court in the speaker's private office where the state's political glitterati shuttled through as the massive trays of ziti and lasagna were consumed pounds at a time.

Shaw would have liked to have been Florio's guy, to serve as chief of staff, to hold the most important job in New Jersey's State House. But Shaw made it appear he had come to grips with disappointment and seemed to be thriving. Until the classic Jersey double cross. Worried that someone might be on to him and his shenanigans (the graft, the bribery, the criminal excess that would ultimately lead to his own undoing), Bobby J turned on Shaw in 1995, casting him off after accusing Shaw of skimming campaign money. With Byrne always playing the role of Rasputin, Janiszewski and his wife, Beth—who really should have been cast as Lady Macbeth in a modern Shakespeare production—summoned attorney Donald Scarinci to their home.

Then, as now, Bob Menendez's guy, Scarinci was the attorney of record for the Janiszewski political organizations. It was a brief moment of détente between Menendez and Bobby J and it was Scarinci who was responsible for managing the peace. To make it all seem right and proper and official, Bobby and Beth informed Scarinci that Shaw was stealing money and needed to be dealt with as soon as possible. They didn't want any publicity or complaints filed with state election regulators, and certainly they were unenthusiastic about the prospect of Shaw telling the press or anybody else about what had happened.

"It had to be kept very quiet," said one Hudson Democrat involved in the episode.

Scarinci laid it out in cinematic fashion, telling Shaw "we could do this the easy way or the hard way," as the story goes. Shaw could fight back and force Bobby J to fire his ass, risking a formal complaint with state election officials and the Attorney General's office. Or he could just part ways with Janiszewski and he would be allowed to continue working for other pols, keeping his business in Hudson County, and earning a living. It was an easy decision for Shaw.

In time, he would get to see Bobby J go to jail. The Hudson County power broker would go down as one of Jersey's highest-profile political crooks and stoolies, after turning state's evidence and helping the feds reel in other pols while admitting he extorted more than $100,000 in payoffs. Like Solomon Dwek nearly ten years later, Janiszewski turned on anyone he possibly could, and those who escaped still treat the episode as a near-death experience.

* * *

After the Bobby J split, Shaw for the first time began having real financial problems. Bobby had spread the word among political insiders that Shaw was misusing campaign cash, and Shaw's old friend and business associate, Frank Robinson, walked out to go to work for Florio and then Doria. Shaw's firm, Rifka Consulting, soon collapsed.

Coming to Shaw's next rescue was Pulver, the union leader. Shaw and Pulver were self-described animal lovers and took over operations at the Hudson County SPCA shelter in Jersey City. Pulver was officially in charge, but he had Shaw run the place. It was an ill-fated arrangement. Their control ended after the State Commission of Investigation found thousands of dollars from the shelter was diverted and skimmed and the conditions at the facility were nothing short of "inhumane."

The SCI, an agency founded during one of New Jersey's efforts to rid the state of the Mafia, found the animal shelter one of the worst in the state. In a December 2000 report the SCI said the shelter run by Shaw and Pulver was

a dirty facility with a depressing atmosphere where animals were crowded into cages, animals were housed in cages that were too small for them, sick and injured animals were unattended, sick animals were caged with healthy ones, a stench permeated the facility, and the workers appeared disinterested and unknowledgeable about the animals. Animals that were healthy when taken to the shelter quickly became ill, many very seriously. In violation of the mandated seven-day holding period for strays, animals were adopted or euthanized within that period of time . . . When the disposal company arrived each week, the shelter's two freezers were always filled to capacity, with carcasses typically strewn on the floor around the freezers.

Shaw avoided public attention from the SPCA scandal, as Pulver and his brother Frank took the hits in print. The insiders, though, knew it was all Shaw.

By 2005, Shaw had declared bankruptcy. He reported in federal court papers he was into St. Michael's Medical Center in Newark for $76,457, Meadowlands Hospital in Secaucus for $43,055, Christ Hospital in Jersey City for $43,200, his cardiologist for $10,767, and even the Jersey City Medical Center ambulance squad for $624. The bankruptcy was terminated three months after it was filed. Still, he remained a desk reference of health problems. In addition to the cigarettes, drugs, booze, and overindulgence in food—or maybe because of them—there was heart disease, cancer, and diabetes that was so severe his doctor ordered Shaw to have a gastric bypass in 2009 in the hope that less food could keep him alive longer. He always had some sort of ailment to battle and nowhere near enough money to pay the medical bills.

Shaw, though, continued to kick around Jersey City looking for a score. He could be seen hanging out at City Hall, talking about a union he was organizing but never quite got together. He was talking about strategy for campaigns he didn't run. And he was working with the other so-called bedbugs of Hudson County who feed off the system. He prided himself on driving around North Jersey in a 2001 Mercedes E430, but "it was a piece of shit," one confidant said. "He liked to say it was a Mercedes, but it was a fuckin' mess inside. It was disgusting."

Still, the most important thing for a guy like Shaw remained access—or the perception of it—that he could sell to an unwitting whale, a lawyer, a developer, anyone with a loose wallet.

When Dwek was sent by the feds to nail politicians, it was Shaw who provided the most critical entrée to the biggest haul on the corruption side of the Big Sting. He opened door after door in Hudson County and brought down one of his few remaining friends, Corzine cabinet member Joe Doria. It was also Shaw who quickly agreed to roll over on others as soon as FBI agents surprised him and took him to the Meadowlands Sheraton for the application of a little pressure the night before the July takedown.

"Jack Shaw would be a guy who'd roll over," one longtime Hudson operative sighed.

When Shaw found Dwek sitting across from him, it was the perfect opportunity. To Shaw, Dwek was a total patsy. A big, clumsy rich guy with fast lips and an open wallet who wanted access. *Well, well, well, if you want access, I'm the guy for you.*

Shaw was more than happy to turn on the chatter, turn up the bravado, and turn inside out the pant pockets of the developer looking to buy influence. *This is gonna be easy.* Have a few sit-downs with the powerful and connected, make Esenbach think he's really on the inside, and then take his money. No different from the Vegas hooker who gets paid before sex and takes off when the john is in the bathroom.

Little did Shaw know that Dwek was operating the greatest double cross of them all—one that would end with the words "you have the right to remain silent" uttered more than 40 times in one morning.

* * *

A shell of the man he once was, Jack Shaw still had his bravado and his chatter during his first encounter with Dwek on February 17, 2009, talking about Jersey City politics. "For the last four years, I've had a very, very good relationship with the mayor."

"Oh, with, ah, Healy," Dwek replied.

"Healy," repeated Shaw.

As in Jerramiah T. Healy, the chief executive of New Jersey's second-largest city.

"Yeah."

"Matter of fact, I understand you want to see him," Shaw said casually.

Soon after, Shaw, the tired, burly fixer from Chicago—now relegated to baggy shirts and khaki pants—was driving a flashy new Mercedes that made his friends more than just a little suspicious.

12

⊶╉╉⊷

The Stripper, the Mayor, and the Manzo Boys

Jack Shaw took out his cell phone and hit Leona Beldini's number from the contact list. She picked up right away. "You know we have a meeting today, right?" he asked. Jersey City mayor Jerry Healy was going to be there. Shaw didn't know it, but Healy already was one of the big targets in the FBI investigation. Ed Cheatam planned to be there as well.

Shaw would be the key to getting Dwek into Jersey City. He was close to Leona and she was even closer to Healy, giving investigators the opportunity for a clear shot at the top elected official in the state's second-largest city. Beldini confirmed the time but voiced her concerns over Cheatam. She told Shaw that Healy might not be "comfortable talking finances" in front of Cheatam, who she suspected was working for one of the other candidates.

"There are too many snakes around. Do you understand what I'm saying?"

She asked Shaw that again. And then again.

When Shaw first presented himself to Dwek, boasting about his political connections, federal investigators were incredulous. "No one had ever heard of this guy," recollected one. "We didn't realize how plugged in Shaw was."

Then they checked Shaw's history and realized he had real juice. He knew Hudson County. He was very close to Joe Doria, now a member of Corzine's cabinet. And Doria had the ear of Bob Menendez, who had long been the focus of interest by federal investigators, with nothing to show for it. If the feds got to Doria, they all wondered where it could go. At that point, said one of those who worked on the case, every day it was "holy shit, this is huge."

First, however, they had to reel in Leona.

Leona Beldini, 74, was a close friend and right hand to Healy, as well as his campaign treasurer for the upcoming mayoral election. She was well-known in Jersey City, serving without pay on the city's economic development agency while continuing to operate a successful real estate agency in town. She also held a ceremonial job as deputy mayor for Jersey City, which was little more than a $66,154-a-year political plum.

For Beldini, a onetime president of the Rotary Club and a candidate for state assembly, being deputy mayor meant performing weddings and standing in for the mayor at ribbon cuttings or speaking engagements. It was considered a part-time job, but the exposure alone didn't hurt her real estate business. She had no vote on city matters and certainly no real authority. Mostly it made her a woman you'd want to meet, a persona at center stage, and center stage was a place she always liked to be.

With her short hair a muted blond, she favored tailored pants suits, silk scarves, and tinted glasses. She had a reputation as a gracious and shrewd businesswoman who could still be hard as nails during a campaign. Long before all that, however, Beldini had a different life and a far more flamboyant career under a stage name that her agent had pulled out of the New York *Daily News* more than 50 years earlier.

Leona had been known as Hope Diamond, the Gem of the Exotics. As a young, shapely, dark-haired burlesque queen, Beldini had been a stripper through the 1950s and '60s from Buffalo to Boston, getting top billing as a headliner in places such as Union City's old Hudson Theater. She had been hot stuff in her twenties, with elaborate costumes, bedecked with sequins, rhinestones, beads, feathers, and furs. As the band wailed, each piece slowly came off until she shimmied wearing little more than her perfume, which some remembered as "exquisite."

Born in New York and raised near Princeton, Beldini told of growing up poor and leaving home at age 17 to escape an alcoholic mother and abusive stepfather. Leona had joined a chorus line as a teenager out of high school and said she began taking her clothes off onstage because it paid an additional $50 a week.

"She was a big name—very well-known on the circuit," recalled Dixie Evans, who runs the Burlesque Hall of Fame in Las Vegas, where Hope Diamond was inducted in 1995. In one rave review, a critic called her

> . . . an imaginative and resourceful performer, who uses her natural endowments in such a way as to make men's minds embark on journeys into fantasy. Backstage in the basement dressing room, she drew her kimono primly up around her well-shaped throat and discoursed solemnly on her

art. "I take my work very seriously," she said, as she stuck a Band-Aid on her blistered left heel. "And I want you to say that I think there's definitely an art in taking one's clothes off . . ."

While she did not make a big deal about it and seldom talked about her past, it was no secret among those who knew her. Nor was she in any way embarrassed by it. The Hudson Theater, she once told a reporter years ago, "was a wonderful place to be in the fifties. It was a wonderful form of entertainment."

Even today, there are those in Jersey City who remember sneaking as teenagers into the long-shuttered Hudson Theater, hoping to get a furtive glimpse of Hope Diamond. Beldini would talk about it with her own excitement. "At the Hudson Theater, we brought in people from all over New York, North Jersey, South Jersey," she said, long before she had ever heard of David Esenbach. "The limousines would pull up; men in tuxedos, women in evening gowns would get out; the place was always packed." Friday night, she remembered, was a particular madhouse. "It was singles night, oh boy," she said. "The curtain would open, and the whistles and screams would not stop for two hours. It was truly an amazing time . . ."

Beldini finally hung up her tassels and feathered boa and tucked away the cheesecake publicity stills of Hope Diamond—some of which hung in her finished basement. She raised a son and a daughter and began selling real estate in Jersey City and did quite well for herself. Healy, a lawyer and municipal court judge, met Leona when Beldini was a member of the city's rent control board and he served as the board's attorney. Over the years, the two became good friends. There were backyard parties and family get-togethers. When asked if he knew of Hope Diamond, Healy gave the guilty, knowing smile of a 10-year-old boy caught flipping through the pages of *Playboy*. "I had heard the name," he conceded. "She didn't hide it."

Healy owned a summerhouse in Bradley Beach, down the Jersey Shore, just a few miles to the south of Dwek's home in Deal. Beldini would come down with her family on summer weekends, and when Healy's wife heard of a house for sale around the corner she called Leona, who quickly snapped it up. Following his election as Jersey City's mayor, Healy named Beldini deputy mayor in November 2004. She was, as she would sometimes say, the person who "had the mayor's back."

Solomon Dwek did not know anything about her. He did not even have any idea what a deputy mayor did, something he had in common with many developers looking to make a legitimate deal. He just knew Leona was close to Healy and that's where he and the FBI wanted to be. As one defense attorney later described it, "If you were running for office, Mr. Dwek wanted to meet you."

* * *

Jersey City had a history rich in corruption, dating to the days of the old Hague Democratic machine during the early part of the last century. Frank Hague, who became known as The Boss, had been a ward heeler in a town rich with patronage and enriched by a lucrative tax base generated by its heavy industry and the railroads that once ran through it. Those jobs and taxes on railroad-owned property meant money and votes for an entrenched party organization that Hague—a tough Irishman with a sixth-grade education and brooding eyes—eventually came to control with an iron fist. He shook down not only the city's business interests and its political hacks but also those in public jobs who were expected to kick back a percentage of their paychecks every week. One of the most powerful big-city bosses in the country, he was able to sway elections, choose senators and judges, and cement the victories of those he favored for governor. Voter fraud was rife, with the names of the dead never culled from polling lists yet somehow always registering as having voted in the most recent election.

Never convicted of any wrongdoing, Hague, with his shakedowns, was the stuff of legend. People still talk of the custom-built partner's desk in his inner sanctum, with a two-way lap drawer that could be pushed outward like a bank drive-thru window, ostensibly to allow visitors to deposit cash-stuffed envelopes. The desk survives, used for years afterward by the city clerk and now in the office of the corporation counsel, who thought it a neat relic until the events of July 2009.

Hague owned lavish homes in Deal and Palm Beach, Florida, an apartment at the Plaza Hotel in New York, and boasted a lifestyle that included frequent trips to Paris. At the time of his death in 1956, he had an estate estimated at $10 million, despite a public salary that never exceeded $8,500. He was ultimately succeeded by John V. Kenny, a Hague foe, who would also be the focus of corruption allegations that ultimately led to a federal conviction in a multimillion-dollar kickback scheme.

In the second half of the twentieth century, Jersey City lost population, industry, and influence, as well as its perch of power. Still, its leaders continued to attract the attention of federal prosecutors. For good reason. Mayor Thomas Whelan was convicted in 1971 on federal corruption charges involving kickbacks from contractors. Gerald McCann, another mayor, was charged two decades later with federal fraud and tax evasion.

Time, meanwhile, was changing Jersey City once again. The Hudson River waterfront was being quickly gentrified into a new community of back-office financial jobs linked to Wall Street, luxury condominiums, and high-rise office towers. An influx of new immigrants, added to the mix of yuppies from New York, had ended the city's long rule under machine politics, and elections were often a crowded free-for-all with as many as 11 candidates for mayor. Everyone thought they had a shot.

Jerry Healy emerged from the last scrum. The son of Irish emigrants, Healy worked his way through college tending bar. From there, he did a stint as an assistant prosecutor in Hudson County and another as a municipal judge before first running for mayor in 1997. With no candidate reaching a majority, Healy found himself in a runoff election against Republican Bret Schundler, a wealthy social conservative. Healy lost but was elected to the city council four years later. He then defeated 10 others in November 2004 in an election to fill the vacancy left by the death of Cunningham, the city's first African American mayor.

Healy was not corrupt like many of his predecessors but was certainly their equal in terms of color. With a crooked tie, thinning, reddish hair turned gray at the sides, and a perpetually unbuttoned white short-sleeve shirt, Jerry Healy was just a regular, affable guy. He was a blue-collar mayor who liked to drink, a diabetic whose sole concession to his health had apparently been to give up regular beer for lower-calorie Amstel Light, which he imbibed more than frequently.

He also had a tendency for the kind of antics that could lead to embarrassing front-page stories in the *Jersey Journal*. There was a photograph that circulated on the Internet showing him naked and slumped over on his front porch one morning. His campaign manager claimed he had been set up by an opponent, who banged on the door in the early hours and had a camera ready when Healy stumped outside. In fine Jersey fashion, he was elected anyway.

Healy said whatever he felt, and could be very funny. He had once been arrested for violating a noise ordinance—at two in the morning. He once even had set up a town hall–style meeting with constituents in, of all places, a local pub. He got into fistfights, although not in the past 10 years, he claimed. "I am what I am," Healy said, without embarrassment, when asked about such episodes. "I like to eat, drink, sing, dance, and laugh, and I make no apologies for that. That's who I am and everybody knows it."

In 2009, he was again running for mayor, in the upcoming May municipal election against a cast that included former Democratic state assemblyman Louis Manzo, who was making his fifth appearance on the mayoral ballot, and L. Harvey Smith, the state legislator and former acting mayor. Leona was in charge of helping raise cash for the Healy campaign.

As the campaign heated up, Jack Shaw called up Leona and told her he had someone who wanted to express his support for the mayor.

* * *

Sitting in another diner with Jersey City housing commission member Ed Cheatam, Shaw told the man he knew as David Esenbach that he had spoken by phone that day with Leona. "She's in Florida," Jack said of Beldini. But she had agreed to get Mayor Healy together with the developer for a meeting. "She will call up and get a date for us within the next two weeks."

Dwek made sure everyone was on the same page. "You spoke to Ed," he said to Shaw. "You know, I could talk openly and everything, right? Like I talk to him . . ."

"Yeah," Shaw reassured Dwek.

"He vouches for you. He's my brother, you understand?"

Dwek was channeling Donnie Brasco, but Shaw didn't seem to mind, or care. "Yeah, we share," he said.

Cheatam piped in on Shaw's behalf. "Me and Jack run in the same circles," he said.

Shaw just said they would set it up with Healy as soon as possible. "We won't go to his favorite place," he promised. Dwek chuckled, as if he were in on a joke he did not understand, as he continued to record the conversation.

"It is the most uncomfortable, little shitty—," continued Shaw.

"Where, what town?"

"—luncheonette," continued Shaw dismissively. "In Jersey City. On the corner of Montgomery and Baldwin. Right across from the Beacon."

The Beacon was a huge, imposing condominium complex developed from the historic old Art Deco buildings that once served as the Jersey City Medical Center. With marble walls, terrazzo floors, etched glass, Egyptian-styled relief carvings, and decorative ornamentation, the hospital had stood on the hill in the center of the city as a grandiose monument to Boss Hague, who built it with millions of New Deal cash during the Great Depression. Overbuilt and overstaffed, the hospital went into decline with the rest of the city. The medical center itself moved out in 2004 and the complex seemed destined for the wrecking ball, despite its magnificent interiors. But with the growing turnaround of the city around the waterfront, the hospital buildings looked like an opportunity waiting to happen, despite their location in the middle of a neighborhood that nobody could walk alone at night. They were sold off to developers and converted into luxury apartments and lofts, in a gated complex that some of the city's elite now call home. Healy's team was planning a political fund-raiser there soon.

The place Shaw was talking about was across the street from the Beacon—a run-down diner with a name that harkened to the days when ambulances ran by what had once been one of the busiest hospitals in the country. It was called the Medical Center Luncheonette, and there was always a seat there for Jerry Healy. It was where Shaw would introduce him to Esenbach. It was where the end of Healy's political career was going to begin.

"Why does he like it?" Dwek asked about the beaten-down joint. Was the food that good?

"Ah, it's cheap, and he always used to go there," Shaw said. He let Esenbach in on the backstory: "The mayor drinks a little."

"That's good." Dwek brightened. "We'll take him to dinner."

Cheatam just about laughed out loud as Shaw continued his story. Everybody in Jersey City knew about the mayor and his fondness for beer. Three years earlier, Healy's taste for the brew had spilled out—yet again—on the pages of all the newspapers after he was arrested and charged with disorderly conduct and resisting arrest outside a bar owned by his sister near his Bradley Beach shore house. Healy said he was trying to break up a lovers' quarrel, but he wound up pepper-sprayed by the cops, handcuffed, face-down on the sidewalk, and then convicted in municipal court.

When the mayor was home in Jersey City and not at the beach, he had his routine, Shaw said: "When he got through drinking at night, he'd go to the luncheonette and have breakfast and stuff. But it's really a little crampy place. So I'll get him over here."

"So what's the protocol with him, I just talk to him and tell him what I want to do?" wondered Dwek.

"Yeah, just talk," Cheatam agreed.

"Just talk to him what you want to do," agreed Shaw. "Don't mention any money."

"No money."

"We'll deal, we'll deal with—"

"Don't tell him, okay," repeated Dwek.

"Tell him you want to contribute."

Shaw knew there were more ways to pay somebody off than the traditional bag of cash. There were legal ways to do it, in a place where "pay to play" was practically a state motto and certainly a cherished way. Kick in—meaning pay enough in political contributions—and you get to play. Engineering and law firms were big-money players in local elections because professional services and emergency repair work did not come under the state's public bidding statutes, and they were frequently rewarded with fat contracts by those they backed. David Esenbach would not have to do anything under the table, Shaw could only be thinking.

Dwek, though, wasn't looking for legal ways to pass cash. "Okay, yeah, call it what you want, yeah," agreed Dwek. "But he'll help me with my approvals and he, he, he understands . . ."

Cheatam made it simple. The key words were always understood. "Just tell him you're willing to work with him. If he works with you, that's it."

Shaw told Dwek he had a "very good relationship" with Healy and he would set up a meeting for them. He, too, talked of getting Esenbach to the table with Lou Manzo, the other mayoral candidate, as "insurance" in the event that Healy lost the election. At the end of the meeting, Dwek gave Shaw a FedEx envelope with $10,000 in cash. "This is just the beginning," Dwek said. Shaw, thanking him, predicted the two would have a long relationship that was good for both of them.

Cheatam received a $5,000 finder's fee for bringing them together.

* * *

Less than a week later, it was Cheatam playing the role of fixer in a meeting with Dwek and the Manzo brothers. Cheatam had told Esenbach a month earlier that Manzo was important because they had to "cover both sides" in the upcoming election. In the crazy non-partisan elections of Jersey City, where votes were pulled across the ballot by multiple candidates running on no party line, one never knew what could happen. Plus, Esenbach was still dangling big cash finder's fees, so each new intro meant *ka-ching* for Cheatam.

Ronald A. Manzo was a stalwart of Hudson politics and older brother of former assemblyman Lou Manzo, who was running against Healy in the mayoral election. They didn't look it and didn't advertise it, but Ron and Lou were both well off. They had inherited family money that traced to a charter bus company their parents and grandparents owned, and each had invested in the insurance business. Lou always left the money stuff to Ron and the pair has constantly fought over the last decades, but they were as tight as any brothers could be. Ron built their nest egg into a fortune through RAM Insurance Agency ("RAM" stands for "Ronald A. Manzo") and a small battery of related companies run out of an office on the industrial west side of Jersey City.

RAM was a typical operation for North Jersey, catering to a poor clientele and specializing in bargain-basement policies with premiums paid through small cash installments every week or every other week. RAM sold what's known as "street-surance." Unlike some street-surance outfits that defraud their customers, RAM's policies were good and the underwriters paid off, but the business was awash in $10 and $20 bills that could never be traced even if someone wanted to. And no one—outside law enforcement—wanted to.

As RAM grew, the small-time operation began to be supplemented with government contracts, and in New Jersey those deals were tantamount to winning the lottery or getting a license to print money. Government agencies always pay their bills, they always need insurance, and unless there's heat from the press or law enforcement, there's really no reason for officials to watch what a contractor is doing as long as the job appears to get done. There was even less of a reason to ask questions when the contractor was a campaign contributor. As the contributions increased, the desire to ask questions decreased proportionately.

Ron also knew how to keep politicians happy: all-expense-paid trips to the Super Bowl (never reported of course), golf outings, and hours-long parties in the backrooms at the hole-in-the-wall strip joints that dot North Jersey's urban landscape.

Over the years, Ron took his money and used it to become a player in local politics. Often, his goal was assisting his brother, the elected official in the family who started as a county freeholder, moved on to the state assembly, and repeatedly sought the mayor's seat in Jersey City. Just as frequently, Ron's donations were fairly standard investments in the world of pay-to-play politics where contractors donate as much as possible to the pols who hand out the contracts. Once those pols get into office, they make sure the contracts go to their donors on the basis that the spoils go to the victors' friends. Perfectly legitimate. Just like law firms and engineering firms, it's done with insurance brokers. If it can be bought, sold, or invoiced, it can find its way onto the contracts-for-cash merry-go-round. Ron Manzo got to be so good at it and so well-known for his political "generosity" that he was sought after by ever more imposing figures on the political scene.

By the time 2000 and 2001 rolled around and Jim McGreevey looked to be headed toward the Democratic nomination for governor, Ron Manzo was getting in tight with the top officials on McGreevey's campaign—for good reason. Manzo was a key fund-raiser and official member of McGreevey's campaign-finance team during 2001. That wasn't all. Manzo had gotten so close to McGreevey's two top lieutenants, Gary Taffet and

Paul Levinsohn, that when they secretly opened a billboard-development business, Manzo signed one of the hush-hush sham advertising contracts that helped the pair reap a windfall.

Forever known in New Jersey's political lexicon simply as "Billboards," the Taffet-Levinsohn development scheme burst into the headlines early in the McGreevey administration and moved steadily from controversy to all-out scandal as prosecutors in Chris Christie's office investigated and the state's front pages ate up the coverage. The case was equal parts simplistic and impossible to believe. As Taffet and Levinsohn—both eventually lost their jobs because of billboards—were running McGreevey's campaign, they secretly formed a small web of companies with an insurance broker from Philadelphia. Through that, they secured rights to erect massive highway signs around the state and quickly built a sizable inventory. Some of the sites they controlled were barred from having billboards through local ordinances, state restrictions, or landowner opposition. That's where politics came in: few were better connected than Taffet and Levinsohn at the time, so they were in the perfect position to either skirt the rules or talk the right people into going along. It was all worth it financially. Billboards located where they're usually prohibited are much more valuable, so the Taffet-Levinsohn stock of signs was incredibly attractive to the big outdoor-advertising firms that see gold along New Jersey's network of highways.

But Taffet and Levinsohn didn't want to just sell their billboards or the development rights they had secured. They wanted their portfolio to bring in top dollar, and for that they needed to have inked advertising contracts on the sites. To do that, they hit up who else but their political friends, donors, lawyers, firms looking for state contracts or favors from McGreevey. Often, Taffet and Levinsohn made their billboard pitches at the end of McGreevey fund-raising meetings—an obvious offer the fund-raisers couldn't refuse. Manzo was one of those advertisers. In the end, Taffet and Levinsohn cleared millions when they sold the business on the virtual eve of McGreevey's ascension to the governorship.

The feds spent years working the billboard investigation and it did yield huge headlines when McGreevey's onetime patron, former senator John Lynch of New Brunswick, pleaded guilty in an offshoot of the probe in 2006. Taffet and Levinsohn were never charged, even though Christie's prosecutors and the FBI believed their whole package of billboard sales was a fraud built on political corruption.

One of the people who rolled over on Taffet and Levinsohn in the billboard case was Ron Manzo—a fact that was only learned after his deeper ties to Taffet were revealed as his troubles and Taffet's grew. Two months before McGreevey abruptly resigned on August 12, 2004, after getting caught in his lies over his relationship to Golan Cipel, the Israeli he had hired as his homeland security adviser, Manzo pleaded guilty in federal court to five criminal counts stemming from an insider-trading scheme. Manzo admitted receiving inside information from a bond trader, who got it from his wife, a secretary at famed New York law firm Skadden, Arps, Slate, Meagher & Flom. Manzo told the feds he passed on the information to his buddy Taffet and then proceeded to help the Securities and Exchange Commission in their pursuit of Taffet. In the end, Taffet paid a civil fine of $725,000. Ron was sentenced to three years of probation and was ordered to pay a $250,000 fine.

"Ron is what he is," said one political operative who has known the Manzos for more than 20 years. "He's a scorpion. Ron is right up there. These are New Jersey's finest."

* * *

Still on probation from the insider-trading and perjury convictions, Ron Manzo was nonetheless deep in the game in Hudson County in 2009. Again running his brother's campaign, Ron remained Lou's permanent political adviser. Ron was out of the insurance business thanks to his felony stock-trading conviction but still had his old RAM office on West Side Avenue in Jersey City and was now dabbling in real estate.

As the election drew closer, he wanted his younger brother to take a meeting with a developer who had taken an interest in the campaign. The election wasn't the only thing on Ron's mind. He had been trying to unload a piece of property and this developer seemed to have money, didn't appear too discriminating, and wanted to get in good with Lou. His name was David Esenbach.

Through Cheatam, Ron set a meeting with Esenbach for Monday, February 23, 2009. Ron promised to get his brother there. Cheatam, who owed his allegiance to Healy, could not be seen with either Manzo. Retribution in Hudson County is always swift and Cheatam could quickly lose his job in Jersey City if anyone knew he was working for Manzo's side. So the four met at a Perkins Pancake House across the river in Staten Island, just on the other side of the Bayonne Bridge.

"This is a guy I work with," Cheatam said, introducing Esenbach.

Dwek smiled and shook hands. He went into the story of the luxury condo project on Garfield Avenue. As he talked, Lou Manzo was trying to figure out in his mind where it was, but all he could see was the chromium-contaminated site. Manzo knew the city streets and, unlike Healy, was not in favor of bustling development in his town.

"They're cleaning the property up. I have a 'no further action' letter from the DEP," said the developer.

That was enough to immediately tell Lou the guy was a full of crap. A "no further action," or NFA, letter was a written determination by the Department of Environmental Protection that there are no discharged contaminants present at a site or that any environmental hazard has been cleaned up. There was no way Garfield Avenue had been cleaned up. For that matter, Esenbach admitted he didn't even own the property. But Manzo the candidate went into his campaign spiel about affordable housing. He was being attacked by Healy as being antidevelopment and bad for business, but Manzo gave his talk about fast-tracking projects that made sense for the city. Even though Lou figured the frumpy Jewish developer at the table was a fast-talking dolt, he played the role of policy-oriented candidate because, well, there could be some campaign contribution in the offing.

"I've been in four or five campaigns," Lou said later. "You meet people who are just bullshit artists. But I'm hoping he's going to write a check."

Over plates of pancakes, Esenbach told Lou his main interest was getting his "approvals" and not "getting jerked around for three years."

"Well, David is going to be doing some contributions to your campaign," interjected Cheatam.

After breakfast, the Manzos left together while Cheatam and Dwek continued speaking in the restaurant's bathroom. They agreed that they would meet again in the next few days. The plan was to bring $10,000 in cash for Lou, which would be given to him through his brother. Two days later, Ron was back at the same restaurant, this time without his brother. Before Ron arrived, Cheatam told Dwek that the campaign manager was "okay with the cash." But Cheatam said he would act as the intermediary and take the envelope himself.

Dwek went into his normal chatter for the surveillance camera. "I don't want to be treated like every other developer in Jersey City," he said. He did not want officials bothering him. "I'm a member of the Green Party," he told Ron. Dwek dealt in cash. It was a line he would use over and over again that he had thrown in by himself. When that was first heard on a surveillance recording, one assistant U.S. Attorney could not believe his eyes and ears and he summoned Howe and Nobile to watch the video on the computer monitor. "We never told him to say he's a member of the Green Party. That's all him," the assistant U.S. attorney said.

Ron raised no objections but told them to avoid using the word "approvals" with his brother. Instead, Ron said to use the word "opportunities." At the end of the meeting, he watched Cheatam accept an envelope containing approximately ten thousand dollars in cash.

"I'm making an investment in you guys," Dwek said.

"I didn't see anything," Ron joked.

"You don't know nothing," agreed Dwek.

Lou, Ron, and Cheatam did not meet with Dwek again until March 4. To Lou, the second sit-down was going to be more annoying than the first. *I know I have to do a face-to-face with the prospective donor to wow him, and then repeat it to say thank you,* he thought. *But come on already.* "Why are we meeting with this guy again?" Lou complained to Ron. "Did he make a donation?"

Ron strung his little brother along: "Well, he wants to make a donation. He just wants to talk to you about some other stuff."

Fine, Lou figured. *What the hell.*

What Lou didn't know—and would come to find out only after his close encounter with a pair of handcuffs—was that his beloved brother was secretly ruining both of their lives. Ed Cheatam was doing his own development deals with Ron. "My brother was trying to get rid of a parcel, ironically, on Garfield Avenue," Lou explained much later. "He had been trying to get rid of it for two or three years, so Cheatam was shopping it around."

All Ron cared about, Lou said, was "he had somebody to buy the property. That's all he was interested in."

Cheatam stood to make probably $100,000 if it sold for a million. Ron was simply working Dwek to buy the property and believed he finally got somebody to take it. But once again, Dwek and the FBI were running the granddaddy of the cons, plotting to double-cross some of the great double-crossers of New Jersey.

* * *

The big lunch meeting with Esenbach, Beldini, and Mayor Healy was set for Friday, March 13, 2009. Two days before, Shaw, Cheatam, and Dwek had dinner together to finalize strategy at the Chart House at Lincoln Harbor in Weehawken, a waterfront restaurant with expansive views of New York City, specializing in seafood and hot chocolate lava cake. Cheatam liked the food there. As usual, the HAWK was recording everything for the FBI from its perch just below Dwek's chest.

"We're seeing the mayor on Friday," Shaw reminded Esenbach. The instructions were not to talk to Healy about cash. Just tell him about the projects the developer was looking to move forward. "Don't talk about nothing else, right?"

"Nothing else," instructed Cheatam. "We're just taking Healy out and say you're the new developer in town and . . . we need as much help from the city that we can get."

Leona, they explained, would be the transfer point for the cash. Esenbach was having trouble, though, trying to keep everyone in place. "And Leona is on the council? Or she's his right-hand man?" he asked.

"Leona is the deputy mayor," Shaw explained once again.

"Oh, so she's with him," clarified Esenbach.

"Yeah."

"And she operates the way we like to operate? Leona?"

"Yeah," said Shaw, as if he had said it too many times before. Shaw told Esenbach that he and Beldini would sit down over the weekend and talk about contributions to the Healy campaign. "Do you have any idea what you want to contribute?" Shaw asked.

"Oh, I don't care. The money means nothing, as long as he'll help me with my approvals, right?"

"Yeah, he will help you with your approvals."

"Yeah, you know me." Esenbach laughed. "I'm not a big contributor, you know."

At the same time, they were still working Manzo, Shaw reminded him, so they were covered no matter who won. "You got Manzo on one side . . . you got him on the other side," said Shaw. "One of the two are going to win."

"Yeah, I don't care," said Esenbach.

The thing of it was, Shaw noted, "they're both friends . . ."

"Of course," finished Esenbach. "Call it donate; call it whatever you want. As long as he helps me out with what I need, with my high-rises, my approvals, fine. What do you think is a good number to go in for?"

"Right now I'd say ten."

"Start off with ten," repeated Esenbach. "Okay, we'll work it out with her."

The third candidate for mayor, L. Harvey Smith, was also being targeted by the trio, although Dwek could not for the moment recall his first name. "Smith, you're still ah, working with, right? What's his name?"

"Harvey," prompted Cheatam.

"Harvey," repeated Dwek. "I can't remember everybody." He reminded them once more that he was paying for access and there was cash for them for each contact they made for him. "The more guys you got around, bring 'em on, because you know, I'm a generous guy."

* * *

Just before 1:00 P.M. Shaw's cell phone rang. He had a Johnny Cash ring-back tune on the phone that would play for callers before he picked up. It could play for as long as two minutes if he did not answer right away:

Hey, get rhythm when you get the blues . . .

Miles away, Tom Ceccarelli, a retired FBI agent now working as a consultant for the Bureau, monitored the federal wiretap on Shaw's phone. Ceccarelli's job was to determine if a call was germane to the investigation. If it wasn't relevant, he was to stop listening and switch off the recording. But first he had to listen to Johnny Cash as he waited for the call to be answered, and he had heard that song over and over again on perhaps 3,000 calls.

He did not particularly like Johnny Cash.

This time, Shaw picked up relatively quickly.

"Jack?" It was Leona Beldini.

"Yes. How are you?"

Ceccarelli kept the recorder going.

"So, still on for one o'clock, right?"

He confirmed the time, telling her that there would be the three of them coming: David Esenbach, Shaw, and Eddie Cheatam. She stopped Shaw.

"What's the mayor's relationship with Eddie now?" she asked. In the tight world of Jersey City municipal politics, everyone always kept score and knew who was on what team. Cheatam had been playing for the other side, and Beldini was hesitant about having him anywhere near the mayor in a discussion over campaign contributions.

"He's raising money for the mayor," insisted Shaw. "I think he's been trying to talk to the mayor. But he is supporting the mayor. He's helping me with raising money."

Beldini sounded dubious. "Why is Eddie coming?" she asked again.

"Because he works for David."

"He works for him? What does he do for him?"

"He's a real estate guy. He's not a Realtor. He just finds real estate opportunities for David. He works on a monthly fee."

Beldini was still uncomfortable. "Okay, yeah, 'cause my only question is that I didn't tell the mayor. I said it was you, this other fellow, Jewish fellow from New York, and myself. And I don't want him to think that I'm pulling one over and bringing somebody else."

"Eddie is a hundred percent with him. He just works for David."

She persisted as she drove, muttering out loud as another car made the wrong turn up a one-way street, "You understand what I'm saying though?"

"I understand and I'll take care of it."

* * *

About an hour later, Dwek walked into the luncheonette where Shaw and Beldini were already waiting. Cheatam had been instructed to keep out of the picture at first, agreeing to pop in only later, after the mayor arrived, to ease Leona's concerns. Shaw made the introductions to Beldini as a waitress hustled over.

"You got some hot tea, maybe decaf tea or something?" asked Dwek.

"Decaffeinated? Lemon?"

"Lemon, yeah please," said Dwek. He looked around. "This is a six-star restaurant we got going here."

"Yeah, this is his favorite place," said Shaw once again.

Beldini nodded. "His favorite place, and they cook special for him. He'll leave a luncheon and not eat and come here."

Shaw hung on to the thread. "I would say well without a doubt the most productive meetings I've had with him—"

"Right here," finished Beldini.

"Right here," agreed Shaw. "Because you go to City Hall, you got fifteen other people they got to be in on the meetings."

The conversation was inane, just like all the hundreds of hours of meetings and phone calls Dwek had participated in since becoming a star informant. They were just going on and on about a place they all agreed was a little shitty hole-in-the-wall where he wouldn't have gone to eat even if it had been blessed by Moses himself, and they wouldn't let it go. As they made small talk, Healy finally popped in. His sport coat was open and tie was undone, hanging around his open shirt like a scarf. The mayor was less interested in meeting Esenbach than he was in getting something to eat. He wanted his lunch. Despite all the talk about what they cooked for him, all he wanted was a bowl of potato salad and an iced tea.

Dwek stood up. "David Esenbach," he said with his hand out.

"David?" asked Healy in his low voice.

"Esenbach. It's a German name." He spelled it out for the mayor.

Shaw quickly got down to business. Esenbach, he told the mayor, had an option on some land and wanted to talk about the mayor's race. "I told him you were the place to put the money," Shaw said.

"I love the city and, ah, you know, I'm from New York and I, you come over here and you're in the city ten minutes," said Esenbach, going into his routine. He knew development from his Ponzi days in Monmouth, so it was second nature to talk about real estate.

"Oh, it's great," agreed the mayor, picking over his lunch and picking up the thread. He knew how to talk up development. "You could hit midtown or downtown Manhattan in a matter of minutes from the city any four PATH stops and ferry stops. You got to go the right hours, though."

As Healy talked, Dwek was transfixed by the mayor. Healy had taken the pepper shaker from across the table and just began dousing the potato salad. The shaking was strong and animated, as if the pepper did not want to come out, and he kept doing it. Shaking. Shaking. Shaking. The shaking went on so long the pepper became a running joke once the video was played in federal court.

"David has an option on the property on Garfield and Caven Point Road," Shaw said.

Dwek piped in. "It's a hedge fund out of Connecticut that controls it; I don't know who the owners on paper are," he said. "With everyone's help, including Jack, we're looking to do like seven fifty."

He was talking 750 luxury condos in a now 25-story building, whose height would continually change throughout the sting. Near a chromium-contaminated waste site off the New Jersey Turnpike. "With everyone's blessing," added Esenbach after a pause.

Healy reached for the pepper again, not looking at Dwek as he stared at the potato salad. Finally he asked the question nobody asked before: "Twenty-five stories there? Is it zoned for that?"

They would work on that, promised Shaw.

"What's the process now?" asked Dwek, laying the groundwork for a payoff offer. The script said he was to complain about the long approval time for a project and then offer something to make it all go faster. "I mean let's say sometime in May or June I'm ready with my plans on Garfield. I need variances and stuff like that how, how does that work in the city?"

Healy was straight with him. "You apply to, show up to the, to the planners, apply to the zoning board of adjustment if you need a variance."

"It's not like a three-year process or something, right?"

"No, ten months," insisted the mayor. "It'll take you ten months."

"Ten months to get my final approval?"

"Yeah, and you know the way to do is there are no secrets. You know you just can't get approved and jam it through . . . The bottom line you know it's gonna be good for the community and good for the city."

Healy would later tell people he thought Esenbach was just strange. He never shut up and what he was selling just didn't add up. "I just wanted to get my lunch done," Healy said.

Dwek went back to his rehearsed speech about being sandbagged on other development projects. "When I was young and naïve, I went into a town they told me I could build a four-hundred-room hotel and then they jerked me around three, four years and I put up a two-point-one-million-dollar deposit and then they approved me for eighty rooms, and I walked away from my money."

"Four hundred rooms?"

"And they approved me for eighty. And they took my blood out. First they told me there was no quorum. Then they told me they don't like the landscaping; then they told me they don't like the lighting; then they told me I needed to put lights on the roof in case of an emergency."

Leona was curious. "Where was that?"

"Not too far from here," said Dwek, making it up as he went along. His cover mixed fact and fiction. His company, he said, was BH Properties, which was actually the front company incorporated years earlier by the FBI for a separate investigation into rigged school-board insurance contracts. He claimed to have 130 LLCs, or limited liability companies, under him, which he did—as Solomon Dwek, and all of them in bankruptcy. He told Beldini he owned about 375 properties across the country, with a lot of them in Florida and the Carolinas, and about thirty parcels in New York City.

The talk briefly broke off as Ed Cheatam walked in and pulled up a chair to join the group at the table.

"Hey, Ed, how are ya?" Leona greeted him.

"Plenty of room," said Dwek, making space so that no one was left out of the video he was shooting. "I'm the only big one around here."

"So did you explain everything to him, Dave?" asked Cheatam.

"No, I'm waiting for you. You're my man."

"Ah, Dave's ready to do some projects in Jersey City."

Healy played by the book. "We have a planning board, a planning department. It's put in a way that's receptive and knows it's important to bring in more development to our city."

"Well, Mayor, we are ready to do some things," Cheatam said, ". . . with your help and your assistance."

"Approvals are the key," said Esenbach.

"Who owns the land now?" the mayor asked.

"It's uh, a hedge fund out of Connecticut that controls it. I don't know the name. I don't know the LLC. You could look that up."

"So you're already hooked into the owner?"

"Yeah. We deal with each other."

Cheatam added that the only issue was to clean up the soil.

"Is the land dirty?" asked Leona.

"Was. It's clean now," assured Cheatam.

Healy had finished his heavily peppered lunch and stood up. "All right, I have to go," he said. "Dave, very nice meeting you. We hope you can be one of the many investors in Jersey City, in our city."

He said his good-byes and Dwek left the table with him to pay for lunch.

"I got it," said Esenbach. "Hopefully many more." He turned toward Cheatam. "Just tell him, you know, I'll help out, you know."

"Thanks, Dave."

Dwek returned to work on Beldini before she also left. "You know, but you can count on me, you know, and my support and stuff."

"Perfect," said Leona. "We'll help each other."

"As long as I don't have no problems with my approvals."

"Well, we should not; if we do everything by the code we never will."

After they left, Dwek got back to business with Jack. "Interesting," Dwek said. "So what's the deal with these guys now? Did you talk to Leona or you're talking to—"

"No, we're gonna meet—I'm going to call her later and then we're probably gonna meet probably tomorrow morning."

"They seem very friendly and very developer friendly and they'll help me on my approvals and that's what counts. I'm not going to have any red tape on some stuff 'cause I really will need them, especially when it comes to zone changes or council support."

Cheatam said they were both watching out for him. "We have all our friends in all the different departments."

Dwek said he liked low-key, under-the-radar guys who operate quietly. "Guys like us," he said.

13

⊷╫╫⊷

March Madness

Each morning in Newark, there was a status discussion among those in Special Prosecutions, who would gather in Jimmy Nobile's office to talk about Mike from Monsey.

There were concerns almost daily about the state of the case. They had already drawn up contingency plans about what would need to happen if they were forced to take the case down immediately. They knew it could be any time, with that possibility growing more and more likely each day. Dwek was meeting new people all the time, playing "Dwek" here and "Esenbach" over there, and working in business and political universes that gave new meaning to the words "it's a small world."

The conversations always opened the same, with Nobile asking bluntly, "Are we still alive?"

In fact, there had been several close calls.

Months earlier, Denis Jaslow, an investigator for the Hudson County Board of Elections and a former corrections officer, had been pulled into Dwek's circle by Khalil in an effort to hook Esenbach up with officials in North Bergen. But Jaslow suddenly became suspicious after a Christmas card he sent to Dwek at the New York address of BH Properties—which was no more than a mail drop for the FBI front company—was returned as undeliverable. Jaslow relayed his dark suspicions to Khalil, who called up Dwek one Tuesday evening in early January.

"I got a phone call from Denis," Khalil told Esenbach. "Doesn't want to do business now with you. Doesn't want to get involved."

Dwek laughed it off. "What's his problem?"

"He said, 'I don't feel comfortable with him. He's wired. He's trying to set me up. He's a federal informer.'"

Dwek was cool on the wiretap, not hesitating for a moment, as he feigned surprise. "A what?!"

"A federal informer."

"I've been developing property for eighteen years," said Dwek evenly. "I mean, what does he want me to do, stop developing?"

Khalil hesitated and said only that Jaslow didn't feel comfortable, but would not immediately get to what had caused him to have second thoughts. Dwek continued to speak calmly, as if talking Khalil down off a ledge. "No one's forcing the guy. If he doesn't want to do anything he doesn't have to," he said. "The guy's a little crazy, I guess."

Khalil finally told him about the Christmas card coming back. "I don't know what that means."

Dwek tried to casually dismiss it. It was just something with the mail, he said. "The post office screwed up. I don't know what that means. He's crazy."

In fact, it had been a mail problem. When Jaslow addressed the envelope, he had put down the wrong floor. On the other end of the line, Khalil finally agreed Jaslow could not possibly be right about Dwek being wired. "I know you're not," he said as the conversation was captured in its entirety by the FBI.

Dwek himself was also jeopardizing the case over and over. He veered so often off the script that to many he was like a loose cannon. At one point, he told Khalil on the phone that he could not make some meeting because he had to go to Boston to meet with ExxonMobil executives. "I'm trying to buy six hundred gas stations," he claimed, playing off recent news reports that the company was selling them. Six hundred gas stations. Roughly 20 percent of the total number of gas stations in a populated highway state like New Jersey. Still, nobody blinked.

At another point he called Khalil one morning to let him know he was not available. "I'm in Florida now," he announced. "I took my jet last night."

There had been nothing on the runway. No Gulfstream IV hangered at Teterboro Airport. Solomon Dwek was still in federal bankruptcy court trying to hold on to his car—which, by the way, was wired for sound by Dwek's good friends at the FBI even as the trustee was attempting to sell it.

In fact, the more the investigation widened, the more the prosecutors seemed willing to take risks. Dwek as Esenbach set up a big dinner one evening with Khalil, Cheatam, and their wives at Ruth's Chris Steak House, another upscale, busy restaurant on the water in Weehawken. It was far from the kind of dark, intimate place one might think a federal informant whose picture had been in the newspapers might feel comfortable doing business. Again, David Esenbach brought his "wife," the agent Khalil knew as Leah but who was really FBI "Undercover Employee 3805." Esenbach had mentioned earlier that his wife was six months pregnant. But she arrived showing no sign of gaining any weight. "She carries small," Dwek quickly explained.

* * *

In Nobile's office, they would get into detailed discussions about problems and game out strategies. They were facing mounting pressure from the federal bankruptcy judge and potential sellers who wanted to go to contract. The feds were committed to not letting Esenbach enter into sales contracts because that would hurt real people. They checked *The Star-Ledger, The New York Times,* and North Jersey papers every day because a single story on the bankruptcy would kill the investigation. They decided that they might be able to survive reports in the small Jersey Shore weeklies or even the *Asbury Park Press* because "Hudson County politicians aren't reading those papers, but the North Jersey press—we knew we were done."

They would also continue to role-play with Solomon to figure out how to take a conversation where they wanted it to go. Everything was rehearsed, despite Dwek's penchant for running wild. In one meeting with Van Pelt, the Republican assemblyman later convicted of taking $10,000 from Dwek, the informant went off on a tangent when he heard the South Jersey politician had kidney problems. "My grandfather had a transplant," Esenbach immediately offered.

"Oh really?"

"Last month. He suffered a long time."

Esenbach began embellishing the story as he went along, improvising a script that had never been written for him: "He's seventy-eight years old. He's going, he's a little crazy. I mean, I like the guy, but he's a little loony. He's seventy-eight years old. He's going three weeks for dialysis. So he goes on the list."

Dwek told Van Pelt that his grandfather went on the list for a kidney transplant, but he short-circuited the process with cash. He bought him a kidney donor. "I said listen, what are you, an idiot? You'll be dead three times before you get a kidney. I said you know, there's ways of doing these things."

Sitting with Van Pelt in Morton's The Steakhouse in Atlantic City, Dwek repeated the very same terms that Levy-Itzhak Rosenbaum put on the table for him in Brooklyn when he began arranging to buy a kidney for his fictitious secretary's imaginary "Uncle Teddy." Dwek did not actually offer the assemblyman a kidney but let him know he could make it happen for $150,000.

"I called him up. I said someone donated a kidney," Esenbach went on. "The donor, you know, the quote-unquote 'donor,' came in. I got a guy in from Israel. We had the surgery last week."

Van Pelt did not bite, but the bizarre story—as crazy as it sounded—had some truth to it. Dwek later testified that his grandfather had indeed purchased a kidney. Solomon, however, said he had not been a party to the transaction.

Meanwhile, it was getting busy out in the field. By March 2009, agents and prosecutors were juggling simultaneous sting operations now involving more than three dozen people and trying to make sure none of them ever crossed paths. During that month alone, Dwek met with his targets at least 26 times. He covered hundreds of miles, shuttling from one secret meeting to another, as the FBI taped every word. It was Jersey City for breakfast. Brooklyn for lunch. Late-afternoon plates of pasta at Casa Dante back in Jersey City and dinner at the Chart House in Weehawken. Dwek talked money laundering with rabbis in synagogues. Bribes for public officials over drinks. And he continually switched identities, often on the same day. One moment he would be Dave Esenbach, madcap real estate developer with money to burn; the next, Schlomo Dwek, real estate mogul trying to pull another fast one. At one point, he called up Khalil. "I've been to Casa Dante too many times for dinner."

He worked at a maddening pace, moving in a web of false identities and fake stories, with meetings lined up like a string of beads—three, sometimes four the same day—involving more cash-filled envelopes and a widening circle of targets who, it seemed, never suspected or second-guessed the outrageous entrepreneur or the easy money. In the mornings before he would set out in his Lexus SUV for the diner of the day and in the evenings before he went to bed, Solomon would work the phone, making one call after another in quick succession, sometimes as Schlomo and two minutes later as Dave. As he disconnected, he would put a coda on each recording.

"The preceding was a consensual call with . . . ," he would dictate, giving the name of the target, the time, the date, and the number at the other end.

* * *

Wednesday, March 4, was a typical day, operating as himself with Mordchai Fish to arrange another cash exchange. It was a cold, windy day, typical of early March in New York, and Dwek was in his car at the corner of Fourteenth Avenue and 39th Street in Borough Park in Brooklyn, on the way to another meet. The HAWK was in place just below his chest and he had his cell phone out, making arrangements for a second team of FBI agents to pick up the surveillance when he arrived. "Are they there?" he asked as he sat behind the wheel, the prearrangements being picked up on the surveillance tape. "If they're there, tell them to be in position in fifteen minutes. As long as there's no traffic, I'll be there in fifteen."

The FBI's routine was to frequently change the chase teams so that nobody "made" the feds. "Dirty it up with the guys if you can," instructed one of the agents over the phone. "Observe as much shit as you can inside. Whatever you can get."

"Just like we did in Williamsburg?"

"I'd tell him it was a hundred, but 'it became fifty because he played with me.' I'd start the meeting like that."

Fish was waiting for him on a street corner as arranged and got into Dwek's Lexus, heading for a grocery store to meet with a couple of guys who had cash in exchange for $50,000 in bank checks Dwek had given Fish earlier. "When we get there, I'll go first," said Fish. "This is just a middleman. The main guy is in Williamsburg. He sends it over here."

"I thought it was Levi from Israel," said Dwek, mostly for the benefit of the FBI agents monitoring the conversation. He had talked a lot about Levi, an Israeli who he was told was a key player in Fish's operation but had yet to meet.

The drop-off had already been arranged by Levi, replied Fish curtly. He didn't say much more. As the Lexus neared Sixteenth Avenue, Fish pointed off to the corner. "It's the grocery store," he told Dwek. They pulled over and got out of the car. They walked in and Fish was handed a white plastic shopping bag as if he had just bought a box of cereal. Fish did not bother opening it as he returned with Dwek to the car and they drove to Congregation Sheves Achim, a small, three-floor tenement-like brick building with air conditioners sticking out of every window, located on a busy street corner a few blocks away and went in. Inside the plastic bag were thick bundles of $100 bills.

Inside Sheves Achim, as the two counted the money, an Israeli came into the room to watch what they were doing. Fish did not pause, nor did he bother introducing the stranger to Dwek, asking only, "How much more *gemoras* are you doing?"

The man laughed at the question, and he introduced himself. "My name is Levi Deutsch," he told Dwek. Here, finally, was the Levi from Israel whom Fish had told him about.

Dwek immediately told Deutsch what he was doing. As always, he had to establish intent so that there would be no mistaking anyone's motives when the case eventually went to court. He was pulling money out of his bankrupt business, right under the nose of the federal trustee and his creditors. There was a lot of cash, he claimed. "A hundred, sometimes two, three hundred a week," he said. It didn't matter what number he pulled out of his head. It was the FBI's money.

Deutsch told Dwek if he was moving that much cash, he should consider joining him as a partner in setting up a charitable organization, through which other people's money could be moved for a fee. "You have people, let's say, who have big checks every day. But I don't deal with people in the street. I just deal with people—big changers. They don't wanna put in all these checks in one."

"They don't want anyone to see what's going on," interjected Dwek. He knew exactly the way it worked. He had been doing it for years at the Deal Yeshiva. But he played the game.

"Yes. But in one account, it's too much money. So we have opened an account, like a charity."

"So it looks good, like a gemach or something?" asked Dwek.

"Yeah. For every check, we take two percent, three percent," Deutsch said. It wasn't illegal in Israel, he claimed, but here he used a charity he had created called Tzedek Levi Yitzak. If they were partners, he said Dwek could use the charity to launder as much money as he wanted.

"What if I put in one million dollars?"

"I could give it back cash to you," said Deutsch confidently. "I have people over here." He also had people with money in Swiss banks.

"You could handle one million dollars a month, no problem?" Dwek asked, sounding surprised.

"Yes." In as little as a week.

Dwek immediately switched gears. He said he was generating a lot of money from the illegal handbag business he had set up. The same story he had used with Kassin about the counterfeit bags. Prada, Gucci, fancy stuff. "They sell for two, three thousand in the store. I make 'em for forty dollars, I sell 'em . . . for two hundred dollars. They're knockoff bags. I have profits."

"If they catch you, you could sit in jail."

That was exactly what Dwek had wanted Deutsch to say. So there was no mistake that everyone knew it was wrong when they saw it played on the video. "And what we're doing with the cash is the same thing here," he told his new friend. "We gotta be careful."

Deutsch encouraged him again to enter into a partnership and talked about the codes they would use on the phone. "Like let's say, when I say I want one hundred thousand dollars, I say 'one cow.'" A cow and a half meant $150,000.

Dwek was going into the dairy business.

* * *

The next day, Thursday, Dave Esenbach was right back to the political corruption business, with three separate meets in New York and New Jersey. There was first a follow-up get-together with Ron Manzo at the same pancake house on the other side of the Bayonne Bridge. Then it was off to Guttenberg, another small Hudson County community along the river, only four blocks wide, directly across from Manhattan's Upper West Side.

Guttenberg had been in the news only a year earlier. Former mayor David Delle Donna and his wife, Anna, had gone to jail after a federal judge declared that the two had put their town up for sale, accepting thousands of dollars in bribes from the owner of a local bar to keep the Alcoholic Beverage Control Board from closing her business. It was another typical Jersey corruption case, which meant there was nothing typical about it. Among the payoffs were cosmetic breast surgery for Anna, a cuddly Yorkshire terrier named Toby, pet insurance for the dog, Macy's gift cards, and more than $10,000 in cash to gamble in Atlantic City.

U.S. District Judge Harold Ackerman sentenced them to four years in prison. He said public corruption was "pervasive" in New Jersey and hoped the sentence would send a message to other politicians. "Public office is a public trust. That's the bottom line. This notion cannot be repeated often enough. It cannot be forgotten," Ackerman declared.

That Thursday's meeting was a quick hit with Vincent Tabbachino, a former Guttenberg councilman and now the owner of a tax preparation business. Tabbachino was in his sixties and had first met Dwek as Esenbach in early February, again through Khalil. "He's a powerful figure. He runs Guttenberg," Khalil had claimed. He also claimed in a taped call that "Uncle Vinnie" was a former NYPD detective and a member of the Gambino crime family.

Tabbachino was no Paulie Walnuts, but at one time had been a Guttenberg cop. Balding and overweight, he had two plastic knees and, instead of a .38-caliber snub-nosed revolver, he carried a broad smile. Yet there was a certain braggadocio to him. He would tell associates, "Nothing gets done in Hudson County without me." Yet he also had a big heart. On Christmas, he would dress up as Santa Claus to entertain kids. A former district governor and active member of UNICO, the Italian-American service organization, Tabbachino was described by others as a jovial type of guy, the type of guy who would lend a helping hand.

Esenbach had gone through the story of the fake handbag business that he had been pitching on the money-laundering side of the case—another dramatic crossover play that could have dire consequences if it went badly. "I've got to get rid of some cash out of the business," he said at the meeting a month earlier.

Vinnie agreed to convert a $50,000 check in exchange for a $5,000 fee. On the surveillance tape, he told Esenbach to make the check out to "Tabbachino Associates" to make it look like a business transaction. Vinnie began paying out the money in increments to avoid the reporting of cash transfers by the bank. It was a money-laundering gimmick called structuring. Tabbacino's cover story would be that the money had been paid in connection with the sale of his mother's house. Vinnie was fighting off a bad cold but had Esenbach come by to pick up a $24,000 installment owed on the transaction. The two discussed using one of Tabbachino's relatives who might be in a position to help Esenbach move his counterfeit handbags.

Then it was off to Jersey City that same day to meet with Mariano Vega, the city council president. Khalil, who was delivering another scalp to Dwek in return for a finder's fee, had again set it up. The location: Casa Dante, the landmark Italian restaurant on Newark Avenue. With a warm interior of dark wainscoting and white tablecloths, it was a place long known for dinner and deals among power brokers and the politically connected. There was little on the menu Dwek would eat—crab cakes, Scungilli Fra Diavlo, Stracciatelle, and Taglio Milanese del Vitello. But food was always just a prop for him, something to pick at while he went through the story line that had been rehearsed with Waldie and the agents over and over again. Even at Casa Dante, which was known as one of the top restaurants in the state, Dave Esenbach paid little attention to what was on the table.

"I never ate," he told people months after it was all over. "I was the cheapest confidential informant the government ever had. I brought Entenmann's cakes with me. Hershey's. Water and fruit platters. They all ate well. They were ordering Chicken Francese, lobster tails. I ate breakfast in the morning and starved all day."

Khalil briefed Esenbach before Vega showed up and described his role on the council. "He's a big boss in Hudson County government," Khalil described Vega.

The arrests began at six in the morning, as federal agents began knocking on forty-four doors in synchronized unison, bringing to light a complex sting operation involving charges of payoffs, political corruption, black market kidneys, and money laundering, in a scheme with international hooks that spanned from the Jersey Shore to Hoboken to Brooklyn. (*Star-Ledger* Photograph © *The Star-Ledger*, Newark)

Solomon Dwek, the Rabbi's Son, in a mug shot the day he was arrested (Photo provided by the Monmouth County Prosecutor's office)

Dwek confers with lawyers in state court in connection with the bank fraud that first jammed him up. (*Star-Ledger* Photograph © *The Star-Ledger*, Newark)

Charles A. Stanziale, Jr., the no-nonsense bankruptcy trustee given the task of sorting out Solomon's complicated Ponzi scheme, even as Dwek was secretly cooperating with the feds. (*Star-Ledger* Photograph © *The Star-Ledger*, Newark)

Chris Christie, now governor of New Jersey, was the U.S. Attorney who gave the go-ahead to launch Dwek in the biggest undercover sting operation in the state's history. "Make it a short leash," he ordered. "Give him six months." (*Star-Ledger* Photograph © *The Star-Ledger*, Newark)

James Nobile, head of special prosecutions in the U.S. Attorney's office. When Dwek first came up on his radar, he cryptically called one of the lawyers tied to the bankruptcy case. "Is this real?" he asked. (*Star-Ledger* Photograph © *The Star-Ledger*, Newark)

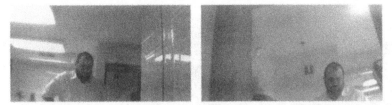

A rare glimpse of Dwek at work. In this never-before-seen photo, Solomon Dwek is captured by his own surveillance camera as he left the men's room of the Meadowlands Plaza Hotel in Secaucus. The video system, called The Hawk, only showed Dwek's point of view as he set up various targets in the long-running federal sting. The only time he appeared on the video himself was when he looked into a mirror. (FBI surveillance video)

Rabbi Eliahu Ben Haim, the principal rabbi at Congregation Ohel Yaacob in Deal and the father-in-law of Dwek's younger brother. He used religious charities to launder at least $1.5 million which he thought had come out of Dwek's bank fraud, an insurance scam, and the sale of knock-off handbags (*Star-Ledger* Photograph © *The Star-Ledger*, Newark)

Rabbi Edmond Nahum, the cantor and rabbi at the Deal Synagogue, where Dwek's father served as principle rabbi. Nahum, according to surveillance tapes, told Dwek to go to Rabbi Saul Kassin. "Kassin is big," Nahum reassured him. (*Star-Ledger* Photograph © *The Star-Ledger*, Newark)

Rabbi Saul Kassin was a revered figure in the Syrian community. The chief rabbi of Sharee Zion, a synagogue located on Ocean Parkway in Brooklyn, Kassin could trace his lineage back to fifteenth-century Spain. "What if someone comes and asks me, 'What's this? This money that you're taking?'" he asked of a check Dwek wanted to exchange. (*Star-Ledger* Photograph © *The Star-Ledger*, Newark)

Shimon Haber, the first target of the sting. Dwek called Shimon, telling him he was looking for development opportunities in Hudson and a way to grease the skids to make it happen. (*Star-Ledger* Photograph © *The Star-Ledger*, Newark)

John Guarini, the key to getting the feds into Hudson County, where thousands of dollars in payoffs would eventually be made by Dwek posing as a crooked developer. A character straight out of a Damon Runyon tale, he always seemed to be working an angle. (*Star-Ledger* Photograph © *The Star-Ledger*, Newark)

Maher A. Khalil, the Jersey City assistant director of health and a member of the zoning board, who came with references. Dwek was told he would "do the right thing" and "get things done." (*Star-Ledger* Photograph © *The Star-Ledger*, Newark)

Jack M. Shaw. Of all of the fixers and middlemen connected to the Jersey Sting, none would prove more critical or colorful than Shaw. (*Star-Ledger* Photograph © *The Star-Ledger*, Newark)

Jersey City Mayor Jerramiah T. Healy was a regular, affable guy who had a tendency for the kind of antics that could lead to embarrassing front-page stories. (*Star-Ledger* Photograph © *The Star-Ledger*, Newark)

Leona Beldini with her lawyer, Brian Neary. Beldini was a close friend and right hand to Healy, and had an earlier life—and a far more flamboyant one—as a burlesque stripper, under a stage name that her agent had pulled out of the New York *Daily News* more than fifty years earlier. (*Star-Ledger* Photograph © *The Star-Ledger*, Newark)

Ed Cheatam (left), walks with his attorney, Alfonso Robinson III. Another low-level Hudson County operative with political hooks, Cheatam had served as vice president of the Jersey City Board of Education. Inside the U.S. Attorney's office, prosecutors could not stop laughing about his name. "Could you imagine this guy goes to trial?" asked one. (*Star-Ledger* Photograph © *The Star-Ledger*, Newark)

Levy-Itzhak Rosenbaum, charged with brokering the sale of black market human kidneys. "I've been doing this a long time," he said. (*Star-Ledger* Photograph © *The Star-Ledger*, Newark)

Levi Deutsch (left), one of the accused money launderers, being escorted from FBI Headquarters. Asked where he got his cash, Deutsch was vague. "Largely diamond business. Other, other things," he said. (*Star-Ledger* Photograph © *The Star-Ledger*, Newark)

U.S. Senator Robert Menendez (left), and Joe Doria, New Jersey's commissioner of community affairs. Doria was targeted by the feds and his home was searched, but he was never charged with any wrongdoing. (*Star-Ledger* Photograph © *The Star-Ledger*, Newark)

President Barack Obama and New Jersey Governor Jon Corzine during a campaign rally for the governor at the PNC Bank Arts Center in Holmdel, just a week before the sting operation was taken down. (*Star-Ledger* Photograph © *The Star-Ledger*, Newark)

Solomon Dwek, with a FedEx envelope stuffed with ten thousand dollars in cash in hand, hooks up with Harvey Smith, Jack Shaw, and Ed Cheatam in the parking lot outside the Malibu Diner in Hoboken. Their meeting was captured by FBI surveillance cameras. "Harvey, I don't want you to call me a cheap skunk anymore," said Dwek, his words captured on tape. (FBI photo provided by U.S. Attorney's office)

One of the most memorable perp walks in New Jersey history. Three mayors, two assemblymen, five Orthodox rabbis. Men and women. Young and old. Some well-known; others a mystery. (*Star-Ledger* Photograph © *The Star-Ledger*, Newark)

Assemblyman Daniel M. Van Pelt leaves federal court. Young and new to the assembly, Van Pelt was eager and he was in debt. (*Star-Ledger* Photograph © *The Star-Ledger*, Newark)

Hoboken Mayor Peter Cammarano. "I could be indicted, and I'm still going to win," he bragged. He served just twenty-three days before he was arrested. (*Star-Ledger* Photograph © *The Star-Ledger*, Newark)

Acting U.S. Attorney Ralph Marra and Weysan Dun, who headed the FBI's Newark Division, at a press conference following the takedown. "For these defendants, corruption was a way of life. They existed in an ethics-free zone," declared Marra. (*Star-Ledger* Photograph © *The Star-Ledger*, Newark)

"Will he take cash?" Esenbach wondered.

No, said Khalil. Vega would be looking for a political contribution in the form of a check. Finally, as the council president arrived, Khalil introduced him as "the most powerful individual in Jersey City." Born in Puerto Rico, Vega was balding, with distinguished silver hair, known for presiding over city council meetings that never seemed to end because of his habit of adding his two cents to every discussion. Khalil told Esenbach Vega was a friend who would be of great assistance on the Garfield Avenue project.

"If I can," agreed Vega. "How can I help?"

Dwek again laid it out for him. He wanted assistance on approvals and did not want to start investing before he knew that he had officials who would assist him. Vega agreed to set up meetings with the director of Jersey City's Housing, Economic Development and Commerce Department. If there were problems, they would resolve them. The council president asked for Esenbach's business card and told him to send a packet of material outlining the proposed project. The talk moved to Vega's reelection campaign in the upcoming May municipal elections. "I'm a generous guy," promised Esenbach, once again.

Vega quickly interjected that he did not want to be involved in any quid pro quo but suggested there were many ways to provide financial support, including contributions to candidates who were political allies. Esenbach told him he did not want to contribute directly but had companies who would contribute. "That's a good way to do it," agreed Vega on the surveillance tape.

"I'll do the right thing," said Esenbach.

* * *

Dwek never stopped talking long enough to listen at any of the meetings. "He sounded like an auctioneer—that kind of quick speaking, telling exactly how it was going to go," complained lawyer Michael Koribanics, who represented one of Dwek's targets in the sting, Guy Catrillo. Koribanics, a former Hudson County assistant prosecutor, complained that Dwek "bulldozed over people, almost like he was naming the terms."

Far more critical was Jersey City criminal defense attorney Peter Willis, who represented Harvey Smith. "He never stops. Never stops. He does the majority of talking," Willis noted. "By his own personality, he is obnoxious. He is pushy. And what's hard to believe is that everybody didn't get up and walk away from the table."

Catrillo was a onetime producer and punk rocker who played guitar for a band called The Bones in the early 1980s. His videos could still be found on YouTube.

He was a senior city planning aide, who also met with Dwek at the urging of Khalil. Catrillo couldn't figure out what Dwek wanted, but Khalil kept bugging him, telling him he wanted Guy to meet his boss. Although Khalil was still on the city payroll, he was spending more and more of his time working for Dwek.

Born and raised in Jersey City, Catrillo, now in his fifties, was very close to Healy. He was also on the ballot for the upcoming municipal elections, running for council in Ward E, the reborn downtown with the entry to the Holland Tunnel and views of Battery Park City in Manhattan. At their first meeting, Dave Esenbach told Catrillo that he was interested in developing real estate in Jersey City and told him about the Garfield Avenue luxury condo project. He thought Esenbach was crazy. Catrillo wondered to himself if this guy had ever gone to this place at night. It was mostly dilapidated lots at night filled with junkies. If he wanted to put in hundreds of luxury apartments, the only place to do it was the waterfront. But Esenbach just kept talking. He said he was looking for officials he could own and who could get him approvals.

They met again on March 16—a cool, dry Monday evening—at the Chart House in Weehawken. On the surveillance tapes, Catrillo, in his soft, earnest voice, told Esenbach that the city council voted on every zoning change.

"That's music to my ears, because I got you opposite me," said Esenbach, who predicted that Catrillo was a shoo-in to be elected to the council, even though Catrillo had virtually no chance against the self-righteous incumbent, Steven Fulop, who acted like he was on a rocket ship to the big leagues.

"But I don't know you," said Catrillo.

"That's right." That's the point, Esenbach said. "That's how we do business. No one knows me. You never saw me. You don't know my name. No trace or nothing, man."

* * *

A day later, Tuesday, March 17, Vega was back on the schedule and asking about the promised plans for Garfield Avenue. "I should have them in about ten days," said Esenbach. Vega noted the state was planning legislation that potentially could assist in defraying some of the infrastructure costs with respect to this kind of development. He told Esenbach most people did not know about the pending change. "You're getting it early, before it got out of the box," he said.

"I'm in good hands," said Dwek.

"Like Allstate," agreed Vega.

Esenbach then gave him a $2,600 check made payable to the election fund of Mariano Vega. The check was later recorded on Vega's campaign finance reports as coming from BH Property Management, 44 Wall Street, New York, N.Y. The same mail drop address Dwek used to establish his bona fides over and over again.

The council president put it in his inside jacket pocket. Dwek then parried with him on the surveillance tape, saying he knew that Vega would help him out and do the right thing. But the council president did not bite. He told the developer that whether or not he helped, he would not string him along. "I know you don't want to be blindsided and have your questions answered up front about what is doable," said Vega. "But I don't want you to think that because you know me, you can fuck the world."

* * *

A few days later, Khalil, Cheatam, Jack Shaw, and Dave Esenbach were together to talk about the ongoing effort with Leona Beldini and Mayor Healy. "So how's my girlfriend Leona doing?" asked Dwek.

"She's doing very good," replied Shaw.

"I thought it was a good meeting on Friday," Dwek said.

"They're very happy."

Dwek was still stuck on the Medical Center Luncheonette, which had not particularly impressed him. "That restaurant's terrific. I'm happy I didn't eat too much food there. I would've been in bed sick, you know."

Shaw said no matter what anyone thought of the hole-in-the-wall diner, it remained the mayor's favorite place. He had known someone who had bought the building across the street from the restaurant, wanting to put in a little Greek take-out joint. Then Shaw's friend applied for the permits to put a handicapped restroom on the first floor and the men's and women's bathrooms down the stairs below. The city inspectors simply refused to okay the plans.

"They go, no, no, no—you can't do that; you got to put all three up on the first floor," said Shaw. "Which is not legally true." The problem was that if his friend did that, there would be no table space for the restaurant. So, said Shaw, he made some calls on behalf of his friend and claimed to have found out the real story. The mayor just didn't want another restaurant taking business from his favorite luncheonette across the street. "So now it's an art gallery."

"Well, listen. That's good," said Esenbach. "He doesn't like competition."

Dwek moved the conversation back to Leona and Healy. What's next? he asked.

Cheatam said Beldini's problem was that she could not take cash.

"I'll do a check or something if she wants to, but the problem is you know the limits," said Esenbach. "I have companies where I'm not a partner. I'm a blind partner, so I mean, how am I gonna do anything significant? Can I give her a check for ten grand from an account?"

"Nah," said Cheatam.

"No," agreed Shaw.

"How do I do that then?"

The way everyone else did, despite some of the strictest campaign finance rules in the country. There were legal limits on how much an individual could give to any candidate. It was a flat $2,600 for the primary campaign and another $2,600 for the general election. But everyone bundled checks. The biggest law firms, engineering companies, and real estate developers in the state could not give any more than the limits proscribed by the New Jersey Election Law Enforcement Commission. However, every lawyer, engineer, and employee of those companies could each give $2,600. It was a way to buy influence without breaking any laws, and every company in the state vying for government business or connections did it. It was done in gubernatorial campaigns and even presidential elections. That's how someone got labeled one of George W. Bush's "Pioneers," by bringing more than $100,000 in donations to the campaign. It's how Chris Christie became U.S. Attorney in the first place and it's just the way the game works.

Shaw laid it out for Esenbach. "It's gotta be broke up," he explained. So if he wanted to give $10,000, he would have to write four checks for $2,500 each from four separate accounts.

Then there was a way to skirt the law entirely. Dwek could give Shaw and Eddie the money and they would take care of it, Shaw said. Left unsaid was that they would find straw donors to give the money to the campaign. Such contributors are donors in name only. They give their own personal checks to a campaign but get reimbursed for it—in this case by Esenbach through Shaw. It's an old-school trick and it's illegal but hard to detect and wouldn't be the first time it happened in a New Jersey election.

"So she'll be okay with that?"

"Yeah," said Shaw. Then, he said, Beldini wanted to talk to him about being the broker on the Garfield Avenue project, as Esenbach had suggested days earlier. If it had been a real project, anyone brokering the sales of the condos would stand to make a whole lot of money.

"She's a very sharp woman," remarked Dwek. "You know I'm sure she can sell those units in a heartbeat. The question is how do I hire her or have her retained without a conflict issue?"

"There is no conflict because it's not a redevelopment zone." (Redevelopment zones are actually managed by the city government, and therefore, city officials have to live by stricter rules on doing business with companies selected to build inside them.)

* * *

To say Maher Khalil was not too keen on Esenbach getting in tighter with Jack Shaw would be a colossal understatement. It was competition for the finder's fees that had been coming to Khalil. Shaw, who was far more connected than he was, could eat his lunch. On Friday just before noon, he was on the phone with the developer. "You're meeting with Jack Shaw? Be careful of him," Khalil warned ominously.

"Who, Jack Shaw?"

"Yeah."

"He's a little sneaky, the guy. Right?" replied Dwek, playing along.

"His word doesn't mean much. He's a shark."

"He's a shark?"

"Be cautious."

Khalil was getting as paranoid as Rabbi Fish. If he wasn't worrying about Shaw, he was getting antsy about getting promoted to a city directorship, which would mean a big jump in pay, under Mayor Healy. Khalil whined about it constantly, and by Sunday afternoon he was back on the phone with Dwek to complain about his bad fortune. "And another thing between you and I," he said. "It seems like I might get fucked out of the directorship with Healy."

"Why? What happened now?"

* * *

The following week established a pattern that made one wonder whether Dwek ever slept. That Monday, he drove again to Casa Dante to meet with Philip J. Kenny, a former operations coordinator for the Hudson County Board of Freeholders. Kenny, who would be elected to the Jersey City Council in May, agreed to take $5,000 in contributions from two straw donors in exchange for helping Dwek obtain development and zoning approvals for a luxury condo project.

Earlier that same day, shortly after 10:00 A.M., FBI agents intercepted a call from Jack Shaw to James P. "Jimmy" King, also a candidate in the May election in Jersey City. According to transcripts, Shaw reminded King they would be meeting Dwek at a restaurant in North Bergen the next day.

"I'd rather just have Esenbach do something, uh, with the, uh, Jimmy—Friends of Jimmy King, with a check or something, and, uh, and I'll talk to you about that," King told Shaw.

"How 'bout green?" asked Jack.

"No, I don't think so. I think I got to talk to you about that privately."

"Well, whatever you do, if he asks you what you need, you need twenty-five hundred dollars—that's the max that David can give you."

"Okay, I will do that," replied King. "I have no problem with that."

"Then we'll work out how we're going to get it to you."

           * * *

The next day, Tuesday, March 24, Stephen Kessler, former chairman of the Ocean Township Sewerage Authority in Monmouth County, was sentenced in U.S. District Court in Newark to a year in federal prison for accepting $15,000 in bribes from one of New Jersey's most prominent engineering firms. Kessler was charged after the second sweeping Bid Rig investigation in Monmouth, headed by Bill Waldie. He admitted that he and former mayor Terry Weldon split kickbacks from the founder of the engineering firm Schoor DePalma, which had been hired to help renovate the township's waste-treatment plant.

In Hudson County, the FBI that day set up multiple meetings in the space of hours for Dwek. He began the day at the Brownstone Diner & Pancake Factory, near the old Jersey City Medical Center. The Brownstone was a longtime favorite of Shaw, who arrived with Eddie Cheatam and Leona.

"So now with Garfield Avenue," Esenbach told Beldini. "I'm gonna have other sites and stuff, obviously across the city. You know Jack and Ed are helping me. I mean, I'm not gonna have any conflict issues, right? With you helping me on voting and stuff like that, right?"

"Voting?" asked Beldini. "No, I'm not a vote."

"She's not a voter," reiterated Cheatam.

"I'm not a vote," she said once again.

It sounded like an old Marx Brothers routine on the tape. Dwek still had not gotten it straight that as a deputy mayor Beldini was in a ceremonial position and had no vote to give on anything. She could pose for pictures and marry people in City Hall. That was about it.

"She doesn't vote on anything," Cheatam explained.

"She cuts the red tape," offered Shaw.

Dwek wasn't put off. He was willing to buy whatever influence he could for the surveillance camera. Leona was still a public official and a way to Healy. "Okay. And other people on the council you'll make sure that they vote positively and stuff like that."

"I can definitely help you get through a lot of red tape," said Leona evenly, sitting to his right.

"I appreciate that."

"But I don't vote."

The talk turned to the upcoming mayoral fund-raiser for Healy at the Beacon complex on the hill. Organized by Beldini and the Jersey City Democratic Committee, it was called Broadway at the Beacon. Tickets were $250, and Beldini wanted Esenbach there and invited his wife as well. He begged off, telling Beldini that Jack and Eddie were the ones who went to the political functions, although he was good for a whole bunch of tickets.

"I don't like going out, you know? I like staying low-key, for good reason," said Esenbach.

"It's on a Saturday night," reminded Shaw, who wasn't a rabbinical scholar but knew enough that the guy in the yarmulke wasn't going to be traveling anywhere on the Sabbath.

"Saturday night, yeah," echoed Cheatam.

"Yeah, right, you don't go out on Saturday night," acknowledged Leona. "And we want people to come. It's gonna be a very elegant affair, so we want people that'll look good."

As she went on about the show and buffet with carving stations and a wine station, Dwek wasn't really interested and tried to steer the conversation back to his main interest. Buying influence.

"Now, you sit on the planning board also or the parking authority?" he asked.

"Parking. I'm the mayor's liaison to the parking authority," said Leona. "I represent the mayor on a few boards."

Okay. He could work with that. "The parking authority, they say also could cause trouble potentially," said Esenbach.

Leona shook her head. "No."

Cheatam corrected him, "No, no, not at all. They don't get involved in the government."

Later slipping into the men's room with Cheatam, Dwek wanted to know how he was doing.

"She's cool with everything, Leona, right?"

"She's cool with everything," agreed Cheatam.

"She doesn't vote on anything?"

"No, she doesn't vote. She sits on all the meetings that she wants to sit in on, okay? She expedites different things, you know? If we run into any problems, then she'll expedite it."

Back in the restaurant, Esenbach told Beldini that she could count on him. He had already given Jack $10,000. "But as the election gets near, I'll give him another ten thousand. You can always count on my support."

"Great, we need it," she said.

He asked about the mayor's campaign fund again and Beldini spelled out the separate accounts geared toward the municipal election. It was a way to evade campaign finance limits. Many candidates set up their own campaign fund and then benefited from separate political action committees that could also accept additional contributions beyond the $2,600 limit. It's another old-school trick. PACs are not allowed to coordinate activities with the campaigns, but policing that is impossible, and Beldini made the intent clear.

"What we're trying to do is to put money into different funds so we can, when we need it, funnel it back into the mayor," she said. "Which everybody does."

The $10,000 Esenbach had given Jack was going to the Jersey City Democratic Committee. He could give separately to Healy for Mayor 2009.

"I think it's a max of twenty-six hundred dollars per person," she explained.

"But we don't have a problem with that." Dave smiled. "I go through them with the cash and then they do whatever they gotta do with it."

"Whatever they have to do, yeah," replied Leona.

"So this ten was for this Democratic thing. I'll do him another ten for Healy, and then—"

"Perfect," she interjected.

"And then you're my person for, obviously, all the real estate."

"Thanks so much," said Leona.

After Beldini left, Cheatam pulled Dwek aside. Ed did not at all like the way the conversation had gone inside. He knew full well what they were doing, but there was no reason for it to be out on the table so openly. That's why he and Jack were there. To act as middlemen and make sure nothing was as blatant as Esenbach was making it.

"You gotta be careful," Ed warned in his low voice. "You got to be very,

very careful. These people—they come back to us and say they don't like talkin' money with you. They don't."

Dwek feigned ignorance. "What's the—I'm generous," he protested. "I want to help them."

"Yes, but help them through us," cautioned Cheatam. Why didn't this guy understand? Maybe they did things differently in New York, but this wasn't the way to do things here. It was the exact same conversation that Shimon Haber had with Dwek in Union City months earlier. Cheatam could not stress enough that he couldn't bring up money to an elected official. "They don't—they can't really talk," he insisted.

"I hear you; I just want to make sure that they're not gonna forget me."

"They know."

* * *

With Beldini gone, the three remained at the Brownstone Diner for the next meeting, Catrillo was on his way and quickly sat down at the table. The video surveillance system was still running, as Garfield Avenue was again put on the table. Catrillo was in campaign mode for the Ward E seat in Jersey City and Cheatam told him that once he was elected, Dave would be looking for his help on development issues.

Catrillo still couldn't figure out what was driving the guy but said he was "pro development" and, if elected, he would look to become the city council's designee on one of the land-use boards. Dave walked him out to the parking lot of the diner and told him he wanted to give him money. Catrillo protested, but Esenbach persisted: "I'm a very generous man."

As they headed to the parking lot, Dwek pulled a FedEx envelope out of his car and gave it to Catrillo. "Tell me you won't forget me. Just say, 'I won't forget you.'"

This guy's a nut, Catrillo was thinking. But he did what he was asked, only later regretting it. "I won't forget you," he replied.

There was $5,000 in cash inside. All of it was captured on tape.

From there, Dwek shifted to the Coach House Diner on Kennedy Boulevard in North Bergen, a popular local diner with dark paneling and a long bar, for the meeting with Jimmy King that had been set up the day before. King was a big guy with steel wire–framed glasses and a shock of white hair, who had the usual Hudson County political credentials. A former councilman's aide and ally of the late mayor Glenn Cunningham, King had enough juice to go on the county payroll at one point as an undersheriff. His ties to Cunningham for a time had also nailed King a $98,000-a-year job as executive director of the Jersey City Parking Authority, where no one who worked for him was allowed to sit on the political sidelines. One former employee hired to perform "community outreach" claimed his hours were cut after he refused to buy a $1,000 ticket to a Cunningham fund-raiser. Others accused him of shaking down employees to pay for a billboard advertising his civic association or threatening some with reassignment if they failed to purchase tickets to political events. King himself was finally ousted after Cunningham's death, and Harvey Smith became acting mayor.

Now King was looking for donations to assist his run for city council in the urban, inland Ward C, a district marked by the Pulaski Skyway and busy Journal Square. He slid into a seat at the diner, where once again the subject was the mythical Garfield Avenue project, now steadily growing in size and scope, even though there were no building plans, site elevations, engineering studies, or a single permit application. This time, Cheatam immediately took the lead before his client opened his big fat mouth. Cheatam explained that Dave Esenbach was a developer who looked for help whenever he went into a new city. Describing the condo project, Cheatam told King they would need zoning changes to make it work.

Despite Cheatam's efforts to take control, Dwek did not wait and quickly moved away from any sense of nuance. "Hopefully I can reciprocate in a small way," he said.

King was cautious. In the wake of his problems at the parking authority, the FBI long before the Dwek operation took shape had come into Jersey City and begun looking over the agency's financial records. No charges were ever brought. "You can always work that out with them guys," King said, gesturing to Shaw and Cheatam.

Before King left, Esenbach spoke privately to the council candidate. "What I wanna do is, maybe, I'll give you five thousand dollars to start." As the election campaign progressed, he would give more and more. "I want a friend on council that will help me when it comes for, uh, votes, zone changes, and junk like that."

After King left, Dwek told the other two what he had promised about the $5,000 payment. To Cheatam, it was like Esenbach had not been listening to a single thing he had impressed upon him. Sure, King and others they were introducing would probably take the cash. "But you have to give it to us and we have to give it to them 'cause they won't touch anything," Cheatam said. His patience was wearing thin.

* * *

The day was not over. Shaw and Cheatam had arranged back-to-back meetings with LaVern Webb-Washington and Lori Serrano, both candidates for the city council who were not likely to win. Esenbach had said he wanted to hedge his bets by covering all sides.

Shaw had reached out to Cheatam on the weekend before, on Saturday morning, remarking how Dave was "planting a lot of seeds" in the upcoming municipal elections, and discussed the timing of Webb-Washington and Serrano. Then on Saturday night after sundown, when they knew Esenbach would mark the end of the Sabbath by turning his phone back on, Cheatam called Dave to talk about other seeds they might sow. "Now, are you interested in Hoboken?" Eddie asked him.

"Hoboken I love!" exclaimed Dwek. "I was going to tell you that when I saw you on Thursday and Friday. I have a property there that someone sent me. It was a large one. I think it's a teardown. I didn't look at it too well because I didn't know anyone in that town and I didn't want to have any problems."

"Hoboken's my town," said Cheatam.

"Your town? That's music to my ears."

Not to be outshone, Khalil, whose competition with Cheatam was getting less than friendly, later shopped his own Hoboken contacts to Dwek. "I have a friend named Russo there . . . he's a councilman; his father used to be the mayor . . . went to jail for taking bribes, shaking down." Michael Russo was a Hoboken councilman and son of disgraced former Hoboken mayor Anthony Russo. The mayor had pleaded guilty in 2004 to taking $5,000 in cash from an accountant in return for city contracts.

"You gotta be smart," said Dwek. "You can't shake down a guy for a couple hundred dollars."

"The kid's a little more mature than his dad," suggested Khalil.

* * *

The meeting with Webb-Washington was a few miles away from North Bergen at the Broadway Diner off West 54th Street in Bayonne, which advertised itself as home to the world's best pancakes. The 60-year-old Webb-Washington was a housing activist and former outreach representative in Glenn Cunningham's state senate office when the then-mayor was also serving as state senator. She was a candidate in the upcoming Jersey City Council election—on the ballot for Ward F, which includes the waterfront Liberty State Park and the small supply bridge to Ellis Island. Shaw and Cheatam introduced Esenbach as a developer with projects in Florida, New York City, and the Carolinas. Still pushing the Garfield Avenue development, Dwek told her flat out he wanted zoning changes to ease the restriction on the number of stories that could be built at the site.

"Density is the key to making money," he said. "I'm looking for your support for zone changes, resolutions, approvals. Stuff like that."

"Oh, definitely," agreed Webb-Washington. "I get that done."

This was getting easier. Dwek had opened a kissing booth at the carnival that is Jersey City politics and they were rushing to line up for smooches. "What I'll do is, I'll give Jack to start, five thousand dollars. As we get closer to the election, we'll meet again," said Esenbach. He told her he would give Jack the envelope but said he didn't want to do it by check ". . . 'cause I don't wanna have any conflicts."

Webb-Washington had absolutely no problem with that. In fact, the clock was ticking. "Can you do it as soon as possible?" she asked.

After she left the diner, they stayed at the same table waiting for the next appointment on their busy dance card. In strolled Serrano, also a candidate for Jersey City Council. Like King, Serrano, 37, had political aspirations that paved the way to a cushy public job in Hudson County for those who picked the right side. The single mother of two who worked for the city's school district, she had once headed the Jersey City Housing Authority before being ousted over claims that she had not completed all of the courses required of public housing commissioners. Close with Lou Manzo, she now was trying to get herself elected to an at-large spot on the Jersey City Council, and Esenbach wanted to help her. Right into a felony.

Again, Cheatam made the introductions, as the tape rolled. "Dave," he said, "is gonna do a development down on Garfield Avenue. He's gonna put some high-rises up, so we're gonna need your support for that once you're on the council."

"Absolutely," said the former housing commissioner.

Esenbach talked about the zoning changes he was looking for to ease the restriction on the number of stories that could be built. "I wanna make sure that once you leave and you're up on the dais . . . you don't forget my name and number . . . I get your vote," he said.

Serrano assured him she would not forget. "I'm not like that," she said. "You can count on me."

Cheatam put nothing out on the table but an offer to contribute to the campaign. "So Lori, we're gonna try to help you out this year," he said. "But the main thing is, when you do get in, don't forget Dave."

"Absolutely," said Lori brightly, as if disbelieving her own good luck.

That wasn't enough to get Dwek what the FBI was looking for. She had to understand he was offering her cash in return for her help after she was elected. "I'll give you, you know, to start, five thousand dollars and then hopefully we'll do more as the campaign progresses," he suggested. "Yeah, as long as I know I got your vote on the council, any zone changes, resolutions . . ." He couldn't be any plainer.

Neither could she. "Right," agreed the strawberry blonde, her words captured on the surveillance video. "You will."

"I don't want to do checks or anything 'cause I don't want any conflicts," he further added, making sure she understood what he was saying. It was important she knew.

That was fine with her. "I know," she told him.

Bingo.

* * *

That evening, Khalil got Dwek on the tapped cell phone. Out of the loop, Khalil knew about the meetings in Jersey City and Bayonne and wanted to know what was going on. Every contact Cheatam made for Esenbach meant that much less money for Khalil. He also needed to tread carefully. If Khalil lost his temper, he could lose thousands, maybe hundreds of thousands, over the course of his dual careers at City Hall and with the developer Esenbach.

"How's Ed Cheatam treating you?" Khalil asked casually.

"Cheatam's good. He's an interesting character, to say the least, but he's a nice guy."

"Don't trust him . . . to be honest with you he's not really in with Healy as much as Jack Shaw." Khalil reminded Dave that Eddie had worked as a Port Authority police officer. "He's a cop, so he's got a cop attitude."

Khalil wouldn't let it drop. In a city swarming with hidden agendas and secret deals, Shaw quickly found out what Khalil was up to. Even past his prime, Shaw was a better, more plugged-in operator than Khalil could be at his best. So the next day, Jack called up Cheatam on his cell phone. Thanks to a federal court order, the feds had already tapped Shaw's line, so the FBI got to listen in. The two swindlers were going to have a problem with the crazy Egyptian. Shaw told Eddie that Maher Khalil had gone straight to Jerry Healy and offered to introduce Dave Esenbach to the mayor.

It could be a comedy. But it was a crisis for the FBI. Federal prosecutors now had sting targets trying to stab each other in the back, in a cutthroat competition over the commissions they hoped to get from Dwek, who was passing around FBI cash and creating a market for corruption. It was like *Glengarry Glen Ross*, with Jack Lemmon and Al Pacino willing to kill each other over a new sales lead. On the set of *The Sopranos*.

Shaw and Cheatam both agreed that Khalil was attempting to impress the mayor to snare the promotion that he continued to obsess over. Cheatam said he had already told Maher he wasn't going to get the directorship under Healy: "I told him that piece has already been given up. I worked it out for Khalil to get it under Manzo, and if Manzo gets in, then that's a different story."

Shaw said he was not so sure that he would give the job to Khalil if Lou Manzo somehow beat Healy in the mayoral race.

Khalil was back on the phone with Dwek later that day. "Ed Cheatam, he's the biggest bullshitter I ever met," Khalil bitched to Dwek.

Dwek, meanwhile, had a new target in his sights. He was looking to get a meeting that would reel in the biggest name yet.

* * *

Joe Doria was the commissioner of the state Department of Community Affairs and had always been close to Shaw. Here was a member of the governor's cabinet and prosecutors wanted desperately for Dwek to talk to him. Now that Dwek was in with Shaw, it was time to try knocking on the door that led to Doria.

"I forgot to ask Jack yesterday," Esenbach said in a call to Cheatam. "Could you ask him to ask Joe Doria if we could meet?" he asked. "I don't know what his schedule is, tomorrow, Friday, Monday, or something. Maybe for lunch or something . . . I have those plans on Bayonne I just want to talk to him about."

Cheatam called him back at seven thirty that evening. "Joe Doria said he can't meet with you this week or next week, so I guess we'll have to wait until you get back," he said. "Jammed up."

14

─◄┼╋┼►─

Hudson County Hardball

"The Senator." Peter Cammarano had already earned his nickname by the time he was in high school. He wore his career goals on his sleeve and seemed to be making all the right moves: college to law school, moving from campaign volunteer to election lawyer and then to council candidate in high-profile, high-octane Hoboken. He worked for one of the state's top law firms and was a protégé to the dean of New Jersey's campaign attorneys, Angelo Genova.

Peter was sure he was headed to the political big time, and to a certain extent, the eventual title was beside the point. "Congressman" was good. "Senator" better. Who knows, maybe even "governor." He was articulate, looked good in a suit, and was incredibly confident. He had the right persona and the right bio, married to another lawyer, father of a young child. Following a hard-fought race in 2005, Cammarano won his first term on the Hoboken council.

Soon after the council election, Genova invited the young associate in for a chat. Angelo had a reputation as an engaging conversationalist and confidant to the politically powerful. In a political universe full of talkers and blowhards, Angelo was also remarkably discreet. One time, he got on the phone with a reporter to offer a no-comment on some political story. When the reporter pressed, Genova asked conspiratorially, "Off-the-record?"

The reporter agreed. Yes. Off-the-record.

"Off-the-record, no comment."

At work—especially in dealing with his subordinate associates—it was all business for Genova. The law firm of Genova, Burns was not a place for friendly chitchat or grand discourses on the meaning of life. Genova himself certainly didn't have the time to ask his lawyers about their dreams and innermost thoughts. So when he called Cammarano into his office, he was not looking to offer a pep talk or pointers for future ordinance proposals. Angelo needed to have a blunt conversation with the man who was the heir apparent to take over Genova's position running the campaign-law practice at the firm.

Where do you see this going? Angelo asked about Peter's politics. He said he had great respect and admiration for people in public office; he had been around them his whole career. But you can't be a lawyer and a politician, said Genova. You have to choose. Council is one thing, but if your plan is to keep going higher, you need to a make a decision.

It was a no-brainer for the ambitious attorney. Voluntarily Cammarano said he would soon be saying good-bye to the fast track in the law and at his tough-to-enter firm. His future was to be a warrior. A political gladiator.

* * *

A lot has been said and written about politics in New Jersey's Hudson County. Blood sport. Hardball. To the death. Hand-to-hand. Not for the faint of heart. The whole gamut. Really, though, one word sums it up: "Armageddon." Every year it's Armageddon. At every level, it's Armageddon. For the school board, for the council, for mayor and Congress, in many ways it looks and sounds like the modern incarnation of the Bible's climactic final battle between good and evil. Politics is a tough business everywhere. And careers can be made or broken with every decision. But in Hudson politics is personal. It is about people's jobs and pensions and it's every day.

Hudson County is broken up into a dozen communities, including some the state's biggest—like Jersey City and Union City. Many parts look and feel like they're straight out of the history of the early twentieth century. Tenement buildings, crowded streets, immigrants of every stripe packed in together in the shadow of the gleaming skyscrapers just a short PATH train ride away in Manhattan. It's a gritty, urban county of newly relocated yuppies looking for a cheaper alternative to New York City who are mingled with off-the-boat Latino immigrants and the bodega and Colt 45 crowds. The homicide and robbery rates are high. Cars are constantly getting stolen or burglarized. The streets can be hard. Like the politics.

More akin to the Commission that oversees New York City's Mafia, or even a low-rent corporate board of directors, the mayors of the 12 Hudson County communities serve as the unofficial council of elders that runs the county's legendary Democratic Party. Boss Hague's Democratic Party. Bobby J's Democratic Party. Despite occasional flare-ups of Republicanism, Hudson is a Democratic county. The Democratic county chairman is often the mayor of Jersey City or selected by the mayor, and there is little in the way of *democracy* underlying the functions of the *Democratic* Party machine. The mayors and chairman decide and it's final. The end. *The governor disagrees? Fuck you! The newspaper questions the propriety? Shove it!* It's how it is and how it's always been.

Over the years, New Jersey and many other states tried to professionalize their government structures by removing some of the patronage and partisan politics. One of the most important efforts on that front was the push decades ago to have officials chosen through non-partisan elections that were supposed to allow the best candidates a chance, regardless of party structure and political bosses. In New Jersey, it was in large measure pitched as an antidote to the one-party rule that bred corruption in places such as Newark and Jersey City. Some communities, like Secaucus, still opted to keep their elections in November with candidates representing the Democratic and Republican parties. But others, like Jersey City, Hoboken, and Union City, embraced the reformist concept of non-partisan elections.

To the insiders, good government—like all things—is best in moderation, and the party bosses in Hudson County and Trenton did not want to open the gates to a total political free-for-all. They came up with the compromise of holding the non-partisan elections in May, making it easier for the organized machines to maintain some level of control amid typically lower turnouts. They figured it was hard enough to get people out to vote in November; no one except those affected most would make it to the polls in the spring when there's no governorship or presidency on the line.

The election dates were rearranged. And the corruption stayed, along with the usual stuff that goes with urban campaigns: stealth wars of rumor and gossip, ethnic battles over turf and who's more black or Puerto Rican, and, of course, the money. Always the money, in ever-growing amounts. There was the obvious money, the cost for producing and airing TV and radio commercials within the most expensive media market in the world, New York City. The cost of brochures, flyers, T-shirts, pollsters, hot dogs, and soda at rallies. And there was the not-so-obvious money. The cash that greases the streets in the days leading up to elections. Street money. And it came in staggering amounts of $10, $20, and $100 bills. *You're knocking on doors, here's your cash. You're taking old ladies to the polls, here's your cash. You're driving a truck pounding out Spanish music and voices imploring people to vote, here's your cash.* The county was littered with the not-so-ancient tales of political operatives holing up for days at a time in their campaign headquarters to make sure that no one came close to the drawers with tens of thousands stuffed inside.

For the benefit of Dwek—and, unwittingly, the FBI—Maher Khalil offered a quick primer on street money during a phone call on May 5, 2009, a week before the municipal elections in Hudson. "If you have a meeting on Tuesday, be careful not to go to the Brownstone," Khalil said of the landmark Jersey City diner. "Everybody's there. And also the feds . . . the state."

Dwek had no idea what he was talking about.

"They go there because election time, that's when everybody's taking. They call it street money."

Long a staple of New Jersey elections, street money flooded the districts on Election Day, especially in urban Hudson County.

One of the by-products of non-partisan spring elections was unpredictability. With no party affiliations, anyone can run as long as they meet the residency and age requirements and produce the minimum number of signatures on a petition. With massive numbers of candidates on the ballot sometimes, elections turn into political roller derby, and winning is tough. Non-partisan elections give victory to the candidate who collects an absolute majority of 50 percent of the vote plus one. Imagine how hard it is to get that when there are a dozen candidates in the field.

Often, the end result is even more craziness than the May election. If no one wins an outright majority, the top two vote getters have the right to compete the following month in a runoff, which can be just as costly and ugly, if not more so. Anyone can win a runoff. Just think: Candidate Smith gets 49 percent of the vote and Candidate Jones gets 15 percent and they're the two top placeholders in the May election. Candidate Smith could very well go into the runoff as the underdog if all the other candidates who lost join forces behind Jones, adding to his original support. Runoffs, therefore, were to be avoided if possible, and that meant raising and spending enough money in the May election to bury the opposition before all hell broke loose.

"Once you're in a runoff, all bets are off," Harold "Bud" Demellier, campaign manager for Jersey City mayor Jerry Healy, candidly told Dwek one day.

It would be in this arena where Dwek would find more targets of opportunity, in far less time, in a feeding frenzy of fund-raising among candidates so desperate for campaign money, in races often decided by a few hundred votes, that many never gave a second thought as to why someone would be so willing to give them an envelope stuffed with $100 bills.

* * *

It was a Saturday night just before 8:00 P.M. in early April when the FBI intercepted a phone call from Jack Shaw to Michael Schaffer. Former Hoboken city councilman, perennial candidate, commissioner on the North Hudson Utilities Authority courtesy of a patronage appointment, Schaffer was just another odd character in a sea of odd characters.

"Did you ever meet Mike Schaffer?" one federal agent asked shortly after the July 23 roundup. "He looks like he just fuckin' woke up behind a bar somewhere. Seriously."

A typical denizen of Hudson County politics, Schaffer had lost his council seat years earlier after his onetime patron, Anthony Russo, was convicted, and he now spent his time just hanging around the game. He was sloppy and never seemed to have anywhere pressing to be. Still, he would don a business suit for no reason some days just to make it seem like he was somebody important going to some critical meeting. He claimed to be a developer and never seemed to be short of cash thanks to money he inherited from his father, who had been a workingman but died leaving a healthy pension after a career at the Port Authority of New York and New Jersey. Schaffer spent most of his adult life saving up what little cash he had by living with his parents until they died, before moving to the posh new Maxwell Place condo complex in Hoboken.

Shaw wanted to talk to Schaffer about the upcoming mayoral elections in Jersey City and Hoboken. He had a guy he wanted Mike to meet, a developer by the name of Dave Esenbach who Shaw said had recently given another official $20,000.

"I know Esenbach will give Cammarano five thousand," predicted Shaw. "We'll probably have to run it through you." The developer was throwing out $5,000 and $10,000 payments to just about anyone running for election in Hudson County, said Jack in wonder. "Cheatam finally found a guy with money."

Schaffer had gotten in with Cammarano early. The professionals and elected officials around Cammarano couldn't figure out the connection or even what he was doing there. Schaffer was always in headquarters, hanging out, talking with the staff, waiting for Cammarano to show up.

Actually, it was a symbiotic relationship. Cammarano wanted the money Schaffer was connected to and Schaffer wanted the reflected glory. One night, after a particularly important political event, Cammarano took off at 11:30 P.M., telling his staff he had to go see Schaffer. They were flabbergasted. *You can't go see him in the morning?*

Cammarano was always late for everything. He didn't focus on anything, didn't take campaigning or fund-raising seriously, and did all the backslapping—yet didn't put in the work, said one Cammarano intimate. "But when Schaffer walked into headquarters, that was it. He'd go right to Cammarano in the back and the two of them would walk out without saying a word."

Shaw arranged to meet with Schaffer and Cammarano at the Malibu Diner in Hoboken in two weeks. The evening before, they connected to confirm the time and date. "We're gonna try to get this kid some money tomorrow," said Jack.

* * *

In a state where shooting political stars have crashed and burned in record time, Cammarano gave off the distinct whiff of another good-looking, hard-charging, well-spoken young man in a hurry. He seemed like a real up-and-comer. His connection to Genova was huge in a universe where Angelo was considered the best of the best, a patriarch of campaign-finance work, labor counsel to governor after governor, and a regular on the PR-essential lists of top lawyers in the state. Peter also made the right moves himself, becoming a fellow at the renowned Leadership New Jersey program and making a point of introducing himself to the top pols and political reporters in the state.

"He had a lot of gifts," said Tom DeGise, the Hudson County Executive and a veteran of the hardest of hard-core Hudson County political skirmishes. "Peter could speak. He really liked the arena of politics."

But he made it seem he was not just a young version of the old-school bosses. He was the new face of the new Hoboken. He wanted to become the first mayor to have been raised outside the Mile Square City, and he was the first mayor to build a coalition of old-time ethnic Hoboken and new-era single, professional, making-the-scene Hoboken.

Behind his back, Peter was constantly being compared to former governor Jim McGreevey. It was only a partial compliment. McGreevey was skilled at the game and he knew how to make things happen. "Peter knew to get higher he would have to have some accomplishments to run on," said one of his confidants. Cammarano pushed his fellow council members to give him the center spot on the council dais so he would get more camera time. He could out-argue, out-articulate the others, and he religiously pored over videos of council meetings to improve his performance.

McGreevey, though, was also a man of many secrets. And that was the other side of the comparison to Cammarano. There were, of course, the unjustified rumors that Cammarano—like McGreevey—was gay and in the closet. It was the kind of talk that had dogged McGreevey for years before he actually came out. But it had never appeared to have any validity with Cammarano. More seriously, there were the real secrets to Peter's personal life and how he did his politics.

Cammarano was a child of divorce. He also had himself sired a daughter while in high school and had been paying support ever since. When he finally decided to enter the Hoboken mayor's race in 2009, Peter had the choice of going public with his history or trying to keep it secret. Despite recommendations from his advisers to put the information out in advance, he decided to keep a lid on it. Not to protect his privacy but in a craven maneuver to tempt his adversaries to use it against him. That way, he figured, he'd be able to use his own secrets as a weapon against his foes in the three-way mayor's race.

It worked like a charm. They played into his strategy and he got to play the wounded, wronged, hounded victim.

Cammarano also got in bed with some of the old-school pols around Hudson County, hoping their support could mean the margin of victory in May and acceptance when the mayors gathered to divide the spoils. He started paying consultants sent to him by other mayors and religiously followed their instructions over the objections of his loyalists. The end result was a campaign that neither looked nor sounded cohesive but was just good enough somehow.

Some of his associates worried over Peter's habit of cutting corners. As a lawyer trained in campaign-finance rules, he knew where the soft spots were and they alleged that he had employed one of the best-known legal end runs in the business: he allegedly had a top campaign contributor pay the salary of his campaign manager, a salary that could easily surpass $2,000 a week in New Jersey. And Peter ran up big bills, which is not uncommon for pols who always figure they'll win and then be able to fundraise enough to cover their debts after they win. What enraged his insiders, though, was the fact that Cammarano was sitting on a decent piece of wealth after his grandmother died and left him her estate. They didn't realize the money was held in a joint investment account with his wife and Cammarano was unwilling to tell Marita anything about his campaign finances. Worst of all, every single one of Cammarano's manipulations would likely have been perfectly legal had he allowed his inner lawyer to do it the right way and set up legitimate political action committees that can—despite the public's antipathy toward them—serve as unbridled supplements to a campaign crew. Staffers can get paid through them. Excessive donations can be made through them. It was exactly the type of sophisticated end run McGreevey used to employ.

As the mayoral election proceeded, those around Peter started noticing a change. An arrogance took over, as did a diminished willingness to do the fund-raising, phone calling, and retail campaigning that is essential to get across the finish line. He also seemed to be getting in tighter and tighter with Schaffer. Cammarano's people started asking one another the same question out loud: "What the fuck is Schaffer doing here?"

           * * *

With Dwek throwing so much chum in the water to attract fish, the smell of money seemed to be driving his middlemen crazy. The simmering competition for illicit commissions among Maher Khalil, Ed Cheatam, and Jack Shaw began to get out of control. The three were always in a foot-race to see who could rake in more cash from Esenbach the whale, and they were playing dirty.

Khalil, who was working non-stop for Dwek, played the victim. He needed the money to support his wife and new baby, and more than anything, he was looking to ingratiate himself with anyone who would help him get a promotion at City Hall. Cheatam and Shaw were the predator sharks. Already in good with Dwek, they would do anything and say anything to minimize Khalil and get him kicked to the curb. They didn't only bad-mouth Khalil to Dwek; they also put the hammer to Khalil directly.

It wasn't long before the FBI agents realized they had a problem on their hands. Agitated, Khalil got on the phone with Dwek to relay a conversation he had just had with Cheatam. "Now he's angry," Khalil said of Shaw. "He wants me out of the picture . . . Ed Cheatam said he has his own political game . . . He [Cheatam] said 'he wants to cut you out completely.'"

Dwek was calm, but his FBI handlers were not. Typically, Dwek would let that kind of stuff just go by the boards as the targets tired themselves out with all their backstabbing. This time was different. Dwek got back on the phone with Khalil and inquired about how much he was making with the city. After doing some quick math, Dwek said he realized it wasn't enough, calculating that Khalil's gross was $50,000 a year.

"Starting May first, I'll give you five thousand dollars every month. This way we'll supplement everything I have to. And we'll keep everyone happy," Dwek said. "Just trying to do the right thing by you. For everything you've done for me, I'm trying to reciprocate."

Dwek buried the point, but it was crystal clear. "I don't need, I don't want, anyone jumping up and down. I don't need anyone talking about me or anything like that."

With the emergency defused, Dwek chuckled and said he would look forward to the elections being over by the summer. "All the chaos," he said, "better be."

* * *

The Jersey Sting, meanwhile, went on, in a state that had no shortage of scandal. Thursday, April 23, was yet another busy day for federal prosecutors. Elsewhere, the FBI was raiding the home of assemblyman and former Perth Amboy mayor Joseph Vas, a month after a state grand jury indicted Vas on charges that he conspired with municipal employees to bill the city for $5,000' worth of clothing, sneakers, and other personal items when he served as mayor.

In Hudson County, Waldie's FBI team of special agents was following Cheatam, Shaw, and Dave Esenbach into another meeting with Jimmy King, the council candidate in Jersey City, at a local diner. Dwek was again talking big about his development plans. "We'll keep you busy. Don't worry," he said. "Once you're in, that's it, man. We, we got our first application coming."

"Does Jack know about the application?" asked King.

Of course, said Esenbach. "It's on, you know, Garfield."

"I don't care what it is. It's done," said King, his conversation all being caught on the HAWK surveillance video. "Name it. Done."

"Just make sure they expedite my stuff."

The four of them walked out of the diner and Esenbach headed for the trunk of his Lexus. Shaw stopped him. "Uh, he wants for you to give it to me," Shaw said.

"So I'll give it to you now, and you'll give it to him now?"

"Yeah," said Jack.

Esenbach nodded. "I got it in my trunk, so let's go," he said. He opened the back and pulled out a FedEx envelope containing $5,000 in cash and handed it to Shaw as King watched. The informant, turning to King, gestured toward the envelope. "Make sure, you know, Jack's on that," Esenbach said, as if it were a campaign contribution to be reported on his campaign finance reports. "Don't put my name on nothing, okay?"

"Nah," agreed King.

"I don't wanna have any, uh, conflict, trace, or anything like that," he reiterated. "There'll be more after you win."

The FBI undercover agents, who had been inside the restaurant during the meeting, saw Shaw hand King the envelope in the parking lot.

That same day, Esenbach, Shaw, and Cheatam had separate meetings set up with Ron Manzo and LaVern Webb-Washington in Bayonne. The housing activist and council candidate continued to promise her support for a proposed zone change for the Garfield Avenue project once she was elected to the Jersey City Council. "Dave, you are on the top of my list," LaVern pledged eagerly. In the diner's parking lot, while sitting in her car, she took an envelope from Dwek. There was $5,000 in cash inside. Telling him she would conceal the source of the cash by identifying it as a personal contribution to her own campaign, she agreed with Esenbach that she did not want his name on "nothing," so that down the line no one could say that she had been bought for her support of Garfield Avenue.

The meeting with Ron Manzo was at the same diner. Again, developer Dave Esenbach was pushing hard to hear the right words, as he promised another cash payment to the mayoral campaign of Manzo's brother Lou.

"Just make sure your brother gets me expedited."

"There's no question," agreed Manzo, winking at Esenbach. "It's only because of good government and has nothing to do with anything else. It makes sense."

With the wink caught on the video surveillance, the meaning of it all seemed clear. "After the election, you'll see another ten," Esenbach told him, adding that he was not to forget the promise made to Khalil for a City Hall promotion under a Manzo administration. "He's in, right? Mr. Director?"

"Yes," said Ron. "But we don't have to mention that."

Dwek and Cheatam left the diner together. In the parking lot, Dwek took a FedEx envelope with $10,000 cash from the Lexus and handed it to Cheatam to hand over to Manzo. "Just make sure he gets my stuff expedited. I told him I'd give him another ten thousand dollars after the election. And another seventy-five hundred dollars for Khalil."

Cheatam took the envelope and went back into the diner. Minutes later, Manzo and Cheatam both emerged. Cheatam gave Manzo the envelope, which was wrapped in a map.

The script and locations remained unchanged for Lori Serrano, next up in the lineup, who met Esenbach outside the diner. He promised the Jersey City Council candidate a copy of his zoning change application as he told her not to let it fall to the bottom of the pile after she was elected. She agreed that his back was covered. As she took another $5,000 in cash, she thanked him for the donation and told him the money would be used in connection with volunteers on the day of the election.

"I don't donate," replied Esenbach. "I invest."

Lori had no quarrel. "I respect that. You're a businessman."

The day was not yet over. At about 5:00 P.M., Dwek as Esenbach caught up with Jaslow, the Hudson County Board of Elections investigator now back on his payroll, and Secaucus mayor Dennis Elwell at the Meadowlands Plaza Hotel in Secaucus.

A lifelong resident of his town, Elwell was a seven-term councilman well regarded because of his service in the Army during Vietnam. He was elected mayor in 1999 and was facing another tough reelection bid in 2009. Elwell didn't know if he would have a serious challenge in the Democratic primary in June and knew one of the surest ways of keeping potential opponents out of a race was with a healthy war chest.

In Secaucus, Dwek's game was a development possibility along Route 3—the heavily traveled highway that connected the Lincoln Tunnel to the Meadowlands Sports Complex, where the New York Giants and Jets play. The conversation was focused mainly on Joe Doria and whether they could count on him for help. Esenbach boasted that he had Doria in his pocket, despite only having just met him through Shaw.

"You friendly with him?" asked Jaslow curiously.

"I never used him for anything. I never asked him for a thing in my life," Esenbach replied. But Doria would be there when needed. "He's my man. I'll use him one day, maybe. But he's a fine man . . . he's in charge of the low-income housing. He's the commissioner. So no grant money goes out in the state without his approval. He's also strong with the mayor of Bayonne."

Once Elwell joined in, he quickly became dubious of the way the conversation was going. "I always thought you're better off to comply with the law than ignore it."

"I wanna invest up front," said Dave. As he noted time and time again, he was a generous guy.

The next day, Harvey Smith, the other candidate for mayor in Jersey City, was on the schedule. Dwek drove to the Perkins Pancake House in Staten Island to meet Smith with Cheatam—who could not afford to be seen with Smith any more than he could meet openly with Manzo—again accompanied by Shaw.

Esenbach again wanted to make sure Smith was on board in expediting a zoning change for Garfield Avenue. As they sat around the table, the legislator got up and excused himself for a few minutes. While he was gone, Dwek asked Cheatam whether Smith's aide, Richard Greene, was to join them. He was to be the middleman.

"He couldn't make it," said Ed.

"So what are we going to do?" Dwek asked. He had an envelope full of $5,000 in cash waiting in the car outside. "Give it to him after?"

Shaw shook his head. "Give it to me and I'll have to give it to him. He won't take it himself."

"But the guy understands I'm looking to get expedited?"

"Oh yeah," said Jack.

Dwek cemented the deal. "Tell him I'll do the five now, I'll do five more after the election. If he wants more, no problem, as long as he helps me expedite the stuff."

When Smith returned, Cheatam told him, "Dave here is a very generous person and he likes working with people. He's going to make a contribution to your campaign. His only thing is that his name is not connected to it, nor my name, nor Jack's name. He'll give you something now and you make the runoff and he'll keep contributing to you, to your success."

Esenbach interjected, "Runoff or you get elected, or both, I told Ed I'll do the five thousand dollars now and then five after the runoff and then after the election. Just don't put my name anywhere or anything like that."

Smith held them up, as if not understanding what they were saying. "I can only put the name on the check that is, who the check's coming from."

"There is no check," explained Cheatam. Then he repeated what he just said: "There is no check. There is no check."

"We don't want to have any conflicts," Esenbach explained to Smith.

Harvey now knew what they were proposing. "I understand and that's going to be difficult for me to deal with," said the assemblyman. He was unwilling to accept cash.

"That's why we want to make sure you go through Rich," said Cheatam, referring to Greene. "We have to figure out a way that we put a contribution like that. We have to come up with checks, because . . . ," he trailed out, and then just said, "We'll deal with it."

As the meeting broke up, Dwek opened up the invisible script he had rehearsed one more time. "So, I'm going to handle everything through Ed."

"I understand," Smith replied.

"Just don't put my name on nothing."

"I understand."

"Just give me your word that you're going to expedite my stuff."

Smith laughed. "I don't do quid pro quos. Ed will tell you how I operate."

That was not what the FBI or the prosecutors wanted to hear.

* * *

The following Monday was the afternoon meeting with Cammarano at the Malibu, a typical Jersey diner of polished stainless steel and turquoise and pink neon, located on 14th Street in Hoboken. The entry on Cammarano's personal schedule for the day put it bluntly: *2pm–3pm Mike Schaffer at Malibu with Peter ONLY.*

Shaw and Cheatam came in with Dwek, and met Schaffer and Cammarano inside. To Cammarano, it was just another private fund-raiser, and he began talking about himself. "I run the election law department at the biggest election law firm in the state of New Jersey," he said. One of his issues for this race, where his opponent, Dawn Zimmer, was looking to put the brakes on new construction, was development. "To the extent there's a pro-development person in this race, that's me."

Esenbach said if he were to look for opportunities in Hoboken, "I wanna make sure that I, you know, you, you're my man."

"You can put your faith in me," said Cammarano. "I promise you you're gonna be treated like a friend."

On the surveillance video, a deal of sorts was ironed out. Esenbach said he would deal through Schaffer, giving him five thousand to start, and then after the election he would do another five thousand. "Just make sure you expedite my stuff," Esenbach said. "Make sure my name is not—I don't want it to show up. I don't want any conflict issues."

"Right, right, right."

"I'm a businessman," said Dave. "Generous guy."

* * *

That Wednesday, Dwek met with Hoboken councilman Michael Russo at the Light Horse Tavern, a pleasant little upscale place on Washington Street in Jersey City. Russo was bad-mouthing Cammarano. Dwek was eating chocolate bread pudding with caramel ice cream. Khalil vouched for Esenbach, whom he had only met a few months ago. "One thing about David: you can trust him. I've known him almost nine years. He's always been a man of his word."

Nine years? Dwek could only smile to himself.

"Sounds like we'll get along fine," said Russo.

"You need something? Boom," continued Khalil. "Call him tomorrow: 'I need five, ten grand for my campaign.' Boom."

As intended, Russo was impressed. "Always nice to have friends like that."

Then they got down to business. "Whatever I do, I'll do through Maher . . . I don't want to do anything in my name. I don't want to have any conflicts," Dwek said.

"You're a smart man," Russo observed.

"I'll give him five thousand next week and you'll work it out . . . and after the election, I'll do the same. It'll be more."

Russo agreed and then the foursome broke up. After that, however, Russo would not take calls from Dwek's middlemen.

"We met him, we never heard from him again. Whatever happened to the guy? He fell off the face of the earth?" asked Dwek of one, weeks later.

"Nah. I think you spooked him."

"He seemed like a nice guy."

Some have suggested Russo was advised by an attorney to stay away from the informant. The feds believe Michael went home and was reminded by his ex-con father that this is New Jersey and money that presents itself too easily is often connected to the feds.

Russo has never answered the question and declined to talk about it. He has never been charged with any wrongdoing.

* * *

With the municipal elections quickly drawing closer, Dwek had his hands especially full on May 6, now just six days before voters went to the polls. He began that Wednesday with breakfast at the Doubletree Hotel in the heart of Jersey City's financial district, where he met Mariano Vega, the city council president, at the hotel's Harsimus Cove Bar and Grill. Dwek, according to the surveillance tapes, told Vega he had brought $10,000 that he would pass along through Khalil.

"You and Ed can figure out how to handle the money. I just don't want my name reported anywhere," Esenbach told Vega, as the tape ran.

Dave also told Vega he was preparing the Garfield Avenue application. The council president said he was meeting with someone on Friday and was going to give a full briefing and he needed to see a draft of the proposal. Esenbach promised they would meet again after the election and told Vega to expect another $10,000 for a victory party.

"That'll buy a lot of pretzels," quipped Vega.

"Just don't put my name on anything."

"No, no," said Vega. "We're going to do it the correct way." He told Khalil to have people write checks.

Then it was to Brooklyn to do another cash deal with Rabbi Fish and Levi Deutsch. They had to wait for Levi to complete the transaction. "He's got the connections," the rabbi said of Deutsch. "His connections."

When Deutsch walked into Fish's small shul in Borough Park, Dwek again told him about his knockoff-pocketbook business, which ostensibly was the reason he was looking to launder cash. "We make the fancy bags. You know, they make the fancy bags? This, a bag like this for three thousand? I make the same bag. I put the label on. It costs me twenty dollars. I sell it for two hundred."

"I know," Deutsch responded, as if tired of hearing the story again.

After the meeting, Dwek got back in his car and drove to New Jersey, returning to the Coach House Diner in North Bergen, where he caught up with Michael Manzo, an independent candidate in the Jersey City election and no relation to Lou and Ron Manzo. Esenbach had his favorite line ready as he proposed a cash contribution. "There's people like Democrat, Republican, but I'm in the Green Party; I don't like any conflicts, you understand?"

Manzo laughed. "Green is like gold, right?"

"That's right, I don't have gold in my house, but green I have. So, you know, if it's okay with you, you know, maybe I'll do five thousand and another five after the election."

Then it was on to an almost celebratory dinner back at Ruth's Chris Steak House in Weehawken to catch up with Shaw and Cheatam.

"How's Garfield Avenue going?" Cheatam wondered. It was a fair question. Esenbach had been at this for months, and so far no one had seen any plans, site elevations, contracts, or permit applications. Nothing.

"I had my guys speak to the sellers, the DEP thing, and the DEP actually looked at the application, and they're coming out, they said, May 20," Esenbach told him. None of that was true. "They're doing a site inspection. Everything's okay. Then they sign off."

He quickly asked about the $5,000 payment that was supposed to go through Greene to Smith.

"I converted it," Cheatam said. "I gave money orders."

"Money orders for five grand?" asked Dwek. "You just have to put different names I guess on it."

Ed and Jack just laughed out loud. "With money orders, you don't have to put any names on it," Cheatam explained.

* * *

On Friday, May 8, the group gathered in Hoboken at the Malibu. *10:30 am–11:30 am—Meeting with Mike Schaffer* was the entry that day in

Cammarano's calendar. The election was the following Tuesday, and Shaw told Schaffer that Esenbach wanted to "invest" some more in the young mayoral candidate. Dwek, as usual, went into his routine about "expedite my stuff" and how he didn't want any conflicts, so his name couldn't show up anywhere. Another $5,000. "Don't put my name—like last time."

"Understood. Understood."

Esenbach suggested that after the election the following Tuesday they might meet on Wednesday or Thursday to celebrate a campaign victory. "I'll give you—I'll do another five."

"Maybe after, uh, we sleep in a little bit on Wednesday," Cammarano said to laughter all around.

* * *

Four days later, Peter won a spot in a Hoboken runoff for mayor, surprising the political establishment. His need for cash now went into warp speed, as the street money flew out the door, and Cammarano wasted no time. Voters were actually still going to the polls in Hoboken when Jaslow called Dwek with the news that Cammarano needed cash. Jaslow didn't realize that Dwek was already hooked into Cammarano through other bagmen, and didn't ask. Jaslow just wanted the finder's fee.

"I got a call from Peter Cammarano," Jaslow said.

"Peter? Yeah," Dwek replied.

"Are you in the neighborhood?"

"I'm not in the neighborhood, no. I'm in the city. Why? What does he want to do?"

"They want to see if you can do something for him."

Jaslow said it was important to get the cash, or a commitment, immediately. "They're trying to get something put together today. They gotta put money on the street."

With his typical cool, Dwek told Jaslow to carry back the message that Peter could count on "five extra" if he won or secured a spot in the runoff.

* * *

After the election results were in, Webb-Washington, who lost her long-shot bid for a seat on the Jersey City Council, thought the gravy train wouldn't stop. She wanted to challenge the vote count and sought out Esenbach to help her financially. Paying the bills of someone who was not—and was not going to be—an elected official didn't particularly interest the FBI.

"Dave, we need a lawyer, I'm in a runoff . . . they're trying to steal it. I need a lawyer. It's up to you now," LaVern told Dwek frantically the morning after the election. "I need a lawyer. People wanted to vote for me who couldn't vote for me. Machines were messed up. I need a lawyer. But I can't hire one; I don't have a dime."

Calmly, Dwek told her to call a lawyer and call him back. He proceeded to disregard her calls and messages from then on.

Lori Serrano may have also thought Dwek would be a sugar daddy for life. In the wake of her election loss, she thought about moving to Florida. Esenbach's backstory included a portfolio of Florida real estate developments, so she figured he could help. Through Cheatam, Serrano reached out to Dwek. This time, Dwek actually followed through by making a call to a legitimate business contact, but Serrano never moved.

* * *

Amid the Hudson elections, Vinnie Tabbachino, whom Khalil had first brought to Dave Esenbach, reentered the picture. Tabbachino had earlier tried to connect Dwek with West New York mayor Sal Vega, who kept putting off a meeting and then, after finally agreeing to sit down with Dwek, sent a lawyer instead. For most of his time in the investigation, Tabbachino offered little except humor. Like the time when he had to cancel a sit-down with Dwek.

"What happened was I got a call from the FBI in New York," Tabbachino said. Dwek was amazed. "I have to go over there today. What it is, it's about, I'm a victim this time . . . The stockbroker I was using, he was getting money back from the broker—not from the broker, from the company, the CEO. So there's a chance of me getting back about twenty grand. They sent a limo over for me. Swear to God."

In the end, the only Tabbachino play that worked out for the feds was Ridgefield mayor Anthony R. Suarez. The mayor was in his second term as leader of the small Bergen County community when Suarez, Tabbachino, and Dwek met at Patsy's Restaurant in Fairview in May. The talk focused on development—as usual—and how a mover like David Esenbach likes to be treated. "I just wanna make sure I got someone in there that, you know, can help me expedite, uh, you know, with my approvals. That's all. And, you know, I wanna make sure I got a friend that will support my stuff."

As the FBI had instructed him, Dwek tried to "dirty up" the conversation. "Did, you know, you told the mayor how we gonna do business now?" To which Tabbachino responded, "He understands everything. I told him

I would take care of whatever had to be done. And I told him that we'd help him out with his, his campaign."

Suarez didn't have an election coming up the way many of Dwek's targets did. But Suarez was a Democrat in the middle of a non-stop fight with the Republican-led town council. A lawyer by day, Suarez refused to allow political attacks against him to go unanswered, and he formed a legal defense fund to sue those he thought were responsible. It was to that fund that Tabbachino said he would funnel $10,000 of Dwek's FBI money, with $2,500 of it making it all the way to Suarez. The mayor never deposited the check. He thought something was fishy and gave it to his buyer to hold.

* * *

The next day in Hoboken, a week after the election there, Shaw, Cheatam, Schaffer, Dwek, and Cammarano reconvened and the talk turned hard and direct and concentrated on the June 9 runoff. Cammarano was in rare form: "Right now, the Italians, the Hispanics, the seniors are locked down. Nothing can change that now . . . I could be, uh, indicted, and I'm still going to win eighty-five to ninety-five percent of those populations." The HAWK got every word, clear as can be. With each syllable, Cammarano more and more became the poster boy for New Jersey's corrupt politics.

"We're breaking down the world into three categories," Cammarano said of those who backed and opposed him. "There's the people who were with us, and that's you guys. There's the people who climbed on board in the runoff. They can get in line. And then there are the people who were against us the whole way. They get ground into powder."

Anyone among that last group looking for construction approvals could just languish for three years, Cammarano announced. Another $5,000 for the boy king.

The June 9 election was close and the results were not immediately tallied. Up by more than 200 votes when the numbers came in off the polling machines, Dawn Zimmer had to wait for a count of about 775 absentee votes. It wasn't until Friday, after all the absentee and provisional ballots were tallied, that Cammarano emerged with a slim, 161-vote victory. Genova had been on hand personally to stand sentry at the county's election office to ensure the ballots were counted properly. Peter had been elected as Hoboken's youngest mayor.

The victory, however, came at a huge cost. When the smoke cleared, Cammarano was at least $85,000 in debt. During Election Day itself, campaign scheduler Jamey Cook-Lichstein remembered the staff writing so many $100 checks to street workers that they ran out of checks. Then they ran out of money and the checks that had been distributed bounced for the rest of the week at the check-cashing kiosks near the city's west-side housing projects.

One month to the day before the takedown, Cammarano's calendar showed one more of the now-familiar entries for the Malibu: *9am–10am Meeting with Mike Schaffer, Jack Shaw, and David. Where: Malibu Diner. Description: Attending: Peter.*

Shaw directed the conversation right where the FBI wanted it to go. Where Cammarano needed it to go because he needed the scratch. "So anyway, we understand you got a [campaign] debt ... the main reason we're here is to see how we can help you, and you've got to tell us somewhere in the neighborhood of what you need."

Dwek weighed in with what had become his own campaign slogan: "I'm a generous guy."

Cammarano confided that the street money checks that had bounced totaled about $19,000 and that he had to take out a $20,000 bridge loan to cover himself. Dwek offered $10,000, provided he could remain invisible on paper. "I appreciate it," the mayor-elect said, grateful for the money.

15

⊶ ✦ ✦ ⊷

Put Him on Ice . . .

On a warm, sunny Wednesday in Hoboken on the first of July, Peter Cammarano was sworn in as the city's thirty-seventh mayor. As he put his hand on a Bible at noontime to take the oath of office, the young lawyer, flanked by his wife, Marita, who held their baby daughter, Abigail, promised to make residents proud. "The motto of the United States is *e pluribus unum*. In other words, out of many we are one," Cammarano declared. "In Hoboken, we are all neighbors. We shall rise or fall, sink or swim, but ultimately succeed together . . ." Most of New Jersey's political elite was in attendance—including Governor Corzine, Newark mayor Cory Booker, and U.S. Senators Frank Lautenberg and Bob Menendez—along with 500 of Cammarano's closest friends at the Schaefer Center at Stevens Institute of Technology in Hoboken.

It was not a day to celebrate democracy for the U.S. Attorney's office. The swearing in of the new mayor had long been a source of concern among federal prosecutors. They had known for months they were going to arrest Cammarano. Then he actually won the election. The question had been whether to allow him to take the oath of office.

The debate had been going on since April or early May, when it first became clear they were going to be arresting Jersey City councilmen—they thought maybe half the Jersey City Council at one point—and they worried that they could throw a major city into chaos. Would the voters and the residents of Jersey City become innocent victims of a government sting? It was a serious question and not an unusual one for prosecutors who arrest elected officials with some frequency. Then Cammarano entered the picture and it was not only members of the governing body who were to be arrested but also a mayor in a city where the position carries full executive authority, like governor or president.

In the first couple of weeks of June, acting U.S. Attorney Ralph Marra convened the full team of case agents and prosecutors in his conference room, the same location where Chris Christie reluctantly sat for the original pitch that would turn Solomon Dwek into a federal cooperator. The agenda for Marra's meeting was more than just a status report on Dwek; it was to plan the grand finale of the behemoth of a case. *Who's getting arrested? Who's going to be offered the chance to roll over on others? When is it coming down?* Planning an assault like the one displayed on July 23 takes some time. There is always an emergency takedown scenario in mind in the event the investigation gets compromised and the whole thing has to end instantly. But luck had been on the side of the feds, and it now appeared they would be able to end the game on their terms, much the way they had played it all along.

A lot of things had to be factored into the timing, not the least of which were vacation plans already on the books for both Marra and the FBI's top agent in New Jersey, Weysan Dun. The FBI said it would take two to four weeks to prepare for the simultaneous arrests and searches and the agents would need another couple of weeks to run out the scams Dwek had been using to get his various targets deeper and deeper in trouble. They had to work it out that Fish would have hundreds of thousands of dollars on hand when he was hit. They needed to find the moment when they believed Levi Deutsch would be back in the United States. And they needed another crack at Joe Doria.

Then, a new problem: Cammarano's swearing in. *Shouldn't we consider taking the case down before he takes office?* The question was raised by Michele Brown, the second most senior official in the U.S. Attorney's office at the time. Brown, a close friend of Christie, who promoted her to the senior staff, had already been accused of secretly aiding Christie's gubernatorial campaign. Within weeks, she would burst into the headlines herself after it was revealed that Christie had lent her $46,000 without reporting it. Brown didn't say she had politics on her mind, though. She was a fairly conservative prosecutor and thought the case should be brought down before Cammarano put his hand on the Bible. Her boss, Marra, was not conservative. It came as no surprise to those in Ralph's office that the boss disagreed with Michele. The calendar was not going to dictate the arrests, he insisted. Marra, along with Jimmy Nobile, didn't think anything should factor into the decision to proceed with a takedown besides the merits of the case—not politics, not inaugurations, not the cycles of Jupiter's moons.

But it was a new day in Washington. The Obama administration was still fresh and Marra figured it was conceivable that Attorney General Eric Holder and his team might be as conservative as Michele. So Marra did the textbook cover-your-ass maneuver and had another member of his senior staff call down to Justice Department headquarters. What did they think? Did Cammarano's swearing-in schedule mean anything?

As distasteful as it may be, the chiefs in Justice said, let him take office. *We break this case open when it's right for us, no one else.*

* * *

By July 1, as Cammarano and council members in Jersey City and Hoboken were taking their oaths of office, everyone working the sting operation was in agreement that it was about time to take it down. The money-laundering stuff was getting stale. There were no more body-parts guys. And the elections were over. Another Jersey City Council candidate getting $500 was not going to make it worthwhile to hold off. The case was also eating up huge resources and the FBI agents were tired. The Dwek team at the FBI consisted of three case agents, plus others going through the recordings and surveillance teams that leapfrogged to the meets. Another team of prosecutors was reviewing the surveillance tapes daily. Even though some line agents wanted to continue the case, the prosecutors and FBI supervisors all knew that Dwek—like every other undercover case—would run out of gas at some point. There would be no construction on Garfield Avenue. There would be no condo complex in Hoboken and certainly no convention center on an industrial wasteland in Elizabeth. Plus, with every new day came the risk that targets could become smart or grow a conscience and "clean themselves" out of the case.

At the same time, the judge in the federal bankruptcy case was getting more than impatient. Dwek's creditors who were out millions of dollars when his real estate empire collapsed under the Ponzi scheme were pushing hard to depose him. In bankruptcy, the goal of those owed money is to preserve assets, and if they could not question him under oath there was increasing concern among the parties that Solomon might be cashing out without anyone knowing. The judge knew it and she wanted Dwek examined. Period.

If that deposition is taken, our investigation is over, period, Marra thought.

Jimmy Nobile and Brian Howe met with federal judge Kathryn Ferguson in Trenton over and over to press for delays. Each time, behind closed doors without anyone outside the Justice Department knowing about it, they were able to convince her to hold off on a deposition order. In November 2008, the judge granted a 60-day extension without explanation. Two months later, 90 days was put back on the clock. But she had had enough. The feds were running out of time and excuses. Ferguson is a tough judge with 20 years on the bench and the kind of encyclopedic knowledge of the law that can overwhelm attorneys. Ferguson had handled some of the most complicated bankruptcies in modern New Jersey history, and a badge from the U.S. Attorney's office was not going to impress her.

In April, Marra himself had to get in the car to go see the judge in Trenton. Marra may well have been the chief federal lawman in the state, but going in for a private meeting with a judge was still a lot like getting called to the principal's office. Yet he had to do it if Dwek was to be closed out the way his prosecutors envisioned. Ferguson went along with another 60-day continuance but left no doubt that it would be the last one.

Marra told the group at his planning meeting that the judge was impatient and that they had all arrived at the endgame of the Dwek case. He wanted Dun and his administrative staff to figure out a day in July. It couldn't be a Monday or Friday because those are tough days to schedule in the summer. It had to be when Marra and Dun would be in town. It couldn't be August because too many people take vacations during that month and the risks of missing targets was too high. It couldn't wait for September because of the unwritten tradition of not doing political corruption arrests or indictments within 60 days of the November election. And it had to be when the FBI was most confident that Deutsch would be in the country, because the feds wanted him and didn't want to try to extradite him—a painful process with an Israeli citizen. Plus, extradition would mean enlisting the aid of the Justice Department's centralized extradition office at the attorney general's headquarters in Washington and involving Washington is never preferable to prosecutors in the field.

Thursday morning, July 23. That's when it would all come to an end.

* * *

June turned into July and everything was going according to plan. Then as July developed, a crisis overtook the Dwek case inside the U.S. Attorney's office. Jimmy Nobile, who had guided the operation since its inception, was suddenly out of the picture.

On Monday, July 13, Nobile walked the familiar path from his office to Marra's, but this was not simply one of the thousands of casual updates the special prosecutions chief provides the U.S. Attorney during the course of months. A law firm had made a job overture to Nobile, and after a career prosecuting cases for the federal government he thought he might actually want to take this leap. But the idea of Nobile leaving the office wasn't the biggest problem for the Dwek case. No, the biggest problem at that moment was that the unsolicited job offer came from a firm connected tangentially to someone involved in the case and it looked like Nobile would have to get out of the matter entirely. Immediately.

Over the years, Nobile had chosen to recuse himself from only a handful of cases, mostly because of job overtures and once because he had a relative by marriage who was related distantly to a target. Nobile had been working this case since Dwek's arrest on the bank fraud. He was unenthusiastic about coming off, especially after Adam Lurie, another senior prosecutor, had left just two months earlier to become staff director to the House of Representatives intelligence subcommittee. But this was a serious opportunity for Nobile. Many of his friends and colleagues had left the office over the years to pursue other interests, and it was likely that his old friend Marra was about to follow that path once the new U.S. Attorney took over.

Job offers could pose no conflict of interest or create obvious conflicts. Those are the easy calls to make. The tough ones come when it's not quite so black and white. Like this one with Nobile. Marra thought it looked like Nobile would have to get out of the Dwek case, but he wasn't certain and, again, he wanted backup from what they call Main Justice in D.C. The decision that came down on July 17 was clear: off the case, no involvement, zero input on prosecuting, investigating, or staffing. Hastily Marra assembled the lawyers on the case in the bland conference room next to Nobile's office in the special prosecutions division. Surrounded by dull beige scuffed walls, with some sitting in the six vinyl chairs, Marra told them that Nobile was out, that Howe would run the show, and that was that.

Nobile was a critical loss. From the beginning, he had been a resource on Dwek as he was on all other corruption cases. A name could come up in an investigation and Jimmy could say, "I remember that name from some case ten years ago." He was the one the FBI went to when Dwek's bank fraud was reported and he was critical in convincing Christie to go along with the cooperation deal. Nobile was a quiet source of calm and steadiness for his subordinates and superiors and he had a silent, confident manner that Marra equated to "Hoboken Zen," given Nobile's life living in the city of Sinatra.

Nobile also had a habit of interrogating his assistants through sessions called the Jimmy Sweats. He might not even know they were called that; that's what the assistant U.S. Attorneys called them. Nobile would pop into his assistants' offices four or five times a day just to ask what's going on, what they were doing with a particular trouble spot. The assistants viewed it as quiet torture. The Jimmy Sweats were critical to keeping Nobile's team focused and out of the "dry holes" that can doom cases.

When Jimmy made a decision, nobody questioned him. He had done these cases for years and there was no doubt who was in charge. Howe, while well liked and competent, did not command the same level of respect, and that quickly began causing problems after Nobile was sidelined. "I wouldn't want to call it a mutiny," one of the lawyers said, "but it was sort of chaotic. There was a lot of internal politics. There were a lot of headaches." No one wanted to think that Howe's physical handicap had anything to do with it. And, truth is, managing a case like Dwek would be hard for the most seasoned of hands. But Howe seemed determined to prove he could handle it by himself. As the final weeks ticked by, Howe's custom-built van broke down, so he took the train to and from work and rode his wheelchair each way between his office and Newark's Penn Station—nearly a mile away. He wouldn't ask for help, even though it would have been offered quickly. He wouldn't even tell anyone about his predicament. "Everyone wished he would ask for help," the lawyer said.

While Howe was acting like he was doing okay, it was clear things weren't working right in Special Prosecutions. Decisions were not getting made quickly and speed was more critical at that point than ever. Inside the team, some people started trying to bigfoot Howe, knowing that Nobile couldn't do anything about it and that few would find out. At one point, Marra dispatched Michele Brown. "Ralph knows what's going on," she told the lawyers ominously. Her job was to tell the gang to knock it off. Marra also moved a loyal and strong prosecutor from Trenton into the team to serve as both a necessary pair of hands at a critical time and someone who would make sure Howe was not being muscled out of control. The biggest problem, Marra found, was that critical information from the FBI was not being shared quickly enough with the whole team of prosecutors. He went so far as to call the FBI supervisor on the case, his old buddy Ed Kahrer, to tell him everyone had to get their act together. "Look, forget about morale. It's damaging our preparation," Marra told him. Kahrer, as invested in the Dwek case as anyone, told Marra he would put the train back on track.

The end result of Nobile's involuntary absence meant that Marra was forced to come in off the bench, basically as a player-coach. Unknown to anyone outside the office, Marra took over the final charging and arrest decisions; he left Howe in control technically, but for the endgame Marra did little but oversee the last chapter of the Dwek investigation. It consumed most of Ralph's days and nights. At one point, he was sitting on his home porch during the final weekend, poring over memos and investigative documents, playing and replaying videos, reading transcripts of Dwek's 3,000 calls and meetings, and "thinking of ways I could fuckin' kill Jimmy. I wasn't sure, you know, drowning. There are so many ways . . ."

* * *

Marra spent nearly his whole professional career in the U.S. Attorney's office. He was a well-known prosecutor with an ability to collect, assimilate, and manipulate complicated fact patterns and win over juries. Outside of his family, Ralph had two great loves: cooking and prosecuting political corruption. In 2002, Chris Christie tapped Marra to become the number two official in the office as a peace offering to those critics who questioned whether Christie deserved the job considering his résumé was devoid of experience as a prosecutor.

The U.S. Attorney's office is best known for its prosecution units, but it also has a civil division, which serves as the federal government's lawyer in New Jersey, and an appellate division. As Christie's "first assistant U.S. Attorney," Marra had tremendous authority over the whole array of functions inside the office. He also had a deep reservoir of credibility with Christie, having been his right-hand man since the very first day Christie walked into the Rodino federal building on Broad Street.

In their time together, Marra helped Christie decide to go after a top fund-raiser to a governor. Marra was a vocal advocate for the decision to raid the offices of the Democratic State Committee. And after Christie seized administrative control of the corrupt University of Medicine and Dentistry of New Jersey, Marra was the one who tried and convicted state senator Wayne Bryant, the chairman of the Senate Budget Committee. The Bryant case was the most notorious prosecution to emanate from the medical school probe.

Marra wanted Christie's job. Not that he was pushing Christie out, but Barack Obama's election in November 2008 made Christie's departure a certainty and Marra wanted to be U.S. Attorney. On his way out the door, Christie said he would be glad to recommend that Marra be named "acting U.S. Attorney" until the new president could nominate a replacement, who would have to be confirmed by the U.S. Senate. Christie had a word of caution: "You probably don't have a chance at the permanent appointment. But if you take the interim appointment, when the new guy comes in, you're going to have to leave. And this has been your whole career."

Christie knew it would be tough for Marra to get the nomination because he had no political hooks with Lautenberg and Menendez, the two
U.S. Senators, who make the recommendation to the president. The temporary appointment, though, virtually guaranteed that Marra would have
to exit after a permanent replacement was nominated and confirmed,
Christie told him, because no new U.S. Attorney would want to keep a guy
who ran the joint for a while. Marra said he wanted the job anyway and
took over on December 2, 2008. With it came responsibility for hundreds
of ongoing matters, including the quickly exploding case of Solomon
Dwek. Marra had been in on the Dwek thing from the get-go and, in fact,
pushed Christie to give the go-ahead for Dwek to go undercover in the
first place. Marra knew the law and he knew the case. He also knew he and
the Dwek investigation were running out of time.

Outside of Marra's line of sight and away from the cameras, a whole
new campaign started with the conclusion of the race between Obama and
John McCain. In a state where law, politics, crime, and headlines create a
powerful alchemy, there is no appointed post more powerful or sought
after than U.S. Attorney. On top of everything else the position has going
for it, U.S. Attorney is one of only a tiny handful of jobs with statewide authority. New Jersey, because of its compact geography and its past as a small
population bedroom for New York and Philadelphia, has only one Justice
Department district. So the U.S. Attorney is the undisputed top federal law-
enforcement official in the state. It is a perch from which many have graduated to lucrative legal practices and judgeships, including a spot on the U.S.
Supreme Court (Justice Samuel Alito is a former New Jersey U.S. Attorney).
And it's the place that revived Chris Christie's dead political career.

As much as Marra wanted to be U.S. Attorney, someone else wanted it
more: Paul Fishman. Paul was himself a well-known lawyer and former assistant U.S. Attorney with a lucrative law firm partnership and serious
chops as a corruption prosecutor. Fishman's first go-round in the U.S. Attorney's office culminated with him holding the same first assistant position
Marra had held under Chris. Paul also could boast a wall adorned with the
pelts of public officials he had convicted, like onetime Passaic mayor Joe
Lipari.

Fishman was the top lieutenant to U.S. Attorney Michael Chertoff,
who later would become homeland security secretary under Pres. George
W. Bush. After Chertoff left the U.S. Attorney's office, Fishman campaigned
to take the top job—aggressively. Paul worked the lawyers and the judges
and eventually convinced Lautenberg to take his name to President Clinton.

The president refused to nominate Fishman. Bob Torricelli, the state's junior U.S. Senator at the time, did not like Fishman. Worse, "The Torch" told intimates, a number of the more senior federal judges in the state were opposed to Paul's ascension to the big chair and, if nothing else, that provided a good political fig leaf—true or not. Fishman, though, wasn't really the issue. Most aptly described as a diabolical genius, Torch hated Lautenberg with an intensity rarely seen in New Jersey since George Washington crossed the Delaware in 1776. For years, Torricelli and Lautenberg, a tough old street kid who had built himself a fortune, co-existed in a state of cold war despite the Democratic Party membership they shared. Cold turned burning hot with Fishman. A close ally of both the president and Hillary Clinton, Torricelli called in a personal favor to get the door shut on Fishman. It was slammed. Lautenberg was livid and threatening retribution.

Fishman left the Justice Department for private practice but never lost his desire for the U.S. Attorney's job. When a Democrat returned to the White House, Paul floored the gas pedal. He worked Lautenberg and the new junior senator, Menendez, and the incoming U.S. Attorney General, Eric Holder. Fishman basically did everything short of having *I love Barack* skywritten over Newark. Then déjà vu. As Lautenberg carried the Fishman standard, Menendez made it clear he had reservations. He wasn't thrilled with Fishman and—like Torricelli a decade earlier—was ticked that Lautenberg was so presumptuous as to believe he had first dibs on all recommendations for presidential nominations. But unlike Torch, Menendez ultimately relented.

On May 15, 2009, the White House announced the president's intention to nominate Fishman to be New Jersey's U.S. Attorney. There was jubilation at Fishman's home in the North Jersey suburb of Montclair. At the U.S. Attorney's office in Newark, you could almost hear the sound of a stopwatch counting down.

Marra and his prosecutors knew Fishman and thought he was a solid lawyer who would do well in the job. But they also knew that if he walked in before the roundup of politicians and rabbis in the Dwek case, he would stop everything in its tracks. *At least two weeks*, Marra figured to himself. *Fishman would want to hold off on the takedown for two weeks. But then rescheduling becomes another complicated equation and, with the election coming, two weeks could quickly become three months.*

"I don't know if I would have pressed the 'pause' button," Fishman said later, sitting in the same room where the Dwek cooperation deal got the green light. "But I certainly would have wanted to wait."

Marra and Michele Brown and Jimmy Nobile and Brian Howe and the rest of the crew did not want to wait for Fishman. The FBI did not want to wait. Plus, they all feared that a wait could prove indefinite or, worse, fatal to the case. The U.S. Attorney has extraordinary authority, and just because hundreds of thousands—if not millions—had been spent, Fishman as the new boss would have been well within his right to review the case and simply exercise "prosecutorial discretion" to turn it off. They just didn't want to chance it.

On October 19, three months after the July 23 arrests, *The New York Times* ran a story based on anonymous sources that said Brown had been secretly aiding Christie and "wanted to ensure that the arrests occurred before Mr. Christie's permanent successor took office . . . presumably so that Mr. Christie would be given credit for the roundup." Yes and no. Brown certainly advocated for a takedown earlier than July 1. She also pushed for it to be done before Fishman came in, something in which she clearly was not alone. Fishman was confirmed by the Senate in the fall and sworn in on October 14.

* * *

Setting the takedown date in stone had an unintended impact on the case.

Well aware that Marra, Howe, and the prosecutors had decided not to charge certain people, the FBI case agents started running their own offense to nail people they felt needed to be arrested despite the prosecutors' call to wrap it up. "The Bureau's like 'fuck them, we're going to get more evidence and make more arrests,'" recalled one prosecutor. Essentially, the FBI was trying to run up the body count. Up until the end, just before midnight on July 22, Dwek was still setting appointments and making wiretapped phone calls. Even in the final months, the money-laundering side of the case was still in full bore, and now even more so. Only a few days before Cammarano was sworn in, Dwek had gotten a voice-mail message from Fish.

"Hello, hello. Hello *shalom aleichem*. Call me," said the rabbi. "Tonight is a *chasanah* ["wedding" in Hebrew]. You know that tomorrow we have to learn. Please. Let's do the mitzvah. Don't delay the mitzvah. This mitzvah can bring you *nachas*."

In Hebrew, *shalom aleichem* is a greeting of extreme warmth. "Mitzvah" means "a good deed," and *nachas* means "pride" and is usually reserved for the way a parent feels about an accomplishment of a child, for the grandchildren, and for the great-grandchildren. Prosecutors translated it as a motivational device by Fish to urge Dwek to set up another profitable money exchange.

It was the same kind of code that meant nothing without context. In an earlier message, the rabbi implored Dwek to be a loyal customer. He just didn't say it that way. "Don't learn with another *chavrusah* [study partner], just with us. Please please please. Be my friend." The next day he just sang on a voice message for a full minute. Then he ended by saying "*hakol muchan*," Hebrew for "all is ready." The feds viewed it as his way of making it clear that he wanted Dwek's business—now.

Dwek had quickly learned the code words. Once, Fish called him and told him he had spoken with another "learning partner" and Dwek wanted to know how to structure the transaction. "Which *mesechta*?" he asked Fish. A *mesechta* is a tractate, or volume, of the Talmud. In the yeshiva, tractates are understood to be massive books that explain and debate Jewish laws covering everything from the observance of holidays and the Sabbath to sex between a husband and wife. It appeared that Dwek was not asking what page of the Talmud Fish was reading from but rather which gemach, or charitable organization, he wanted on the check that would trigger a felony money-laundering transaction.

In May was another of the meetings being set with increasing frequency now with Fish and Deutsch at the Brooklyn synagogue. Once again, Dwek went through his explanation of his counterfeit handbag business. "We make the fancy bags," he told Deutsch, the Israeli courier. "You know. This—a bag like this for three thousand? I make the same bag. I put the label on. It costs me twenty dollars. I sell it for two hundred."

"I know," Deutsch said. "I understand."

Dwek persisted. "We make 'em, we ship 'em, and we make money," he continued. "The money comes into New York, and we ship it overseas to another bank. We wire it. And then it comes back to New Jersey to the bank."

Asked where the cash he was exchanging for the check came from, Deutsch was vague. "Largely diamond business. Other, other things," he said.

The next day, Fish and Dwek went to a bakery in Flatbush to pick up the cash. After first parking his Lexus near the corner of Fourteenth Avenue and 44th Street, Dwek and Fish picked up Deutsch. The money, said the rabbi, was at a bakery, "because he bakes the money."

"How is it he has so many *gemoras*?" asked Dwek.

"Oh, the bakery's just the middleman."

"What's the source? Where's it from?"

"This is all from diamonds," said Fish.

Deutsch piped in. "It's not drug money."

The bakery was located on Avenue M in Brooklyn, where they met

Binyomin Spira, who was recorded giving them a bag full of cash, which prosecutors claimed was in exchange for the checks Dwek had delivered the day before, minus the commissions that had been agreed to earlier. Out of earshot of Fish, Deutsch suggested to Dwek a new arrangement.

"I want to make a little more. I should make something. I don't make a very lot."

Like Shaw and Cheatam in Jersey City, Deutsch was looking to cut out the middleman. He wanted to cut out Fish.

* * *

On the political side of the sting, prosecutors and FBI remained resolutely determined to get Joe Doria, a former speaker of the state assembly, to the table. Long a fixture in county and state politics, Doria was a big man and a big name. After the Democrats lost control of the Assembly in '91 and Joe was relegated to leading a legislative minority, he took on an additional role as mayor of his hometown of Bayonne, south of Jersey City and north of Staten Island. After a tough first year in office, Governor Corzine wanted to make Doria the education commissioner to both shore up the state ed department and add some legislative muscle to his operation. Corzine couldn't give Doria that job—which Doria really wanted—because the governor couldn't bring himself to fire the woman already serving as commissioner. Instead, Corzine recruited Doria to become his commissioner of community affairs—a post of critical importance to local officials and builders across the state. The Community Affairs Department, among other things, has jurisdiction over the finances of every one of New Jersey's 566 cities and towns, oversees all construction and building inspections, runs a mortgage agency, and controls development projects throughout New Jersey.

Short, round, and bald, Doria was as likable as they come. He liked laughing, liked teaching, and he especially liked politics. Sure, he was a Hudson pol and a top guy in the political game. But he was different from the norm. While he could play hardball, Doria was educated and, in contrast to so many of his peers, was as soft around the edges as the others were rough. And he was smart, with a doctorate from Columbia University.

The feds, though, had long viewed Doria as the stereotypical fat, backslapping Hudson County hack, if only because he had lived so long and survived so many wars. The FBI and the U.S. Attorney's office had an uncomplicated view of Hudson County politicians. To them, there were only two types: the crooked and the dead. The reality was that some of Doria's allies were thieves and, what the hell, he had a good relationship with the now-convicted Bobby J. Finally, the feds salivated, someone was going to walk them into Doria's inner sanctum.

Jack Shaw early on had made it clear he had access to Jerry Healy and Joe Doria—two ranking political officials he claimed to Dwek were on the take—and that he could sell that access. To the feds, it was a huge break in the case. With Healy, the feds had visions of repeating what had happened so many times before by arresting the mayor of one of New Jersey's biggest cities on corruption charges. But with Doria, now that was a whole different order of magnitude.

Back in Newark, Marra and his prosecutors were intrigued by what was coming in via surveillance recordings and FBI reports. Marra and Nobile had deep ties to Hudson County. Both were native sons and had spent careers prosecuting some of the county's top officials for the types of bribery, corruption, and fraud that have been Hudson's hallmark for time immemorial. The two kept tabs on Hudson County, they thought about Hudson County, and, most important, they followed the political goings-on in Hudson County. They knew, for instance, about the massive redevelopment project going on at the two-mile-long man-made peninsula once called the Military Ocean Terminal at Bayonne. In the nineties, the Army pulled out and took 3,000 jobs, leaving behind vacant—yet prime—waterfront real estate jutting into New York Harbor south of the Statue of Liberty, a straight shot across the water from the Brooklyn-Queens Expressway. Redeveloping MOTB (pronounced "mot-bee") was supposed to lead to a renaissance. However, Nobile and Marra had long heard reports that the project was corrupt and stories that Doria might be orchestrating it or, at least, in on it. On top of that, they harbored suspicions that Bob Menendez, now the senator, was connected in some nefarious way to the project. They had never been able to verify any of it, however.

Menendez and the U.S. Attorney's office had a long history, some of it good but, more recently, all of it bad. In 1980, Menendez was used by prosecutors in that office to help them convict Menendez's mentor, Bill Musto, at the time a state senator and the occupant of the Union City's mayor's office that Menendez would ultimately take over. Menendez recalled it as a trying and eye-opening time in his life, when he realized that his surrogate father was a crook. His efforts to help win the Musto conviction were a centerpiece of his 2006 Senate race against Tom Kean Jr.

More than 25 years after the Musto affair, during that very same campaign for the Senate, the U.S. Attorney's office—under the control of Chris Christie—took on an even more central role in Menendez's life. That time, Menendez wasn't a star witness for the feds. To the contrary, he looked to be the hunted. Two months before that election, federal prosecutors very publicly subpoenaed records connected to a rental deal between Menendez and a community-service agency that won federal grants. The controversial subpoena would multiply into a small series and it became a critical element of the election, Kean hammering repeatedly that Menendez was under "federal criminal investigation." Feds went further by subpoenaing records related to the work of former Menendez aide Kay LiCausi, who had been romantically linked to Menendez. Inside the U.S. Attorney's office, Christie authorized the first subpoena in 2006, ignoring the potential effect it could have on the Kean-Menendez balloting.

It was a move that infuriated Democrats, who accused Christie of issuing the subpoena specifically to affect the election. They also charged that Christie, who was on an initial list of U.S. Attorneys to be fired by the White House during the Bush administration, was able to save his beloved job by hitting Menendez during the campaign. Christie, however, was not alone in going after Menendez. It was Marra who pushed most aggressively for the subpoena to be issued. Ralph made no secret that he was not the least bit convinced by LiCausi's testimony and others' that said Menendez had done nothing improper.

Marra and Nobile knew that Menendez was tight with Doria and that he had been pushing for the Marine Ocean Terminal redevelopment. Plus, they knew that LiCausi—now in private practice as a lobbyist and government-affairs consultant—was working for Royal Caribbean Cruise Lines, which had a plan to use the revitalized terminal for passenger boarding. The feds long believed that Menendez told businesses who to hire, despite LiCausi's denials under oath. They saw the Bayonne project as a way into the secret world of Bob Menendez, if only they could make Doria roll over on the senator.

Shaw had reached out directly to Doria first in February 2009 with what was for him a typical request: lunch at the Brownstone Diner in Jersey City. Shaw told Doria he had "a guy who wanted to do affordable housing in the Meadowlands. This is a friend." Unlike code words used by Dwek's money-laundering connections, there was nothing hidden or clever about Shaw's language. Doria knew the deal and played along.

Doria was well aware Shaw was bad news and in bad shape. It was obvious and, even if it wasn't, Doria's key advisers were constantly reminding him to "stay away from Jack." Shaw's game was simple. If he could introduce a businessman or a developer to Doria, Shaw would get himself a commission, a finder's fee. If the meet turned into a project, the fees would grow and compound. If the meet turned into nothing, Shaw still got his payment. To Shaw, people like Doria were the product. He was certainly selling.

Doria knew how it worked. But it was a no-impact way to help out a guy who was the embodiment of "down on his luck." Doria felt sorry for Jack.

"He had all kinds of problems," Doria confided to an intimate long after the July 23 arrests. "He was being injected four times a day with insulin. He would carry around those kids' boxes of juice so if he was going into insulin shock he'd take a quick sip. He was in terrible health. And he did the gastric bypass operation because the doctor said if he didn't do that and improve the diabetes, he'd be dead. So I always felt sorry for Jack Shaw. I shouldn't have, but I did. I would say, 'He's harmless.'"

Shaw, however, wasn't harmless. And Doria never took precautions. He would meet with Shaw alone, no record of what was said, no staffer to witness and vouch. Shaw would call Doria's longtime secretary and suggest a lunch or a dinner, and like clockwork, Joe would be at the right spot, at the appointed time. So when Shaw called to meet at the Brownstone, Doria showed up to be introduced to Dave Esenbach and listen to his spiel about a proposed 200-condo development in the Meadowlands.

To most people, the "Meadowlands" means a sports-and-entertainment complex, home of the Giants, Jets, horse racing, rock concerts, and the 2014 Super Bowl. But "The Swamp," as the sportscasters call it, is way more than just the complex. The Meadowlands is a 30.4-square-mile environmentally sensitive zone along the Hackensack River that cuts through parts of 14 towns and is protected by state laws written to reverse decades of use and abuse in a region that had once been nothing but a dump for garbage, abandoned cars, and victims of the occasional mob hit. To protect the area, the state took control of construction and development in the Meadowlands through an agency now called the New Jersey Meadowlands Commission. As the head of community affairs in the governor's cabinet, Joe Doria was the chairman of the Meadowlands Commission. That made Doria hugely important to developers looking to build in the Meadowlands zone.

Dwek's initial meeting with Doria did not go anywhere. Soon afterward, though, Dave Esenbach was already offering up some big talk about his supposed hooks into the gregarious cabinet member, as he outlined to yet another of his targets a new scheme for a real estate project that would never be built, this one in the Meadowlands town of Secaucus.

"If Doria's on it, we can work with him," Esenbach said. "I have people that know him . . . I'll tell you, if Doria has control and I want five hundred condos, I'll get them. You understand? I decide how many I want, where I want, when I want them, and when I want my approval. He doesn't say nothing."

Dwek went on, boasting that he could score state grants from Joe in a heartbeat. "Doria: he'll throw me ten million dollars. I never used him for anything. I never asked him for a thing in my life. He's my man. He's in my pocket. But I never used him. I'll use him one day, maybe. But he's a fine man . . . He's in charge of the low-income housing. He's the commissioner. So no grant money goes out in the state without his approval."

In May, Shaw brought Dwek to see Doria at the Meadowlands Commission offices—without telling Doria the informant would be tagging along. Cheatam was there, too, though he said nothing and Doria couldn't figure out what he was doing in the room. On Esenbach's supposed agenda was another fictional condo complex, this time in Carlstadt—a small community next to East Rutherford and just 2.5 miles away from the Meadowlands Racetrack. Dave also wanted to discuss a land deal he was working on in run-down Trenton. He wanted Doria to "expedite" approval processes so he could move his fictitious deals along quickly. No FedEx envelope ever appeared, however.

Doria told him he could push his people, but there would be no short-circuiting health and safety. Doria also told Esenbach to send a formal letter about the Carlstadt deal to the staff at the Meadowlands Commission and to copy him in on it. On July 14, Esenbach's letter—actually written by the U.S. Attorney's office—was dispatched: "Please allow me to introduce myself and advise you that our company is looking to purchase property . . . under the control of the New Jersey Meadowlands Commission."

Doria's name was at the bottom and the letter was signed: *David Esenbach, CEO.*

* * *

The FBI also wanted to take a last-minute pass at a new target, one that was extremely important and highly sensitive. On May 27, Eddie Cheatam and Dwek were talking on the phone as usual when Cheatam suggested there were development opportunities and pols on the take in Trenton. Cheatam wanted Dwek to meet longtime mayor Doug Palmer.

The ugly state capital was a testament to urban decay and government neglect. When the heavy industry left for the south and west, the city was gutted. Over the years, state and local officials spent considerable effort and cash boasting about developments to come and the city's rebirth, but little has grown in Trenton besides hopelessness. That's not to say there have not been attempts to put the city back together and even some pockets of economic activity. The state has invested in its facilities and there has been some private-sector construction. After all, the city has a great location along the Delaware River, if ever anyone really decided to make a go at it. But for the most part, Trenton is a disgrace compounded by the fact that the gold dome of the State House glimmers ironically within spitting distance of crack dens and gang shootings.

Reigning over it all for the last generation was Doug Palmer, the dapper, well-spoken, African American mayor who became a national leader among city officials. To observers, it seemed Palmer always knew how to impress, which buttons to push, which friends to make. To some in federal law enforcement, he seemed to have a whiff about him that wasn't quite right. They were equally leery of Palmer's wife, Christiana Foglio-Palmer, a good-looking affordable-housing developer whose friends included some of New Jersey's top political operators, such as former senator Bob Torricelli and deposed Middlesex County Democratic boss John Lynch.

Cheatam told Dwek he had a "partnership in Trenton" with the Palmers and suggested that they go and try to run their routine of expedited approvals for cash in the state capital. Cheatam, in the end, couldn't arrange a meeting with the Palmers, but the feds kept pressing. On July 6, Dwek took the Palmer idea to Joe Cardwell, knowing that Cardwell had at least a glancing familiarity with every top-tier African American politician in the northern two-thirds of New Jersey.

"This guy Palmer seems to be a rough guy," Dwek said of the way Palmer insulated himself.

As the tape rolled, Cardwell said not to worry: "I've known him very well. Matter of fact, I'm in the process of doing some work with his wife, some state work." Cardwell said Palmer was no problem and suggested sitting down with the county executive in Mercer County, which includes Trenton. The Mercer County Executive was Brian Hughes, the son of the late New Jersey governor Richard Hughes. The FBI was uninterested in Hughes because the agents did not have the proper legal "predication" to believe he might be on the take, so they did not authorize Dwek to approach him. The FBI wanted Palmer.

After some jostling back and forth on the phone, Dwek convinced Cardwell to reach out and set up a meeting with Palmer. The fictitious developer Esenbach wanted to build on eight and one-half acres near the city's arena, now called the Sun National Bank Center. Dwek didn't give Cardwell precise coordinates, but the zone around the arena looks like a southern version of Garfield Avenue in Jersey City.

"We'll touch base with the right people," Cardwell said. "We'll touch base with the decision makers."

Dwek was pleased. "A meeting together never hurts."

It also didn't happen before the roundup.

* * *

Yet another failed approach in the final days involved David Hepperle, a former member of the Guttenberg planning board and school board.

Months earlier, Vinnie Tabbachino had hooked Dwek up with Hepperle, who thought he was working on a legitimate $100 million high-rise development with Manhattan views when Dwek started inquiring about rigging a school district contract.

"Look, why do you want to jeopardize the project for twenty thousand dollars or thirty thousand dollars?" Hepperle said to Esenbach. Dwek soon realized Hepperle was playing for real. He suggested that Hepperle run for mayor with his financial backing.

Hepperle didn't want to run for mayor and he didn't want to get involved in a bid-rigging scheme. He wanted his project. At the time, Hepperle owned a pizza place with a great location in town, but he wasn't making real money and he wanted the real estate project Esenbach had put on his plate. "It was such a big deal, you had to eat crow," Hepperle explained later when the sting came to light. Hepperle's end would be 2 percent commissions to start.

Dwek kept stalling Hepperle but eventually offered up mock plans for the project, courtesy of the FBI, complete with schematics and floor layouts. By April, it appeared Esenbach and Hepperle were moving quickly to signing their contracts and getting their deal off the ground. But something was still wrong. "Vinnie, you gotta tell him to knock it off," Hepperle told Tabbachino after a handful of meetings when Dwek would talk about paying off public officials as a member of the "Green Party." Dwek was blatant about it and Hepperle told Tabbachino there could be trouble.

"Don't worry; we're gonna talk to him," Vinnie reassured Hepperle, joking that they would "take him out back and choke him."

They were supposed to go to contract on Monday, July 20. Suspiciously, Dwek canceled and rescheduled for 24 hours later. Hepperle, though, had already become uncomfortable and was growing leery of Esenbach. A few days earlier—on a lark—Hepperle went online to Google the name David Esenbach and found exactly nothing.

"I didn't know if he was a fed, but I knew he wasn't who he said he was," Hepperle recalled.

Hepperle stopped talking to him.

* * *

With the clock continuing to tick down, the case agents and prosecutors started setting the pins for July 23.

Dwek got Levi Deutsch on the phone on the morning of July 6, looking to push back their latest laundering transaction. Deutsch was angry at the delay, but he was being set up. The FBI wanted to make sure there would be money to seize when they arrested him. "I was in the hospital. You gotta wait two weeks," said Dwek, trying to put him off. "The week of the twenty-first. Can you do two to three hundred *gemoras* for me?"

In Union City, the surveillance tapes documented Dwek throwing some more checks at Moshe Altman to convert through his washing machines. "How's the money coming along? Is it tight this week or is it good?" Dwek asked.

Recalling that Dwek had expressed discontent at their last meeting over the slow turnaround pace for cash, Altman told Dwek, "You gave me a hard time last week." Dwek said he would have another "hundred," meaning $100,000 pulled out of his counterfeit handbag business, sometime after July 13.

Prosecutors also decided it was time to get Levy-Itzhak Rosenbaum—still known in Special Prosecutions only as "Kidney Guy"—back in the game, weeks after Uncle Teddy suffered his supposed medical crisis. About an hour after getting off the phone with Deutsch, Dwek reached out to the kidney broker in Brooklyn. His secretary's uncle was finally on the mend, Dwek was recorded telling Rosenbaum. "He's in Florida, but he's getting better," said Dwek on the call being recorded by the FBI. "And I'm wondering, are you around next week or are you away?"

"No, I'm here."

"Okay, so next week maybe I'll come see you. I think the secretary wants to come, too. I'll find out. And then maybe the week after we'll bring the uncle in for those tests and everything else."

"Where is he now?" Rosenbaum asked in his heavy accent.

"He's in Florida, but he's coming back the week of the twentieth."

"Aha, so he's getting better?"

"Yeah, yeah, yeah. He had, I don't know, he had pneumonia; he had bronchitis; he had some crazy things. But he's much better now, I'm hearing, and he's coming," Dwek reassured Rosenbaum. "So maybe next week I'll come see you with her, we'll see what the procedure, whatever we gotta do, is, and then the following week we'll bring him up. You're still in the same place in Flatbush?"

"Yes, yes, yes."

In one brief conversation, Dwek set up Rosenbaum for the feds and made sure that he would be home when they came to arrest him.

Dwek and Sarah, the undercover agent, drove from New Jersey back to the house in Brooklyn a week later and met Rosenbaum. Sarah confirmed that Uncle Teddy was now in good health and ready to proceed with a kidney transplant. Rosenbaum said they would first need to take a blood sample to start the search for a suitable donor.

"I am what you call a matchmaker," Rosenbaum explained for them, and the surveillance video. "I bring a guy what I believe he's suitable for your uncle," he said. The donor would then be checked into a hospital to ensure a proper match. "My obligation to you is to bring you a person [who] will have it done. If for any reason, for any reason, he will—the guy I will bring you will not go through, then I have to bring you somebody else."

The blood sample would be frozen and sent to Israel, where Rosenbaum's contacts would work to find a prospective donor. He wouldn't say who they were or even how much they got paid. Only that they were healthy and all ranged from 20 to 40 years in age.

"How long have you been doing this for?" asked Sarah, the undercover FBI agent.

"Ten years," said Rosenbaum, who said he had brokered quite a lot over that time. "Quite a lot," he repeated. The most recent one just two weeks earlier.

Dwek got back to the money. "What's my balance?" he asked. "A hundred and forty thousand you told me?"

It was $150,000, said Rosenbaum, after the deposit Dwek had already put down. "It went up. It's hard to get people." Israel, Rosenbaum said, had passed laws prohibiting the sale of human organs. He told Dwek to bring another $70,000 the following Thursday.

Would he accept checks made payable to several charitable organizations?

"I prefer you do it with cash." Rosenbaum would not say how much the donor got out of that. "Don't worry about it," was all he would say.

Sarah asked whether Rosenbaum would be available to meet Teddy the following week. "How about Thursday morning?" asked the FBI agent.

The Thursday she was talking about was July 23.

* * *

In Hoboken, one week before the takedown, Shaw and Cheatam met Cammarano and Mike Schaffer one last time on July 16, still pushing another real estate deal. By now, Dwek was starting to slip. Asked by the new mayor about the property's exact location, Esenbach was just not sure. "I think it's, it's a parcel of land or something that's available," he said. "And then on Hudson Street there's an apartment building that's all rentals now and the whole building might be coming on the market. Maybe there's an opportunity to go higher, add some density, go wider."

As he fumbled over the details, Esenbach got to the point of the matter. He asked if he had the mayor's support.

"Yes," said Cammarano. "Wholeheartedly."

"At least I bet on the right horse this time," joked Dave.

"Yeah. You did," said the mayor.

In the wake of the costly runoff, Cammarano was still trying to raise money to erase his campaign debt, and Esenbach told him he was there to help. "I'll give Mike ten thousand, you know, green," he said. "Just make sure my name, like the other times. Don't put my name on nothin'. I don't need any, uh, issues."

The group left the diner and walked into the parking lot, where Dwek and Schaffer walked to the Lexus. Dwek opened the trunk and pulled out a FedEx envelope.

"Don't put my name like—"

Schaffer interrupted with a laugh. "I know. I know the drill."

Dwek walked back to Cammarano, who was talking with Shaw and Cheatam.

"I'll be in touch with you next week," said the mayor.

"I'll take care of the other ten," promised Esenbach. "Just, you know, make sure I have your support . . . expediting my stuff."

"Yeah, yeah. I'm with you."

That afternoon, Cheatam called Esenbach to plan what he did not know would be a last meeting with Doria for the following Tuesday.

"Joe at eight thirty A.M. at the Bayonne diner," Dwek told Cheatam.

"I need two Federal Express envelopes coming from you so we can put these letters into it. They want to show they received it that way," said

Cheatam. "We don't want to hand them to them. We want to show we sent it through the mail."

* * *

As the prosecutors and the FBI prepared to pull the curtain back on their monumental case, the New Jersey political calendar was at its most heated point. The race for governor was in its final, frenzied months and Jon Corzine and Chris Christie were at the center, slugging it out now like street brawlers.

Corzine's very weakness had lured Christie into the race and the former prosecutor loved calling the incumbent timid. It drove Corzine bananas. In seven years running the U.S. Attorney's office, Christie fully inhabited—and basked in—the role of chief federal lawman in New Jersey. You could see it on his face. In his strut. He loved the news conferences on courthouse steps to decry another public official trading on elected office. He eagerly traversed the state for speaking engagements in all corners, no matter how long the drive. And he was the rage of the press who provided clippings that wouldn't stop. Lengthy TV interviews with him trumpeting his efforts to clean up corruption and gangs. Announcement after announcement, laying out stings that nailed politicians, informants who fingered politicians, greed that destroyed politicians.

The big, flamboyant, tough-talking prosecutor had his critics. Christie came under harsh scrutiny in 2007, after *The Star-Ledger* revealed that he had appointed former U.S. Attorney General John Ashcroft, his onetime boss, to a lucrative 18-month monitoring contract involving a medical device company that had been under investigation over kickbacks to orthopedic surgeons—a deal estimated to be worth as much as $52 million to Ashcroft's law firm. And a $300 million fraud settlement negotiated with Bristol-Myers Squibb included a provision for the company to endow a professorship at Seton Hall Law School, Christie's alma mater.

Democrats argued Christie was not prosecuting criminals as much as waging a jihad against the infrastructure of the state's reigning political party. Defense attorneys, noting the majority of the office's corruption convictions involved Democrats, claimed his motives were political. Christie responded, saying his office worked on the Willie Sutton principal. Like the famous bank robber said to have claimed that he robbed banks "because that's where the money is," Christie said his people went after Democrats because that's where the corruption was.

In a state where the Republican Party had fallen into a money-starved malaise, Christie was the one point of pride. Party leaders wanted him to run for governor in 2005, but he passed. They took another crack at trying to get him to run for the U.S. Senate in 2006 and 2008; again, no luck.

Then Barack Obama came along. Christie was still only 46 years old at the end of 2008 and he could easily have opted to put off running for another four or eight years, but by the summer of '08 it was clear to Christie that Obama was going to beat John McCain. As a result, most of—if not all—the U.S. Attorneys in the country would be replaced. Christie certainly would be gone. He started looking around at the options. Corporate counsel or governor. That's what it came down to.

After having watched his political career end a decade earlier when voters threw him off the Morris County freeholder board, Christie was ready for a comeback and some validation. His resignation as U.S. Attorney was effective December 1, 2008. Thirty-eight days later, he decided to see if all that "leader" talk was true.

"If you're looking for the same old stuff," Christie declared, his trademark bombast dripping into the newspapers, "you've got the wrong person."

* * *

As Republicans toasted their new fortune, Jon Corzine was literally living through his winter of discontent. The onetime CEO of Goldman Sachs and a name in the Rolodex of the rich and powerful from Manhattan to Dubai, Corzine now was the political neophyte who had bought his way to the most powerful governorship in the nation. And he was increasingly on the verge of being dismissed because of his poor popularity and inability to connect with Everyman, New Jersey.

When he was pushed out at Goldman Sachs in 1999, Corzine cashed out a fabulously wealthy man, locking up a $400 million payday that was certain to grow larger and larger as Goldman stock appreciated in the coming years. Yet even in his fifties, Corzine was still impatient. Soon after he was deposed, Corzine's appetite settled on the cutthroat politics of his adopted home state of New Jersey. It was a world of dank VFW halls, packed black churches, and greasy bagmen with pockets full of cash.

Once in the game, Corzine was totally out of his element. He knew it. His friends knew it. Certainly, his enemies knew it. But Corzine was determined to win, so it didn't matter and he jumped in full speed. To go from unknown to king, Corzine showered his fortune from one end of Jersey to the other. Ministers with community groups got Corzine cash, as did political bosses looking to finance rookie candidates. Corzine once handed Democratic boss George Norcross a signed blank personal check with instructions to fill in the amount as he liked. The first-term governor was openly called the Bank of Corzine and the Democratic Party's "cash register," and the checkout line was always long. On top of his donations, Corzine broke all sorts of campaign-spending records. Even in a state with a history of electing blue-blooded millionaires to high office, Corzine stood alone. He spent more than $60 million to win the seat in the U.S. Senate in 2000.

The Senate appealed to Corzine because of its global prominence in finance and diplomacy. He took on a big role, made the rounds of the news talk shows, but soon grew bored. The Senate is nothing if not slow, and when Corzine got there he was a very junior member of the minority party and, to top it off, an ultraliberal in the world of post-9/11 neoconservative George W. Bush politics. Corzine figured that he would have to serve long past his own death if he wanted to get to a position of leadership and influence. With Corzine feeling stuck in that bottleneck of seniority and tradition, the governorship started to appeal to him because of its executive authority and command of the news cycle.

With the surprise resignation of McGreevey, and enough money to scare away most of the other challengers in his party, Corzine jumped in. He spent $40 million to finance his 2005 bid, winning easily over Republican Doug Forrester, another wealthy contender who used his own money to fund his campaign.

Yet it soon became clear that as adept as Jon Corzine had been at trading bonds and running Goldman Sachs, he was as awful a politician. He looked down on backroom operators such as Jim McGreevey and brawlers such as Bob Menendez for not having his pedigree, but those were the guys who knew how to connect with voters, how to stay on message, how to explain their positions, and how to fight when necessary. In New Jersey, it's necessary a lot. Corzine could do none of that. He was personable and eager to try to talk people into his viewpoint, but the hallmark of his politics—more than liberal or Democratic—was simply ineptitude.

He could not deliver a speech or a sound bite and was apt to blurt out whatever it was he had just been told in private. As the insiders say, he was "tone-deaf" to both the politics on the ground and what the political class was thinking.

Once the 2008 presidential election kicked off, the governor had already decided it was time to move on from the claustrophobic State House in Trenton. He was tight with the Clintons and did everything he could—short of selling his testicles—to get Hillary Clinton the Democratic nomination, with an eye toward an appointment in the new administration. In addition to his forceful endorsement of Clinton, Corzine traveled the states to stump for her, and when her candidacy was gasping its dying breaths Corzine even offered to help bankroll do-over primaries to win Clinton the nomination.

Secretly, Corzine was also trying to hedge his bets. He offered to dispatch trusted aide Tom Shea to assist with Obama's effort, even as Corzine was publicly working Clinton's side of the street.

Still, as June and July of 2008 passed Corzine began to realize that Hillary's loss meant his immediate future now appeared to lie in Jersey and he may well need to run and win reelection as a sign of his own vindication. The governor summoned his senior advisers to a private meeting at the home of his business manager, Nancy Dunlap, at her top-of-the-line Manhattan digs overlooking the entrance to the Holland Tunnel. The group was in agreement: reelection, though difficult, was certainly not impossible. *We're likely to face Chris Christie and he is beatable and it appears we may have a Democratic president in the White House. So that will help. Plus, this is New Jersey. It's a blue state through and through and has gotten ever more blue in the decade since Christie Whitman and the Republicans ran the roost at the State House.*

Then came the collapse. The ballooning prices of the national housing market had fully burst, the economy—as Corzine had been saying for months—was in the throes of recession, and suddenly the population of the United States was pissed. At the world. Pissed at Wall Street. Pissed at anyone and everyone who carried even the faintest odor of the boys at AIG, Lehman Brothers, and, yes, even Goldman Sachs.

In late 2008, Corzine convened his top people again at Dunlap's home. Again, he asked if he should run. This time, everyone said no. Only Corzine thought he could win. The governor battled through the end of 2008 and first half of 2009 as Christie ran a remarkably smart, steady, and disciplined race. When July 2009 dawned, Corzine was in bad shape in the polls and among party loyalists, but it appeared he might be finally gaining some adrenaline, something that could vault him out of the summer and into the fall homestretch. It looked like it was—at long last—coming together and the image that gave the Corzine team some hope was the form of the sweating, smiling new president, Barack Obama, standing off Exit 116 of the Garden State Parkway.

* * *

Following the meeting with Dave Esenbach on July 16, Cammarano drove down the parkway to the PNC Arts Center in Holmdel for Corzine's rally with Obama in hopes of getting close to the president. Maybe a picture.

It was the president's first political trip since taking office and he was greeted like the rock star he was the day he won the presidency. Thousands lined up in the typical July swelter. Corzine beamed onstage. All of the state's top Democrats were there. Corzine's campaign handed out signs that said: OBAMA CORZINE, as if they were running mates.

"I'm proud to stand with a man who wakes up every day thinking about your future and the future of New Jersey," Obama told the cheering crowd of seventeen thousand. "Jon's a leader who's been challenged to govern in extraordinary times."

Sweating and shouting, Corzine stood alongside Obama and, pumping his fist, said, "Now, with a partner in the White House, there is no limit to what we can accomplish."

* * *

Twenty-four hours after Obama left New Jersey, on the Friday before the bust, Dwek had a last meeting with Harvey Smith. Shaw, Cheatam, and Dwek met the legislator at the busy Malibu diner in Hoboken. "Well, I made two calls yesterday," said Smith.

"You're a man of your word," replied Dave Esenbach.

"I only do business one way."

Smith had notes outlining what he had done on Dave's behalf. As the tape rolled, Smith told them he had called the state Department of Environmental Protection on the Garfield Avenue project, as well as a second proposal they had pulled out of thin air for Bayonne on Route 440. "You need a letter from the mayor that he supports it, I mean I'm just giving you my point of view, a letter from the mayor as well as whatever lawyer you use."

"I appreciate your support."

What wasn't said was that Dwek was already trying to reel in the mayor of Bayonne, Mark Smith (no relation to Harvey Smith), and the local Democratic chairman, Jason O'Donnell, who was on his way to becoming the mayor's director of municipal services at City Hall. Harvey Smith told Dwek there was a state Department of Transportation official he knew who was willing to help him out as well. "If you need, if my clout isn't enough, he'll make a phone call down the road to let him know how [he] supports this project." As he got up, he told Esenbach that he was "trying to find me a new way of making a living."

They left the diner and went to the parking lot, the surveillance tape showed. "Okay," said the legislator, patting Dwek on the shoulder and walking toward his Ford Flex, parked nearby.

Dwek, finally adhering to Eddie Cheatam's repeated urgings, made him the middleman. A FedEx envelope with ten thousand dollars cash came out of the trunk of the Lexus and Dwek handed the envelope to Cheatam, who followed Smith to his big SUV.

Eddie was seen leaning into the open passenger side window and then returned empty-handed. "He said 'thank you,'" he told Esenbach.

Dwek ambled over to Smith's car. "Harvey, I don't want you to call me a cheap skunk anymore," he kidded.

"Hey, it's not about that," replied Smith. "It's just about—it's just about the fact that I'm a straight guy."

"Just like me," said Dwek. "We do business our own way."

* * *

Monday evening just before eight o'clock, Dwek got Rabbi Fish back on the phone and arranged for him to have a huge haul of cash at his place so the FBI would find it on Thursday morning when they raided. Dwek claimed he was closing on a big deal and needed the money right away.

"So everything is already, *Yom Chamishi bah-boker.*" Thursday. In the morning.

"Can we learn?" asked Fish.

"We have to make it a big learning. This is the deal now, because I have the closing at nine thirty. I need three hundred *gemoras* by you and we do, instead of the usual *maaser* [tithe], we'll do twenty percent for whatever it is because of all the things. But I have to be out because the closing's nine thirty."

"The question is . . ."

"I need the names on the *gemoras.*"

"I understand, but the question is, we spoke last time do you have to have all the *gemoras* on the spot?"

"Yeah, yeah, everything there. So make some miracles happen. Call me back with the names and I'll see you then by your place," said Dwek.

"You mean . . . if I put things together, you have to understand one thing: if you don't show up . . ." Fish was worried that he would be left holding the bag if Dwek arranged a big cash transfer and then failed to come through with the checks to cover it.

"No, no, no, no," Dwek reassured him. "I sold a different building. I have everything ready. There's no problem. There's no no-showing-up. It's all ready. *Mezuman* [ready cash]." He told Fish that he would be there at nine in the morning and they would do it fast.

"Okay," agreed Fish. "*Shalom uvrachah.*"

Good-bye and be blessed.

* * *

Doria met Dwek on Tuesday, July 21, for the third and final time. As usual, the commissioner was by himself—no staff or driver—when he arrived at the Uptown Broadway Diner, near his home in Bayonne. Shaw had arranged the gathering. Again, Cheatam was there unannounced, serving no apparent purpose. Doria was on time for the quick stop at 8:30 A.M. Dwek was late, arriving just as Doria was ready to take off. Dwek wanted Doria to look at the plans he said he had had drawn up for the Carlstadt project.

"I don't need to see them," Doria said to Dwek, as Esenbach, who was getting more insistent. "It needs a variance." The commissioner got up to leave. In that ever-so-familiar pattern, Dwek followed Doria out, trying to get him to go to the trunk of his car. "I don't have the time; I don't want to see them; I don't need them," Doria said, growing more impatient and irritated.

Only days later, Doria confided in his closest friends that he was actually "running away from Dwek who was . . . chasing me. What's wrong with this guy? He said to me, 'What should I do?' I said, 'Do whatever you gotta do. Talk to Jack. I told you what to do.'" Weeks later, after the events of July 23, Doria would return in his mind to that moment around nine o'clock that morning. *Should I have realized something was odd and reported it to the attorney general or some other law enforcement agency? Should I have taken the plans? What if Dwek had secretly hidden cash inside the plans and I never found it? How would that look?*

But if Dwek had actually given him money, he knew he would have run to the authorities immediately.

The next day, Wednesday, at Barelli's Restaurant in Secaucus, Doria saw Shaw yet again. This time, the agenda was not Esenbach but a real developer Shaw was working with—one who employed Shaw's longtime companion and had transformed the old Jersey City Medical Center into the Beacon complex. Before the commissioner left the meeting, he turned privately to Shaw. "Jack, I don't want to meet with that guy anymore. He's obnoxious. What the hell's he doing, chasing me to my car for? I don't like people chasing me to my car. I just don't care."

Then things began focusing for Doria. But not fast enough. As his old friend Jack Shaw pulled away, Doria saw the crumpled guy who always seemed to be scratching for clients drive off in his brand-new black Mercedes.

That's weird, he thought.

* * *

The scene in the U.S. Attorney's office in Newark was not quite chaos. "Chaos" would have been too strong a word. But it wasn't a well-oiled machine. Some of the assistant prosecutors doing a last read-through of the criminal complaints were stressed. "I wish Jimmy was here," one kept muttering.

Jimmy Nobile was always a calming presence when he was at the helm, showing no outward worries. Even his occasional popping of Rolaids antacid tablets had a soothing, therapeutic effect on his team. He knew everything and had been through this kind of fire drill so many times before. He knew the protocols with the magistrate judges. He knew it backward and forward. And he was not there. Because of his mysterious recusal from the case, he was sitting alone in his office. Down the hall, Brian Howe was visibly exhausted. In the run-up to the takedown, he had been routinely coming to work at 5:45 A.M. for the past five or six months. Now it was all catching up to him.

In Washington, the Department of Justice was alerted to what was to come down. The Jersey Sting was going to be a national story and the communications staff at DOJ wanted to push it out aggressively. They liked the case, they liked the number of bad guys to be rounded up, and they liked that it was all occurring in the New York City media market, which magnifies even the most minuscule hiccup into a 75-point headline.

It's a big case, a good case; it's going to make a lot of news, Justice officials thought. Memos, press releases, copies of the complaints were e-mailed to Washington, making the senior people at the home office even more excited about the news that was about to break.

On Wednesday afternoon, the FBI began to make its play, just hours before agents were to begin fanning out across New York and New Jersey to haul in Solomon's catch. Agents knocked on the door of Moshe "Michael" Altman. The real Mike from Monsey, the unofficial moniker of the case. Even though Altman never succeeded in serving up government officials to Dwek and his FBI handlers, the feds never lost their interest in seeing whether Altman could take them down a road that would lead to corrupt politicians. Early in the case, Altman had told Dwek in recorded conversation that he had previously passed a bribe to Albio Sires. At the time Altman made that comment, Sires was a Democratic congressman representing Hudson County and a stretch of urban New Jersey that runs along the state's northeastern shore down to gritty Perth Amboy, across from Staten Island. According to Altman's story, the bribe had been given to Sires while he was mayor of West New York, the town neighboring Union City—where so much of Altman's development work had been centered before he met Dwek, and when Sires was also speaker of the state assembly.

A tall, thick Cuban native, Sires had come from nowhere to take over the state's third-most-powerful job and quickly became a well-liked and well-known figure in Trenton. To federal prosecutors, Sires was always viewed as one of the ones that got away. In 2002, the U.S. Attorney's office indicted Sires' chief fund-raiser and one of his closest friends, Rene Abreu, on 42 counts of bank fraud, bribery, and extortion. The case grew out of a corruption investigation, though the final result didn't have much to do with politics. Abreu was ultimately convicted, but the feds really didn't want him. They had told Abreu repeatedly that they had a Get Out of Jail Free card waiting for him if he would roll over on Sires. Abreu wouldn't, and his trial was turned into a discourse on Christie's political ambitions by Abreu's attorney, Christie critic Gerald Krovatin.

Years later, when the feds heard Altman utter Sires' name, they grew interested. Very interested. The problem was they couldn't use Dwek to go after Sires. Though Altman was advertising a political target, he was part of the money-laundering side of the case, which meant he knew Dwek as Dwek, not Esenbach. And Altman was, obviously, unaware that Dwek had turned state's evidence. To get where they wanted with Altman, the feds realized they could be putting their whole case in jeopardy. So to make the Altman play work to snag Sires, the agents devised a strategy of approaching Altman quietly and privately to try to entice him to roll over separate from Dwek. That would keep Solomon's two identities and cooperation arrangement intact and allow them to go after Sires.

There were risks: What if Altman refused to cooperate and then got on the phone and blew the lid off the case? What if he started calling the money launderers and told them what happened? The feds never really got to know the rabbis and their associates well enough to gauge whether one of them might shoot Dwek between the eyes and feared that could be a real possibility with hundreds of thousands of dollars and years of prison time on the line.

The feds decided they would put off an Altman approach. They would still make it, but only after everything else was signed and sealed. So just before the July 23 arrests, a small team of FBI agents was dispatched to surprise Altman. As Dwek was making his final plays with Fish and the others, Altman was being told he had two choices: help the government implicate the congressman or learn what it's like to feel handcuffs and to make bail. The whole team knew that if Altman decided to cooperate with the authorities, the takedown would have been put off. Indefinitely.

Altman considered the possibilities. He gave serious thought to taking the FBI's offer and going the way of his associate Solomon Dwek. Ultimately, though, Altman said no deal.

It didn't end with that. The alleged money launderers, in many ways, were always the biggest risk in the case. They had the cash and contacts to leave the country, and the agents and prosecutors needed to surprise them so they could seize the huge stacks of money the targets were sitting on. Approaching Altman could backfire, badly—just 12 hours before the takedown.

"We had to put him on ice," said one of the feds.

So they locked Altman up. It served to keep him out of circulation and off the phone and, as a fringe benefit, could have a psychological effect that might make him more willing to cooperate. What could be more motivational, they figured, than a night in jail. And they didn't just lock him up in some country club minimum-security joint or a sterile location like the FBI's Newark offices. They stashed Altman at "Green Street," the hard-core city lockup in downtown Newark. Not a lot of white-collar crooks there. Green Street was the home of the corner whores, gangbangers, and repeat-offense dead-enders who call Newark's nighttime home.

With Altman unwilling to deal, it was a go for the July 23 takedown. The FBI's commanders were notified, as was the U.S. Attorney's office in Newark. First things first, however. Get to Dwek. Solomon was home in Deal with his wife and kids, waiting to learn the results of the Altman move. With a call from his FBI handlers, Dwek knew it was red alert and that he needed to start the process of letting Pearl in on the cascading secrets that had overtaken his life. The arrests would begin in 12 hours.

Before the couple could share the moment of great confession, they needed to get out of the house. The feds wanted Dwek and his family nowhere near their ranch in Deal as the assault occurred. Safety was the most obvious concern, and everyone in the Syrian community knew where the family lived. Also, the Dwek family home is maybe 50 feet off a public street and the feds had no interest in dealing with the press that would quickly converge.

"We're going away for a couple of days," Solomon told Pearl. "Get the kids packed."

As hard as it is to believe, Dwek confided later that his wife put up no resistance to news of the surprising summer vacation. The women of the Syrian community were typically compliant with the orders of their husbands, and Pearl did what she was told. Plus, it was the summertime; the kids weren't in school. A couple of days away would be okay, she figured. The family quickly left the Shore and headed to a North Jersey hotel often used by the FBI to stash witnesses who needed to stay local but had to be kept out of sight.

Solomon continued in his dual informant role through the night as the setups for the pols and money launderers were finalized. At the same time, the FBI began its invasion of the New Jersey and New York area. The feds paid a visit to Jack Shaw and took him to the Meadowlands Sheraton in Secaucus for a little discussion. In Jersey City, the feds showed up on the doorstep of Mariano Vega. They had a photograph of Dwek and they asked if he knew him. The same guy who had promised to pass along $10,000 to him through Khalil, not two weeks before.

"No," said Vega. The agents asked him if he had ever spoken with any real estate developer regarding a project on Garfield Avenue. Vega again said no.

Peter Cammarano was tending bar that evening, celebrating his birthday, and seemed to be having a great time.

Harvey Smith had left the state with his wife and grandson to drive down to Virginia.

Anthony Suarez, the mayor of Ridgefield, had headed to the Jersey Shore.

At eleven twenty-five that evening, Dave Esenbach received a frantic call from Maher Khalil, who had just spoken with Tom Fricchione, a former Jersey City councilman whom he had introduced to Dwek months earlier.

Fricchione, it seemed, had just been visited by the FBI.

16

◄┼ ┼┼►

Takedown

In the early-morning dawn of Thursday, Guy Catrillo was awakened by a loud knock on his door at precisely 6:00 A.M. There were six federal agents waiting outside, some wearing the familiar blue windbreakers with FBI stenciled in yellow across the back. Still groggy from sleep, Catrillo had no idea at first what they wanted.

"Where's your dog, Spooky?" demanded one.

The Jersey City planning official thought for a moment and wondered how they knew the name of his dog. Then they asked him if he had talked with someone named David Esenbach. They presented Catrillo with a warrant for his arrest. Understanding came suddenly like a cold shower, waking him up to the realization that this had nothing to do with his dog.

Catrillo had last spoken with Esenbach in April and even then felt there was something wrong about him, with his big plans for an unlikely real estate development on Garfield Avenue. On a call with Shaw, he remarked, "Dave's style is not right for some people."

But Jack told him they should continue to meet because Esenbach was "talking a substantial number."

In fact, Esenbach had set him up and everything Catrillo said months earlier was on tape. Remembering all the Verizon trucks that had been around the house recently, Catrillo figured they had been staking him out for days. Any way he looked at it, he knew he was royally screwed. He didn't feel like he had too much to hide.

"There's ten thousand dollars in my slipper that belongs to you," quietly admitted Catrillo. He had put $10,000 of the $15,000 in cash given to him by Esenbach under his bed for safekeeping. After losing the council election, he had not used most of the money.

They searched him, threw him a lime green polo shirt, and took him to a government-issue Ford Escort waiting outside. One of the agents asked if he was willing to cooperate: "No one will know we were here." Catrillo politely declined, telling them he would prefer to speak to a lawyer, and then gave them directions on how to get to Newark. They were from out of town and didn't know how to get out of Jersey City.

In the light morning traffic it was just a short drive to Newark, and they soon pulled into the back of the FBI building. Catrillo looked, startled, through the tinted glass. There was Leona Beldini, in handcuffs, being led out of another car. *Leona? What is she doing here?* Inside the building, where he was fingerprinted and photographed for mug shots, he saw Jack Shaw. And a man with a long beard and a hat. And Mariano Vega. *What the hell is this all about? Just who is David Esenbach?*

Leona woke to the same knock at her door, where she, too, was presented with a warrant for her arrest. She was allowed to get dressed as the agents waited. Before they took her to the car, she made a call to a friend, leaving a voice message that sounded almost cheery: "Hi, this is Leona. I'm here with some guests from the FBI. I need some representation," she said.

An hour down the parkway in Elberon, a group of agents from the FBI's Red Bank office were arresting Rabbi Eli Ben Haim at his home not far from the beach. Another team of FBI, IRS, and investigators from the Monmouth County Prosecutor's office were searching the summer residence of Rabbi Kassin in Deal. By then, news of the takedown had begun to spread and Andy Mills, a photographer for *The Star-Ledger,* found his way to Kassin's house. A woman inside, still in her robe, paid no attention to the FBI or the boxes of documents being pulled out. She just zeroed in on Mills, standing at the curb of the street. She jumped up as he started to raise his camera. "Get the hell out of here!" she yelled at him. "Get the hell out of here!"

As Mills continued to shoot, she yelled to the agents, who ignored her as they walked in and out of her home. "Stop him!" she angrily demanded. "He can't do that." One of the federal agents tried not to laugh as he walked by Mills, who couldn't care less. "Boy, she gave you the business," the agent muttered.

At the Deal Synagogue, a minyan had already gathered for morning services when the feds entered the building on Norwood Avenue at the appointed hour. Four FBI agents came looking for Rabbi Edmond Nahum, the cantor who shared congregational duties there with Rabbi Isaac Dwek. One of the congregants, engrossed in prayer when the agents came in, stood staring in disbelief with others as they escorted Nahum into his office and locked the door behind them.

Nahum looked apprehensive. Nobody knew what was going on, but he was well aware exactly where this was all going after they brought up Solomon's name. Nahum had passed the kid off to Fish but was on tape telling Dwek to spread the money around. A short time later, Nahum, in his black coat, was led out through the glass doors of the synagogue. Above the entrance was a gold inscription in Hebrew: THIS IS THE GATE OF THE LORD THROUGH WHICH THE RIGHTEOUS WILL ENTER . . .

In Flatbush, Levy-Itzhak Rosenbaum was at home just as expected. The kidney broker intended to keep his appointment that morning with Schlomo Dwek and his secretary. Long before they were scheduled to show up, however, there was the 6:00 A.M. knock at Rosenbaum's door. Outside were agents from the FBI's New York office, lending assistance to the New Jersey operation. He was allowed to dress in his usual white shirt and black pants and was led out in handcuffs.

Mordchai Fish's small *shtiebel* in the Borough Park section of Brooklyn is an unwelcoming fortress-like corner building with peeling gray paint and security bars on the lower windows. The FBI arrived there at 6:00 A.M. and recovered $300,000 in cash. He, too, was arrested.

In Belmar along the Jersey Shore, Lou Manzo had stayed overnight at his summerhouse. He was scheduled to be on the radio that morning with Jim Gearhart, who presided over the top-rated morning-drive show on New Jersey 101.5 FM, a popular station once known mostly for its local traffic reports that had built a legion of listeners by rallying against taxes and corruption. At 6:30 A.M., Manzo got a call from an unknown number. He thought at first it was Gearhart's producer and flipped open his cell phone. The voice on the other end was unfamiliar and identified himself as an FBI agent. "We have a warrant for your arrest."

Manzo thought it was some kind of joke. "Who the fuck is this?" he demanded.

The agent explained again that they were planning to arrest Manzo on extortion charges. "Look. I know you think this may be a joke, but here's a number you can call to verify who I am," he said. "If you turn on your TV, you'll be seeing some of this."

Manzo turned on the television. On the local NBC station, reporter Jonathan Dienst was narrating the parade of arrests: "The mayors of Hoboken, Secaucus, [and] Ridgefield were among forty people arrested in early-morning raids across New Jersey this morning as federal officials unveiled a long-ranging probe into public corruption and international money laundering, officials said. FBI and IRS rounded up various elected officials and several rabbis across the state in what is being described as one of the biggest investigations of its kind in Jersey's scandal-plagued history . . ."

There was live video showing Peter Cammarano being led into the FBI building in Newark. There was Leona Beldini in a dark brown housedress, along with a bunch of people Manzo had known for years. Vega. Guarini. Jimmy King. Manzo's brother Ron. In the middle of it, a group of Orthodox Jews in black. Manzo was transfixed as he watched. The FBI wanted him to drive back up to his home in Jersey City, where they said they would wait for him. He got into his car and began calling around, looking for a lawyer.

* * *

Within the noisy command center high up in the FBI building, Weysan Dun, the special agent who headed the Newark Division, had several difficult phone calls he had to make himself just before the operation was launched. One was to the police chief Tom Comey in Jersey City. It had already been a sad week in Jersey City. Five officers had been seriously wounded in a shoot-out with a pair of armed robbery suspects. Among them was Marc DiNardo, a 10-year veteran of the police department who served in an elite emergency response unit. DiNardo did not make it. The father of three had died of his injuries at Jersey City Medical Center just two days earlier, on Tuesday.

"I really have to apologize for doing this, but we're making some arrests this morning," said Dun, from the relative quiet of an office borrowed from one of his senior deputies. "We'd appreciate you don't say anything to the media, but it is happening momentarily."

Outwardly, it was a courtesy designed to keep good relations. But it was really an added measure to help ensure the safety of the FBI and IRS agents stomping around the city. The FBI chief then made another call to the state's top law enforcement official, Anne Milgram, New Jersey's attorney general.

* * *

Inside the Rodino building in Newark, acting U.S. Attorney Ralph Marra had arrived early in the morning, along with all of his senior staff and the lead members of the special prosecutions unit. Howe, who had had less than four hours' sleep, was in his office before 6:00 A.M.

The public affairs officer, Michael Drewniak, was putting the finishing touches on a packet of press releases and criminal complaints that would be distributed to the media. The phones began ringing off the hook with the first arrests and he was now fielding an endless barrage of calls—on two cell phones and a desk line—from reporters who needed quick confirmations to get something on the air or send a crew to a location. It was going to be a busy day. Prosecutors had been arranged in teams based on the various segments of the Dwek investigation. Some were handling the alleged money launderers and alleged kidney broker. Others were to oversee the arraignments and bail hearings for the corruption cases.

Marc Larkins, the executive assistant U.S. Attorney and number three official in the federal prosecutor's office, was also getting calls—one from a former colleague now working in the office of Corzine's chief counsel. The governor's lawyer was fishing for information. "You know I can't tell you," Larkins told her. She persisted, trying to rephrase her question in order to get an answer. Each time, Larkins gave her the same old song and dance. All would become clear in due course.

* * *

As the story continued to stretch out on television, no one outside the investigation yet realized the full scope of what had happened. The names of those being arrested were coming out one by one as they showed up in handcuffs. Not until the criminal complaints were unsealed did it become obvious that this was unlike any other big bust that had ever happened in New Jersey. In addition to the mayors, there were five Orthodox rabbis, a number of Israelis accused of being cash couriers, the Jersey City deputy mayor, and the president of the Jersey City Council. The list included political operatives, candidates in the recent municipal elections, two New Jersey legislators, and, what seemed incredible to everyone, someone charged with brokering black market kidneys.

The mystery was what could possibly link it all together. No one yet knew that these were separate, parallel investigations and that Dwek had been living two lives, pulling in people on both sides. Dwek's name had still not surfaced, nor had the disclosure that there had been an informant in the case.

Word quickly leaked out that Joe Doria might be involved. At the Department of Community Affairs in Trenton, a top official was mystified by all the talk when reached by a reporter for *The Star-Ledger*. As they spoke, he suddenly had to hang up. "The FBI is here," he said in a low voice.

At Doria's contemporary home in Bayonne, another team of agents had come knocking on his door as well. Not to arrest him but to question him. They knew money had gone from Dwek to Shaw and they knew Shaw was advertising that the cash was going to Doria because he was on the take. But there was no evidence that the cash had been passed on to Doria. Or that he even knew what Shaw had been up to. Now with the operation winding down, there was no longer any reason to play it subtle. The money the feds had given to the longtime political fixer was marked, and they had already searched Shaw's apartment for the cash. Nearly $40,000 was given to Shaw; only $25,000 was found in his apartment. If he had given it to Doria, they were determined to find it. Their banging on the front door went unanswered. They knocked some more. Still no answer. Could they have the wrong address? They knew the well-kept home near the park was listed in Doria's name. Why would he not answer? The agents went back to their cars. Maybe, they thought, Doria was at the other home listed in his name. They called there.

Doria had two sisters who were both nuns. Sounded like the start of a joke—hey, have you heard the one about the politician who has two sisters who are nuns? But it was true, and when they were not at the convent they stayed in a house that Doria owned near his own in Bayonne. The FBI called over and got Sister Beatrice on the line.

"Is Joe Doria there?" an agent asked, after identifying himself.

"He doesn't live here," she said.

"Where is he?"

"Home."

"Where's that?"

"You're the FBI," she replied. "You should know."

Only in New Jersey would you find a nun mouthing off to the FBI at six in the morning. But truth is, there had never been a whiff of scandal around Doria and it was just completely beyond the realm of possibility to Beatrice that the FBI would want her brother. She thought it was a prank call.

* * *

Josh Zeitz, a onetime congressional candidate who traveled all day every day with Gov. Jon Corzine, was speeding up the New Jersey Turnpike shortly after sunrise when his cell phone rang. On the other end was one of the troopers on Corzine's state police security detail, calling from the governor's Maxwell Place condo in Hoboken.

"There are some FBI agents here and they've taken away someone," Zeitz was told.

The hairs on the back of his neck went up. For days, Corzine and his closest aides had been hearing chatter in political circles that something big was coming down and it could be any day. With Chris Christie, the former U.S. Attorney, now the Republican challenger to Corzine, corruption, they worried, was likely to be a cornerstone of the campaign. There was mounting suspicion that some kind of surprise was going to come out involving corrupt officials just before the election. After all, it's New Jersey and politicians are always being arrested.

"It was in the system," described Corzine long afterward. But nobody had a clue what *it* might be about.

The night before the raids and that morning's formal notification from Dun, in fact, Milgram had received another vague call, this one from Marra, alerting her that there would be some political arrests the following morning. But the attorney general, who had been growing increasingly distant from the governor who had appointed her, hadn't given Corzine the heads-up.

Corzine was still asleep in his penthouse, with its views of the Empire State Building, when the trooper called Zeitz. The day was supposed to be spent on political business—large and small. There was a senior-center event outside Elizabeth, a high-end house party on a leafy block near Seton Hall University, and preparations for the much-anticipated announcement of Corzine's running mate. It was the first time in modern New Jersey history that lieutenant governor nominees would be on the tickets, and Christie had already announced his.

In painfully typical style, Corzine had jerked from candidate to candidate—politician to minister to businessman—in a public spectacle that had the distinct feel of the bumper cars at a boardwalk amusement park. Corzine wasn't thrilled with his final decision, but he had finally made one and it was a relief to his whole team. The running mate would be Barbara Buono, a state senator from Central Jersey with a law degree and the chairmanship of the powerful budget committee on her résumé. She was five years younger than Corzine, attractive (by New Jersey political standards, very attractive), and a capable debater and public speaker. She was a strong choice but not Corzine's first, and the governor, his staff, and even Buono herself all knew it.

Everything would change after the call to Zeitz.

Juggling coffee cup, cell phone, and steering wheel, Zeitz turned on the radio somewhere around New Brunswick and quickly got a sense of what was going on. Then he started hitting speed dial. He managed to reach Bill Castner, the top attorney in the governor's office, but the connection sucked. Unable to make himself heard the first couple of times, Zeitz finally shouted into the phone to tell Castner about the arrests in the governor's building: "They're here! They're arresting people in his goddamn building!"

Before then, no one associated with the governor knew that Michael Schaffer, one of the 44 people on the list to be arrested, lived in Corzine's building on the Hoboken waterfront, just two floors below. Schaffer had scored the apartment because he had raced to Jersey City for the first-night public offering in which the developer sold units on the spot at bargain-basement prices to people with money.

"He could bite me in the ass, I wouldn't know him," the governor later recalled. But the scandal, the crisis, the catastrophe for Corzine's Democratic Party was—quite literally—now inside the gates. Imaginations raced as they wondered how close to the governor this was going to go.

Zeitz called and woke up the governor. "Don't answer your phone," he instructed.

* * *

Jerry Healy was shaken awake by one of his daughters. "They locked up Leona and a whole bunch of people," she told her father.

Healy wondered what kind of nightmare he was in but padded over to the television in the living room and began watching what the world was now seeing. Then something jogged in the mayor's memory as he recognized one of the FBI agents escorting somebody in handcuffs. She had been in his City Hall office only the day before with another agent. They said they wanted to talk to him regarding some kind of Bernie Madoff spin-off involving money laundering. The agent asked whether he knew somebody named David Esenbach. Healy had scratched his head. He was not good with names, even with those he knew. Even months after, he would refer to Dwek's alter ego as "Eisenbeck."

"It's possible," admitted the mayor. "I meet lots of people all the time. I don't recall, but there's a guy upstairs who can check it."

They never showed him a picture and he never gave it a second thought. If the meeting was 10 minutes, it was a long time. Now he began to get a gnawing feeling as he continued to watch. He wasn't sure what it was all about, but as soon as he saw the FBI woman he knew she hadn't come to him to talk about Bernie Madoff.

* * *

The FBI agents went back to the first address they had for Doria and tried knocking on the door once again. But there was still no answer. The feds had a growing suspicion that Doria was in the back of the house, shredding something, flushing something. They were not sure if they had the authority to bust in.

The truth was that Doria just plain couldn't hear them knocking and ringing the bell. His front door opened to a breezeway, sealed off by a heavy wooden interior door. That opened into a living room with a cathedral ceiling. Upstairs, all the way in the back, is the room where Doria and his wife, Maribeth, slept. To conserve money in the summer, they often turned off their central air conditioner and used a window unit in their bedroom, closing the door to keep the cool air in. Doria also suffers from sleep apnea, so at night he wore a breathing machine that blew air into his face and noise into his ears.

With FBI supervisors finally instructing the team to resort to a battering ram ("They should have taken the goddamn door," one chief said back in Newark), an agent on the street finally got the bright idea of calling Doria's house phone. The commissioner answered immediately, his voice sounding a lot like a guy who was sleeping. Still in his pajamas, Doria went downstairs. Outside, the FBI and Bayonne cops were waiting. Across the street were reporters, already alerted that Doria might be a target.

As Doria awoke to the situation, his phone continued to ring. One call came from Augie Torres, the political columnist and opinion editor at the *Jersey Journal*. "Heard they raided your house," Torres said. "What is it about?"

"Augie, they're here," Doria snapped back. "I don't know what it's about."

The agents let Doria's wife and daughter leave and gave Joe the chance to change into street clothes. They showed him videos and interviewed him for two hours.

"You took money from Jack Shaw," they accused.

He denied it.

"You're lying," said one. Then they played on their laptop two scenes of Dwek handing Shaw cash, saying it was for Doria. On another video, he could see Shaw telling Dwek he was setting up a meeting with the president of St. Peter's College in Jersey City—where Doria earned his BA and later was an administrator—so the informant could pay for a new "Joe Doria Scholarship Fund." It would be a favor to Doria, who was reluctant to accept a bribe himself, they claimed.

The agents asked Doria about cash. He told them he didn't need cash the way some people do. He was earning $141,000 a year, his wife was a school administrator, he owned a rental property in town, plus, "I don't have any bad habits. I don't drink; I don't run around; I don't go to Atlantic City."

The agents, playing good cop/bad cop like they did in the movies, finished their questions and then called for the 10-person search team. As the FBI scoured Doria's home for the next two hours, Doria's phone kept ringing. Reporters, political allies, associates, advisers. A couple of his closest friends telling him to stay strong and refuse the inevitable calls to resign. It was not long before Castner and the governor's chief of staff, Ed McBride, were on the line, in what would be only the first of several conference calls with Doria that day. They wanted to know what was happening and whether Corzine had anything to worry about as he struggled against falling poll numbers in a tough reelection bid.

Doria had taken his share of lumps over the years. During his time as Assembly speaker, one newspaper used Doria and his girth to illustrate government bloat. More significantly, his ability to push through unpopular legislation wound up undoing him when he was blamed for engineering the enactment of Gov. Jim Florio's wildly unpopular $2.8 billion income tax hike in the early nineties. Doria didn't dream up the tax hike, but he got blamed for it and the subsequent "Florio debacle" that saw the legislature swing from Democrat to Republican—with veto-proof majorities—in the 1991 election.

Doria's history with Florio loomed large when the Democrats retook control of the Assembly in 2001. And it was at the heart of McGreevey's decision to publicly double-cross Doria by engineering a play that would keep him from returning to the speakership even though Doria was in line for it. Doria's allies never forgot or forgave that McGreevey maneuver. By the time Corzine became governor, it was ancient history, as Doria had rebounded strongly and transformed himself into a sought-after state senator and master manipulator of the Byzantine legislative process. Early in Corzine's term, the governor literally begged Doria to join his administration. In the end, Corzine named Doria to lead the Community Affairs Department. That very appointment would make Doria a target for the feds and Solomon Dwek after Jack Shaw said Doria was on the take.

After some initial discussion, both Castner and McBride felt Doria could hold on to his job, though the political advisers around Corzine had a different take. They insisted Doria had to go. Corzine pondered what to do.

At his Bayonne home, Doria could only sit and watch as the FBI searched every book. Every drawer. They missed an envelope marked "rent money" with $1,400, which Doria handed to them. Joe also offered the agents something to drink, but they declined because they had their own water and snacks, which they carried inside two large cardboard evidence boxes. In the end, the agents left with three things that fit in their pockets: the $1,400 in cash, plus $1,000 more—some to clean his mother-in-law's headstone and the rest that was given to his daughter for her birthday—a copy of the girl's college account records, and Doria's own St. Peter's pension statements. No charges were brought against the commissioner.

The agents finally left carrying the empty evidence boxes as if they were full of documents, exiting through the front door in full view of the press.

"You walk out with those two boxes, people are going to think you took two boxes of material," Doria complained. It wasn't fair.

"We can't help that," the lead agent replied.

* * *

Inside the lockup at the federal courthouse in Newark, many of those arrested were still shell-shocked, trying to figure out what had happened. For some, the lightbulb went on very quickly. Others professed total ignorance of what they had done wrong.

Leona was trembling in the holding cell, which had two benches and a commode out in the open. "What did we do here?" she asked.

Shaw looked like he was going into a diabetic coma. "They're trying to make me say I gave money to Doria and I didn't," he murmured to Lou Manzo. "These guys. Guantánamo has nothing on these guys." Shaw's death sentence may have already been sealed by that point. Five days later, he would be discovered dead in his apartment at Portside Towers in Jersey City. Valium was among the dozen prescription drugs in his apartment.

Anthony Suarez, the mayor of Ridgefield, was sitting in a light T-shirt and white beach shorts. He had been on his bicycle for a morning ride, as he vacationed on Long Beach Island, when he got a call on his cell phone from the FBI. They had a warrant for his arrest. He went back to his house without changing and then got into his car, driving north on the Garden State Parkway to turn himself in. His pale blue shirt read: PROPERTY OF RIDGEFIELD POLICE.

Khalil, who had introduced Dave Esenbach to Catrillo and so many others, was contrite. "I'm sorry, Guy," was all he could say to Catrillo. One by one, the Hudson County contingent got wise to the fact they had all dealt with the same man. Esenbach had been the nexus. While nobody had yet told them all, some—like Jack Shaw—had already been shown the videos of the sting in an effort to convince them to cooperate. It was clear that Dave was no ordinary fast-talking developer with money to burn. Dave was FBI.

The Orthodox Jewish defendants kept to themselves, many speaking in Yiddish. Finally, one of them just said a name, as if he was spitting it out.

"Dwek," he said with guttural disgust. The Rabbi's Son had betrayed every one of them. They had helped someone who was already facing federal charges in his schnookie bank deal, and he had taken them down with him. As they heard the others talking about David Esenbach, it soon became clear that they were all victims of the same guy. One told Manzo there was no Esenbach: "His name is Solomon Dwek. He screwed money from everyone."

Manzo, who spent a lot of time at the Jersey Shore, immediately knew the name of Dwek and the story of his $50 million bank fraud. It was no secret down in Belmar.

"He's not the best man in the world," Ben Haim told Catrillo. "I know his father very well. I knew him since he was a little boy."

John Guarini, the taxi inspector who gave Dwek the first opening into the world of political bribe offering, was in a rage and could be heard shouting in an adjoining cell. "That motherfucker! That motherfucking bastard. I'm going to kill him," he yelled, others recalled. "Yeah, I took money from that fucking cocksucker. I'm a businessman." Someone told him to shut up, but Guarini continued to rant and rave: "I brought that motherfucker around. The FBI is stupid. They don't know anything."

It was getting old after a while and no one was in the mood. "John, shut the fuck up," said another. "This place is fucking wired."

One of the U.S. Marshals shouted back, "Shut up, you motherfucker. You can't talk to the prisoners."

Catrillo sat down on a bench. It seemed to him like a bad Fellini film.

* * *

Throughout the morning, aides to the governor began appearing one by one at his Hoboken condo as though it were some sort of wake. They were stunned as they continued to watch the televised images of the rabbis and many of their acquaintances and political allies being led in handcuffs to and from the FBI building. A meeting with top campaign staffers, scheduled for the morning, was quickly canceled. So was a diner stop with the editorial page editor of *The Bergen Record*. A visit to a senior citizen center was taken off the schedule as well.

After breaking every speed limit on the way, Zeitz arrived at Corzine's place around 7:00 A.M., followed soon afterward by campaign manager Maggie Moran and all-purpose consigliore Tom Shea. They watched for hours as they went through the governor's coffee and the pretzels, Cheetos, and the rest of the salty snacks he kept in his cupboard. The video footage continued in its endless loop while a steady flow of calls came in and out. Political allies from around the country, friends of the governor, anxious White House staffers. Everyone wanted to know what the hell was going on and the decision was unambiguous—no one did. There had always been a fear that some new revelation of political corruption would become a serious distraction during the campaign, and that had "been baked into the cake," the governor later explained. But he never had any idea how truly bad the day would get. "The noise got pretty loud," he said.

On one conference call with aides and advisers, the whole scene was brutal, grim.

The most important people in Corzine's political organization had been unenthusiastic for months about the governor's running for reelection. The voters, according to the polls, certainly were not warm to the idea. Now, with the footage searing into his brain like a laser, Corzine's mind—with its capacity for split-second billion-dollar calculations—was racing.

* * *

In the U.S. Attorney's office, there were dozens of cameras set up, focused on a podium in the seventh-floor conference room. CNN, the national news networks, the local TV stations, and reporters from *The New York Times*, *The Star-Ledger*, the *Daily News*, and other newspapers all squeezed into the long room as Drewniak passed out briefing sheets. All the seats were taken, with people lined up along the walls on both sides, and prosecutors from the office stood to get a glimpse of the action.

The feds were calling the operation Bid Rig 3, as if it were a continuation of the initial Monmouth County investigation into local corruption that had been launched 10 years ago. They even referred to it as a decade-long probe. But this was different, and wasn't really spun off anything that had come earlier. Nobody had ever seen anything like this.

It turned out to be the single biggest press conference ever held inside the U.S. Attorney's office—so big, in fact, that dozens of chairs had to be removed to make room for the formidable array of TV cameras that needed space. Many staffers of the U.S. Attorney's office, usually free to watch press conferences, were told to stay at their desks. There was simply no space for anyone who did not have to be there.

Ralph Marra took his place behind the microphones, with Weysan Dun to his left, Brian Howe to his right, and others from the special prosecutions division lined up behind them, including David Bocian, Sandra Moser, Mark McCarren, and Maureen Nakly. The four assistant prosecutors would soon be on their way to marathon arraignment sessions.

"Today we're here to announce the takedown of a large-scale, dual-track investigation," began Marra. "On the public corruption side, the

FBI and IRS have arrested and noticed for arrest twenty-nine individuals, including assemblymen and mayors, underscoring more than ever the pervasive nature of public corruption in this state. On the other side, the FBI and IRS have arrested and summoned fifteen members of connected international money-laundering rings, including five rabbis and their associates as outlined in the complaints. These rings, led by clergymen, cloaked their extensive criminal activities behind a façade of rectitude."

Marra went through the arrests: Daniel Van Pelt. Peter Cammarano. "The politicians willingly put themselves up for sale," Marra said somberly. "For these defendants, corruption was a way of life. They existed in an ethics-free zone and they exploited giant loopholes in the state's campaign finance rules."

Those charged with money laundering, he said, painted a disgraceful picture of religious leaders acting as crime bosses. Marra, cameras clicking continuously, charged that the rabbis used charities set up to do good works as vehicles for laundering more than $3 million in illicit funds.

"The rings were international in scope, connected to Deal, New Jersey; Brooklyn, New York; Israel; and Switzerland; and they trafficked in the cleaning of dirty money, all across the world," he continued.

Dun called the arrests unprecedented.

"The list of people we arrested sounds like it should be the roster for a meeting of community leaders. But sadly, they weren't meeting in a board meeting this morning. They were in the FBI booking room."

Then he told the press about the search warrants on the offices and home of Joe Doria, the office of the president of St. Peter's College, and the Deal Synagogue, where Dwek's father was rabbi. For Doria, the disclosure and public announcement meant his time in the Corzine administration was about to come to an end.

Marra and Dun never identified Solomon Dwek. The criminal complaints filed in the case only referred to a cooperating witness, a "CW" who had been charged in a federal criminal complaint with bank fraud in May 2006. While it soon became an open secret that the CW was Dwek, the government for months afterward refused to confirm it.

"The fact that we arrested a number of rabbis this morning does not make this is a religiously motivated case. Nor does the fact that we arrested political officials make this a politically motivated case," said Dun. "It is not about politics. It's certainly not about religion. It is about crime and corruption. It's about arrogance. It is about a shocking betrayal of the public trust. It is about criminals who use politics and religion to cloak their criminal activities and enrich themselves while betraying those who trusted them."

Ed Kahrer, also at the podium, said the themes of the day had included deceit, abuse of power, and betrayal of trust. "New Jersey's corruption problem is one of the worst, if not the worst, in the nation," he intoned. "Corruption is not only pervasive; it has become ingrained in New Jersey's political culture . . . It is a cancer destroying the core values of this state."

Less than 90 seconds into the press conference, Howe, who had looked sick before anyone began talking, whispered quietly to Nakly and moved his wheelchair backward and away from the podium and the bright lights. After working nearly around the clock in the last 24 hours on the highest-profile case of his career, the pressure of bringing it all home had finally caught up to him. He retreated to Marra's nearby conference room, where he was loaded up with Gatorade to try to keep him hydrated. He rested for a time before going home early. They wanted to have him rushed to the hospital, but Howe resisted.

The presser was a frenzy of reporters shouting over one another, some using Ralph's first name to get his attention, others hoping that proper decorum would help them get a word in edgewise and hollering, "Mr. Marra!" With a faint look of pleasure on his face, Marra got hit with questions from all over the spectrum: What was the CW's role? Will Doria face charges? Tucked in the middle of the round-robin was a typical query for a New Jersey corruption-bust press conference: "From what you've heard through the investigation, do you have any confidence that the cycle of corruption can end?" He had a ready answer.

"There are easily reforms that could be made within this state that would make our job easier, or even take some of the load off our job," he replied. "There are too many people that profit off the system the way it is and so they have no incentive to change it. The few people that want to change it seem to get shouted down. So how long that cycle's going to continue I just don't know."

* * *

Healy watched the press conference, carried live, still in his living room with his family and aides. At first, as the arrests were being made and it became clear that many of those caught up in the whole thing were Jersey City officials or city employees, the mayor was despondent. "This looks pretty bad for the city," he said out loud.

His deputy mayor was under arrest. So was the city council president and, it seemed, just about everyone who had been on the ballot. It was like a huge bomb had been dropped on the city. With the press conference, though, Healy's depression turned to anger. In his mind, they had crossed over the line. It was a political lynching. "It's a fucking Chris Christie press conference," Healy grumbled. "It's a fucking campaign ad."

Whatever happened next, Healy was now sure the governor's race was over. He thought Jon Corzine had been damaged beyond repair and that the U.S. Attorney's office and FBI had publicly cast their votes for their old buddy Chris.

* * *

Soon after he was elected as mayor, Peter Cammarano assembled a new team to run the city. Like him, they were 30-something professionals, many of whom he had gotten to know through Young Democrats groups. They viewed their gigs as investments in their résumés and their futures. Anyway, they figured "it's not like Pete's going to get indicted or something." Like people outside Cammarano's circle, they viewed the young mayor as being on his way to bigger and better and so he was too smart to do something stupid.

Suddenly, their world seemed very, very different early on July 23. Phones started ringing at the homes of Cammarano's aides, each one telling another to turn on the television and trying to figure out what they should do. Some of them, with little children at home, had to switch from Barney the Dinosaur to Newark perp walks. Others, without kids, were still asleep, only to be awakened by the news.

"Peter has been taken in by the FBI as part of a large-scale operation," said the voice on the other end of the phone after awakening Hoboken's chief city attorney, Steve Kleinman. "It's big."

Kleinman couldn't believe it until the phone rang again. "I guess you're going to have an interesting day in City Hall today," said the second voice, instructing him to turn on Channel 5. "I saw them walking people in and out of the FBI in Newark. At that point, we realized that this was real."

Soon they all descended on their city offices near the Hudson River waterfront to await official word. At the city's ancient City Hall, a surreal calm overtook the administration as they waited in suspended animation for the news. They didn't want to say it out loud, but their first concerns were themselves. *Was I in some meeting with somebody?* One person reached out to the state attorney general to ask her what was happening. She said she didn't know.

The city's top people, both those who came in with Cammarano and the holdovers, gathered in the mayor's own private office to watch the only television in the building. They kept refreshing their computer screens to see if there was anything new on the Web or any official arrest documents released by the U.S. Attorney's office. Though crowds started to build elsewhere in town, City Hall was disturbingly quiet.

"There were rumors flying around about a lot of things that day. Names that were thrown about, turned out to be inaccurate, stories about a second round of arrests," Kleinman said. "Nobody knew whether there was going to be another shoe to drop."

Cammarano had been in office only three weeks and not made a single significant government decision. The day before, on his birthday, Cammarano took his senior staff out for a round of lunchtime burgers at Five Guys near City Hall. As the next morning began, his people were in his office watching the end of his career and answering e-mails that were pouring in.

What's going on in Hoboken? was the simple message showing up on BlackBerrys.

Finally, the arrest complaints were posted on the Internet and dueling realities took hold: the charges were not associated with city business, so there was some relief; and Cammarano was in huge trouble. *This is no joke,* Kleinman realized.

"They were very serious [accusations] and they were understandable," Kleinman said. Cammarano was actually an old-school waterfront thug who became a criminal to win power.

At lunchtime, many of the same people who had gone out with Cammarano the day before gathered again, this time at O'Neil's on Bloomfield Avenue. "Who knows if any of us are going to be working here tomorrow, so I might as well have a beer," Kleinman said. He ordered a cold one.

* * *

After the televised press conference, Castner and McBride almost immediately called Doria back. Dun's comments about the search warrant now made it seem like the commissioner was maybe two steps away from indictment. Whatever it meant, Corzine and his political advisers had decided they couldn't leave an already-unpopular governor with a member of his cabinet under mounting suspicion.

"What I had to do with Joe Doria bothered me a lot," Corzine said many months later. He didn't want to fire Doria and knew that it would allow the presumption of guilt to overtake any residue of innocence. But "it was a pile-on time," Corzine said. The governor still turns sour, his mood darkens, when the Doria moment is raised. "It would have been a disaster for him to stay there. Personally. He would have been dragged through the mud by people, particularly during a political campaign . . . I still think he's one of the most honorable people I've ever worked with, but that doesn't mean he wasn't going to get destroyed."

On the phone, Castner and McBride told Doria they needed his resignation. If he wouldn't offer it, Corzine had authorized them to fire Joe. One of Doria's advisers told Joe between calls that Corzine could go fuck himself. "Tell them you'll resign, but only if Corzine has the balls enough to call himself and tell you. He doesn't have the balls."

Doria understood that message, but he also understood the political reality and that his time in Corzine's administration had died as soon as the FBI came knocking at his door. "You know, you guys are young," Doria said after telling Castner and McBride he would step aside. "Get out of this business while you still can."

Soon Corzine did call, over the objections of his lawyers and advisers who thought Doria had become poison to the governorship. Corzine spent 20 minutes trying to explain to Doria the necessity of his resignation and the fact that it was his political aides who made him do it. Doria never turned in a resignation letter. He simply slipped into retirement as quietly as he could. Then he retained John Azzarello, a former assistant U.S. Attorney and counsel to the 9/11 Commission, and one of the state's top criminal defense lawyers.

* * *

Behind an army of gun-toting guards inside the well-cooled citadel that is the Department of Justice in Washington, senior officials were watching Marra and Dun hold their news conference in Newark. With the election of President Obama, a whole new crowd had taken over the massive department, headquartered about halfway between the White House and the Capitol. For all their loyalty to the Democratic Party, prosecutors are prosecutors and, down deep, they love nothing more than a good, headline-grabbing case that shows the world that cops still beat the robbers.

"It was not the first time that, when watching a press conference, the people in D.C. realized the U.S. Attorney had gone beyond what the U.S. Attorney Manual allows," a Justice Department official said. "The FBI guy, he was out there also."

Not long after Marra and Dun came down from the podium, Marra and his staff learned for the first time that Washington was pissed. The calls were low-level, coming in to Marra's spokesman, Michael Drewniak, from the AG's press office in Washington. But they were a signal of trouble to come. In D.C., they wanted to know why Marra said what he said about policy and politics and they questioned whether the acting U.S. Attorney had gone too far in his comments. The type of guy who's never going to be confused for a diplomat, Drewniak reminded the Washington communications people that Marra's comments were in the press packet that had been sent to the Robert F. Kennedy Department of Justice headquarters 24 hours earlier. And, if that wasn't enough, he suggested that the folks in D.C. could go screw themselves.

* * *

In Hoboken, the state troopers who stood permanent sentry around the governor were asked to change their routine and remain outside his apartment that day as the debate continued over how Corzine would respond.

The episode was a psychological game changer. The ultracompetitive governor who could cheat death in a highway wreck and beat them all on Wall Street had finally come to the same conclusion even the most mediocre pollster could discern: the race was lost. The campaign was never going to focus on corruption and, in the end, that's not the issue that drove voters away from Corzine, according to the exit polls. But corruption was Christie's core reason for existence and the very essence of his rise to prominence. Christie rode a caravan of crooked pols to the Republican nomination, and as was obvious from the live shots on the tube that humid morning, Corzine was way too close to the worst parts of New Jersey politics.

Later in the day, a grim-faced Corzine held a press conference with Anne Milgram, his attorney general. Corzine doesn't hide his emotions well and he looked ashen and angry. On television it appeared Corzine would have been just as comfortable throwing the lectern across the room as he was using it to hold his notes. "Any corruption is unacceptable—anywhere, anytime, by anybody," Corzine told reporters. "The scale of corruption we're seeing as this unfolds is simply outrageous and cannot be tolerated."

His aides left Hoboken. Campaign manager Maggie Moran, for one, had to get to Corzine headquarters in Trenton to address the troops. *Here's what's happening. Here's what we're doing. Here's what we know.* She couldn't offer much beyond what they were watching—like everyone else—on television.

* * *

Christie had spent the summer doing low-impact, low-cost public events designed to keep the budget down while making sure he was in the papers and on television. The Republican was participating in New Jersey's public-financing system, so his budgets for the primary and general election were set in stone (not including the outside groups that can help but are separate from the campaign). With his war chest empty after the June primary, Christie's organization was raising money while the candidate was treading water, hoping to keep the momentum going.

A key element of Christie's strategy was to force the unpopular incumbent to spend time and money in core Democratic areas. It would serve to distract Corzine from the real game, which was independent voters in the suburbs. So Christie got in his SUV and proceeded to spend much of July traipsing around the inner cities of Newark, Plainfield, Elizabeth, Perth Amboy, Camden. For public consumption, Christie told reporters he was in the cities because he was fighting for every single vote. But that was nonsense. "I wanted him to have to play on his own turf," Christie said later. "Every day he's not in Hamilton or Woodbridge or any of the towns where the election is going to be won was good for us."

Christie's bizarre-looking Republican-on-the-city-streets gambit was in full swing when the FBI and IRS went storm-trooping around the metro area on July 23. The candidate was on the road early when he heard the first reports on the radio: "Forty-four politicians arrested in an FBI sting." The former U.S. Attorney had been hearing, like Corzine, that something big was coming down. Christie knew the Solomon Dwek sting had been in full force since he left the prosecutor's job in December. But Christie said there was no way of knowing if the "something big" he had been hearing about was that or any one of the other major cases that were brewing when he left. *Forty-four pols arrested in one sweep doesn't make sense. That's not something I know about*, Christie thought. "I knew there were cases pending. I know of cases that are still pending, I assume, that aren't public."

On his way to an event in Hudson County, Christie and his driver started hearing the first accurate reports of what was going on in Newark. They knew they were headed into the nucleus of the takedown. Later Christie would be confronted with accusations that he had been briefed on the roundup and that it was an effort to aid his campaign. Exhibit A would be the fact he was in Hudson that day, perfectly situated to greet the press focused on the big story. He still scoffs at those accusations. "If in fact you knew, you wouldn't be there," Christie contends.

As much as he could, Christie listened to the coverage of the takedown that day and was learning as the stories developed. Suddenly, with one word—"Doria"—the Christie–Corzine campaign was now part of the big takedown. As crazed as Corzine's campaign had become, Christie's was serene. Nothing was changed. Christie's running mate was already in place. Christie himself suffered none of the chaos engulfing Corzine. "He is so disciplined," one of Corzine's aides said enviously during the race.

Once it was clear that Dwek was the informant, Christie obviously knew what was about to come as it happened. But in interviews since, he insisted he had not been forewarned and maintained that he had no idea how large the case had gotten. He said he got his information the same way Corzine did, through political backchannels. Christie had been scheduled to go on a block walk that day along a street in the Hudson County community of West New York. Addressing the media in a barbershop that afternoon, he called the arrests "just another really tragic day for the people of New Jersey."

* * *

Cammarano's aides finished their lunches and their beers at O'Neil's and they were back in their offices for a full afternoon of What the Fuck! They found little had changed. No work was being done, city business was in a state of paralysis. There was, however, one thing on the agenda: mayoral succession. The lawyers went through the law and the city's charter to determine how a mayor resigns if he wants and what happens if he does.

Then, on a day full of surprises, came another big one. Without warning, Cammarano's mother walked into City Hall. Reporters and photographers had set up camp outside the mayor's home. His mother—visiting from out of town—didn't want to deal with the press just to get back inside. *What do you say to her? What do you do? This is terrible,* they thought. She looked stunned.

* * *

One by one, the accused were brought into federal court, bound in ankle shackles and handcuffs. Lawyers for many argued that Dwek, who was facing 30 years in jail, had set everyone up at the behest of the government in an effort to get himself out of a jam.

Entrapment, they told reporters. Coercion. A bad guy making others go bad to get himself off the hook.

"He obviously worked with the government to set people up," said Terry Ridley, attorney for Lori Serrano. Michael Bachner, the lawyer for Rabbi Mordchai Fish, charged that Dwek had used his relationships to manipulate innocent victims. It's an assertion everyone agreed with, but it did not matter.

During the hearings, which ran into the evening, bail was set, ranging from $25,000 to $3 million for most of the defendants, who were required to surrender their passports and to limit their travel to New York and New Jersey. As Shaw finally walked out of the courthouse with his girlfriend, he gravely shook the hand of Catrillo. "I want to apologize if I got you into anything," he said. "Good-bye." It was the last time Guy would see Jack alive.

Healy went to see Leona when she was finally released on bail. He took her out to dinner.

Despite the Gawker.com headline, not everyone had been arrested. Tom Fricchione, the former Jersey City councilman and assistant director for the Hudson County Department of Corrections who served as Phil Kenny's campaign treasurer during the city council election and had met with Dwek through Khalil, was never named in the case. He would die in December at the age of 64, of natural causes. The county prosecutor said there was nothing suspicious about his death; the political chatterers in Jersey City insist he either was killed or committed suicide because he had agreed to roll over on others.

Kenny, elected to the council in May, was also not named or charged that day. His role in the case would not even surface until October 2009, when he made a surprise visit before a federal judge in Newark and admitted that he had accepted $5,000 from Dwek.

Al Santoro, the former head of the Ocean County Democratic Party who had spent time on Esenbach's dime in Atlantic City—and served as Dwek's connection to GOP assemblyman Van Pelt and the Ocean County GOP chairman, George Gilmore—also was not immediately connected to the case. It was not until December 2009 that Santoro's involvement was revealed, in a plea deal where he acknowledged accepting $6,500 in bribes.

Harvey Smith remained in Virginia during the arrests. But the FBI had never been that concerned that any of those involved in the political corruption cases would try to run. Like Manzo, they called him up and told him to come back to New Jersey.

Yolie Gertner, one of the lesser-known people charged on the money-laundering side of the case, just plain disappeared. Oddly enough, during the takedown a man named Yolie Gertner did show up to turn himself in. He had not been arrested by agents. He had just heard that the FBI was looking for him. As it turned out, there was more than one Yolie Gertner in Brooklyn and this wasn't the one they were seeking. The quiet cash courier was never found. Authorities believe he fled to Israel.

The Dweks spent the prior night and that day at the hotel in North Jersey serving as an FBI safe house. Solomon's arrest in 2006 had shaken his wife badly. She also knew he was in bankruptcy. The bankruptcy, in fact, was Solomon's cover as he left the house every day while working with the FBI. All Pearl ever knew of the past three years was that her husband was leaving for a day of working with the bankruptcy trustee to unravel and sell off his assets, or perhaps he was meeting with his attorneys on the bank fraud. For three years, as Solomon played the central role in an international sting, Pearl knew nothing.

The next morning, Dwek finally told his wife. She was furious.

"It was much worse than any way you can put it," was all he said later. "She took the kids and left."

Pearl Dwek was angry at her husband for turning state's evidence and for helping the feds arrest other people in her community, members of her faith. She didn't care about the pols, but Pearl was an observant Jew, a proud member of the Syrian Jewish community, and now, without her knowledge or assent, her husband had become a predator preying on her own. Given the choice, Pearl would have preferred Solomon serve his full prison sentence instead of going to work for the FBI.

Solomon, too, was getting less and less thrilled with his choices. He watched the arrests on television and immediately began having second thoughts. Each and every one of the people arrested had become an associate or comrade to Dwek. Solomon had no friends, and Khalil and Fish, in fact, had become companions to the adrenaline junky con man. During hours of calls and meetings, they bantered about the world and the weather, politics, religion, you name it.

"I liked most of the people I dealt with. Van Pelt was a nice, warm guy. They were good people. Nice people. I liked them," Dwek would tell someone later. "Khalil—I built a relationship with the guy. I don't have bad feelings about that."

Now, on July 23, Dwek watched television as these people were walked into jail, went to court, and emerged later with careers and lives in tatters. He thought to himself, *I wouldn't do it again.*

17

⫸✛✛⫷

Rogues and Cronies of Thieves

The press had a field day. Reporters and headline writers couldn't have dreamed up a better story to break up the midsummer doldrums of stand-alone beach photos and petty crime at city pools.

The New York *Daily News*: "FROM BOGUS MOGUL TO FBI'S BUSI-EST RAT: How son of rabbi worked full time to bring down dozens in federal probe" and "MEET THE FLIMFLAMMING INFORMANT BE-HIND BUSTS."

The *New York Post*: "RABBIS IN MONEY WRINGER—LAUNDERED MILLIONS IN SYNAGOGUE AND CHARITY SCAM."

The *Jersey Journal* went for brevity: "CHARGED."

The *Trentonian* also got to the point: "SCHMUCKS."

The New York Times mused that the dialogue of the criminal complaints seemed straight out of an introductory screenwriting class for a crime movie.

The *Jerusalem Post* lamented the Jewish angle: "5 US rabbis nabbed in vast corruption scam. FBI Agents storm into New Jersey synagogue during prayers. Three mayors, 2 legislators also among 44 suspects arrested on charges ranging from multimillion dollar money-laundering to selling Israeli donors' kidneys."

The *Irish Times* employed a TV allusion: "FBI sting exposes scams to rival any 'Sopranos' plot."

The calls for resignations came immediately.

In Hoboken, angry residents gathered in the rain the following week, demanding that Cammarano just leave. Standing outside Hoboken City Hall, they chanted, "F-B-I! F-B-I! F-B-I!" Cammarano did not immediately take the hint. The 32-year-old mayor said he did nothing wrong, even as his wife left with their young daughter, first saying she needed to get away from the noise and then filing for divorce.

Dawn Zimmer, still the president of the Hoboken City Council after having lost the mayoral election, said it appeared Cammarano could not be forced out. "We're in a difficult situation," she told reporters. "The public is asking for the council to take action, and often asking for action it does not appear we can take." Working with the city's attorneys and state fiscal monitors to explore all options, Zimmer noted that even a recall election could not occur until a mayor had remained in office for one year.

In Ridgefield, where officials passed a resolution calling for the resignation of Mayor Anthony Suarez, a borough council meeting turned raucous with 150 protestors, who spilled into an overflow room set up by police at the local community center. Nicholas Lonzisero, the councilman who sponsored the resolution, said Suarez should do the right thing. "We can ask him to resign. We cannot force him to resign," he told reporters. "The quicker he resigns, the quicker we can put this crisis behind us and begin the healing."

Suarez, who received some hugs from supporters outside before entering, trembled as he read a statement. "I want to assure you all that I am completely innocent," he said.

In Secaucus, Mayor Dennis Elwell was also under mounting pressure.

In Jersey City, Mayor Jerry Healy suspended without pay six of the eight officials caught up in the federal sting but dismissed a call for his own resignation by a small group of city activists. "I have done nothing wrong and have a duty to serve the people of Jersey City who elected me to this office," said Healy, who was never directly named in the criminal complaints that came down but was an obvious piece of the whole investigation.

Healy did, however, get another visit from Donnie Russ, one of the three FBI case agents. "Your friends are talking to us," said Russ, a tall man with broad shoulders and trim, brownish-blond hair. "People you think are your friends are talking to us. People you don't know are talking to us."

Healy looked back impassively.

"We think it's in your best interest to be talking to us," Russ told him.

In Trenton, there was a push to amend the state constitution to require the replacement of lawmakers who are indicted. "It's impossible to be taken seriously in your job if you're under criminal indictment," insisted Monmouth County Republican assemblywoman Caroline Casagrande. "If you were a police officer, or a teacher, you would not be permitted to continue working while facing criminal charges."

And the governor continued to press for all elected officials caught up in the federal sting to head for the door, even as he looked for ways to remove them from office. "I really think it is very hard for any of the folks that have indictments to be able to function effectively," Corzine said.

Assembly Speaker Joe Roberts, a South Jersey Democrat who wears the scars of a generation of political battles, was in his car on the day of the arrests when he heard from Bill Castner. Corzine's chief counsel had been Roberts' right-hand man for years and the two remained close. Castner briefed the speaker, who after all his time at the State House had grown accustomed to days like this. *I've had all too much experience with this type of thing,* he thought.

Roberts was not a lawyer but an accomplished businessman who had made a fortune operating pubs along the shore. His uniform-like business suits never betrayed the fact that he was a Parrothead devotee of singer songwriter Jimmy Buffett. Though Roberts knew what it was like to hear Assembly members were arrested for corruption, he quickly discerned from the cell-phone briefings that the Dwek takedown was a whole new thing.

Van Pelt and Harvey Smith were the first Assembly people in Roberts' era who were charged with crimes that were tied to their responsibilities as state legislators. Before that, the Assembly members who had been nailed got hit with charges stemming from their campaigns or dealings in other government offices. This time, the crimes alleged took place in the house. "It affected our institution," Roberts said later. Soon afterward, he would announce his retirement from politics, although his decision to leave the game had been made before the FBI started arresting members of the Assembly that morning.

At the end of his career, Roberts was at the end of his rope. *Enough was enough,* he thought. By nightfall, Roberts had stripped Van Pelt and Smith of their committee assignments—a measure that had become fairly common in the wake of legislators being charged with crimes. What was unexpected was Roberts' announcement six days later that he was suspending the pay and benefits of the two Assembly members. He couldn't fire them, but he could take their money.

Roberts was joined by Corzine, who called on the three mayors arrested to step down. In Secaucus, Elwell gave up fastest. On July 28, Elwell became the first to resign his post; he also withdrew from the fall mayor's race. Cammarano continued to resist. He arrived at his City Hall office before 7:00 A.M. the day after his arrest in order to beat the press that had started making camp in Hoboken. Later that day, Peter walked down the stairs and stood in front of a bank of cameras to say, "I have no intention of resigning my office. I believe that I am fully capable of carrying out my oath of office and duties of office."

With protests continuing and growing outside his home and office, Cammarano held out a week before "no intention of resigning" turned into a statement read by the city's lawyer, Steve Kleinman: "It had been my hope and expectation that I could remain in office and perform my official duties until I had the opportunity to resolve the legal charges against me in court. Regrettably, it has turned out that the controversy surrounding the charges against me has become a distraction to me and an impediment to the functioning of Hoboken government." Cammarano reiterated his innocence. He pleaded guilty eight months later.

Corzine insisted that all the mayors arrested resign. Anthony Suarez in Ridgefield refused. His lawyers refused. His lawyers were on the phone back and forth with Corzine's office and they still refused. Suarez just wouldn't go. His attorneys issued a statement saying: "In the past, Governor Corzine has not personally succumbed to political pressure but has instead vindicated his rights through the legal process. We admired the Governor's resolve in those situations. We merely request that Governor Corzine grant Anthony Suarez the same consideration." Privately, Suarez's attorneys told Corzine's aides that their client would be in office longer than the governor would. They were right.

* * *

Immediately after the takedown, the governor switched gears on his running mate. As if reopening a war wound that had finally healed, Corzine decided not to tap Middlesex County senator Barbara Buono after all. Just as it is with the selection of a vice presidential candidate, choosing a running mate for a statewide race has one ground rule above all others: the candidate must do no harm. Then, and only then, you look to see if the running mate helps, where, how, and what's the best way to put that person to use. When Corzine first settled on Buono, he made it clear to his team he wasn't going with his first choice or someone he trusted completely. Indeed, the governor worried that Buono might well spend more time preparing for her political future than helping with his political agenda. Still, that was okay—until July 23. The issue of harm now loomed large.

Buono had had an on-again, off-again relationship with Democratic boss John Lynch. At one point in 2002, Lynch had encouraged Buono to run for Congress. Buono had insisted over and over that she bucked Lynch plenty, but to Corzine at that moment the senator just seemed too close to one of the state's notorious political warlords.

Corzine's mind raced. *How about the state's attorney general, Anne Milgram?* She was young, aggressive, and viewed as bright, and had spent years fighting with some of the state's most potent political leaders, including the Democratic boss of Union County, Ray Lesniak. Just a week before the Dwek arrests, Milgram's office had seized computers from the Board of Elections in Essex County as part of an investigation into election fraud that was targeting allies and friends of the oldest of the old-time New Jersey political bosses, "Big Steve" Adubato in Newark.

Milgram, Corzine thought, *would be perfect.* Then again, she wouldn't, he realized. Democratic leaders would kill him the way his 2007 auto wreck didn't. Plus, who knew if Milgram would even be willing to join Corzine on the suicide mission? After the fact, those close to Milgram said she would sooner have had Christie's face tattooed on her forearm than run for lieutenant governor.

Corzine went round and round all day on the selection. Finally late into the afternoon, Maggie Moran phoned to say as emphatically as she could, "I need the decision by five so we can have the signs made up for tomorrow." At last, a drop-dead deadline. Corzine was good with those.

Forced to decide, the governor returned home emotionally. His first choice all along had been an old Jewish grandmother from the state senate, Loretta Weinberg. A political brawler, Weinberg had the distinction of having fought the bosses, including Bergen County Democratic chairman, Joe Ferriero. Corzine had bankrolled Ferriero's organization over the years—including one time in 2005 when he had his elderly mother dispatch a $37,000 contribution to the Bergen Democrats. But he never liked Ferriero and, when Ferriero tried to block Weinberg from moving from the Assembly to the Senate, Corzine threw his weight behind the old lady. July 23, Corzine said, "Seal the deal." Put Loretta's name on the signs.

Within 24 hours of the arrests, Corzine's camp started leaking the news.

On Friday, a group of key aides and consultants gathered from around the country at the stately governor's mansion in Princeton. Drumthwacket was designed to look like the White House and since the 1980s has served as the executive residence for New Jersey's governors. It was used by at least one of New Jersey's governors (who didn't live there full-time) as a sort of highway motel where he could meet his sexual partners of the moment. It was used by Christie Whitman (who also didn't live there) as a convenient place to stay midweek when she needed to be in South Jersey early in the morning. And it was used by Jim McGreevey, who did live there, for the critical days of meetings and soul-searching that led to his famous "gay American" confession—the speech that ended McGreevey's career and led to Corzine's rise to power.

Corzine and the team met in the informal second-floor residence of the mansion. There, for the first time, Corzine made it clear that he realized he could very well lose the election.

* * *

That same morning, Chris Christie and his wife, Mary Pat, awoke to a reality ushered in by a *Star-Ledger* headline that trumpeted the words "Walk of shame; Wide-ranging corruption scandal snares officials and religious leaders." At their large home atop a quiet hill in Republican Morris County, the Christies took in a political landscape flattened by a blast called Dwek and had a quiet husband-to-wife conversation. The Republican candidate, like everyone else on the inside in the game of New Jersey politics, viewed Corzine's money as the single most important factor in the election. So Christie—like the rest of the insiders—figured that the wealthy incumbent could find a way to pull out the election. *We're winning and it's looking good, but he's probably going to find a way to leg it out.* To that point, though, Corzine hadn't found his path to a comeback. He was floundering, missing critical opportunities and allowing the independent polls to drive home the story line that Christie was pulling away.

With the carnage of July 23 fresh in everyone's minds, Chris turned to Mary Pat and said he finally thought it was possible that they would need to prepare for a life as governor and First Lady. Mary Pat looked at her husband and stared for a few seconds. "Really?" she said. She thought about that before answering, "You know, I think you're right."

That weekend, during Christie's weekly Sunday night conference call with his high command, the conversation focused on the arrests and Corzine and Doria. On the call were Christie, Mary Pat, Christie's brother Todd, strategist Mike DuHaime, campaign manager Bill Stepien, finance chairman Bill Palatucci, and media consultant Russ Schriefer. Christie was still thinking back to how Corzine had responded to the takedown. After the governor had held his press conference with Milgram, Chris thought to himself, *This guy's like a gift; he's a gift. It just looked so fake and she just looked like she was there under duress . . .*

The consensus on the call was simple: *Nothing has changed for Chris. We have no idea what the impact will be, but it is all upside for us. If it keeps the media and Corzine preoccupied, good. If it doesn't, so be it. Keep going and let the story, the reporters, and the mess that is Solomon Dwek drive Corzine crazy.*

* * *

Those arrested in the sting began seeking out the state's top criminal defense attorneys. From the very first afternoon when they were herded one-by-one into federal court, many were already being accompanied by some of the state's most well-known lawyers—the "go-to" guys who were always on the short list of calls when one was in serious legal jeopardy. Former New Jersey attorney general Peter Harvey, in the courthouse for another client, said it was like a gathering of the Who's Who of the legal community.

Cammarano retained Joseph Hayden Jr., a former prosecutor who had defended onetime NBA star Jayson Williams on manslaughter charges. Famed New York lawyer Gerald L. Shargel, known as a tough litigator who defended mob boss John Gotti, was brought to help represent Rabbi Kassin. Justin Walder was representing Rabbi Nahum, and Henry Klingeman, another former federal prosecutor, was representing Joe Cardwell.

John Farmer Jr., dean of Rutgers Law School and the former New Jersey attorney general, thought they would need all the legal talent they could afford given the public's view that those arrested were undoubtedly guilty. "There is no presumption of innocence anymore," he said.

Many in the Syrian Orthodox community flatly refused to believe the charges. David Ben-Hooren, a member of Kassin's congregation and publisher of a conservative monthly newspaper, told reporters on the day of the arrests that when the facts came out he expected that everyone would find out that the rabbis never broke the law. "I believe they're going to be vindicated," he declared. "Knowing those rabbis for many years, I know that they devoted their lives to charity, and there's no way that they benefited from any of those activities."

Others said the case was nothing but lies. In Flatbush, a campaign was started to inundate prosecutors with letters of support for Rabbi Kassin.

In Deal, a young man grabbed the notebook of a reporter on Norwood Avenue and followed him for blocks, urging people not to speak with him. At the Deal Synagogue, one older member of the congregation came barreling through the glass doors to the sanctuary as a TV crew approached. "Get the fuck out of here! Motherfucker. Get out of here! How dare you!" he thundered in a tirade of biblical proportion, ranging from full-throated rage to the verge of choking back tears. "You want to make trouble? Huh? You want to make people happy, right? You looking for problems? Just get out of here, you assholes!"

He gestured wildly, the pent-up emotion of a sad day now just coming out, almost as a sob of realization as his voice broke and he deflated in sorrow. "You work for the paper. You work for the paper. I know that you make ten dollars an hour, but this is not going to make you a promotion," he said, almost pleading now. "Just go home! And keep quiet! And leave people alone. And don't hurt people."

He finally turned his back on the TV crew and others seeking comment. "Get out of here! Everyone!"

By Saturday morning, the furor had yet to die down. For the congregations in Brooklyn and Deal, there would even be some biblical reference to it all during Shabbat services. Every week, the *parsha,* or reading, for Jewish congregations around the world follows the same schedule, as the Torah is steadily wound forward on its annual cycle. That Saturday was the final Sabbath before the observance of Tisha B'Av, one of the saddest, most solemn days on the Jewish calendar, mourning the destruction of the ancient Jewish temples in Jerusalem. The readings that Sabbath included a prophecy from Isaiah. It spoke of the culture of corruption and sin that had overtaken the Jews who occupied Israel more than 2,500 years ago and seemed to echo eerily as it was recited in Hebrew on July 25, 2009:

> Alas, she has become a harlot, the faithful city that was filled with justice,
>> where righteousness dwelt—but now murderers.
> Your silver has turned to dross; your wine is cut with water.
>> Your rulers are rogues and cronies of thieves,
>>> everyone avid for presents
>>> and greedy for gifts . . .

18

⊸┼╂┼⊱

"I Am Guilty, Your Honor . . ."

Brian Neary was one of New Jersey's better-known criminal defense attorneys. His clients over the years had ranged from celebrities such as the late rhythm-and-blues singer and songwriter Wilson Pickett and hip-hop stars Foxy Brown and DMX to police officers accused of wrongdoing, and murderous Chinatown gang members. A native of the Greenville section of Jersey City and a graduate of Hudson Catholic High School, where he had played point guard against much bigger opponents, Neary had gone on to the University of Notre Dame and New York University School of Law before landing a job with the Hudson County Prosecutor's office.

On this day, January 27, 2010, he sat in the fifth-floor, wood-paneled courtroom of U.S. Judge Jose Linares in Newark, where he was representing Leona Beldini. For the first time in her life, the 74-year-old Jersey City deputy mayor and onetime burlesque star felt totally naked under the spotlight. Six months since the arrests that stunned the state, the story of how it all played out was going to be told for the very first time by the government's star witness, Solomon Dwek.

Neary was itching to take him on.

Bookish in his dark-framed glasses and signature bow tie, Neary leaned back in his chair, chin resting in the palm of his fist. Assistant U.S. Attorney Sandra Moser gave her final approval to the makeup of the jury. "Your Honor," she finally told the judge, "we are satisfied."

The defense attorney got to his feet, stretched his head around like a boxer about to get into the ring, took off his jacket, and then slid off his sweater. Moser glanced over with a bemused smile at the *Rocky* moment. "I thought the silk robe was coming out," the young blond prosecutor said quietly.

"Just getting the warm-ups off," replied Neary, pulling out a granola bar and a bottle of water for the early-afternoon ramp-up of the long-awaited first case that would go to trial in The Jersey Sting. The jury was sworn in and given instructions from the judge.

Assistant U.S. Attorney Thomas Calcagni, prosecuting the case with Moser, launched the opening salvo. He addressed the jury from a lectern in the center of the courtroom. "The people of Jersey City, like people everywhere, are entitled to a government free from corruption," said Calcagni in his carefully scripted opening. "To never put themselves above the law. The duty to not take bribes."

Calcagni paused and then looked straight at the jury. "This is a case about a Jersey City official who took that duty and stood it on its head. This is a case about a Jersey City official who took bribes. It's as simple as that. And that official . . . ," he continued as he turned and pointed dramatically to the woman at the defense table, ". . . is Leona Beldini."

* * *

When Jack Shaw left the federal courthouse on July 23, he was smiling. He talked with the reporters assembled outside and told them he was innocent. Inside the lockup he didn't look well, and some of the others arrested were worried about his health. At 6:30 P.M. on July 28, the Hudson County Prosecutor's office was notified that Jersey City police were at the scene of a "suspicious death." The cops had rolled up shortly after 5:00 and the unconscious man on the floor was pronounced dead at 5:50 P.M. The prosecutor's office dispatched a Crime Scene Investigation team from its homicide unit. Lying on the floor, shirtless, wearing a pair of black shorts and black knee-high socks was Jack Shaw.

Through all the years of corruption and chicanery in Hudson County, the prosecutor's office has remained remarkably untouched by it all. With no reason to change the protocol, the investigation into Shaw's death was led by Prosecutor Edward DeFazio and his detectives.

"There are no signs of forced entry, robbery or apparent trauma or signs of a struggle," the official report said. The lock wasn't jimmied. Security tapes were checked. Almost immediately, DeFazio started hearing conspiracy theories about Shaw being murdered, Shaw being ordered to kill himself, Shaw voluntarily killing himself because he knew too much. "I'm sure a few people imagined it could be some sort of homicide due to the part he played in this criminality," DeFazio said. "But that clearly was not the case. And that was very apparent early on."

A career prosecutor who prides himself on a Jersey City accent thick as August humidity, DeFazio would ask the reporters who called which theory they were thinking of, which movie was popping to mind. When *The Godfather Part II* was mentioned—the scene where one Mafioso slit his wrists in a bathtub—DeFazio said, "Oh, that's a good one." But his investigators were on the scene of Shaw's death for hours and his office spent five months going over and over the case before deciding they would never be able to say exactly how Shaw died. They could figure out what killed him but not how it happened. "From the start it was thought not to be a homicide," DeFazio said. "It was either an accidental overdose because he was involved with all these medications or a suicide." No note was found.

The coroner said: "The victim had a long medical history, including gastric bypass in 2009, diabetes, hypertension and a heart condition. The victim was on numerous medications . . . The victim has been depressed and unable to sleep recently . . . There was no alcohol in his system."

Shaw was found in his home office, near a desk, a few feet away from what was described as a "decorative Egyptian mummy" sarcophagus. Shaw had two desks: one for typical office work and a second where he painted the metal military figurines that were his hobby. On one desk investigators found a number of Tramadol pills—a narcotic-like drug prescribed to patients suffering severe chronic pain. In the apartment, more than a dozen prescription medications were found.

The final report was dated December 9, 2009. Cause of death: acute Valium toxicity. Manner of death: undetermined.

* * *

The week after the arrests in New Jersey, a legal symposium was held by ultra-Orthodox leaders in Borough Park. The packed event held a surprise. The Grand Rabbi of the Spinka Hasidic sect, Naftali Tzi Weisz, who pleaded guilty in his own money-laundering scandal, came into the room to give an emotional speech of contrition in Yiddish and broken English.

"Unfortunately we have to admit in public that things happened that were not supposed to happen. We must have to express our wish that these matters will never happen; we have to commit that in the future this will never happen again," the rabbi said.

* * *

The guilty pleas began coming in less than two months after the arrests.

In early September, Maher Khalil and Guy Catrillo both admitted taking bribes from Dwek. Under questioning, Khalil not only acknowledged taking $72,500 in bribes but also implicated others—Mariano Vega, Ed Cheatam, and Vinnie Tabbachino. In the short proceeding, also held before

Judge Linares, Khalil said he accepted $20,000 in bribes on behalf of Vega and funneled them through straw donors to the Jersey City Council president's campaign fund. He said he took another $5,000 for Cheatam. Vega, he said, also personally took $10,000 from the informant, at the time still only known to him as Dave Esenbach. Khalil's lawyer, Michael F. Pedicini, said his client had regretted his actions. "He decided to take responsibility for this and move on with his life."

Catrillo admitted taking $15,000 in bribes.

Two weeks later, another pair of public officials pleaded guilty. Cheatam said he took $70,000 in bribes and introduced Esenbach to an array of Democratic officials, including Harvey Smith, Peter Cammarano, former Secaucus mayor Dennis Elwell, Lou Manzo, and Leona Beldini. "I'm surprised he didn't implicate his mother," said Peter Willis, a lawyer for Smith. Cheatam also claimed he moved $15,000 in illegal contributions to the campaign of Jersey City mayor Jerry Healy, in exchange for his help to secure approvals for the Garfield Avenue luxury condominium project that never existed. He was widely expected to be cooperating and testify in any future trials.

"Unfortunately, Mr. Cheatam is living up to his name," said John David Lynch, a lawyer for Lou Manzo. "He's cheating the truth."

Denis Jaslow, the Hudson County board of elections investigator who at one point was convinced Esenbach was an informant and then inexplicably changed his mind, admitted accepting $15,500. He confessed to introducing Dwek to Joseph Castagna, a Jersey City health officer, and Jersey City Council candidate Michael Manzo, who was no relation to Lou Manzo.

Six days later, Jimmy King also pleaded guilty, telling Linares that he accepted between $5,000 and $10,000 from Dwek while running for the Jersey City Council. In exchange, King had promised that if elected he would help secure zoning changes for the Garfield Avenue project.

In October, Phil Kenny, the Jersey City councilman who until that point had not been publicly implicated, became the next shoe to drop. He unexpectedly came into court and pleaded guilty to accepting $5,000 from Dwek, becoming the case's forty-fifth defendant. Because of Kenny's guilty plea, he was required under law to resign from the council.

Hours later, Mariano Vega, the Jersey City Council president who had resisted calls to quit, finally agreed to temporarily relinquish his leadership post but refused to step down from the council. Vega also later amended his campaign finance reports, adding four payments totaling $10,000 from donors tied to Dwek. One was Vinnie Tabbachino. On the amended report, Vega listed Tabbachino's occupation as "FBI operative."

Asked about the changes, Vega remarked, "There were some things that needed to be corrected."

Jersey City housing advocate LaVern Webb-Washington was the seventh to plead guilty, admitting she took $15,000 from Dwek in return for her promise to secure his zoning approvals. She ultimately pleaded quilty in September 2010.

Then came Dwek himself.

* * *

More than three years after the $50 million bank fraud that launched him as an undercover informant in the biggest criminal sting in New Jersey history, The Rabbi's Son briefly emerged from the shadows in October 2009 in appearances before judges in state and federal court to plead guilty to his crime. Dwek's appearance was not accidental. The feds needed their key witness to unmask himself so they could use him at the trials that were about to begin. He arrived first at the federal courthouse in Newark shortly before 9:00 A.M. Security was tight for the man now called *moser* by his community, disavowed by his father, hated by the ultra-Orthodox, and for the very first time publicly acknowledged by the U.S. Attorney's office to be the "cooperating witness."

Nobody was taking any chances with his safety. He was brought in by U.S. Marshals in an FBI caravan that included two black Chevy Suburbans with dark tinted windows. One parked parallel to the courthouse, shielding the vehicle carrying Dwek from photographers as it rolled into an underground garage. About an hour later, Dwek emerged from a secured entrance to Linares' courtroom, in a dark suit with a light blue tie and black velvet yarmulke.

Dwek stood in court, tapping his fingers on the defense table during parts of the hearing, nervously adjusting his steel-wire glasses and touching his face, shifting his weight from foot to foot while glancing around at the courtroom crowded with reporters. Other times he just smiled, touching his hands lightly to the table in front of him or clasping his hands together. He answered questions from the judge clearly and directly in a perfunctory 30-minute appearance to enter pleas to bank fraud and money laundering in connection with the two bogus checks totaling more than $50 million that he tried to deposit at the PNC Bank.

"I am guilty, Your Honor," he declared, firmly and without hesitation, in a plea arrangement that left him facing between 9 and 11 years in prison.

Afterward, Dwek poured himself a cup of water, smiled, and nodded at federal prosecutors. He shook hands with Sean McCarthy, one of the

FBI case agents who had been his shadow for the past three years, and with the federal bankruptcy trustee, Charlie Stanziale, who was in the courtroom at Dwek's request. "Thanks for coming," he told Stanziale. Then Dwek walked back through the secure door of the courtroom, accompanied by U.S. Marshals.

Later in Freehold, the scene was repeated before Superior Court Judge Thomas Scully. There, Dwek pleaded guilty to state charges in connection with the $10 million loan from Amboy Bank to purchase 30 Broad Street in New York—most of which was used to pay off other investors in his Ponzi scheme.

* * *

Number eight of those to plead in the corruption sting was Mike Manzo, the failed council candidate, who admitted in December to taking a $5,000 bribe. Nine was in court the next day. Al Santoro, the former head of the Ocean County Democratic Party who until that point had yet to be publicly connected to the case, made a surprise appearance, admitting to accepting $6,500 in bribe money in exchange for introductions to officials to secure development approvals—including Assemblyman Daniel Van Pelt, the Waretown Republican.

Former Dwek employee Charles Amon was the tenth defendant to enter a guilty plea, on December 14, admitting he took $1,500 in exchange for his introduction to Jeff Williamson, the Lakewood Township housing inspector.

In January, Shimon Haber stood solemnly in court, fingertips pressing down on the glass top of the defense table, as he waived indictment and pleaded to one count of conspiracy to launder money.

Leona was the first to go to trial.

* * *

Beldini sat impassively at the defense table, looking alternately at Tom Calcagni and the jury. Her glasses were off and she had a tissue clutched in her right hand as the prosecutor paced in front of the jury.

"It's really all about the tapes," Calcagni said in his opening remarks. "It will be like you're in the room with them. You will see and hear exactly who said what to whom. You will see her repeated assurances that she will uphold her end of the corrupt bargain. You will see them. You will hear them. You will be there with them."

Calcagni told the jury how Beldini met Dwek through Cheatam and Shaw and the deal Dwek was pushing on Garfield Avenue. How he wanted assistance in return for payments disguised as political contributions.

"The project never got off the ground. The project wasn't real. Garfield Avenue wasn't real. David Esenbach wasn't real," Calcagni said. "Solomon Dwek was a convicted criminal. He defrauded friends, family, and institutions. His crimes were extensive. But don't lose sight of the audio- and videotapes that will be played for you. The tapes will prove the case."

Neary sat slouched in the red leather chair next to Beldini, saying nothing as the prosecution laid out its opening. When Calcagni finally ended, the defense attorney, scrappy and theatrical, lived up to his reputation as he slowly got up.

"This case is about a man who stole four hundred million dollars. Let me repeat that. Four hundred million dollars," he said, laying out the Ponzi scheme that Dwek had run long before he was caught passing bad checks. "It should have ended when he passed two twenty-five-million-dollar checks. But it didn't."

Once Dwek was caught, he began a new scheme—this time to keep himself out of jail, using Shaw and Cheatam to score introductions to politicians. "Ed Cheatam—you will learn how appropriately named this individual was," Neary seethed.

Neary likened Dwek to a dark magician and fast-talking auctioneer. "He repeats over and over, continuing to say words that have no meaning other than to him." Leona, Neary said, had come to politics out of her involvement in civic organizations. She was as close to the mayor as a blood relative and was there to protect his back. "For that, the government gave her a new name. Defendant."

* * *

The parade of pleas continued. Jeff Williamson pleaded guilty in late January to accepting $17,500 in return for promising to overlook code violations. Itzak Friedlander, who was tied to Altman's real estate operation, pleaded guilty in April to conspiring to launder some $175,000 for Dwek.

A short time later, Yeshayahu Ehrental and Schmuel Cohen also entered pleas to their roles in the money-laundering operation. In separate hearings before U.S. District Judge Joel Pisano, Ehrental and Cohen said they supplied hundreds of thousands of dollars to Rabbi Eli Ben Haim to help launder $1.5 million for Dwek. During the hearings, both men said they worked a contact in Israel to supply Ben Haim with cash. They pleaded guilty to operating unlicensed money-transmitting businesses. A day later, Arye Weiss entered a similar plea.

Peter Cammarano, the former Hoboken mayor who had been video-taped boasting about grinding political opponents "into powder" and predicting that not even criminal charges could prevent his election, followed. Eyes downcast, he admitted accepting $25,000 in illegal campaign contributions. "After he finishes the criminal process, I expect he will rebuild his life and once again be a positive member of society," said his attorney, Joe Hayden.

In August, Cammarano was sentenced to 24 months in prison for his role in the sting.

Walking without hesitation to a lectern in the middle of the courtroom as if he were still a practicing attorney, the former mayor expressed "profound regret" for his actions.

"I have nobody to blame but myself," Cammarno said. "I know I let down friends, my family and supporters and the people of the city of Hoboken. I will spend the rest of my days, whatever comes, making amends for my conduct in this case."

Cammarano is telling people he is writing a book. Federal law prohibits him from making any money from it.

* * *

The jury saw the black-and-white videos, one after another, of Dwek and Beldini and $10,000 in tickets purchased for a Healy fund-raiser.

"The mayor knows, you know, where the tickets came from? He appreciates the way I do business, right?"

"Absolutely," Beldini answers.

Dwek talked money and real estate and payoffs.

Neary hit repeatedly on the point that Dwek never personally put a bribe into Beldini's hand. "She never took a dollar, did she?"

Dwek snapped back, "She got the money through a middleman."

The prosecution called four witnesses, including Dwek. Neary did not call one, focusing instead on his aggressive cross-examination.

In their closing arguments, federal prosecutors told the jury that Beldini demonstrated her guilt by talking of cutting red tape and "flipping the pile" to ensure that Esenbach's applications were on top.

"You saw it. You heard it," the prosecutor said. "The United States has proved it beyond a reasonable doubt."

Neary said Dwek was a "con man par excellence and a thief of first rank" who duped Beldini into making seemingly incriminating statements using the skills he had honed as the architect of a $400 million Ponzi scheme.

* * *

In the months afterward, a number of elected officials revealed they had also been the focus of Dwek's sting but never took money or meetings. In Hoboken, council members Dawn Zimmer (who would replace Cammarano as mayor) and Beth Mason told reporters that overtures from Dwek had been received by their camps.

And there were those who had no idea how much of a target they had been. Immediately after the arrests, Albio Sires realized that Dwek, posing as Esenbach, had tried to set him up, because Tabbachino wanted to arrange a meeting with the congressman in 2009. That overture, however, went nowhere. Sires' in-state aide, Richard Turner, who doubles as the mayor of Weehawken, got the request and waited barely seconds to say there would be no sit-down.

The continued focus on Sires by federal prosecutors pissed him off. "I don't know why they have a hard-on for me. I don't even know who this guy Altman is. If I met him, I met him at some sort of event," Sires said. "It's amazing, these guys. They get a hard-on for somebody. I'm just confounded by this effort by the feds that somehow I'm corrupt. For twelve years I was mayor and there never was anything other than that stupid fuckin' corrupt police chief I inherited."

* * *

After a nine-day trial, Beldini was convicted by a jury of eight men and four women on two of six corruption counts for taking bribes. Neary had spent much of the trial trying to paint Dwek as the heavy, and was successful. One of the jurors on his way out of the courthouse said the informer was clearly a bad guy. But that did not mean he was not credible. "I don't think he lied," said Michael Cuppari, 25, of Cranford.

Leona was sentenced in June to three years in prison. With her voice shaking, she told Judge Linares she had never been so afraid. "I stand before you facing the most terrifying moment of my whole life," she said.

Linares, though, reminded her she could have walked away from Solomon Dwek. "Any reasonable person listening to him would know he was a crook," Linares said.

Assemblyman Daniel Van Pelt, caught on tape accepting an envelope stuffed with $100 bills, also tried his luck before a jury. He was convicted as well in late May.

* * *

After Jack Shaw died, some of the feds said Healy and Joe Doria ought to be grateful, that Shaw's death saved them. The truth may be just the opposite. Healy lost the support of Bob Menendez and left the county's Democratic chairmanship. He also has not made up his mind on whether he will run for mayor again, but the smart money is banking on Jerry bowing out. As for Doria, the feds spent months and months trying to see if the missing $15,000 crept somehow into Doria's life while no one was watching. If, as Shaw told Lou Manzo in the lockup, Shaw never passed any money to Doria, then solving the mystery of the missing money will be impossible. If Shaw never passed Doria any cash, then Shaw's death will wind up being a last slap in the face for the one guy who never abandoned the fixer from Chicago.

* * *

Within days of the takedown, inside the top echelon of the Corzine camp the governor began openly talking about aborting his campaign. The message that Corzine might abandon the effort was relayed to the White House. Then it was withdrawn. The worst thing for a candidate is ambivalence, and the people in Washington needed to know what the hell was going on in Jersey.

The White House had been worried for a while already and now the president's men insisted on finding out what was happening, what Corzine was thinking, what he was going to do, if he would stay in the race, if he did could he win, and should Barack Obama play any additional role in what could well be a kamikaze mission on the New Jersey Turnpike. Corzine was getting regular calls from Obama counselor Valerie Jarrett. Even more frequent were the conversations between White House political director Patrick Gaspard and Corzine campaign manager Maggie Moran.

A meeting was set for August 10 at the home of Corzine's girlfriend on Fifth Avenue. Coming up from D.C. was Obama strategist David Axelrod and Gaspard, who wanted to meet with Corzine, Shea, Moran, state Democratic chairman Joe Cryan, political consultant Steve DeMicco, and Jamie Fox, the king of the state's political operatives.

In many ways, Fox was key. He had worked for Jim Florio and Bob Torricelli and managed the ugly conclusion of McGreevey's governorship. Fox was also a bridge to the Obama organization, having worked with Axelrod and the president's campaign manager, David Plouffe. Fox was an usher at Plouffe's wedding and the two remained in day-to-day contact even throughout the heat of the 2008 presidential campaign. Fox also was a mentor and close friend to Tom Shea. By the summer of 2009, Fox had built his boutique lobbying and public affairs firm into a successful concern and he had no desire to leave that for a sweaty sprint with a governor he didn't like very much in a campaign that may well have already been lost. Plus, what nearly no one knew at the time was that Fox had already made his decision and wanted no part of the governor's campaign. He had worked out a mutual non-aggression pact with the Christie camp. As long as Fox stayed out of the game, Christie and his boys would neither attack him nor hold a grudge against him or his clients in the future.

President Obama had already campaigned for Corzine and made a public show of support for a man who helped put him in the U.S. Senate. Back in June, a *Star-Ledger* reporter was invited to meet with the president at the White House so Obama could put out the word: "I think very highly of Jon Corzine. I think he's a terrific public servant . . . I'm confident that he can win reelection." So the White House already had serious skin in the game.

Before the Manhattan sit-down, Gaspard made calls to New Jersey to first determine who, if anyone, could mount a replacement campaign so late in the season. Was there anyone popular enough to actually pose a challenge to the juggernaut that Christie had become? Would Newark's popular young African American mayor, Cory Booker, be interested? Could he win? Booker was interested, but the mayor's pollster, Joel Benenson, said it was a fool's errand. Benenson had run the numbers and Booker would lose to Christie. Worse than that, it would damage Booker's future chances of running for governor, and at just 40 years old Booker had plenty of time to wait. Hell, Booker could hold off until 2017 and still be the "young" guy in the race.

If not Booker, who? The only answer was Richard Codey. He was state senate president and, as a result, became acting governor after McGreevey's resignation and before Corzine won. Codey had wanted the job in his own right, but Corzine and his wallet shoved Codey aside in 2005. Codey was legitimately viewed as the man who had saved New Jersey's Democratic Party after McGreevey, and he parlayed that into serious statewide popularity—something that only increased after he took on a talk radio shock jock who mocked his wife's battle with depression.

Irony is the rule in New Jersey politics, and by July 2009 it seemed Codey was poised to take over Corzine's campaign. The problem with that was Codey had never been seriously tested in a statewide race. In 2005, the Republicans gave Codey a pass so they could train their sights and spend their limited resources on Corzine, who was actually running. In many ways, the GOP opposition to Corzine actually helped Codey's popularity shoot up, because he kept his luster while Corzine was getting body-checked every day.

The White House was told by some of its most trusted New Jersey voices that Codey could be a problem because no one knew if he could raise enough money to compete with Christie and whether he had any skeletons or enemies or both that could reveal themselves in the race to Election Day. It was a story line pushed each day more aggressively by South Jersey Democrats aligned with George Norcross, Codey's avowed enemy. And it framed the way the decision would be made in the West Wing. If the White House was to be so bold as to switch candidates, it had better not blow up in the president's face. *If we do this, we own this. And if we own it, it better work.*

The day before the secret sit-down in New York, Corzine and his crew gathered at the official beach house of the governor, a secluded waterfront getaway near Seaside Heights. On the table were deli sandwiches from one of New Jersey's famed roadside convenience stores. The group knew what was at stake. They did a dry run of the presentation and they prepared for the possibilities. They believed there was a chance that Axelrod would blow his lid. That he might say the president was out of the picture, that Corzine could sink or swim on his own but that he could forget the White House's phone number. They feared Axe might tell Corzine the president of the United States—the leader of his party—wanted him out of the race.

Seven months earlier, Corzine had summoned his top aides to Manhattan to ask whether they thought he should run for reelection and if he could win. That night, Corzine was the only one who didn't think he should get out. Now, he was heading back to Manhattan uncertain how the evening—perhaps the campaign—would end. Corzine's private schedule for August 10 recorded it simply as a New York visit with three and one-half hours blocked off. With the doors shut, Axelrod opened up with a stunning show of calm and understanding: "I want to be clear about this: The president's your friend. The president supports you in this election. If you believe that I'm here to ask you to leave the election, that's not true. But we have concerns."

With that, Corzine's team went into the presentation. DeMicco did a PowerPoint on turnout targets. Cryan went through the local political landscape. Maggie discussed the money. Axelrod and Gaspard were worried. For the first time they learned about the Corzine chaos and realized it was pretty much caused by the candidate, not the staff. They were stunned when they heard Corzine was getting multiple sets of poll numbers and not paying attention to any of them. They couldn't believe it.

They were used to the Obama campaign, where discipline was religion and campaign science was like Scripture. They were looking at a scene where "no drama" was a foreign language. Yet they remained surprisingly calm even as some of Corzine's advisers in the room hoped the governor would be pushed harder.

Axelrod told Corzine that Obama wanted a commitment the governor would bound into action, spend enough money, and get really aggressive, really fast.

Within a few days, Maggie and Gaspard hatched the plan to bring in Benenson. He was Booker's pollster, yes, and McGreevey's before that. But Benenson was still basking in a newfound fame that came with serving as Obama's lead pollster in 2008. Corzine's longtime pollster Mark Mellman, unable to convince Corzine of anything, had tried to quit a few times, but Corzine wouldn't let him go. Now, Mellman was out, Benenson was in.

With Benenson's ties to the White House, his hard edge and fanatical loyalty to his cause, Corzine's campaign had finally found some cohesion and footing and passion. They didn't know it was already too late.

* * *

Immediately following the take downs, Corzine had called for the mayors to resign but did not ask the same of the others who were arrested—the commissioners, the patronage appointees, the members of the council. That last group was important. Republicans accused Corzine of having a double standard designed to help himself. If Jersey City Council members were forced out, that could well have meant some of the most effective players in Hudson County get-out-the-vote efforts would have been ousted by a man who needed their help on Election Day. Corzine said that was not his motivation, he only wanted to force out those directly in charge of government spending and administration.

No matter. Jersey City sat out the election anyway. Corzine's campaign was banking on more than 76,000 votes coming in from Hudson. Privately, they insisted they were satisfied with Hudson's turnout, but that didn't tell the story.

"There was no Hudson operation in the campaign and if it weren't for Hoboken and Union City there would have been nothing," said one of the Hudson County organizers. In years past, Hudson was ground zero for gubernatorial politics. Rallies, concerts, fund-raisers. Democratic candidates basically took up residency in the county to maximize turnout, and Corzine, who had lived in Hoboken since 2002, was no different. At least not in 2005, when he won the governorship in a rout. From the day of the takedown, on July 23, until Election Day, three and a half months later, Corzine attended only a couple of small events in Hudson, did nothing in Jersey City, and did little but slip in and out of the county when necessary. There was no Jersey City presence at all because many of the key people, including Joe Cardwell and the county's Democratic chairman, Jerry Healy, were pushed to the side. In the case of Cardwell and others who were arrested on July 23, they were just lying low hoping to keep the heat at bay. They wanted no part of campaigns or elections—not for a while.

With Healy, it was more complicated. With Healy, the arrests turned him radioactive. On the street and among fellow mayors and political leaders, there was a real suspicion that the mayor rolled over to protect himself and that he went to work for the feds. Healy knew it and he knew that's why people weren't talking to him. "Your number one job as county chairman is fund-raising," Healy told people in the wake of the arrests. "How the hell am I gonna raise funds? I don't wanna have any more fuckin' fund-raisers for anything. Who the hell's going to talk to me?"

Behind closed doors, Healy was emphatic that the collapse of the Hudson County Election Day operation proved the true motivation behind the July 23 arrests. "It was all about the November 3 election."

Others go further. They say Chris Christie's goal and legacy as U.S. Attorney was the systematic dismantling of some of the state's leading political organizations, in Bergen, Hudson, and Middlesex. They argue that Christie came to office while the Democratic Party was riding high and heading toward its zenith in New Jersey. They say he was determined to bust it down. They openly criticize him for using a strike force of federal agents and the vast resources of the Justice Department to go after politicians to benefit himself and his party instead of fighting gangs and fraud and the things that are always said to "really matter to people."

Christie laughs at that: "That's the kind of thing that's said by people who were never in that office."

Chris Christie won his crusade to become governor in November 2009, becoming the first Republican to win a statewide election in New Jersey in more than a decade. Outpolling Corzine by more than four percentage points, he beat the well-funded incumbent despite a barrage of negative ads criticizing Christie.

Dwek's attorney, Mike Himmel, ran into Christie a few months later. "I told you he would be one of the greats!" the lawyer said of Dwek.

Unconvinced for so long, Christie acknowledged it: "Yes, you did."

Corzine and his surrogates spent much of the time between July 23 and Election Day criticizing Christie for the way he ran the U.S. Attorney's office and the people who took over after he left. They attacked Michele Brown for being too close to Christie, for being beholden to Christie because of the money he had lent her, and charged that she served as a pipeline of confidential information to the Republican candidate. Corzine and the Democrats also went after Ralph Marra, first alleging he rigged the Dwek arrests to occur during the campaign in order to pay Chris back. Then they went after Marra for his comments during the July 23 news conference. Over and over, Corzine would say things like "The politicization of the office is the issue." The governor and his allies complained about slow responses to freedom of information requests made to the U.S. Attorney's office, and when they received the documents they used them to again go back and hit Christie and Michele. For months, Democrats would whisper to reporters that Michele was Christie's "girlfriend," a charge that both were aware of and shrugged off.

With Corzine back on Wall Street, his tune has changed. Now he says he does not believe the massive corruption and money-laundering sting had anything to do with his defeat, nor does he think the Dwek case was orchestrated as a political ploy by Christie and his allies: "I think that would be an extraordinary abuse of power. The election was lost because unemployment was ten percent. People were hurting."

Loretta Weinberg agrees with Corzine and, no matter the discomfort caused by the Dwek case, "the behavior can't be excused," she said. Weinberg remains in the New Jersey state senate with Barbara Buono and the two joke about the lieutenant governor contest that had political observers riveted for a brief, fevered time during the summer of 2009. For her part, Buono had some of the best luck of all during the governor's race. Losing out on the number two spot saved her time, trouble, and effort, and she is saddled with none of the damage that comes with an election loss as she settles into her new role as Senate majority leader with an eye toward making a move up—including a possible run for governor.

Also remaining in the state legislature is Joe Cryan, the state Democratic chairman and loyal Corzine lieutenant during the campaign. Now the Assembly majority leader, Cryan is the state's only ranking Democratic leader who remains publicly committed to the agenda Jon Corzine pushed during his four years as governor. Cryan believes the events of July 23 were orchestrated for Christie's benefit and his view is "validated," he said, by the fact that so many people involved now have powerful, high-paying jobs in Christie's administration. The Dwek case to Cryan marks the final act in a career at the U.S. Attorney's office in which Christie played the role of backroom boss with a badge.

"It was political. Marra was over-the-top. The timing of the thing was not about luck," Cryan said. Christie "used his office as a political stronghold along the way. God bless him, but it doesn't excuse the behavior. Look, there's no sympathy for the people who did this [took bribes]. That's a losing argument, because there are people who committed the crimes. But why did Dwek end up in Hudson and not Morris? It certainly does make you scratch your head."

When he thinks back to July 23 and the aftermath, Cryan said the only word that captures it is "shock." He said "it took the wind out of everything. Made all of us question everything. The day after those arrests was the longest day of the campaign. From a Democratic Party standpoint, as chairman it was a devastating emotional blow all over the state. It set us back. There was nothing else going on for three to four weeks, maybe longer."

The simple truth is, Cryan said, "as a state chairman, I could've brought back FDR, it wouldn't have mattered. This went all the way through the campaign."

* * *

In politics, you decide how you feel based on the outcome. By that measure, Christie's campaign was a success and he says he loves being governor despite the ugly road it took to get there. But when he looks back at 2009, Christie now acknowledges openly that he never would have imagined Michele Brown and Ralph Marra would have been subjected to the pummeling they got. Christie is convinced they did not deserve it. He allows that he may have been naïve and he has not stopped apologizing for his "mistake" of omitting the loan to Michele from his tax returns and federal financial-disclosure reports. Were it not for the loan, the Corzine camp may well have taken a pass at going after the U.S. Attorney's office because of the high regard it is held in. "I felt awful for them and I felt incredibly responsible. These are dear friends. Put aside they're colleagues," Christie said of Brown and Marra. "I don't know that I can blame Jon Corzine for it. I don't know what he had to do with it. I hope never to know who exactly was responsible for it. But it did real damage to both of them. I think it was unfair. It was the worst time of the campaign for me."

Michele Brown has never spoken publicly about the controversy that swirled around her. She has told friends that it would do her no good and would only serve to further hurt her husband, because every time the loan is mentioned so is the fact that Brown needed the money because her husband lost his job. She is now a key member of Christie's senior staff at the State House, overseeing all appointments, including nominations to the state supreme court and the governor's cabinet. Brown has told intimates she knows that people openly gossip about her relationship with the governor and that she can do nothing about it. She, too, admits to naïveté, that she should have realized she would become an issue in the campaign and, by extension, so would the U.S. Attorney's office, but she is adamant that, as a career prosecutor, she doesn't think "politically."

On August 25, 2009, Michele left the U.S. Attorney's office a little while before 5:00 P.M. and, on her way out, sent a one-page letter to Marra's secretary: "I do not want to become a distraction from the critically important work we do."

The news that Brown had quit was still not universally known when Marra sent a memo to the staff at the U.S. Attorney's office saying he had accepted her resignation with regret: "I know how distracting these transitions can be, and this one has been made more difficult as the Office has been unfairly drawn into a political campaign." Brown has said she would have quit right after Christie did if she could have known how the campaign was going to play out.

* * *

In March, Lou Manzo held a press conference—without the approval of his attorney—to accuse the FBI and federal prosecutors of using both him and his brother as pawns to help Christie become governor. Manzo brought campaign finance records showing contributions to Christie's campaign from employees of the U.S. Attorney's office and a long list of former federal prosecutors who joined Christie's administration.

"I think it's obvious when you connect the dots that there was an attempt to use a government sting as an effort to help Christie's election," Manzo charged.

In May, four of the most serious counts against the Manzo brothers were dismissed by Judge Linares, who ruled they could not be charged with extortion under the Hobbs Act because neither held public office at the time. In other words, Linares said you can't be bribed for official action if you're not in a position to take the official action. But just prior to the ruling, a federal grand jury returned a superseding indictment charging the Manzos with additional counts of mail fraud.

Many believe that the additional indictment was handed up out of spite because the U.S. Attorney's office doesn't like its motives challenged or questioned. The current U.S. attorney, Paul Fishman, dismisses that. "I think folks think we care more than we do about what he said at his press conference," Fishman said in May. "It's a perfectly legitimate indictment backed up by the evidence and it has nothing to do with what Mr. Manzo said or didn't say at his press conference."

After a generation as one of the great odd characters of Hudson County politics, Manzo says his meetings with Dwek and subsequent arrest have left him a financially broken shell of the man he once was. "I don't know when I'll leave the earth. But July 23, 2009, is the day I'll put on my tombstone."

* * *

Ralph Marra announced the arrests and charges on July 23; then he went back into his private office to share a couple of quick attaboys with his prosecutors and the guys who run the FBI in New Jersey. Quickly he had to switch gears and get down to preparing for a hearing that had long been scheduled for the next day: the sentencing of former state senator Wayne Bryant. It was a big case but nothing compared to Dwek. After court, Marra was again surrounded by reporters who had more questions about the busts announced 24 hours earlier. Marra didn't have any more answers, but it was a big story, so everyone was scraping for follow-ups. Marra was glad to oblige. "Unfortunately, there is a climate of corruption in the state that very much needs to end," he told the press.

Marra ended the day and then went off to his annual vacation down at the Jersey Shore. Ralph was joined by his wife and three kids for their traditional pilgrimage to the beach, where they were trailed by the afterglow of the international news story he had announced. He knew there had been some crankiness from Washington, but he disregarded it as just the usual internecine squabbling between his press office and the one at Main Justice. Plus, he got a congratulatory note from Lanny Breuer, the assistant U.S. Attorney general who headed up the Justice Department's Criminal Division, so everything seemed to be going well.

Then on August 18, as Christie was trying to explain away his loan to Michele Brown as an "oversight," the Associated Press reported that Marra was the subject of an internal investigation over the comments he made during the July 23 news conference. The report, filed by the Associated Press' Justice Department reporter in Washington, said the ethics probe focused on whether Marra's statements violated government policy because they aided Christie's campaign. The first Marra heard of the investigation was from a reporter who immediately called for comment after the story appeared on the AP wire.

Publicly Marra said nothing and scoffed at the news. Behind closed doors, he was fuming. He and his aides first tried to pin down what was going on and quickly learned that a complaint had been lodged against him. That led to an initial inquiry—a far cry from an "investigation." Marra said he tried to invoke department rules that require the source of a complaint to be revealed to the subject, but his superiors wouldn't give him that information. He also said he answered every question posed to him both in writing and during a subsequent interview and he insisted his comments that day were well within the boundaries. He requested that an investigation be undertaken in Washington to find the source of the leak and that the department issue a statement saying clearly that he was not under investigation.

Over the following months, Marra said he was able to figure out two things: the complaint was filed by someone in the Justice Department, not opposing counsel as is usually the case; and that the actual letter submitted to the department's Office of Professional Responsibility accused him of timing the Dwek arrests to help Christie. Along with the questions Marra was asked, he was instructed to address "allegations that the announcement of these charges was inappropriately timed to influence the outcome of the New Jersey gubernatorial election." After watching Christie fend off for seven years accusations that he was using the U.S. Attorney's office for political gain, Marra said he never thought through the political implications of the Dwek case or how he could get caught up in the Christie–Corzine cross fire.

"I'm just expendable," Marra said. "Some people up here had enough of a contact down there to orchestrate this thing and to leak it. By attacking the office, of course, they're further attacking Chris. I'm pretty disappointed. [The Justice Department] . . . let themselves be used politically and they didn't stop it and that's terrible."

Shortly after Fishman arrived in the U.S. Attorney's office, Marra was told he was not going to be allowed to remain on the senior staff. Ralph could stay as a prosecutor in the office and go back to trying cases if he wanted, but corruption was out. Marra carried the whiff of Christie, Fishman said, and corruption cases pursued by Marra would bear the unavoidable taint of somehow being done at the behest of the new governor. Marra said Fishman's concern was ludicrous, but he had decided on his own to leave the office anyway. He started looking for corporate counsel positions in the private sector and then Christie offered him the position of chief attorney to the New Jersey Sports and Exposition Authority, which, among other things, runs the Meadowlands sports complex.

With Marra following close behind Michele Brown in going to work for Christie, some critics say it is perfectly clear in retrospect that Dwek was designed exclusively to aid the Republican's campaign. "I don't really care. There's always an election in New Jersey," Marra said.

"The ongoing gubernatorial contest had absolutely nothing to do with the timing of the indictments and arrests. The factors that determined the timing of the indictments and arrests were the sufficiency of the evidence, the logistics of conducting simultaneous arrests of forty-four subjects and search operations at multiple locations, operational security, and investigative strategy," he said. "These are the factors that are considered in the planning and conduct of any arrest and search operation and the takedown of the Bid Rig investigation was handled no differently."

* * *

At the U.S. Attorney's office in Newark, the key players in the Dwek case remain. Jimmy Nobile is back in charge. Brian Howe is doing his thing. And half a dozen other lawyers have been enlisted to handle the various trials that are on the docket for the next two years. But many of the most important members of the supporting cast are gone. In the front office, Paul Fishman, who inherited a huge number of prosecutions connected with Dwek, has been inscrutable to those trying to get a read on how he feels about the case. Fishman was glad to speak to the press after Beldini was convicted and he insists the office is fully invested in pursuing the remaining defendants.

Fishman also made it clear that he would not green-light an indictment of Jersey City mayor Jerry Healy as part of the Beldini case. To some, that was a signal Fishman was unenthusiastic and believed that Healy was clean. Fishman also was not shy to say in an interview that Dwek's efforts were not quite as impressive as some have suggested because the informant simply went out and brought back a couple of dozen different cases tied together only by Dwek. It's not like he was able to net 44 defendants in one case, Fishman said.

But Fishman is an inscrutable guy. He doesn't betray much. And one of the things he won't talk about is the fact that he approved a continuing investigation of Jerry Healy to determine whether any other federal criminal laws were broken by the mayor in cahoots with his friend Leona Beldini. Fishman wanted the FBI to investigate Leona's real estate projects, her job, the whole gamut.

Fishman also has refused repeatedly to close out the Doria investigation. Many in the political world insist that Doria isn't guilty of anything and the simple fact of having the file left open is an affront to God and all that is good and just in the world. The only problem is, the prosecutors and the FBI are still not convinced. During the search of his home, they found records showing that Doria's wife has a seven-figure bank account in her name. The agents did not take the records during the search, mainly because the warrant did not include Maribeth's bank documents. No matter. After they left Doria's house and office, the FBI and IRS went to his bank and got the account information that way. The feds continue investigating. Fishman won't comment.

Doria and his lawyer also won't comment. They are trying to lie low and allow the feds to exhaust themselves and their avenues by investigating as much as they want—to the point of having no alternative but to close out the matter. Doria has never been interviewed or even asked casual questions since that first round of inquiry on the morning of July 23. Were he questioned, Doria would have told prosecutors that the bank account that appears suspicious represents nothing more than the money left over from his late father-in-law's estate, coupled with his in-laws' remaining investment income and $300,000 netted off the sale of his in-laws' house. The account looks sizable, but as Doria has told intimates, it needs to be because it's the money used to support his mother-in-law, whose nursing home bills exceed $8,000 a month.

* * *

Less than two weeks after the July 23 roundup, on August 4, the Power List of the 100 most influential people in New Jersey politics was posted by the Web site PolitickerNJ.com. The roster is an annual rite that pays homage to the connected, the kingmakers, and the very plugged in. It's loaded with lawyers, lobbyists, political operatives, media personalities, and even a couple of backroom bosses. In the wake of the Jersey Sting, the 2009 list featured Ralph Marra at number 10, with the number 1 spot going to the state's G-man-in-chief, Weysan Dun.

It was the second accolade to come Weysan's way since the big takedown. On July 24, FBI Director Robert Mueller reached out to offer his compliments.

Then, most important, on November 19 Dun announced he had gotten the transfer he was angling for. Dun got to go back home to Omaha to head the Bureau's operations in Nebraska and Iowa, a posting that would allow him to live in the same house as his wife, who remained at their home in Omaha during his absence.

Justice Department officials made it clear they were not happy with his comments during the July 23 news conference. Months later, Christie said Dun's comments were beyond the pale. "He would never have gotten away with that if I were U.S. Attorney." Christie said he would have instructed Dun in advance to stay away from commenting on Doria because no one had been charged in that segment of the case and it was politically sensitive. Marra said he didn't coordinate statements in advance and had no problem with Dun's words. "It was just the Bureau's normal policy of confirming searches," Marra said. For as long as he can remember, Marra said, the FBI has confirmed a search when agents do one so people know that it's not just some guys wearing blue windbreakers. He said it's also important so neighbors don't worry that something more serious is going on, like a terrorism investigation or a murder probe.

* * *

Weysan Dun had no apologies for his remarks at the July 23 press conference. He said his comments were carefully crafted to ensure they were balanced and neutral so as to avoid benefiting any candidate or political party.

"I emphasized the fact that the investigation had been ongoing for ten years, thus transcending multiple administrations representing both major political parties. I also pointed out there had been two previous rounds of arrests during the course of the ten-year-long investigation in which sizable numbers of public officials of both political parties had been charged and arrested," he said. "The decision to confirm locations where search warrants had been executed was carefully considered. It is important to remember search warrant affidavits are a matter of public record and readily available to the press. Also, the FBI generally confirms the execution of search warrants so as to assure those who may have witnessed the activity that it was a legitimate law enforcement operation."

Dun said he had heard nothing but positive feedback from the public and from headquarters regarding the arrest operation and press conference. Plus, someone from the highest ranks of the Corzine administration sought him out at a public event in the days after the arrests to thank and compliment him on the fair and balanced nature of his remarks. He declined to identify the official.

In July of 2010 after a year-long inquiry, Marra, along with Dun—who had never been informed he had been the subject of the Justice Department investigation—were both quietly cleared of stepping over the line in their comments.

In a letter from the Justice Department's Office of Professional Responsibility, the two were informed they had acted properly. "Based upon the results of our investigation, we concluded that you did not violate any professional obligation and thus did not commit professional misconduct or exercise poor judgment in this matter," wrote Mary Patrice Brown, acting counsel for the office.

Marra still wonders why there even was an inquiry. "We had so many facts in the record and affidavits that we had a lot of evidence to talk about," he said. It never troubled him that he was investigated. "It troubles me that it was leaked and nothing was ever done about it."

Dun said he had been surprised an inquiry was even initiated. "I was confident my comments were consistent with DOJ guidelines," he said.

* * *

In June, Rabbi Eli Ben Haim stood before U.S. District Judge Joel Pisano in a dark suit and yarmulke to admit that he had used religious charities to launder up to $1.5 million.

"How do you plead to this charge?" asked the judge.

"Guilty," Ben Haim said.

Michael Schaffer admitted he gave $25,000 in illicit cash campaign contributions to Peter Cammarano in a scheme to obtain the former Hoboken mayor's official influence regarding Dave Esenbach's real estate development projects.

Jeffrey Williamson, the ex–Lakewood Township housing inspector, was sentenced to 37 months in prison. Charles Amon, Dwek's former property manager, was sentenced to a year and a day in prison.

In August, Suarez narrowly escaped recall in a special election in Ridgefield.

* * *

"You know what a friend is, Mr. Dwek?" Beldini's lawyer, Neary, asked one day. "Have any friends? How many are not FBI agents?"

Dwek did not answer right away. Finally, he replied, "It is a very difficult question to answer."

"You don't have a father as a friend, is that correct?"

It was correct. His father, with whom Solomon once prayed three times a day, had all but disowned him. At services two days after the arrests, Rabbi Dwek gave a sermon that was so critical of his son's work for the FBI that word began to spread that the Dwek family was treating Solomon as though he had died. A rumor that the Dweks sat Shiva for Solomon turned out to be apocryphal, but the rhetoric was so strong that the

U.S. Attorney's office contacted the rabbi and directed him to cool it. Death threats were coming in against Solomon, and the feds believed that Dwek's father was inciting them.

Neary continued pushing Dwek: "You don't have a mother as a friend, is that correct?"

Again, The Rabbi's Son hesitated. "No."

"Don't have Uncle Joey as a friend?" Neary pressed. The Uncle Joey Solomon had scammed out of $60 million.

Dwek looked down and could not immediately answer. Finally he put his hand to his face and said, "No."

The pauses grew longer. The answers came slower.

"Don't have all the members of the Community you stole money from?"

"No."

The court turned quiet. Dead quiet. The room was filled with cold emptiness, with absence, with a lifetime of bad decisions draped over Solomon like the graduation gown he never got to wear. Then, finally, after all the millions of dollars, all the lies, all the families destroyed, all the phony profits, all the elaborate stories, all the FedEx envelopes stuffed with cash, Solomon took off his glasses in silence and wiped the tears that suddenly welled from his eyes.

Finally, Solomon Dwek cried.

New Epilogue for the Paperback Edition

Deep within the ugly, industrial heart of Newark—near the Turnpike and the truck depots and the sewage plants and chemical factories—the Essex County jail rises over the horizon. Squat but imposing, it's called a "correctional" facility but it's designed to do nothing of the sort. It warehouses the worst of what North Jersey has to offer until the system moves them to state prison or sends them back to the streets. It is the largest facility of its kind in New Jersey, forbidding and set behind a moat and razor wire that have one message: If you don't need to be here, don't.

Beyond the ramp, the gray antiseptic waiting area, the loud double and triple locks that keep the insiders from getting out, a familiar-looking figure sits surrounded by a swarm of armed guards. There in his yellow prison-issued jumpsuit, no yarmulke, with a slight smile on his face, is the master criminal, Solomon Dwek.

He starts with small talk, but it holds little interest for him. He blanches at discussion of his family. He wants to cooperate, he says, with the pair in front of him, to finally tell the world his story, but then he recoils. He wants his lawyer, but says his lawyer won't return his calls. Then nothing. A long wind-up, but no pitch. Dwek didn't want to come clean. The game was long over, but he was spoiling for yet another con.

It wasn't immediately clear, but it would crystallize soon enough.

As for Dwek's presence here, in jail, that was another matter altogether. He was not supposed to be here, but Solomon—named for history's wisest man—had dug another hole for himself yet again.

* * *

In the months since the takedown of July 23, 2009, new revelations continue to spill out, almost every week it seems. Testimony emerging from the trials that have taken place to date still has the ability to surprise. One moment, Solomon Dwek is narrating a surveillance video clip, as he uses the stock, cliché phrases that became a part of the script throughout the investigation. *I don't know you. You don't know me. Say no more . . .*

"I was instructed to make clear that I was a corrupt developer," he explains on the stand.

The next moment he talks almost indifferently about the widespread money laundering he was doing before he got caught, naming friends and relatives in the Syrian community who poured cash into the Deal Yeshiva in exchange for donation kickbacks—people who have so far not been charged with any criminal wrongdoing.

As of this writing, thirty-one of forty-six people charged have pleaded guilty, including Joe Cardwell, Rabbi Kassin, Rabbi Fish, Levi Deutsch, and Ron Manzo—and in just the past year. Four others were convicted at trial. Charges against one were dismissed and another of those charged died. Yolie Gertner, the mysterious cash courier who disappeared as the arrests came down, is still a fugitive; his whereabouts unknown. Maybe he is in Israel. Some say London. The FBI figures Yolie has seen American shores for the last time.

But Solomon Dwek, the fast-talking, quick-witted real estate investor who convinced a bank to give him $25 million at a drive-thru window, turned out to be far less effective on the witness stand than federal prosecutors hoped when they launched him in 2006.

That became clear—painfully clear for the feds—during the trial of Ridgefield Mayor Anthony Suarez. The boyish-looking Democrat, who steadfastly maintained his innocence throughout, refused to resign even as Governor Corzine and his aides hammered away at him, both publicly and in private. At one point, the mayor's lawyers told the governor's chief counsel that Suarez "is going to be in office longer than Corzine." What was uttered as bluster ended as prophecy.

The Suarez trial pitted the government against one of the state's top defense attorneys, Michael Critchley, a tough, street-smart litigator who hit Dwek hard during cross-examination. Critchley, a bull of a man with equal appetites for expensive cufflinks and the jugular, always comes to trial very well prepared. By the time he got Dwek on the stand, Critchley had built a mental hard drive of Dwek's personal history and previous testimony, and had become an expert in the psychology of the Rabbi's Son. He knew Solomon was a liar and a con man who would say anything to work a mark and he was eager to offer his clinical assessment that Dwek was a sociopathic disgrace to the cause of justice. While the government had its surveillance videos, Critchley was ready to paint a picture of Solomon he was certain would make jurors loathe the man.

Critchley also had something else going for him. He, like few others, knew the government's case against Suarez was weak—another byproduct of Jimmy Nobile's surprising eleventh-hour withdrawal just before the takedown. The charges against Suarez never would have been brought under more careful review. Ralph Marra acknowledged as much during a detailed and candid postmortem at Rutgers University Law School late in 2011.

Suarez had been charged with bribery and extortion for allegedly taking $10,000 in exchange for promising to support building projects proposed by Dwek. "It took only two meetings," the federal prosecutor told the jury during his opening argument. Suarez, who had met Dwek in 2008 through Vinnie Tabbachino, was raising money to cover legal fees in an unrelated political lawsuit. Posing as David Esenbach, Dwek said he would contribute. In exchange, he wanted help securing permits to build in Ridgefield.

"I wanna make sure I got a friend that will support my stuff," Dwek told Tabbachino during a meeting at Patsy's Italian Restaurant in Fairview.

In testimony that followed, the jury quickly learned that Suarez had turned down a $10,000 cash payment passed to him through Tabbachino in the familiar FedEx envelope. When Tabbachino gave the mayor a check for the same amount made out to his legal fund, Suarez at first accepted it. That, however, wasn't the end of it. After conferring with his own lawyer at the time, former federal prosecutor Henry Klingeman, the mayor wrote "VOID" on the check and told Dwek he wouldn't give his projects preferential treatment.

Critchley studied Dwek while he testified during the Beldini trial and said he was a "dangerous witness" whose flaws were now coming back to haunt the U.S. Attorney's office. He was ready to pounce when he got Dwek on the stand.

"Critch," as he's known by the initiated, began by bringing up a scheme that had never been disclosed, where Dwek and a partner arranged to pay life insurance premiums for people with terminal illnesses who couldn't afford them. Another simple scam. When death finally came, the families of the insured got 10 percent, while Dwek split the rest between his partner and his father's religious school. Fit Dwek's MO to a tee. All profit, no heavy lifting, no sophisticated computers, no Wall Street pump-and-dump shenanigans. A partnership that yielded bucks for everyone involved— and of course something for the yeshiva.

"How much money did you make investing in people's death?" Critchley asked in a masterful moment prosecutors knew they'd regret. The lawyer's question hung in the room like pall and, in an instant, Dwek the Swindler was transformed into Dwek the Merchant of Death who preys on the barely breathing unable to outrun their mortality.

"The yeshiva made about $125,000," Dwek admitted.

"It was kind of diabolical, right?"

"Objection!" shouted the prosecutor.

"Okay," conceded Critchley. "I'll use a different word—it was kind of sleazy."

"Yes," Dwek replied, shrugging his shoulders.

Defense attorneys insist that "Perry Mason" is fiction and that they're lucky to worm their way into one juror's head deeply enough to plant the smallest seed of doubt. But Critch got his "Perry Mason" moment. And Suarez was soon found not guilty of taking $10,000 from Dwek. It was the first time a public official had been acquitted of federal corruption charges in New Jersey in more than a decade.

Suarez's codefendant in the three-week trial did not fare as well. Tabbachino, always jovial and smiling in court, claimed his talk on the surveillance tapes, as Dwek sought approvals for a fictitious development project in Ridgefield, was just bluster. "He likes to B.S.," his attorney, Anthony Kress, told the jury. Tabbachino was still smiling—even while standing to hear the jury's verdict—as he was convicted for attempted extortion and bribery.

Critchley makes no effort to hide the disgust he feels toward the entire Dwek operation.

"It's one thing to send out a witness like Dwek when crime is actually occurring. It's fair game if someone's involved in ongoing criminal matters," he complained. "I get a little concerned and frightened when you send someone like Dwek out to entice people into committing a crime."

He said he still wonders why the government didn't use an FBI undercover agent, rather than Dwek. "Maybe they didn't realize what they were dealing with and got blinded by the thought of the mother lode," he suggested.

Former Assemblyman L. Harvey Smith was also acquitted.

Prosecutors thought they had the former Democratic assemblyman cold. "Stop talking," he could be heard on the surveillance video tape shown to the jury, interrupting the man he knew as Dave Esenbach, as Dwek looked to arrange a $5,000 payment. "Stop talking. 'Cause you make me feel like I might want to pat you down, to see if you got . . ." Videos and photos showed Dwek taking a FedEx envelope out of the trunk of his Lexus and passing it to Smith through an intermediary.

Stung by the Suarez verdict, the U.S. Attorney's office held back Dwek as a witness in the trial. Instead, they put on Ed Cheatam, the former Jersey City Housing Authority commissioner and board of education member who first introduced Dwek to Smith, as the key witness. Cheatam, who had already pleaded guilty in the case, did even worse on the stand than Dwek—and it wasn't because his name sounds like a punch line. In his closing arguments, defense attorney Peter Willis pointed out the government's new star witness was unconvincing and frequently unsure of himself.

Smith took the stand in his own defense and said he did not know there was cash inside when he accepted the envelope. He also said he did not open it until he got to his office. Putting his own narration on surveillance video, Smith said he was simply trying to get away from Dwek.

"I meant for him to shut up," he replied when asked why he had made the comments. "He was annoying. We're in a parking lot in Hudson County and the things he was saying could lead to misinterpretation that I didn't want to be in the papers."

At the same time, Smith, a tall, outgoing longtime pol, came across as very likeable in the December 2010 trial that finished up just before the holiday. The jury was out only three days before coming back to find Smith not guilty of taking $15,000 in bribes. It was an early Christmas present. Prosecutors and defense lawyers were equally stunned by the outcome.

"Praise the Lord!" cried out Smith's wife, Gail, as the jury foreman reached the last of the six not-guilty verdicts. Her six-foot-five husband slumped over the defense table and wept.

Charges against Richard Greene were later dismissed when the government decided that they had no case against him.

* * *

Joe Doria, the likeable Democrat from Bayonne, was also finally cleared, more than two years after he awoke to the FBI pounding on the door of his home in a futile search for marked FBI money. Never charged or even questioned, Doria was seen as a victim of the political fallout, after he was forced to resign as head of the Department of Community Affairs amid Corzine's faltering reelection campaign. But in September 2011, the U.S. Attorney's office sent Doria a rare letter saying they had closed their investigation.

"Based on the evidence of which we are currently aware, no charges will be brought by this office regarding the circumstances that led to the search," Jimmy Nobile wrote.

*   *   *

In the most bizarre aspect of the whole case, the man charged with brokering black market kidney transplants—Levy-Itzhak Rosenbaum—never went to trial but ended in a plea bargain. Truth is he never had any plans to contest the charges. Rosenbaum knew the feds had him dead to rights from the start and all he could do was try to negotiate himself into the shortest-possible prison sentence. In October of 2011, Rosenbaum pleaded guilty in federal court to helping Dwek make arrangements to procure a kidney for his "secretary," later identified as FBI agent Jessica Weisman. At the same time, Rosenbaum admitted arranging transplants for three other New Jersey patients with failing kidneys—all of whom underwent surgery in unnamed American hospitals after paying Rosenbaum. None of the patients or hospitals was named, nor were they charged.

Rosenbaum, in a dark suit and a heavy accent, told federal Judge Anne Thompson the three actual transplants took place in December 2006, September 2008, and February 2009, after he was paid between $120,000 and $140,000 by the recipients. The donors all came from Israel, and earned just $10,000 for giving up one of their healthy kidneys.

"The son told me the father has kidney failure," Rosenbaum told the court of one transaction. "I helped him."

Rosenbaum's attorneys depicted the broker as a sought-after professional providing a legitimate medical service to those in need, like a midwife or hospice nurse. "Each of the recipients was suffering from kidney failure, was enduring the pain and serious health dangers associated with kidney dialysis and was facing death unless a transplant was arranged," the attorneys said.

*   *   *

Some parts of the story, meanwhile, remain a mystery to this day.

When the FBI deployed Dwek into Hudson County and unleashed him into the spring election campaign, Jersey City Mayor Jerry Healy was the top target on their list. The point of the pyramid. If they couldn't get to the man himself, the feds wanted to get as close as possible, thinking that someone close to him would eventually roll over on Healy. They got to Leona Beldini, Healy's friend and deputy mayor, and they got to political allies and advisers. What was never disclosed by the FBI and the U.S. Attorney's Office is how high Solomon Dwek actually infiltrated Healy's organization and his campaign.

People around Healy often explain that the mayor himself was never involved with anything illegal because his top aides were not. Even Beldini, they say, was not as high up or inside as her title and public persona would lead you to believe. But Dwek did make it all the way into the high command of the Healy campaign. The top.

Solomon Dwek got to Buddy Demellier.

Harold "Bud" Demellier has long been a major player in Hudson County politics, with strong ties to the Hudson County Democratic Organization. A high-profile campaign strategist with an imposing height and bearing, he served as Healy's campaign manager. He also has a $127,800-a-year job as director of the county's department of roads and public property.

And for months, he was on the payroll of none other than David Esenbach.

FBI surveillance video that has never been publicly released shows that Dwek met regularly with Demellier, who was never named or charged in the long-running federal probe. Demellier does not deny it and when asked directly about his involvement with Dwek, acknowledged he was paid $20,000 in cash. But he said it was legitimate, that he was acting as a consultant—even while on the county payroll—and there was nothing wrong with it. "This was someone I thought was involved in a syndicate that had money," he said in an interview in his seventh-floor corner office. The same office that can be seen in the surveillance video. The office where Demellier presides over the county's roads, bridges, and the motor pool.

Dwek, in meetings with Demellier, talked constantly about getting zoning approvals to build his bogus condo development atop a chromium waste site in Jersey City, while Demellier, on the video, told him what lawyers to hire to signal to city hall that he was connected. Buddy's introduction to Dwek began in one of the step-by-step processes that became a hallmark of the long-running federal sting. Maher Khalil, the then–Jersey City assistant director of health and a former member of the zoning board, who has already pleaded guilty in the case, put Dwek—as Esenbach—in touch with former Jersey City councilman Tom Fricchione. Fricchione introduced Esenbach to Demellier.

Fricchione, who died in December 2009, was also never arrested. However, according to the surveillance tapes, he frantically called Khalil the night before the July 23, 2009, takedown in the corruption and money-laundering scandal that stunned the state and told him he had just been visited by the FBI. It is not known if Fricchione had decided to cooperate with authorities. But a Freedom of Information Act request filed with the FBI for his file was denied because it was "part of an active investigation."

Several of those arrested in the case were approached by the FBI the night before the arrests and asked if they would cooperate. At least one of the defendants in the case, Guy Catrillo, said on the day he was arrested the FBI told him that no one yet knew of his arrest, and he had an opportunity to help himself if he agreed to cooperate. He declined.

On surveillance tapes obtained by the authors, Dwek can be heard talking about Demellier with Khalil as far back as October 2008, when the informant said he worked out with Demellier the best way to get cash to Mayor Healy—who was never accused of any wrongdoing, or even directly named, in the sting. Healy appeared to have never known Esenbach when he met him months later in a meeting set up by Jack Shaw, another Hudson County political "fixer" who died five days after his arrest in the corruption sting.

"He's a lot stronger than the mayor," Khalil said of Demellier.

During the call, Dwek claimed Demellier told him, "If you want to do cash, go through me. Don't deal with the mayor."

According to the tape, Dwek said Demellier said there was no problem "as long as I don't give it to the mayor. I give it to him for the mayor . . . I'll give the guy ten so there'll be enough to go around."

Days later, Dwek met Fricchione for the first time in a meeting set up by Khalil. According to transcripts of conversations between Khalil and Dwek, the gathering did not go well. "I got a call from Tom—he's not too happy," Khalil told him. "He said the words you were using in the meeting . . . you know, he just felt uncomfortable about buying this person. He doesn't operate like that."

"I know I've got to be careful," said Dwek on the tape.

By the end of October and beginning of November of 2008, Dwek and Fricchione were moving quickly. In a November 4th phone call, Khalil told Dwek to bring the next day two FedEx envelopes each holding $10,000. One was for Demellier and the second for Fricchione. Demellier is "a lot stronger than the mayor," Khalil said, promoting the value of the conquest. And Demellier was also in a position to help Khalil win that City Hall promotion he coveted so badly.

By the time the Healy reelection effort was in full swing a few months later, Demellier and Fricchione were in steady contact with Dwek, the surveillance tapes show. It was as though he was a member of the inner circle. They seemed glad to share their campaign info, they chatted about poll numbers, political strategy, and Healy's $3 million budget and financing operations. Six weeks after the election, Dwek moved in for the kill. It took place amid wide smiles at a Hudson County administration building in Jersey City. There, in his large office with panoramic views, Dwek and Khalil sat with Demellier and Fricchione. As the tape rolled, Bud bragged about his political skill, talking about victories past. "He set us up," Demellier said of a previous adversary. "Once he did that, I buried him. We made him into a racist, which he's not, but we made him into one real quick."

Dwek said he was finally moving ahead with getting the approvals in place to build the massive Garfield Avenue project in Jersey City. Demellier instructed him which lawyers to bring on board. Demellier threw in another boast about a lawyer he mentioned: "I'll call him and tell him to expect it . . . Actually I'm on his payroll for various things in other places."

"The first thing is, you know, what I paid you so far, that I wanna go toward the Jersey City thing," Dwek told Demellier and Fricchione. "And then for future stuff, we'll work on other arrangements."

Demellier responded, "Get the application in."

Then their attention shifted to Bayonne, where Demellier first earned his political stripes. Immediately, Demellier took out his BlackBerry and dialed over to Bayonne City Hall, leaving a message for the mayor's chief of staff. "A friend of mine, I understand, submitted some drawings . . . when you get a chance give me a call, we can chat a little bit about it."

Demellier, in an interview more than a year after *The Jersey Sting* hit the papers, said he had a consulting company called DUB Inc., and agreed to help Esenbach look for development opportunities. "He never showed any knowledge of zoning laws," Demellier recalled. "He never had any building plans. I got irritated a little because he had no plans."

Esenbach, he said, "always talked crazy." But he said he never tried to sell influence and never told him he would help get him approvals. He said Dwek never gave him money for Healy's campaign. Demellier at first said he had never spoken to the FBI, then, a few minutes later, he said he only spoke to the FBI once, when one of the agents connected to the case called in the wake of the July 2009 arrests. He recalled being phoned two days after the takedown, but oddly "they didn't ask me anything."

Demellier said he is not a cooperating witness. "People that know me know that's not something they should believe."

Marra said he had nothing to say about Demellier. No vote of confidence for the mayor's campaign manager, no explanation about why or why not Demellier was looked at by prosecutors. That's the way it goes when someone is neither arrested nor exonerated. No-man's-land.

In the end, though, Demellier could well prove to be one of the luckiest people to have ever sat across a table from Solomon Dwek/David Esenbach. Inside the U.S. Attorney's office in the days leading up to the arrests, Demellier was an active topic of conversation. The feds had him on tape taking money and agreeing to aid Dwek in securing approvals. Even with Demellier's anticipated explanation that he was acting as a "consultant," the feds knew they could make a play on Buddy and let him take his chances with a jury. And juries in New Jersey are notoriously impatient with public officials accused of corruption.

But something told the feds to hold off. Maybe Fricchione could be flipped; maybe Demellier himself. The feds wanted Mayor Healy and Demellier could take them there. Maybe someone else would come out of the woodwork and point an incriminating finger at Bud, strengthening the case against him and giving him all the more incentive to turn on Healy. Maybe one of the lawyers on Marra's staff had a sinking feeling about that one part of the case and, with the number of defendants quickly approaching fifty, there was no need to proceed with anything that wasn't a sure thing.

Demellier says that he has never been asked to return the $20,000 Dwek gave him. And asked if he ever mentioned to Healy about his work with Dwek or his conversation with the FBI, he replied, "I don't remember."

After Demellier's involvement with Dwek was revealed in *The Jersey Sting*, political opponents called for Demellier's head. He insisted he had done nothing wrong and had been acting as a consultant, on his lunch hour, when he met with Dwek. He remains director of the Hudson County department of roads and public property, but lost some of his most lucrative campaign clients. Some will no longer take his calls, believing him to be wired.

Sources close to the investigation now say Demellier was cooperating with the FBI. The feds, they say, have not decided what to do with their old friend Bud. But if there is to be yet another act in *The Jersey Sting*, those involved with the case say it is likely to focus on Bud Demellier.

* * *

In Hoboken, the poisoned well of the city's politics was thrown into yet another great upheaval with the release of *The Jersey Sting*. Details about the ill-fated administration of Peter Cammarano cast new light on what had gone on but, at the same time, helped many finally come to understand the tragedy of their young, handsome mayor.

What was not expected, however, were the revelations about some of

Hoboken's other leading political figures. Chief among them were disclosures that councilman Michael Russo had met with Dwek and made it appear he liked the dubious way Dwek did his business and that he would be willing to accept a bribe, although he never did. The news would have been problematic no matter when it arrived, but, coming as it did while Russo was seeking reelection, added fire to yet another already-overheated Hoboken campaign.

Quickly, Russo dismissed the matter, saying anybody who said he would take a bribe was "lying." So there could be no questions, the authors of *The Jersey Sting* posted online a copy of the FBI surveillance video of the meeting and it clearly showed the conversation quoted in the book. Beyond that, the recording gave viewers a deeper glimpse into Russo's political thinking.

"All things being equal, I'll always make sure my friends are heard before anyone else," the councilman said at a point that would surely make good-government advocates cringe.

The video went viral in Hudson County and, in record time, forced Russo to change his spin. He told a reporter with *Patch.com* that "as boastful as the meeting became, at no time did I suggest that I would engage in any illegal activity." And he went on to say he believed the video had been manipulated to cast him in a negative light. Ultimately, the recording—which was not edited—had no impact on Russo's political career as he thumped his opponent nearly 2–1 at the polls. On his Web site, Russo called the contest "one of the toughest campaigns of my life," but proclaimed bombastically "this election was about the heart of Hoboken. And I can tell you that the heart of Hoboken is beating strongly!"

* * *

Solomon Dwek today is in federal prison. He was transferred there from the confines of the Essex County lockup where he spent the first few weeks of his most recent incarceration. How Dwek landed back in the slammer is yet another story of the lies of the Rabbi's Son catching up to him.

Throughout the trials, Dwek—having pleaded guilty to the bank fraud that led to his cooperation deal with the feds—had been free on $10 million bail. He spent every day on "house arrest"—though he was not home—surrounded by bodyguards. He wore an ankle bracelet that monitored his comings and goings. He remained in touch with his wife and kids, but he would not see them for weeks at a time. He socialized with no one, did not go to the movies, listened to no music. He continued aiding the bankruptcy trustee in his efforts to liquidate what remains of his assets, working with the FBI agents who served as the only social connections in his life. And he was able to follow his beloved New York Yankees.

The house he had provided for his brother was put to auction. His own house in Deal, which was in Pearl's name, was put up for sale for $1.6 million. The real estate listing called it a "beautifully custom home" with built-in cabinetry, inlaid marble floors, a double kitchen and a backup generator. It sits on a quiet, tree-lined street in a quiet Jersey Shore neighborhood. Even now, it looks so plain and average on the outside that it's hard to imagine that an arch-criminal, a super-informant, lived there. The Realtor in charge of the sale avoids mentioning Dwek's name.

It has yet to be sold. Pearl, meanwhile, filed for personal bankruptcy, claiming she owes up to a total of $500,000 to creditors.

Solomon's family moved from New Jersey after the five kids were forced out of the religious schools they were attending. They reappeared some time later in Pikesville, an Orthodox Jewish neighborhood just outside of Baltimore, far from the Syrian community. Their reemergence into public view led to an additional controversy after Dwek was seen in a Kosher pizzeria and the owner captured a quick picture of him with a cell phone camera. Then he posted it online. There was an angry outcry from many that Dwek was living among them and some in the neighborhood criticized the local rabbinical council for giving safe passage to an enemy of the Jews. Dwek's father, the rabbi, was forced out of the synagogue he had built and led in Deal for so many years. Rabbi Eli Ben Haim was also fired from his congregation.

The FBI's Ed Kahrer, the assistant special agent in charge who had supervised the Big Rig investigation and recently retired, said despite Dwek's issues, he was a very good source. "He worked very hard," Kahrer said. "I found myself liking Solomon. He is devoted to his children; to his family."

But at the same time, he said a source remains a source. "They are not your friend."

The aftermath of the investigation was a time of great stress for Dwek. Cut off by much of his family and friends, and attacked in court, Kahrer said Solomon was alone and depressed.

"We would counsel him. Try to talk to him about how he did what he could for his family," he said. "You remind him he tried to do the right thing."

But those in Dwek's situation go through a series of emotional stages, as they come to terms with the consequences of their actions.

"It's like a grieving process they have to go through. And it is not going to go away overnight," Kahrer said.

Estranged for a time from his wife, Solomon and Pearl later got back together in Baltimore and had a sixth child last year, a boy. They named him Rafael—Hebrew for "healer." Perhaps the child can help mend the family his father tore apart.

* * *

Dwek was expected to stay out of trouble while awaiting his sentencing. Having won the mother of all reprieves, the FBI and federal prosecutors figured Dwek would do whatever he could to prove he was no longer a crook. It was certainly a logical assumption. The bankruptcy proceedings continued and he was scheduled to be a witness in several upcoming trials. Dwek was on call for all of it and, despite the beating he took under cross-examinations, he gave the feds every reason to believe he was—at long last—playing by the rules.

Then came the missing rental car.

It was a small matter, really. Dwek had rented a car on behalf of a friend, who for some reason did not return it on time. Hertz reported it as stolen, which led to a criminal warrant being filed in Baltimore. Then it came to the attention of the FBI. At first, Dwek's FBI handler assumed the warrant was a case of mistaken identity because the police report incorrectly described Dwek as African American—an error later attributed to the difference in driver's license coding between New Jersey and Maryland. And Dwek immediately denied any knowledge of the rental—a 2010 Nissan Versa. He also filed a false affidavit with Hertz regarding the incident, before finally claiming to have rented it on behalf of an acquaintance.

U.S. District Judge Jose Linares, who presided over Dwek's plea and has seen most of the defendants in *The Jersey Sting* go through his courtroom, exploded when he was told the government informer misled the FBI.

"He has proven to be a consummate defrauder and an extremely cunning liar," Linares declared in a remarkable tantrum. The judge revoked Dwek's bail and immediately sent him to jail to await sentencing, ruling Solomon had violated terms of his cooperation agreement with the government. Federal marshals took him into custody on the spot, as Dwek removed his belt, his dark jacket, and pale blue tie, handed them over to a friend in the courtroom, and silently walked out.

Federal prosecutors are praying that Linares cools off by the time he sentences Dwek because they fear the judge is so pissed off he might throw the book at Solomon despite his work as a cooperator. The episode brought to an end the $12,500 monthly stipend Dwek had been receiving from the federal bankruptcy trustee trying to sort out the remains of his failed real estate empire. The money was going to support his wife and children.

* * *

Days after he was taken into custody, Dwek received a visit from an administrator at the jail who carried a message from the authors of *The Jersey Sting*. Solomon had long known about the book that traced his exploits with the government, and had been ordered not to read any of it while trials were still pending. He said he would meet with the authors, who were given a private audience with the Rabbi's Son as he sat in the cafeteria of the Essex County jail, in his yellow jumpsuit and black slippers.

The interview lasted less time than it took to get through security. Despite agreeing to the sit-down, and confirming it just before its start, Dwek had nothing to say for once in his life. He had only wanted his visitors to get his attorney on the phone for him.

"Talk to my lawyer."

Chapter Notes

The dialogue between Solomon Dwek and his former real estate partners came in large part out of hundreds of pages of transcripts, sworn depositions, civil complaints, legal briefs, and other material filed as part of the massive federal bankruptcy case—which is still ongoing—and the earlier state civil docket.

Dwek's conversations with those targeted in the Jersey Sting were drawn from the dozens of remarkably detailed criminal complaints and affidavits filed by the U.S. Attorney's office. In some cases, the narrative was supplemented by additional FBI surveillance recordings of other meetings Dwek had set up with many of those charged, as well as individuals who have not been accused of any wrongdoing. All depositions of Dwek cited in the chapter notes were taken as part of the bankruptcy proceedings that were filed against him.

Some of the sourcing on the dialogue recorded by the FBI is specifically cited in the notes following to differentiate the cases from which the recordings were taken. Other conversations of those connected with the case were based on interviews, in some cases with the guarantee of anonymity being extended to the sources, and based on the best recollections of individuals who were there or participated in conference calls.

1. Everyone in New Jersey Was Arrested Today . . .

Most of this chapter was written from the notes and reporting of the authors, who covered the story of the arrests on July 23, 2009, along with their colleagues at The Star-Ledger. Subsequent interviews with the players, including an extensive sit-down with Weysan Dun, who then headed the FBI office in Newark, and with former acting U.S. Attorney Ralph Marra, filled in many of the blanks.

More than 300 FBI and other federal agents were in position . . . Ted Sherman and Joe Ryan, "Walk of Shame: Wide-ranging Corruption Scandal Snares Officials and Religious Leaders," *The Star-Ledger*, July 24, 2009.

The 60-year-old veteran Democrat had been visited by FBI . . . Joe Ryan, "Official Accused in Sting Charged with Lying to FBI," *The Star-Ledger*, December 18, 2009.

"The ships are out there; they're on their way . . ." Josh Margolin and Ted Sherman, "Arrests Shine Spotlight on an Unknown Crime Fighter," *The Star-Ledger*, August 2, 2009.

He had given thousands of dollars . . . State and federal campaign finance reports.

2. The Rabbi's Son

"The property wasn't exactly there . . ." U.S. District Court Criminal Complaint: *United States v. Itzak Friedlander, a/k/a "Isaac Friedlander,"* July 23, 2009.

The Syrian Jews were different . . . Zev Chafets, "The SY Empire," *The New York Times*, October 14, 2007.

It was all about location . . . William Neuman, "Paying Any Price to Live Here," *The New York Times*, June 25, 2006.

"Recession, schme-cession," Dwek replied . . . Transcript of surveillance video during meeting with Mordchai Fish.

Theirs was a closed society . . . Chafets, "The SY Empire."

Many with money began buying property in nearby Deal . . . Jacqueline Mroz, "Deal Gone Sour," *New Jersey Monthly*, September 2009.

The uncle of Dwek's wife . . . Deposition of Solomon Dwek, June 22, 2007.

"I've known him for many, many years . . ." Deposition of Kenneth Cayre, taken as part of the bankruptcy proceedings against Solomon Dwek, August 28, 2007.

"I'm a person that does due diligence . . ." Deposition of Isaac Franco, taken as part of the bankruptcy proceedings against Solomon Dwek, August 22, 2007.

Federal charges were filed claiming the school had submitted false statements . . . Stipulation and Settlement Agreement between The United States and the Lakewood Cheder School Inc., October 25, 2006.

"I would sleep there and come home not too often . . ." Deposition of Solomon Dwek, October 15, 2009.

He was the owner of a major New York–based apparel company . . . Adjmi Apparel Group Web site.

"Jack didn't have too much experience . . ." Deposition of Solomon Dwek, October 14, 2009.

"Solomon was a snot-nosed kid . . ." Jason Method, "Unusual Real Estate Deal in '93 Got Dwek Started," *Asbury Park Press*, August 20, 2006.

"My husband used to—he was very good about helping boys out . . ." Deposition of Rachel Adjmi, January 7, 2008.

"You're putting me out of business . . ." Deposition of Solomon Dwek, October 15, 2009.

Their oldest was Isaac . . . Deposition of Solomon Dwek, June 22, 2007.

Dwek's father put him on the payroll of the Deal Yeshiva . . . Federal 990 tax filings by the Deal Yeshiva.

Dwek wore $13 white short-sleeve cotton shirts . . . Deposition of Solomon Dwek, June 22, 2007.

"Do you and your family need four cars?" . . . Deposition of Solomon Dwek, June 22, 2007.

"He exploded on the scene" . . . Interview with Christopher Siciliano, who knows the real estate market in Monmouth County firsthand and spent several hours pointing out the extent of Dwek's empire before the collapse.

Philip Konvitz, an aging, longtime Monmouth County political power broker . . . John P. Martin, "Developer's Graft Case Dismissed," *The Star-Ledger*, April 4, 2003.

Solomon became a prolific contributor . . . In depositions, Dwek detailed his political contributions to the Bush and Cheney campaign. Federal and state campaign finance records confirmed that Dwek and his wife gave nearly $200,000 in contributions to various political campaigns, both Democratic and Republican.

Non-kosher hors d'oeuvres such as shrimp kebabs . . . Lisa Getter, "Fundraisers Are Collecting by the Bundle for Bush Camp," *Los Angeles Times*, April 2, 2004.

Cayre had made a fortune in the record and video business . . . Alexis Muellner, "Development Partner Has Miami Rhythm in His Roots," *South Florida Business Journal*, October 11, 2002.

"We had made up a profit participation agreement . . ." Deposition of Kenneth Cayre, August 28, 2007.

He did not request any appraisals from Dwek . . . U.S. Bankruptcy Court: Amended complaint by Charles A. Stanziale Jr. as Chapter 11 Trustee of Solomon Dwek v. Bear Stearns, Inc., Kenneth Cayre, KLCC Investments, LLC, and KLC Foundation, June 9, 2008.

He wired $12 million to Dwek on June 30, 2005 . . . Cayre complaint.

"He took me to the hospital, showed me, actually, a plaque . . . Deposition of Isaac Franco, August 22, 2007.

"You're my nephew. I don't know anything about real estate . . ." Deposition of Joseph Dwek, September 11, 2007.

The terms were the same that Solomon had with Jack Adjmi. U.S. Bankruptcy Court: Complaint by Charles A. Stanziale Jr. as Chapter 11 Trustee of Solomon Dwek v. Joseph Dwek, Yeshuah LLC, Joseph Dwek Family Limited Partnership, and Mark Adjmi, March 4, 2008

3. The Schnookie Deal

"They never attended any closings . . ." Deposition of Solomon Dwek, October 13, 2009.

". . . the bank and Scharpf were fined for helping bank executives expense their political contributions." Jennifer Micale, "Expense-Accounts Misused," *The Home News Tribune*, January 8, 2003.

"It was also the bank that McGreevey turned to . . ." Jonathan Schuppe and Josh Margolin, "Troopers Drove McGreevey to Cipel Visits: Sources Say Governor's Use of His Security Detail Made Some Officers Uneasy," *The Star-Ledger*, August 25, 2004.

The loans . . . were edging toward Amboy's legal lending limit . . . *U.S. Bankruptcy Court: Complaint by Charles A. Stanziale Jr. as Chapter 11 Trustee of Solomon Dwek v. Amboy Bank, Amboy Bancorporation, George E. Scharpf*, February 8, 2009.

"It's too expensive to purchase outright" . . . *Stanziale v. Amboy Bank*, February 8, 2009.

"Do you want the mortgages recorded?" . . . *Stanziale v. Amboy Bank*, February 8, 2009.

Ike Franco was increasingly suspicious about what was going on . . . Certification of Isaac Franco in support of application for a preliminary injunction in New Jersey Superior Court, *Isaac Franco v. Solomon Dwek, et al.* May 11, 2006.

"When I was refinancing these deals through my bank, there was a due date of when these loans would be paid back . . ." Deposition of Isaac Franco, taken as part of the bankruptcy proceedings against Solomon Dwek, August 22, 2007.

"I didn't want to believe he was dishonest . . ." Deposition of Isaac Franco, August 22, 2007.

Franco, he said "always told them that I was running a legitimate business and two minutes before that he was telling me I'm a crook and a liar . . ." Deposition of Solomon Dwek, October 14, 2009.

Franco began ramping up the threats . . . The remarkable series of e-mails between Ike Franco and Solomon Dwek were part of the case file in Stanziale's complaint against Franco, seeking to recover any profits from his investments with Dwek.

"I got three hundred deals. I'm making a lot of money . . ." Deposition of Joseph Dwek, September 11, 2007. The e-mail traffic between Dwek and his uncle was included in the case file as exhibits.

"I have no idea what he's talking about" . . . Deposition of Kenneth Cayre, taken as part of the bankruptcy proceedings against Solomon Dwek, August 28, 2007.

It was an invitation for fraud across the state . . . Nikita Stewart, "Group Sues over Deed Backlog," *The Star-Ledger*, August 13, 2003.

Dwek began executing a series of loan and credit agreements . . . *U.S. Bankruptcy Court: Adversary complaint by Charles A. Stanziale Jr. as Chapter 11 Trustee of Solomon Dwek v. HSBC Bank, NA; Isaac Franco; Elyse Franco; and PNC Bank, NA.* December 10, 2007.

The Deal Golf Club dated to the early 1890s . . . From the history of the Deal Golf and Country Club, on the club's Web site.

Members had received a letter from club president William C. Barham . . . Bob Cullinane, "No Deal on Dwek's Offer to Buy Golf Club," *Asbury Park Press*, August 22, 2006.

"I didn't have a cash flow . . ." Deposition of Solomon Dwek, October 13, 2009.

Yeh immediately called up Dwek . . . Deposition of Solomon Dwek, October 13, 2009.

"He used to call my house midnight or two in the morning . . ." Deposition of Solomon Dwek, October 15, 2009.

"IF THE 5.2M IS NOT IN MY ACCOUNT IN THE NEXT 5 MINUTES I WILL COME THERE AND BREAK YOUR NECK!!!!!!!!!!!!!!!!!!!" *U.S. Bankruptcy Court: Amended Complaint by bankruptcy trustee Charles A. Stanziale v. Isaac Franco*, November 3, 2009.

"You know, Solomon's outside making the deposit . . ." Deposition of Michelle Penix, taken as part of the bankruptcy proceedings against Solomon Dwek, April 12, 2007.

Lassik recalled a bank security official telling her, "Solomon Dwek is well-known . . ." Deposition of Dorothy Lassik, taken as part of the bankruptcy proceedings against Solomon Dwek, April 12, 2007.

Solomon had a history over overdrafts on his accounts at the PNC bank in Eatontown . . . Deposition of Maria Quintans, taken as part of the bankruptcy proceedings against Solomon Dwek, May 24, 2007.

The 4:00 P.M. meeting at HSBC . . . Details of the meeting were drawn out of the depositions of

Solomon Dwek; his uncle, Joseph Dwek, and Isaac Franco, September 11, 2007, and George Wendler, January 11, 2007, which were all taken as part of the bankruptcy proceedings.

Dwek was back in New York for a second round with HSBC . . . From depositions of Solomon Dwek October 13 and 15, 2009, Joseph Dwek, September 11, 2007, and George Wendler January 11, 2007, all taken as part of the bankruptcy proceedings against Solomon Dwek.

At PNC, it was a crisis . . . Deposition of Michelle Penix, April 12, 2007.

"Ikey, something's weird" . . . Deposition of Isaac Franco, August 22, 2007.

"You gypped me. You conned me" . . . Deposition of Joseph Dwek, September 11, 2007.

"I was very busy signing" . . . Deposition of Solomon Dwek, October 14, 2009.

That night, Dwek called his uncle . . . Deposition of Solomon Dwek, October 15, 2009.

4. You Have No Idea What You're Messing With . . .

Lehrer just flat out mocked the matter from the bench . . . Walter Olson, "Judge Who Scoffed at Dispute Between Former Law Partners Is Reversed," *Overlawyered*, September 18, 2008.

The appeals court ordered Lehrer to reduce a $3 million jury verdict . . . Kathy Barrett Carter, "Judge Who Wouldn't Cut Award Has Case Taken Away by Panel," *The Star-Ledger*, November 21, 2003.

Lehrer read and then reread Kearney's filing . . . Interview with Alexander Lehrer. February. 2, 2010.

One of his first headline cases . . . William Kleinknecht and Fredrick Kunkle, "Arrested Banker's Records Offer Rare Details of Cash Laundering," *The Star-Ledger*, August 22, 1999.

"Sometimes I had a beard . . ." Bob Cullinane, "Special Agent Close By as Cash Changes Hands," *Asbury Park Press*, August 12, 2007.

"I was the guy who took the risk . . ." Nancy Shields, "Land Deal Scrutinized Price of Ocean Township Tract," *Asbury Park Press*, January 26, 2003.

The FBI also had been told that Dwek had paid off a mayor . . . Ted Sherman, "The Prior Lifestyle of FBI's Prize Jersey Informant," *The Star-Ledger*, March 21, 2010.

A legend in the office . . . John P. Martin, "Prosecutor Shuns the Limelight," *The Star-Ledger*, January 15, 2007.

Brian Howe . . . Interview with Brian Howe, April 16, 2010.

Sliding off a muddy trail . . . David Voreacos, "Prosecutor Inspires with Passion for Life," *The Record*, July 8, 2000.

Appearing after his arrest . . . John P. Martin and Tom Feeney, "Rabbi's Son Charged in $50 Million Bank Scam," *The Star-Ledger*, May 12, 2006.

"A week ago, it was just me in a courtroom . . ." *Asbury Park Press*, May 13, 2006.

"Judge Names Fiscal Overseer to Tally Up Claims vs. Dwek" by James W. Prado Roberts.

"I am the only graduate of the University of South Dakota Law School that you will ever meet . . ." James W. Prado Roberts, "Fiscal Agent Built Firm from Humble Start," *Asbury Park Press*, August 23, 2006.

"He's an ambulance chaser at best . . ." Deposition of Solomon Dwek, May 6, 2007.

Attorney Robert Weir, representing Dwek that day, said his client had wanted to work out the claims against him . . . James W. Prado Roberts, "Judge Names Fiscal Overseer to Tally Up Claims vs. Dwek," *Asbury Park Press*, May 13, 2006.

"He always pays . . ." James W. Prado Roberts, "Creditors: Dwek Owes $298.1M," *Asbury Park Press*, June 1, 2006.

5. "Do I Really Want to Get in Bed with This Guy?"

He had been named U.S. Attorney for New Jersey by Pres. George W. Bush . . . John P. Martin, "A Savvy Lawyer Tests His Mettle as U.S. Attorney," *The Star-Ledger*, February 5, 2002.

Harrison "Pete" Williams, the highly respected senator from his home state . . . Robert Cohen, "Ex-Sen. Williams Is Dead at 81," *The Star-Ledger*, November 19, 2001.

"Here was a guy held in such high esteem by so many people and he turned out to be a crook . . ." Josh Getlin, "Locking Up N.J.'s Bad Guys," *Los Angeles Times*, February 27, 2003.

Soon after arriving in January 2002 ... John P. Martin and Josh Margolin, "Christie Quits, Setting GOP Wheels in Motion," *The Star-Ledger*, November 18, 2008.

Within days of Christie becoming the new U.S. Attorney ... Ana M. Alaya and John P. Martin, "Paterson Mayor Accused of Graft," *The Star-Ledger*, January 25, 2002.

Nobody in Christie's conference room could forget Michael Guibilo ... John P. Martin, "Ex–FBI Informant Is Guilty of Three Bank Heists," *The Star-Ledger*, February 11, 2006.

Hemant Lakhani, a British exporter, who was arrested in an airport hotel suite near Newark for trying to sell missiles ... John P. Martin, "How 2-Year Sting Brought Down Missile Deal," *The Star-Ledger*, April 4, 2004.

McKenna, a top aide to Christie ... Chris Megerian, "McKenna: The Self-made Man Safeguarding the State," *The Star-Ledger*, February 28, 2010.

He received 85 letters in two weeks reporting suspicion of corruption ... Maryann Spoto, "Words to the Wise Jersey Official: Resist Corruption," *The Star-Ledger*, June 18, 2005.

6. Point of No Return

"Do you consider yourself to be an observant Jew? ..." Deposition of Solomon Dwek, October 15, 2009.

The initial sit-down was with Brian Howe ... Deposition of Solomon Dwek, October 13, 2009.

"I told them there were certain threats ..." Deposition of Solomon Dwek, October 13. 2009.

Dwek had more than $1 million in cash stashed away ... Ted Sherman, "The Prior Lifestyle of FBI's Prize Jersey Informant," *The Star-Ledger*, March 21, 2010.

Waldie's team of case agents had gone undercover ... Tom Feeney and Maryann Spoto, "The Man Behind the FBI Sting," *The Star-Ledger*, February 24, 2005.

"Based out of an office suite ..." Feeney and Spoto, "The Man Behind the FBI Sting."

"Our boss knows that you're influential ..." *Criminal Complaint U.S. District Court, United States of America v. Raymond O'Grady*, February 22, 2005.

He then offered a little bravado ... John P. Martin, "Snared in Corruption Sting," *The Star-Ledger*, February 23, 2005.

Joel tried hard not to laugh out loud ... Bob Cullinane, "Who's on the Take? FBI List Lengthens," *Asbury Park Press*, August 9, 2007.

A federal jury deliberated just three hours ... John Martin, "Monmouth Official Convicted of Taking Bribes," *The Star-Ledger*, June 9, 2006.

Weldon later had the book thrown at him ... Jeff Whelan, "Ex-Mayor Gets Harsh term in Graft Case," *The Star-Ledger*, August 28, 2007.

In July, meanwhile, the FBI and IRS paid a visit to the business offices of the Deal Yeshiva ... John P. Martin and Maryann Spoto, "FBI and IRS Agents Grab Records at Deal Yeshiva," *The Star-Ledger*, July 12, 2006.

There was a 116-foot dinner boat ... Deposition of Solomon Dwek, October 15, 2009.

"I kept on pumping money in and money was going out the back door ..." Deposition of Solomon Dwek, October 15, 2009.

"He's probably in the building right now ..." Bob Cullinane, "Dwek Playing Active Role in Liquidating His Assets," *Asbury Park Press*, August 24, 2006.

"From day one, there's always been a question as to whether Mr. Dwek was being forthcoming" ... James W. Prado Roberts, "Dwek's List of Assets Cause for Skepticism," *Asbury Park Press*, December 6, 2006.

His efforts to use $37,800 of his seized assets to pay for tuition ... James W. Prado Roberts, "Judge: No Tuition for Dwek Kids," *Asbury Park Press*, January 11, 2007.

7. Mike from Monsey

Solomon and Shimon had gotten involved more than a year earlier ... *U.S. Bankruptcy Court: Adversary complaint by Charles A. Stanziale Jr. as Chapter 11 Trustee of Solomon Dwek v. Shimon Haber and Adar Holdings LLC*, February 9, 2009.

One building owner had been fighting for years ... Ted Sherman, "Union City Is Racked by Zoners' Testimony," *The Star-Ledger*, December 20, 2009.

Dwek did not know much about Hudson County ... Deposition of Solomon Dwek, October 15, 2009.

Upstairs, Dwek explained what he was trying to do . . . *U.S. District Court Criminal Complaint: United States v. Moshe Altman, a/k/a "Michael Altman,"* July 23, 2009.

Two weeks later, Dwek's name was back in the news . . . James W. Prado Roberts, "Dwek Ally Pleads Guilty," *Asbury Park Press,* March 22, 2007.

A *gmach,* sometimes transliterated as *gemach,* was essentially an Orthodox charity . . . Ted Sherman, "Feds Battle Charity over $500,000 Linked to Corruption Probe," *The Star-Ledger,* January 10, 2010.

The federally appointed trustee in the case was veteran attorney Charles Stanziale . . . Based on interview with Stanziale, May 11, 2010, and bankruptcy court filings.

A few days later, on June 26, Dwek returned to Altman's office . . . *U.S. District Court Criminal Complaint: United States v. Itzak Friedlander, a/k/a "Isaac Friedlander,"* July 23, 2009.

Amon, who would plead guilty less than five months after his arrest, talked freely to Dwek of slipping money to Jeffrey Williamson . . . *U.S. District Court Criminal Complaint: United States v. Charles Amon, a/k/a "Shaul Amon,"* July 23, 2009.

On a rainy Wednesday morning, Dwek met Guarini . . . *U.S. District Court Criminal Complaint: United States v. John Guarini,* July 23, 2009.

Jersey City at the time had been coming off one of the largest building booms in its history . . . Steve Chambers, "Building Boom: The Wholesale Revitalization of Jersey City Is Exciting, but Not Without Growing Pains," *The Star-Ledger,* May 21, 2006.

It was a ludicrous proposal . . . Amy Sara Clark, "Who'd Believe It?" *Jersey Journal,* August 11, 2009.

That same day, Dwek also met with Jeff Williamson . . . *U.S. District Court Criminal Complaint: United States v. Jeffrey Williamson,* July 23, 2009.

8. Religious Retreat

Arye Weiss was expecting Dwek . . . *U.S. District Court Criminal Complaint: United States v. Arye Weiss,* July 23, 2009.

A decade earlier, two Orthodox rabbis and 10 others were charged with laundering $1.7 million in drug profits . . . Robert D. McFadden, "Rabbis Listed Among Suspects in Laundering of Drug Profits," *The New York Times,* June 17, 1997.

In June 2007, Dwek arranged a meeting with Nahum . . . *U.S. District Court Criminal Complaint: United States v. Edmond Nahum,* July 23, 2009.

"I would tell him to write a check . . ." Deposition of Solomon Dwek, October 14, 2009.

Ben Haim had given Dwek $3.1 million . . . *U.S. Bankruptcy Court: Adversary complaint by Charles A. Stanziale Jr. as Chapter 11 Trustee of Solomon Dwek and SEM Realty Associates, LLC v. Eli Ben Haim and Congregation Ohel Eliahu,* May 23, 2008.

Dwek met Ben Haim at his home in Elberon . . . *U.S. District Court Criminal Complaint: United States v. Eliahu Ben Haim,* July 23, 2009.

Kidnap victim Anna Cardelfe, a six-year-old from Spring Lake . . . Kate Coscarelli, Brian Donohue, and Mark Mueller, "Little Anna Is Home Safe," *The Star-Ledger,* November 10, 2001.

Haber had already contributed to the committee . . . Campaign finance records filed with the New Jersey Election Law Enforcement Commission.

"You need four thousand dollars . . ." *U.S. District Court Criminal Complaint: United States v. Shimon Haber,* July 23, 2009.

Saul Kassin was a revered figure . . . Joe Ryan, "Syrian Rabbi's Arrest Casts Shadow," *The Star-Ledger,* November 29, 2009.

Kassin retrieved a large accounting ledger . . . *U.S. District Court Criminal Complaint: United States v. Saul Kassin,* July 23, 2009.

In December, the U.S. Attorney in Los Angeles had announced the arrest of Grand Rabbi Naftali Tzi Weisz . . . Tiffany Hsu, "Jewish Leader Held on Money Laundering Charges," *Los Angeles Times,* December 20, 2007.

The 37-count indictment alleged that Weisz and Zigelman had solicited millions . . . *U.S. District Court Indictment: United States v. Naftali Tzi Weisz,* December 19, 2007.

It was only later learned that the whole scheme unraveled after a longtime Spinka contributor, Robert Kasirer . . . , agreed to cooperate . . . *U.S. District Court Trial Memorandum: United States v. Naftali Tzi Weisz*, January 22, 2009.

Dwek walked into Kassin's dining room . . . *U.S. District Court Criminal Complaint: United States v. Saul Kassin*, July 23, 2009.

9. Kidneys and Fish

The law actually dated to 1984 . . . Margaret Engel, "Va. Doctor Plans Company to Arrange Sale of Human Kidneys," *The Washington Post*, September 19, 1983.

The outrage was immediate . . . Laura Meckler, "How Much Is That Kidney in the Window? A Radical Idea Goes Mainstream," *The Wall Street Journal*, November 25, 2007.

Rosenbaum apparently had his own network of connections . . . Brian Kates and William Sherman, "Peddling a Pound of Flesh," *Daily News*, July 26, 2009.

"I'm in real estate" . . . *U.S. District Court Criminal Complaint: United States v. Levy-Itzhak Rosenbaum*, July 23, 2009.

He had told neighbors he worked in construction . . . David Porter and Carla K. Johnson, "Arrest Shakes Transplant Industry," Associated Press, July 26, 2009.

A positive cross-match shows the donor and patient do not match . . . United Network for Organ Sharing. "What Every Patient Needs to Know," 2009.

On March 10, 2008, Guarini met Dwek again . . . *U.S. District Court Criminal Complaint: United States v. John Guarini*, July 23, 2009.

He had once sat on Jersey City's Ethical Standards Board . . . Jason Fink, "Council Abolishes City Ethics Board," *Jersey Journal*, February 13, 2003.

Mayor Jerramiah T. Healy's liaison to the city's large Egyptian community . . . Christian Niedan, "Hundreds Attend Memorial Service for Murdered Jersey City Family," *Jersey Journal*, February 21, 2005.

Entering the diner, Guarini saw Khalil and made the introductions . . . *U.S. District Court Criminal Complaint: United States v. Maher A. Khalil*, July 23, 2009.

Guarini took his reward . . . *U.S. District Court Criminal Complaint: United States v. John Guarini*, July 23, 2009.

A series of early-morning raids . . . Jeff Whelan and Guy Sterling, "A Crime Sweep Targets Reputed Mobsters," *The Star-Ledger*, May 9, 2008.

Inside was a box with logos from the *Power Rangers* . . . *U.S. District Court Criminal Complaint: United States v. Eliahu Ben Haim*, July 23, 2009.

Dwek found himself beginning to do a lot of business with Mordchai Fish . . . *U.S. District Court Criminal Complaint: United States v. Mordchai Fish*, July 23, 2009.

"If anyone ever asks you, you didn't see me . . ." *U.S. District Court Criminal Complaint: United States v. Yolie Gertner*, July 23, 2009.

10. The Fixer

For 20 years, Joseph Cardwell was one of the go-to guys in Jersey City . . . "Bumps in the Road for Cardwell, Jackson," *Jersey Journal*, February 21, 2005.

The story and characters were as bizarre as any comic-book writer could dream up . . . Jeff Whelan and Josh Margolin, "Menendez Dumps a Close Adviser Caught on Tape Seeking Favors," *The Star-Ledger*, September 28, 2006.

Khalil gave Dwek a brief lowdown . . . *U.S. District Court Criminal Complaint: United States v. Joseph Cardwell*, July 23, 2009.

Cardwell's paper also came up with a novel method of securing the lucrative legal notices . . . Ken Thorbourne, "Jersey City Pays Weekly for Ad," *Jersey Journal*, September 19, 2007.

A state grand jury indicted a former Jersey City municipal court chief judge . . . Rick Hepp, "Ex-Judge Indicted in Ticket Fixing Case," *The Star-Ledger*, July 15, 2008.

Dwek brought over a $25,000 bank check . . . *U.S. District Court Criminal Complaint: United States v. Edmond Nahum*, July 23, 2009.

At the end of July, Dwek and Cardwell again met . . . *U.S. District Court Criminal Complaint: United States v. Joseph Cardwell*, July 23, 2009.

Dwek sat down with Santoro . . . *U.S. District Court Criminal Information: United States v. Alfonso L. Santoro,* December 3, 2009.

The meeting with Carl . . . Ken Thorbourne, "Czaplicki Admits He's 'JC Official 3' in Feds' Complaint," *Jersey Journal,* July 27, 2009.

He had parlayed his political connections over the years . . . Ted Sherman, "Patronage Still Deep at Sewage Agency," *The Star-Ledger,* May 8, 2005.

"Is he cool?" *U.S. District Court Criminal Complaint: United States v. Joseph Cardwell,* July 23, 2009.

A week later, political corruption was again on the front page . . . Josh Margolin and Jeff Whelan, "FBI Raids Offices of Bergen Democrats' Chief and Attorney," *The Star-Ledger,* August 22, 2008.

Dwek, it seemed, had come up with a new scam behind their backs . . . Deposition of Solomon Dwek, October 14, 2009, as well as interviews with several of the players.

At the end of Bush's term, one of the few pardons the president did grant was to Isaac Toussie . . . David Stout and Eric Lightblau, "Pardon Lasts Just One Day for Developer in Fraud Case," *The New York Times,* December 25, 2008.

After a series of false starts and reschedulings . . . Details of these meetings emerged out of the trial of Daniel Van Pelt. In addition, Van Pelt sat down for an interview following his conviction.

On May 19, 2010, a jury called him a liar . . . Maryann Spoto, "Van Pelt Convicted of Bribery, Extortion," *The Star-Ledger,* May 20, 2010.

Christie tendered his resignation . . . John P. Martin and Josh Margolin, "Christie Quits, Setting GOP Wheels in Motion," *The Star-Ledger,* November 18, 2008.

11. The Man from Chicago

Cheatam thought the delivery method clever . . . *U.S. District Court Criminal Complaint: United States v. Jack M. Shaw, Edward Cheatam and Leona Beldini,* July 23, 2009.

A raconteur who looked like Santa Claus . . . Chris Megerian, "Friends Say Shaw Played a Gentler Game of Politics," *The Star-Ledger,* July 30, 2009.

Everyone knew he was a Chicago guy . . . David W. Chen and David M. Halbfinger, "Before Death, a New Jersey Political Operative's Descent," *The New York Times,* July 31, 2009.

Onetime boxer, hard-edged kid from Brooklyn . . . David Wald, "Feisty Florio Develops a More Personal Touch," *The Star-Ledger,* October 29. 1989.

Shaw was the quarterback who called some of the most important plays . . . David Wald, "Hudson Dem Factions Told to Resolve Dispute," *The Star-Ledger,* June 16, 1991.

Shaw and Pulver were self-described animal lovers and took over operations at the Hudson County SPCA shelter . . . Jason Fink, "Shelter Hit on Cruelty, Money," *Jersey Journal,* April 26, 2001.

"I've had a very, very good relationship with the mayor . . ." *U.S. District Court Criminal Complaint: United States v. Jack M. Shaw, Edward Cheatam and Leona Beldini,* July 23, 2009.

12. The Stripper, the Mayor, and the Manzo Boys

She shimmied wearing little more than her perfume . . . Ted Sherman and Joe Ryan, "Big Sting Trial Takes Spotlight," *The Star-Ledger,* January 24, 2010.

The Hudson Theater, she once told a reporter years ago, "was a wonderful place to be in the fifties . . ." Peter Weiss, "Back to Burlesque for One Day Only," *Jersey Journal,* October 21, 2000.

"We brought in people from all over New York . . ." Laurence Chollet, "When Stripping Was a Career Move," *The Record,* March 3, 1995.

Jersey City had a history rich in corruption . . . John Farmer, "Jersey City Once Ruled New Jersey Politics," *The Star-Ledger,* May 17, 2009.

"I am what I am" . . . David Porter, "Jersey City Mayor: No Apologies for Who I Am," Associated Press, July 13, 2007.

"She will call up and get a date for us within the next two weeks" . . . *U.S. District Court Criminal Complaint: United States v. Jack M. Shaw, Edward Cheatam and Leona Beldini,* July 23, 2009.

The Beacon was a huge, imposing condominium complex... Antoinette Martin, "A New Lease on Life for Jersey City Complex," *The New York Times*, February 27, 2005.

He was arrested and charged with disorderly conduct... Carly Rothman, "Jersey City Mayor Arrested at the Shore," *The Star-Ledger*, June 19, 2006.

Cheatam had told Esenbach a month earlier that Manzo was important because they had to "cover both sides"... *U.S. District Court Criminal Complaint: United States v. Louis Manzo and Ronald Manzo*, July 23, 2009.

Forever known in New Jersey's political lexicon simply as "Billboards"... Josh Margolin, "Former McGreevey Aides Reaped a Bundle in Billboard Sales," *The Star-Ledger*, May 7, 2003.

Manzo admitted receiving inside information from a bond trader... Josh Margolin, "Federal Billboard Probe Digs Deeper," *The Star-Ledger*, August 31, 2004.

As he talked, Lou Manzo was trying to figure out in his mind where it was... Based on interview with Lou Manzo, April 7, 2010.

The big lunch meeting with Esenbach... *U.S. District Court Criminal Complaint: United States v. Jack M. Shaw, Edward Cheatam and Leona Beldini*, July 23, 2009.

Hey, get rhythm when you get the blues... Lyrics from "Get Rhythm," written and recorded by Johnny Cash.

He did not particularly like Johnny Cash... Testimony during the trial of Leona Beldini, of Tom Ceccarelli.

13. March Madness

"My grandfather had a transplant"... Transcript of surveillance video taken by Solomon Dwek of Daniel Van Pelt at Morton's The Steak House at Caesar's Hotel and Casino, February 21, 2009.

During that month alone, Dwek met with his targets at least 26 times... Ted Sherman, "Pasta and Payoffs: How FBI Snitch Led Multiple Lives and Orchestrated a Nonstop Series of Stings," *The Star-Ledger*, October 25, 2009.

Former mayor David Delle Donna and his wife, Anna, had gone to jail... Jeff Whelan, "Ex–Guttenberg Mayor and Wife Get 4 Years for Taking Bribes," *The Star-Ledger*, October 25, 2008.

A jovial type of guy... Shawn Boburg, "Ridgefield's Suarez Remains 'Confident,' Councilman Says," *The Record*, July 25, 2009.

His habit of adding his two cents... "Political Insider," *Jersey Journal*, May 14, 2005.

Stephen Kessler, former chairman of the Ocean Township Sewerage Authority... Joe Ryan, "Shore Ex-Official Jailed for Taking Bribes," *The Star-Ledger*, March 25, 2009.

Catrillo still couldn't figure out what was driving the guy... Interview with Guy Catrillo, March 12, 2010.

Others accused him of shaking down employees to pay for a billboard... Earl Morgan, "King Allegedly Got Workers to Pay for His Billboard," *Jersey Journal*, January 6, 2005.

Former Hoboken mayor Anthony Russo... John P. Martin, "Ex–Hoboken Mayor Admits Extortion," *The Star-Ledger*, September 30, 2004.

14. Hudson County Hardball

A lot has been said and written about politics in New Jersey's Hudson County... Doug Daniels, "Welcome to Jersey City Politics; It's Been Rough, Corrupt and Downright Weird for More than a Century," *Politics Magazine*, May 1, 2008.

Over the years, New Jersey and many other states tried to professionalize their government structures by removing some of the patronage and partisan politics... Fred J. Aun, "Law Lets Towns Shun Party Politics," *The Star-Ledger*, May 10, 1998.

Schaffer was just another odd character in a sea of odd characters... Carly Baldwin, "Schaffer Plans to Stay on Job, Defying Zimmer," *Jersey Journal*, April 6, 2009.

"We'll probably have to run it through you"... *U.S. District Court Criminal Complaint: United States v. Peter Cammarano III and Michael Schaffer*, July 23, 2009.

In a state where shooting political stars have crashed and burned in record time... Josh Margolin, "A Shining Star's Alleged Dark Side," *The Star-Ledger*, July 26, 2009.

Thursday, April 23, was yet another busy day for federal prosecutors ... Tom Haydon, "FBI Raids Homes of 2 Perth Amboy Ex-Officials," *The Star-Ledger,* April 24, 2009.

"I don't care what it is. It's done," said King ... *U.S. District Court Criminal Complaint: United States v. James P. "Jimmy" King,* July 23, 2009.

"Dave, you are on the top of my list" ... *U.S. District Court Criminal Complaint: United States v. LaVern Webb-Washington,* July 23, 2009.

"I respect that. You're a businessman" ... *U.S. District Court Criminal Complaint: United States v. Lori Serrano,* July 23, 2009.

The entry on Cammarano's personal schedule for the day put it bluntly: *2pm–3pm Mike Schaffer at Malibu with Peter ONLY* ... Interview with Cammarano campaign scheduler Jamey Cook-Lichstein, May 9, 2010.

15. Put Him on Ice ...

On a warm, sunny Wednesday in Hoboken on the first of July, Peter Cammarano was sworn in as the city's thirty-seventh mayor ... Carly Baldwin, "Cammarano Voices Theme of City Unity," *Jersey Journal,* July 2, 2009.

The calendar was not going to dictate the arrests, he insisted ... Interview with Ralph Marra, June 9, 2010.

Paul worked the lawyers and the judges and eventually convinced Lautenberg to take his name to President Clinton ... Bill Gannon, "Senators Heading for Fight Again," *The Star-Ledger,* February 22, 1999.

The New York Times ran a story based on anonymous sources that said Brown had been secretly aiding Christie ... David M. Halbfinger, "Christie May Have Gotten Improper Aid," *The New York Times,* October 19, 2009.

"I know," Deutsch said. "I understand" ... *U.S. District Court Criminal Complaint: United States v. Levi Deutsch and Binyomin Spira,* July 23, 2009.

After a tough first year in office, Governor Corzine wanted to make Doria the education commissioner ... Tom Hester, "Governor Selects Doria as Head of Community Affairs," *The Star-Ledger,* September 22, 2007.

In 1980, Menendez was used by prosecutors in that office to help them convict Menendez's mentor, Bill Musto ... Deborah Howlett, "Transcript Shows Late Shift Against Boss by Menendez," *The Star-Ledger,* June 22, 2006.

Two months before that election, federal prosecutors very publicly subpoenaed records ... Jeff Whelan and Josh Margolin, "Feds Probe Menendez Rental Deal," *The Star-Ledger,* September 8, 2006.

Christie came under harsh scrutiny ... John P. Martin and Jeff Whelan, "$52M-plus Payday for Christie's Old Boss," *The Star-Ledger,* November 20, 2007.

Corzine's appetite settled on the cutthroat politics of his adopted home state of New Jersey ... David Wald, "Summit Millionaire Hints at Democratic Bid for Senate," *The Star-Ledger,* March 26, 1999.

To go from unknown to king, Corzine showered his fortune from one end of Jersey to the other ... Ted Sherman, "Smart Money: How Corzine Paid for a Win," *The Star-Ledger,* June 8, 2000.

It was the president's first political trip since taking office ... Claire Heininger and Josh Margolin, "Obama Stirs Crowd at Rally for Corzine," *The Star-Ledger,* July 17, 2009.

On the Friday before the bust, Dwek had a last meeting with Harvey Smith ... *U.S. District Court Criminal Complaint: United States v. L. Harvey Smith and Richard Greene,* July 23, 2009.

In 2002, the U.S. Attorney's office indicted Sires' chief fund-raiser ... John P. Martin, "Developer Sentenced to 87 Months for Fraud," *The Star-Ledger,* June 29, 2005.

The feds paid a visit to Jack Shaw ... Josh Margolin and Chris Megerian, "New Twists in Corruption Probe," *The Star-Ledger,* July 31, 2009.

16. Takedown

One of the congregants, engrossed in prayer ... Wayne Parry, "Arrests Put Spotlight on Syrian Jewish Community," Associated Press, July 23, 2009.

In Belmar along the Jersey shore, Lou Manzo had stayed overnight at his summerhouse . . . Interview with Lou Manzo, April 7, 2010.

Weysan Dun . . . had several difficult phone calls he had to make himself . . . Interview with Weysan Dun, December 4, 2009.

"There are some FBI agents here and they've taken away someone" . . . Interview with Jon Corzine and Josh Zeitz, April 27, 2010.

17. Rogues and Cronies of Thieves

In Hoboken, angry residents gathered . . . Brian Whitley and Carly Rothman, "A Growing Outcry for Officials to Quit," *The Star-Ledger,* July 28, 2009.

Immediately after the takedown, the governor switched gears on his running mate . . . Josh Margolin and Claire Heininger, "Weinberg Is Governor's Pick for Running Mate," *The Star-Ledger,* July 25, 2009.

Those arrested in the sting began seeking out the state's top criminal defense attorneys . . . Ted Sherman and Brian T. Murray, "After the Big Sting, the Big Guns Are Hired," *The Star-Ledger,* August 16, 2009.

Many in the Syrian Orthodox community flatly refused to believe the charges . . . Paul Vitello, "Syrian Sephardic Communities Shaken by Charges," *The New York Times,* July 24, 2009.

18. "I am Guilty, Your Honor . . ."

Brian Neary was one of New Jersey's better-known criminal defense attorneys . . . Thomas Zambito, "Brian Neary for the Defense," *The Record,* May 9, 1997.

The prosecutor's office dispatched a Crime Scene Investigation team from its homicide unit . . . Joe Ryan, "Drug OD Killed Pol Caught in July Sting," *The Star-Ledger,* January 6, 2010. Also based on later interview with Edward DeFazio, April 14, 2010.

The week after the arrests in New Jersey, a hastily arranged legal symposium was held by ultra-Orthodox leaders . . . Nathaniel Popper, "Ultra-Orthodox Rabbis Begin to Question Their Own Insularity," *The Forward,* August 7, 2009.

Then came Dwek himself . . . Ted Sherman and Joe Ryan, "What We Now Know About Solomon Dwek," *The Star-Ledger,* October 21, 2009.

Note: Corzine's behind-the-scenes deliberations over his faltering campaign, described here for the first time, were drawn from interviews with Corzine, as well as with many insiders with close ties to the governor.

A meeting was set for August 10 at the home of Corzine's girlfriend on Fifth Avenue . . . Josh Margolin and Claire Heininger, "Corzine Shuffles Campaign," *The Star-Ledger,* August 11, 2009.

Back in June, a *Star-Ledger* reporter was invited to meet with the president . . . Josh Margolin, "President Promises to Support Corzine," *The Star-Ledger,* June 25, 2009.

Chris Christie won his crusade to become governor in November 2009 . . . Josh Margolin and Claire Heininger, "It's Christie; Hungry for Change, Voters Ditch Corzine," *The Star-Ledger,* November 4, 2009.

In May, four of the most serious counts against the Manzo brothers were dismissed . . . Joe Ryan, "Ruling Entangles Corruption Sting Cases," *The Star-Ledger,* June 2, 2010.

"You know what a friend is, Mr. Dwek?" Michaelangelo Conte, "A Lonely Man: Key Witness Is an Outcast," *Jersey Journal,* February 4, 2010.

Cast of Characters and the Roles They Played

The Informer and Those Close to Him

Solomon Dwek: Onetime high-flying real estate speculator who got jammed up over a $25 million check

Isaac Dwek: Solomon's father and rabbi at the Deal Synagogue

Pearl Dwek: Solomon's wife

Michael Himmel: Dwek's defense attorney and former assistant U.S. Attorney

The Ponzi Scheme and Bankruptcy

Jack Adjmi: Wealthy Syrian community businessman who helped Dwek begin his real estate venture

Mark Adjmi: Jack's son

Ken Cayre: Former record and video producer, uncle of Dwek's wife

Joseph "Joey" Dwek: Solomon's uncle and Jack's son-in-law

Isaac "Ike" Franco: Businessman and Dwek investor

Barry Kantrowitz: Real estate broker and a partner of Dwek

Dennis Kearney: Attorney for PNC Bank

Dorothy Lassik: PNC Bank branch manager

Alexander Lehrer: Monmouth County Superior Court judge

Donald Lomurro: Attorney and special fiscal agent appointed by Lehrer

Michelle Penix: PNC Bank teller supervisor

Eli Seruya: Chief financial officer for the Adjmi companies

George Scharpf: President and CEO of Amboy Bank

Charles A. Stanziale Jr.: Federal bankruptcy trustee

The U.S. Attorney's Office

Christopher Christie: U.S. Attorney for the District of New Jersey, later elected governor of New Jersey

Ralph Marra: First assistant U.S. Attorney, later acting U.S. Attorney

Paul Fishman: U.S. Attorney for the District of New Jersey, succeeded Marra

Michele Brown: First assistant U.S. Attorney/chief counsel

Charles McKenna: Executive assistant U.S. Attorney and chief of criminal division

James Nobile: Assistant U.S. Attorney and head of special prosecutions division

Thomas Eicher: Assistant U.S. Attorney, deputy director of special prosecutions division

Brian Howe: Assistant U.S. Attorney and later deputy director of special prosecutions division

Thomas Calcagni: Assistant U.S. Attorney assigned to special prosecutions

Mark McCarren: Assistant U.S. Attorney assigned to special prosecutions

Sandra Moser: Assistant U.S. Attorney assigned to special prosecutions

Maureen Nakly: Assistant U.S. Attorney assigned to special prosecutions

The FBI

Weysan Dun: Special agent in charge of the Newark Division

Edward Kahrer: Assistant special agent in charge who supervised Dwek operation

William Waldie: Special agent who headed Bid Rig investigation out of Monmouth County

Sean McCarthy: FBI case agent assigned to the Dwek operation

Donald Russ: FBI case agent assigned to the Dwek operation

The Defendants

The first targets, leading to a two-track investigation into political corruption and money laundering

Moshe Altman, 39, Monsey, N.Y.: Hudson County real estate developer and member of the Hasidic community

Shimon Haber, 34, Brooklyn, N.Y.: Union City developer/associate of Altman and member of the Syrian community

Political Corruption Cases

Charles Amon, 33, Lakewood: Dwek's property manager

Leona Beldini, 74, Jersey City: Jersey City deputy mayor and former burlesque star known as Hope Diamond

Peter Cammarano III, 32, Hoboken: Mayor of Hoboken

Joseph Cardwell, 68, Jersey City: Hudson County political operative

Joseph Castagna, 53, Jersey City: Jersey City health officer

Guy Catrillo, 54, Jersey City: Jersey City planning aide

Edward Cheatam, 61, Jersey City: Commissioner with Jersey City Housing Authority

Dennis Elwell, 64, Secaucus: Mayor of Secaucus

Itzak Friedlander, 41, Union City: Altman associate

Richard Greene, 45, Jersey City: Aide to Assemblyman L. Harvey Smith

John Guarini, 59, Bayonne: Jersey City building inspector

Denis Jaslow, 46, Wall Township: Investigator for Hudson County Board of Elections

Philip J. Kenny, 53, Jersey City: Jersey City Council member

Maher A. Khalil, 39, Jersey City: Member of Jersey City Zoning Board of Adjustment

James P. "Jimmy" King, 67, Jersey City: Head of Jersey City Parking Authority

Louis Manzo, 54, Jersey City: Mayoral candidate and former assemblyman

Michael Manzo, 53, Jersey City: Jersey City Council candidate.

Ronald A. Manzo, 65, Bayonne: Brother of Louis Manzo and political adviser

Alfonso L. Santoro, 70, Beachwood: Former head of the Ocean County Democratic Party

Michael Schaffer, 58, Hoboken: Commissioner on North Hudson Utilities Authority

Lori Serrano, 37, Jersey City: Jersey City Council candidate

Jack Shaw, 61, Jersey City: Political consultant who died days after being charged

L. Harvey Smith, 60, Jersey City: State assemblyman and former mayor of Jersey City

Anthony R. Suarez, 42, Ridgefield: Mayor of Ridgewood

Vincent Tabbachino, 68, Fairview: Owner of a tax preparation business

Daniel M. Van Pelt, 44, Waretown: State assemblyman and former mayor of Ocean Township

Mariano Vega, 59, Jersey City: President of Jersey City Council

LaVern Webb-Washington, 60, Jersey City: Housing activist and Jersey City Council candidate

Jeffrey Williamson, 57, Lakewood: Lakewood building inspector

Money-Laundering Cases

Eliahu Ben Haim, 58, Long Branch: Principal rabbi at Congregation Ohel Yaacob in Deal

Schmuel Cohen, 35, Brooklyn, N.Y.: Ran cash house in Brooklyn

Levi Deutsch, 37, Brooklyn, N.Y.: Israeli source of cash

Yeshayahu Ehrental, 65, Brooklyn, N.Y.: Ran cash house in Brooklyn

Mordchai Fish, 56, Brooklyn, N.Y.: Rabbi of Congregation Sheves Achim in Brooklyn

Yolie Gertner, 30, Brooklyn, N.Y.: Allegedly a cash courier, remains a fugitive

David S. Goldhirsh, 30, Brooklyn, N.Y.: Allegedly a cash courier

Saul Kassin, 87, Brooklyn, N.Y.: Chief rabbi of Congregation Shaare Zion in Brooklyn

IM: Unindicted conspirator, at the center of a worldwide money-laundering operation

Edmond Nahum, 56, Deal: Cantor and now rabbi at Deal Synagogue

Abraham Pollack, 40, Brooklyn, N.Y.: Allegedly ran a cash house in Brooklyn

Lavel Schwartz, 57, Brooklyn, N.Y.: Rabbi in Brooklyn, brother of Fish

Binyomin Spira, 28, Brooklyn, N.Y.: Allegedly ran cash house from his bakery

Naftoly Weber, 40, Brooklyn, N.Y.: Allegedly ran cash house in Brooklyn

Arye Weiss, 54, Brooklyn, N.Y.: Ran cash house in Brooklyn

Human Organ Trafficking Case

Levy-Itzhak Rosenbaum, 58, Brooklyn, N.Y.: Real estate broker tied to black market kidney operation

The Politicians

Jon Corzine: Former CEO of Goldman Sachs, onetime U.S. Senator and governor of New Jersey

Carl Czaplicki: Director of housing and former chief of staff to the mayor of Jersey City

Joseph Doria: Commissioner of the state Department of Community Affairs, former Assembly speaker, state senator, and mayor of Bayonne

Jim Florio: Former congressman and governor of New Jersey

Jerramiah T. Healy: Mayor of Jersey City, Hudson County Democratic chairman

Robert Janiszewski: Former Hudson County executive, former federal inmate 25038-050

Frank Lautenberg: U.S. Senator

Robert Menendez: U.S. Senator and Hudson County Democratic powerhouse

Albio Sires: U.S. Representative; former mayor of West New York and Speaker of the Assembly

Brian Stack: State senator and mayor of Union City

Dawn Zimmer: President of the Hoboken City Council, later mayor of Hoboken

Bibliography

Aron, Michael. *Governor's Race: A TV Reporter's Chronicle of the 1993 Florio-Whitman Campaign.* New Brunswick, NJ: Rutgers University Press, 1994.

Brown, Erica, Ph.D. *Confronting Scandal: How Jews Can Respond When Jews Do Bad Things.* Woodstock, VT: Jewish Lights Publishing, 2010.

Chafets, Zev. "The SY Empire." *The New York Times,* October 14, 2007.

Cohler-Esses, Larry. "An Inside Look at a Syrian-Jewish Enclave." *The Forward,* August 7, 2009.

DeHaven, Judy. "Amboy Exec Discusses Loan Situation." *The Star-Ledger,* November 22, 2006.

Dwek, Poopa. *Aromas of Aleppo: The Legendary Cuisine of Syrian Jews.* New York: HarperCollins, 2007.

Ellis, Charles D. *The Partnership: The Making of Goldman Sachs.* New York: Penguin Press, 2008.

Endlich, Lisa. *Goldman Sachs: The Culture of Success.* New York: Touchstone, 1999.

Kiener, Ronald C. "Airing the Syrian Laundry." *Religion in the News* (Leonard E. Greenberg Center for the Study of Religion in Public Life, Trinity College), Fall 2009.

Lagnado, Lucette. "A Community Shaken." *The Wall Street Journal,* October 3, 2009.

Lowenstein, Roger. *When Genius Failed: The Rise and Fall of Long-Term Capital Management.* New York: Random House, 2000.

Margolin, Josh. "The Man at the Center of It All." *The Star-Ledger,* July 24. 2009.

Margolin, Josh, and Chris Megerian. "New Twists in Corruption Probe." *The Star-Ledger,* July 31, 2009.

Margolin, Josh, and Ted Sherman. "Graft Sting's Key Witness to Plead Guilty to Bank Fraud." *The Star-Ledger,* October 20, 2009.

Martin, John P., and Tom Feeney. "Rabbi's Son Charged in $50 Million Bank Scam." *The Star-Ledger,* May 12, 2006.

Martin, John P., and Maryann Spoto. "FBI and IRS Agents Grab Records at Deal Yeshiva." *The Star-Ledger,* July 12, 2006.

Neuman, William. "Paying Any Price to Live Here," *The New York Times,* June 25, 2006.

Patton, Phil. "Jeans in the Genes: Why the S.Y.'s Are Sportswear's Chosen People." *New York Magazine,* May 22, 1989. pp. 40–51.

Roffé, Sarina. "Our Crowd." *Religion in the News* (Leonard E. Greenberg Center for the Study of Religion in Public Life, Trinity College), Fall 2009.

Ryan, Joe. "Official Accused in Sting Charged with Lying to FBI." *The Star-Ledger,* December 18, 2009.

Ryan, Joe, and Maryann Spoto. "A Real Estate Mogul Who Used His Wiles to Help Net Dozens." *The Star-Ledger,* July 24, 2009.

Sherman, Ted. "Brooklyn Man Admits Scheme to Launder Cash." *The Star-Ledger,* January 15, 2010.

————. "Creditor Targets Payments to Dwek." *The Star-Ledger,* November 19, 2009.

————. "Feds Battle Charity over $500,000 Linked to Corruption Probe." *The Star-Ledger,* January 10, 2010.

————. "A Guy Trying to Buy His Way Out of Trouble." *The Star-Ledger,* July 25, 2009.

————. "In Fallout of Fraud Sting, IRS Joins Hunt." *The Star-Ledger,* December 6, 2009.

————. "Pasta and Payoffs: How FBI Snitch Led Multiple Lives and Orchestrated a Nonstop Series of Stings." *The Star-Ledger,* October 25, 2009.

Sherman, Ted, and Josh Margolin. "Behind the Scenes, Feds Hunt for Defendants Who Will Flip." *The Star-Ledger,* July 31, 2009.

Sherman, Ted, and Brian T. Murray. "After the Big Sting, the Big Guns Are Hired." *The Star-Ledger,* August 16, 2009.

Sherman, Ted, and Joe Ryan. "Big Sting Trial Takes Spotlight." *The Star-Ledger,* January 24, 2010.

————. "Walk of Shame: Wide-ranging Corruption Scandal Snares Officials and Religious Leaders." *The Star-Ledger,* July 24, 2009.

————. "What We Now Know About Solomon Dwek." *The Star-Ledger,* October 21, 2009.

Sutton, Joseph. *Magic Carpet: Aleppo in Flatbush.* New York: Theyer-Jacobb, 1979.

Acknowledgments

It began with Edward Hyde, Viscount Cornbury and third Earl of Clarendon.

Known for his cross-dressing, bigotry, and incompetence even before he was dispatched to the New World as first royal governor of the colony of New Jersey in 1703, Lord Cornbury's tenure would be marked for the corruption and legacy of graft it would usher in for the tiny state sandwiched between the twin powers of New York and Philadelphia.

The three centuries since have done nothing to make New Jersey seem any less than perfectly hospitable to official misconduct, political chicanery, and corruption. Boss Hague, Abscam, Jim McGreevey. All have helped cement New Jersey's status as first of equals for bribing, skimming, squeezing, self-dealing, and shakedowns among those in the power.

In the days after the takedown of July 23, 2009, New Jersey went through another of its peculiar rituals. The Questioning. It goes like this: *Why Jersey? What is it about Jersey? Why are we such a laughingstock? Can anything be done? Why doesn't this happen in Idaho or Maine or even Wisconsin?*

With New Jersey's great senses of sarcasm and gallows humor, the quickest answer at the local barbershop or dry cleaner was basically "who the hell cares about Idaho?" Some were even eager to watch late-night television to see how Solomon Dwek, the rabbis, and the pols would look after being run through Jon Stewart's wringer or David Letterman's monologue. (For the record, Letterman said he was non-plussed: "Big deal. Call me when they start talking about hookers.")

But it doesn't really end with that. The Questioning is real. People feel a connection to where they live, and while they might knock their home, they're not in love with the idea that outsiders are the ones doing the mocking. After the Dwek takedown, many people thought seriously about New Jersey and why it seems to deserve the black eye it gets. In bars around Hoboken, for instance, there was a hush that blew through each time Peter Cammarano's perp walk was replayed on the news. The quiet was followed by questions posed in an answerless loop.

Because the Solomon Dwek case was so huge and led to coverage so intense, the Questioning this time seemed to be wall-to-wall. The prosecutors got the questions. Politicians got them. Lawyers got them. Certainly, reporters got them. Theories abounded. Satisfying responses were absent.

Both Chris Christie and Jon Corzine count themselves among the officials, political scientists, and psychologists who believe that New Jersey is a victim of the simple, petty greed that has afflicted the human race since Adam and Eve. They say it only seems to exist more inescapably in New Jersey politics and government because there are just so many daily opportunities for corruption presented by layered public agencies without anywhere near enough oversight. Put hundreds of school districts and hundreds of town governments and hundreds of sewer agencies and parking authorities into Idaho, the logic goes, and you'll get New Jersey–style corruption there, too. Take the locks and alarms from the bank, they say, and the money will disappear.

Maybe.

Others, like the white-collar defense lawyers who make a good living thanks to federal corruption busters, say it's nothing more than culture and history with a healthy dose of careerism. After a century of graft, the Mafia, and bad politicians living off patronage, New Jersey lawmen know they can score big headlines and nice promotions by arresting public officials on the take. So they do. The problem with that logic is that it disregards the reality that a lot of the corruption that has been found in New Jersey and continues to exist is real, not imagined. No matter how good Dwek was, he would never have made one case if no one took a bribe or laundered a cereal box full of cash.

Or maybe New Jersey just has more resourceful people looking for a shortcut. Or maybe New Jersey just has more stupid public officials and they would do well to get better at it if they want to remain free.

The truth of *The Jersey Sting* is that some religious leaders and some political figures thought they could cash in while hurting no one but Uncle Sam, who wouldn't miss the money anyway. They thought they were committing victimless crimes. And in the case of the Kidney Guy, he was alleged to believe that he was actually helping both the donors who needed money and the recipients who needed a few more years with their families, had a few more weddings to attend, wanted to dance at a few more Bar Mitzvahs.

In the end, the Questioning leads to exhaustion. Not answers. With more than 8.7 million people, New Jersey is a compact, jam-packed landscape of people and traffic and great food and poverty and bad apples and wealth and farms and mountains and pollution and mayors and councilmen and do-gooders and evildoers. It's tempting for people to think about *The Sopranos* and *On the Waterfront* and Dutch Schultz and Solomon Dwek and conclude that New Jersey is a unique breeding ground for crime and corruption.

But that requires you to forget that New Jersey was also the home of Albert Einstein, Thomas Edison, Buzz Aldrin, Philip Roth, Bruce Springsteen, Yogi Berra, Meryl Streep, and Woodrow Wilson.

* * *

The idea for this book came weeks after the events of July 23. Had it come that day or in the immediate aftermath, we probably would have disregarded it because we—and every other reporter on the story—were having a tough enough time just keeping track of what was going on. That day stands as one of the most remarkable in our years of covering politics, law enforcement, and corruption in New Jersey. As the news began to develop with lightning speed—accompanied of course by rumors, innuendo, unsubstantiated gossip advertised as hard facts, and outrageous speculation—even the actual true details seemed wildly unbelievable. Both of us were in the *Star-Ledger* newsroom that morning, and when the initial reports surfaced that there were allegations of the sale of body parts it was Josh who turned around and declared, "Someone's got to be smoking crack." There was no way that could be true. But it was.

Working in the newsroom of a daily newspaper on a major breaking story like this was as chaotic and crazy as the scene in the FBI command center across town. With our colleagues, we were chasing down even the barest of details, from the Jersey Shore to Brooklyn, on a real-time deadline, posting what we learned online as we confirmed it. Unlike the FBI, we didn't know exactly what we were chasing until we found it.

Like many newspapers, *The Star-Ledger* has been struggling with the collapse of advertising revenues and shrinking circulation, as readers and advertisers migrate to the Internet. But even with our diminished resources, we managed to put dozens of people on the story that day and the coverage we generated made us proud. We won an award from the American Society of Newspaper Editors for our coverage. We were also gratified to be finalists for the Pulitzer Prize in deadline reporting.

Then came the idea of a book.

We had been working on an in-depth follow-up piece, carefully going through the dozens of criminal complaints that had been unsealed. The documents were incredibly detailed, with times and dates of meetings set up by the FBI, accompanied by actual transcripts of conversations secretly recorded by surveillance video. The thick pile of papers filed by prosecutors simply cited a litany of charges against each individual defendant in no particular order. There was no context to any of it and no way to follow the seemingly random events on Solomon Dwek's path, to understand this complex con man as he moved from Bible study to a life of crime to a secret identity working with the FBI.

Over a period of time, we began putting the information into an electronic database that could be sorted by date, time, and place. Soon, the calendar of Dwek's life as an undercover informant began to emerge. It offered an intriguing narrative, showing meetings that followed on top of meetings, with successive targets of an investigation growing by the day. We also began looking at the thousands of pages of records filed in bankruptcy court, which quickly filled in many of the blanks that sketched out Dwek's life, leading up to the Ponzi scheme, the bank fraud, his days as a high-flying real estate developer, and beyond.

Stories written off that reporting appeared in *The Star-Ledger*. But the narrative behind the story continued to grow as we both spoke with sources connected to the case. A continent away, Bill Gannon, a former colleague, had a chance conversation in California with Andy Ross, a literary agent who had been well aware of the New Jersey corruption case. A series of phone calls ensued. The way Andy recalled it, he had loved the story from the moment that he had seen it in *The New York Times*. "I kept telling everyone I knew what an amazing book this would be. I kept thinking of it as a sort of true version of a Carl Hiaasen novel, filled with colorful scoundrels. Only instead of Good Ole Boys in South Florida, it would be about Orthodox rabbis and sleazebags in New Jersey and Brooklyn. I really, really wished I had a project like this to work on."

Andy called Ted. Ted called Josh. With that, we embarked on a project that seemed to become more strange and amazing the more we dug into it.

We are proud of this book, and we are equally proud of the journey it took to get here. We have met new people, established relationships with new sources, and become closer with many of those we had known only casually through these last years. They offered us time and understanding and more than a little humor and encouragement. Even those not fond of the press or the prosecutors or, certainly, Solomon Dwek, made themselves available to us for hours over the course of days, nights, and weekends for months. Of course, most of them insist on staying anonymous and the best way we can thank them is to live up to our obligations to protect them. But as you—our anonymous sources—read this, please remember how very much we appreciate all that you have done for us. As for those who can be named, there are many people to whom we are grateful. Words don't cover the debt we owe, but we are reporters after all, so that's what you're getting.

Our families, Ted's wife, Rosanne, and daughter, Aliza, and son, Matthew, and Josh's wife, Karen, and daughters, Brooke, Julianna, and Rebecca, gave us much support and patience during months of interviews and research. They gave up evenings and weekends, and the best we can hope is that they find this book to have been worth it.

We could not have proceeded without the encouragement and cooperation of the people we work for at *The Star-Ledger*: David Tucker, our editor, critic, and loudest cheerleader—who constantly is pushing us to shine light in dark places—when he is not writing poetry; Kevin Whitmer, the newspaper's executive editor, who green-lighted our work; and editors Tom Martello, Tom Curran, and Suzanne Pavkovic. We are also indebted to our longtime editor, Jim Willse, who always insisted that perfection may well be found with one more call or one more draft. And we must say thanks to our publisher, Rich Vezza, and to the Newhouse family, a group of people who still care about the news.

Our colleagues on the paper who have been reporting daily on this story since it broke were also key. Thanks to Joe Ryan, Brian Murray, Maryann Spoto, Chris Megerian, Jeff Diamant, and Sue Livio, who unselfishly offered their insights, assistance, and confidence. And our special thanks to Giovanna Pugliese, who helped us assemble the photos shot by a team of *Star-Ledger* photographers, and Bumper DeJesus, for assistance with capturing the images from the video surveillance recordings.

Among the people who can be thanked publicly, two stand out: Chris Christie and Jon Corzine. For nearly a decade both men have granted us a level of access and candor that is truly rare in this era of professional image consultants and 24-hour PR managers. The readers of *The Star-Ledger* have, for years, gotten to know these men and, thanks to them, the real story about the way things work, don't work, and should work. As we researched this book, the current and former governors of New Jersey spent hours answering our questions, filling in the blanks, and explaining context in ways that allow this project to cover all the angles—even some that may not be terribly flattering.

Weysan Dun, the special agent in charge of the Newark Division, spent hours with us to give us details that had never been disclosed. Former acting U.S. Attorney Ralph Marra sat down with us, as did the current U.S. Attorney, Paul Fishman, and Charles Stanziale, the federal bankruptcy trustee on the Dwek case. Each of them made this project better. Thanks also go to Walter J. Greenhalgh of Duane Morris, LLP, counsel to the committee of unsecured creditors in the bankruptcy case.

We are grateful for the technical assistance provided by Rebekah Carmichael of the U.S. Attorney's office and Susan McKee of the FBI, and for the help we got from our former colleague Michael Drewniak, who was involved in so many different ways. Thank you as well to our attorneys, Anthony Pantano and Tom Cafferty, for helping us with the type of stuff reporters know nothing about.

Ellen Zimiles and Martin Ficke taught us more about money laundering than we could ever write about and Erica Brown, who was a great resource recalling her childhood in Deal, was very helpful on issues of religious morality and generously shared with us her manuscript for her book, *Confronting Scandal.*

And, of course, none of this would have been possible without Phil Revzin and the staff at St. Martin's Press who shepherded this book and loved this story as much as we do.

From Ted Sherman:

Writing a book is often a solitary experience. And yet there were people all around me, even after the kids went to bed and my wife went upstairs for the night. When I began working as a reporter, my parents, Alice and Bernie, had framed my very first front-page story and put it up on their dining room wall, where it stayed until they died. They shared everything I wrote, and I wish they could have read this book. Their support and encouragement was always felt and there is not a day that I do not think of them.

Thanks to everyone in my family—including my brother, Dr. Michael Sherman, who laughed at all the funny parts and helped me out with the medical stuff, my sister Elaine, and my aunt Rita and uncle Elliott Cohen, who seem to have a sixth sense (or perhaps a Google search set up) alerting them any time one of my stories goes up online. Also, my aunt Sonia Lerner, who knows just about everyone in Brooklyn and helped me connect with sources in the Syrian community there.

And a special thanks again to Bill Gannon, and to David Schwab, Rabbi Steven Bayar, Amy Dantus, and other friends who shared their insight and knowledge.

From Josh Margolin:

I got into newspaper reporting 20 years ago with the encouragement of five people: my parents, sister, and grandparents. My mother and father, Ellen and Joe, have always been great fans even in those first months after I decided not to go to law school. So has my sister, Fredda. And my late grandparents, Belle and Julie Blaushield, have truly been the inspiration to a life built on chasing stories, ticking off government officials, and trying to figure out what some arcane statute means at the wee hours of the morning. The lessons Poppy and Grandma taught me made me the man I am, and their memories sustain me each and every day. I wish they were here.

Also, thank you so, so much to my in-laws, Barbara and Will Roth. You know what you mean to my family and me, and I am fortunate to have walked into your life so many years ago.

Finally, a few words about four people who did not live to read *The Jersey Sting.* Mike Levine, Dee Murphy, Mark Pittman, and Mike Dorman. At different points in my career, all of them were to me editors friends, mentors, and co-conspirators. Their direction, guidance, and affection formed the foundation for the reporter I am, and I will forever measure myself against them, their work, and their standards. Their DNA lives in every paragraph I write.

Index

CPSIA information can be obtained
at www.ICGtesting.com
Printed in the USA
LVHW031911080319
610001LV00001B/102/P